650.142
En27c
2010

FOND DU LAC PUBLIC LIBRARY

P9-CRB-063

# Cover Letter Magic

Fourth Edition

## Trade Secrets of Professional Resume Writers

Wendy S. Enelow and Louise M. Kursmark

**Cover Letter Magic, Fourth Edition**

© 2010 by Wendy S. Enelow and Louise M. Kursmark

Published by JIST Works, an imprint of JIST Publishing
7321 Shadeland Station, Suite 200
Indianapolis, IN 46256-3923
Phone: 800-648-JIST Fax: 877-454-7839 E-mail: info@jist.com

Visit our Web site at **www.jist.com** for information on JIST, free job search tips, free tables of contents and sample pages, and ordering information on our many products!

Quantity discounts are available for JIST books. Please call our Sales Department at 800-648-5478 for a free catalog and more information.

Trade Product Manager: Lori Cates Hand
Series Editor: Susan Britton Whitcomb
Cover Designer: Aleata Howard
Interior Designer: designLab, Seattle
Page Layout: Toi Davis
Proofreaders: Linda Seifert, Jeanne Clark
Indexer: Cheryl Lenser
Printed in the United States of America
14 13 12 11 10 9 8 7 6 5 4 3 2

Library of Congress Cataloging-in-Publication Data

Enelow, Wendy S.
Cover letter magic : trade secrets of professional resume writers / Wendy S. Enelow and Louise M. Kursmark. – 4th ed.
p. cm.
Includes index.
ISBN 978-1-59357-735-3 (alk. paper)
1. Cover letters. I. Kursmark, Louise. II. Title.
HF5383.E4787 2009
650.14'2–dc22
2009036718

All rights reserved. No part of this book may be reproduced in any form or by any means, or stored in a database or retrieval system, without prior written permission of the publisher except in the case of brief quotations embodied in articles or reviews. Making copies of any part of this book for any purpose other than your own personal use is a violation of United States copyright laws. For permission requests, please contact the Copyright Clearance Center at www.copyright.com or (978) 750-8400.

We have been careful to provide accurate information in this book, but it is possible that errors and omissions have been introduced. Please consider this in making any career plans or other important decisions. Trust your own judgment above all else and in all things.

Trademarks: All brand names and product names used in this book are trade names, service marks, trademarks, or registered trademarks of their respective owners.

ISBN: 978-1-59357-735-3

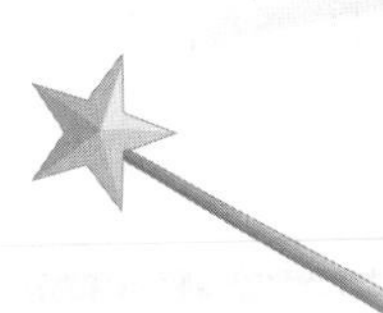

# Contents

## Part IV: Appendixes....................................................389

# Introduction

## The Cover Letter Is How It All Starts

Whether you're selling yourself for a new position or proposing a new book, product, service, or advertising campaign, you begin with a cover letter. You write a letter in an attempt to generate interest, enthusiasm, and action from your reader. That is precisely what we did to interest JIST in publishing this book. And, see, it worked!

**WENDY S. ENELOW, CPRW, JCTC, CCM**
President, Career Masters Institute
119 Old Stable Road, Lynchburg, VA 24503
Phone: 804-386-3100 Fax: 804.386.3200
wendyenelow@cminstitute.com

**LOUISE M. KURSMARK, CPRW, JCTC, CCM**
President, Best Impression Career Services, Inc.
9847 Catalpa Woods Court, Cincinnati, OH 45242
Phone: 513-792-0030 Fax: 513-792-0961
LK@yourbestimpression.com

Michael Farr
President
JIST Publishing
8902 Otis Avenue
Indianapolis, IN 46216-1033

Dear Mr. Farr:

Writing high-impact cover letters and job search communications is what we do best. That's why we have teamed together to write a new book, *Cover Letter Magic.* This publication is designed as a job seeker–friendly guide to developing powerful cover letters that get candidates noticed, not passed over. And it's packed with more than 100 cover letter samples, all written by members of the Career Masters Institute, a prestigious professional association whose membership includes resume writers, career coaches, career counselors, recruiters, and others in the careers and employment industry.

Let me briefly highlight the qualifications Louise and I bring to the table:

- We are published authors with more than a dozen books between us, all written since 1995.
- We have both been featured contributors to *National Business Employment Weekly* and countless other print and online job search publications.
- Both of us have had resumes and cover letters featured in numerous other JIST publications written by David Noble and Michael Farr.
- We have both earned our CPRW (Certified Professional Resume Writer), JCTC (Job & Career Transition Coach), and CCM (Credentialed Career Master) designations, clearly demonstrating that we are at the top of our industry.
- Combined, we have more than 25 years in the resume writing, cover letter writing, job search, coaching, and career marketing industries.

Enclosed is a detailed outline of our proposed publication, along with essential marketing information. I hope that you will give our proposal serious consideration; we think *Cover Letter Magic* will be a valuable addition to the JIST library of top-notch career publications. I'll follow up with you in two weeks.

Sincerely,

Wendy S. Enelow, CPRW, JCTC, CCM

Enclosure

Your job search is no different. You have a commodity to sell—*yourself*—and you must approach your search campaign just as you would any other sales or marketing campaign. You begin by identifying the key features and benefits of that product (you!) and then work to develop a resume and cover letter that clearly communicate those specific points. It's that easy, yet that complex.

In this book, we focus almost exclusively on cover letter writing, although we do include a brief, yet solid introduction to resume writing in chapter 17, "Winning Resume Strategies." Although you might think that writing job search materials is all the same, the difference between writing resumes and writing cover letters is dramatic. They are two entirely different documents, each with its own structure, strategy, and agenda.

*Tip* If you have not yet written your resume, are having trouble with one section, are questioning the wording that you used, or are uncertain about its overall effectiveness, we recommend that you pick up *Résumé Magic*, the companion to this book, by Susan Britton Whitcomb, CCMC, CCM, NCRW, CPRW. Susan's book is one of the most comprehensive resources we've ever seen. It covers virtually every topic imaginable related to resume development, strategy, writing, and production. No matter how obscure your questions are, you will find the answers in *Résumé Magic*.

If your need is more specific—if you have the bones of a good resume but need to fine-tune it, or if you seek resume tips for a specific function or industry—we suggest that you refer to one of our *Expert Resumes* books. With 11 books, covering industries from computer and web jobs to military-to-civilian transitions, the *Expert Resumes* series provides specific strategies and on-target examples that will help you create a great resume or polish your draft into a star.

Consider the following. When you're writing your resume, you're writing a document that you hope to use over and over, for almost every job search opportunity, advertisement, or referral. Of course, at times you might have to modify your resume a bit, and in some situations you might have two or three different versions (depending on your objectives). The bottom line, however, is that you are writing a single document that gives a broad-based overview of your entire career.

The cover letter process is entirely different from resume writing. Almost every time you write a cover letter, you are writing a unique letter to a specific person for a particular reason and with a unique message. That process, in and of itself, requires that you tailor your letters to each individual situation.

> *Tip* To optimize the impact of your cover letters and the response that they generate, you must be willing to invest the time and energy to create customized letters that sell you for a specific opportunity. Anything less will reduce your chances of capturing your reader's attention and being offered the opportunity for an interview.

## How This Book Is Organized

Cover letter writing is an art that requires you to write a brief, hard-hitting document that catches a reader's attention. If you're not an experienced writer or haven't used your writing skills in years, this can be a daunting task. But have no fear. We've made it easy for you with *Cover Letter Magic!* Here's how the book is structured.

The Introduction explores the purpose and objectives of cover letters and why they are so important to your job search. The Introduction ends with the top 10 strategies for writing winning cover letters.

Chapter 1 contains a comprehensive discussion of the nine different kinds of cover letters. You'll learn to identify the one that's right for each particular situation you encounter.

In chapter 2, you'll begin your preparation by developing your cover letter strategy and your key "selling points." This up-front work will make the actual writing of your cover letters much simpler and faster; you won't have to plan and write each letter from the ground up.

Then it's time to write. In chapter 3 we'll coach you in the process of writing a winning cover letter, from the strategy behind the words to the actual words themselves. We'll teach you how to write the three essential sections of every cover letter and give you a cover letter checklist to guarantee that your letters are appropriate, on target, and designed to produce results.

Chapter 4 follows with the unique characteristics of electronic cover letters—their similarities to and their differences from the more "traditional" cover letter.

Chapter 5 furnishes you with tools of the trade, so that you can improve the visual presentation and impact of your cover letters. Fonts, format, and paper are just a few of the topics we'll cover. Then we'll move on to discuss related technology issues such as mail merge, e-mail broadcast campaigns, and other PC-based methods for cover letter reproduction and distribution.

Before we begin reviewing actual cover letter samples, chapter 6 rounds out our discussion with answers to frequently asked questions (FAQs). Should your letter *always* fit on one page? When should you discuss salary in a cover letter, and when is this topic best left for the interview? This chapter also includes tips and tricks from the top—insider strategies gleaned from our decades of experience in writing cover letters for every imaginable job search situation.

Chapters 7 through 13 are what this book is all about: more than 100 "real-life" cover letters written by professional resume writers, career coaches, career counselors, recruiters, military and government transition specialists, and others in the career and employment industry. These letters were used in actual job search campaigns—successful campaigns with powerful resumes and cover letters as their foundation. Chapter 7 shows the "magic" of before-and-after cover letter transformations. Chapters 8 through 11 include letters for blue-collar/trades positions, young professionals/new graduates, mid-career professionals, and senior managers/executives. Chapter 12 is devoted to technical and scientific professionals and, in chapter 13, you'll find cover letters for people who are making a significant career change, from one field to another. You can quickly identify the chapter that is most pertinent to your situation and use the examples in that chapter as inspiration for your own cover letters.

Chapter 14 is dedicated to writing winning thank-you letters, the strategy behind them, and the style in which to present them. Also included are several outstanding samples that will help you make your thank-you letters work as powerful marketing tools.

In chapter 15, after you've read more than 200 pages showing the rules for writing powerful cover letters, we'll show you cover letters written by recruiters. Many of these letters break all the rules!

Chapter 16 introduces what we call "next-generation" cover letters, incorporating innovative approaches for special circumstances. Like everything else, job-search strategies evolve over time, and these cutting-edge documents might be just what you need to provide yourself a competitive advantage in the employment market.

In chapter 17, we share information on writing winning resumes. Learn the best strategies, formats, and presentations for developing resumes that are powerful and well-positioned and produce the results that you want—interviews and offers! Chapter 18 shares our time-tested tips for keeping your career moving in any economy.

Finally, the Appendixes provide valuable career resources to help you plan and manage your winning job search campaign.

Throughout the book, "Tips" and "Examples" are highlighted with special symbols. These sections provide quick insights to enhance the section you've just read, further explain specific strategies, and share insider strategies we've developed in our many years of writing cover letters. And perhaps most importantly, you'll find numerous "Action Item" lists that give you detailed and specific activities to complete as you go about the task of writing your own cover letters.

## The Purpose and Objectives of a Cover Letter

Every time you sit down to write a cover letter, ask yourself the following question: *"Why am I writing this letter?"* Believe it or not, your answer will always ultimately be the same—"to ask for an interview." Bottom line, there is no reason to forward your resume and cover letter other than to ask for an interview.

> *Tip* There are exceptions to this "rule." Consider the letter you write asking someone to pass along your resume to someone they know (to ultimately get an interview with them) or the letter you write when forwarding a copy of your resume to a friend for feedback (so that you can ultimately send it to someone else and get an interview with them). What about the letter you write to an old college professor who is now serving on the board of directors of a Fortune 100 company, asking for contact names and referrals (so that you can ultimately get an interview)? These are not what we traditionally refer to as cover letters; and therefore, the "rule" of asking for the interview does not apply to these situations.

Now, if writing your cover letters were only that easy—just a quick little note asking for an interview! Unfortunately, nothing worthwhile is ever that easy. Before you can ask for the interview, you must accomplish several objectives in your cover letters. These include the following:

- **Introducing** yourself and clearly defining "who" you are—a welder, teacher, sales manager, accountant, computer programmer, aerospace engineer, historian, chef, graphic designer, purchasing agent, security manager, or CEO.
- **Highlighting** your most notable qualifications, experiences, credentials, skills, and achievements.
- **Identifying** the value you can bring to the organization.
- **Capturing** your reader's interest in you, your resume, and your availability.
- **Motivating** the reader to call and offer you the opportunity for an interview.

What's more, whenever possible, you want to relate your qualifications, experiences, credentials, skills, and achievements to the specific needs of the company or recruiter to whom you are writing the letter. Sometimes this information is readily available (such as when the job advertisement lists the company's needs); other times you'll have to do some research (perhaps by talking to someone who already works at the organization); and on occasion you will not be able to find it. Whenever you are able to obtain company information, use that "market intelligence" to present your qualifications as they relate to that organization's needs. Position yourself as the best solution to the specific needs, challenges, or issues you have identified. Here are some examples:

- If you know that the company is looking for a production supervisor with extensive SAP experience, tell them about the SAP project team you managed.
- If you know that the criminal practice firm you're applying to is in desperate need of an experienced paralegal, be sure to highlight the fact that you have six years of experience as a paralegal for a criminal practice firm.
- If you know that the hospital you're applying to has had tremendous problems with retaining its JCAHO certification, write about your years of experience managing relationships with JCAHO accreditation personnel.
- If you know that an electronics firm wants a candidate with experience selling into both large and small accounts, relate your sales successes with both emerging companies and Fortune 100 accounts.

When writing your cover letters, picture this: You've taken each career experience, responsibility, and project you've ever had and laid them all out on a table. Every time you write a letter, you're going to look at everything on that table and then choose what to include based specifically on that company's needs.

What if you've been unable to learn much about the company and its specific needs? In that case, the best strategy is to make "educated guesses" about needs and concerns you can address for that company. A cover letter that presents you as a solution to business challenges is much more effective than one that simply presents your qualifications.

> *Tip* One-third of the individuals to whom you write a letter will never read it; one-third will always read it; and one-third might read it if the resume is interesting and catches their immediate attention. When writing your letters, remember that you are always writing to the latter two categories of readers—the ones who are most likely to read your letter and take action (such as extending you the opportunity for a personal interview). Because you do not know which readers fall into which categories, all of your cover letters must be powerful, well written, and well presented.

## The Importance of Cover Letters in Your Winning Job Search Campaign

You might be wondering whether you need to use a cover letter at all. The answer to that question is simple and straightforward: *Every job seeker must have a cover letter.* There are virtually no exceptions to this rule, unless a particular company or recruiter has instructed you to forward just a resume, without a cover letter. (This rarely happens.)

At other times you might find that a cover letter is optional but not mandatory. A good example of this situation is when you are submitting your resume in response to an online posting. We strongly recommend that you take the time and make the effort to submit a cover letter with your resume, even when you are not required to do so. Why not give yourself every opportunity to stand out among the intense competition of an online job search? A well-written cover letter will set you apart from the pack; and isn't that your ultimate goal?

There is no doubt that a great cover letter can make the difference in whether you get noticed or passed over. A great cover letter can be a powerful marketing tool that does all of the following:

- Positions you above the competition
- Sells your qualifications and your successes
- Demonstrates your knowledge, experience, and expertise
- Creates excitement, enthusiasm, and action (and thus, an interview)

What is it about your cover letter that can do all of this? Is it the words that you write? Is it the style or the tone of your cover letter? Is it the visual presentation? Is it the color of paper that you choose and the type style that you use? Is it the specific achievements that you highlight? The years of experience you have? Your educational credentials? Yes—to all of the above!

As we will show you hundreds of times in this book, your cover letters can have a tremendous impact on the quality and success of your search campaign. To best demonstrate this concept, let's look at a typical job search situation in which you are contacting a company to express your interest in employment opportunities. You don't know of any specific job openings at the company. And you might not even know a specific person to address the letter to. This kind of letter is sometimes referred to as a "cold-call" letter.

Now, what are you going to send to that company? First, you will include your resume, full of factual information about your experience, educational credentials, and more. Your resume, in and of itself, is a powerful tool to sell your qualifications and highlight your achievements. However, the typical scenario is that you will prepare just one resume and use it for every employment contact you make—including cold calls, newspaper ad responses, online posting responses, networking communications, and more.

Your cover letter serves a different purpose. It is designed as a personal introduction to who you are, custom-made for that specific opportunity, and allowing you the chance to communicate a great deal of information about yourself—both the personal you and the professional you. In theory, you're taking excerpts from your resume—the most important excerpts as they relate to a specific position—and rewording them to communicate the same concepts, qualifications, experiences, and accomplishments, just in different words. It is not a good idea, however, to type word-for-word the exact language that you've already used in your resume.

*Tip* Your cover letter should complement your resume, not repeat it verbatim!

## The Rules: There Aren't Any!

Cover letters can be fun to write, although you might not think so. In fact, there may be little that you find fun at this point in your job search. But with the right perspective and a positive attitude, you will find that writing cover letters affords you great flexibility. There is no one set format in which they must be written. There is no one style in which they must be presented. There are virtually no rules to writing cover letters, other than a few basics, which we cover in "The Top 10 Strategies for Writing Winning Cover Letters," which follows. Because they are so flexible, cover letters allow you to positively present just those skills, qualifications, achievements, and credentials that you want to bring to a specific reader's immediate attention.

*Tip* Cover letters allow you the opportunity to "paint the picture you want someone to see while remaining in the realm of reality." You can pick and choose the skills and qualifications you want to highlight in each letter based on the requirements of a particular position. Cover letters give you the platform to create a vision of who you are that relates directly to the company's or recruiter's hiring criteria, while remaining 100 percent accurate and honest.

One of the other advantages of cover letters is that you can be creative in both content and presentation. There is no one standard format that you must follow. In the chapters that contain sample cover letters (chapters 7 through 13), you will have the opportunity to review more than 130 letters that are unique in their wording and style, striking in their visual presentation, and successful in generating interest and interviews.

## The Top 10 Strategies for Writing Winning Cover Letters

1. **Make it easy for someone to understand "who" you are.** Are you a sales representative, actuary, nurse, college professor, chemical engineer, restaurant manager, customer service agent, or architect? Be sure to clearly communicate that information at the beginning of your cover letter. Don't make someone read three paragraphs to find this critical information. No one is going to take the time and energy to figure it out!

2. **Use a unique and professional format when writing and typing your cover letters.** Make your letters visually attractive and distinctive, avoiding overused "standard" formats or templates. Take a look at all the samples in this book to see how creative yet professional you can be in writing the text and designing the presentation.

3. **Highlight your most relevant qualifications.** Use your cover letters to highlight your skills, experiences, qualifications, honors, awards, and credentials that are directly relevant to the company's needs and the type of position and/or career path you are pursuing.

4. **Shine a spotlight on your most relevant achievements.** Be certain to highlight your career successes, results, and accomplishments that will be most meaningful to the letter's intended audience.

5. **Include information that you know about the company or the position for which you are applying.** If you know any particulars about the company to which you are writing (for example, core issues, challenges, market opportunities, products, services, staffing changes, or management changes), be sure to address those items in your cover letter. What's more, relate specifically how your experience can meet the company's needs and provide solutions to its challenges.
6. **Explain why you want to work for this company in particular.** Do you want to work for the company because of its reputation, financial standing, products, services, personnel, location, or market potential? Why *this* company? Everyone likes a good "pat on the back" for a job well done. Companies are no different. Tell them what they're doing right that caught your attention.
7. **Be sure that your cover letters are neat, clean, and well presented.** Remember, cover letters are business documents, not advertising materials. They should be attractive and relatively conservative, not "over-designed."
8. **Double-check, triple-check, and then have someone else check your letter to be sure that it is error-free!** Remember, people don't meet you; they meet a piece of paper. And that piece of paper—your cover letter—reflects the quality and caliber of the work you will do on their behalf. Even the smallest of errors is unacceptable.
9. **Keep your cover letters short!** Cover letters are not essays. We recommend a one-page letter in nearly all circumstances.
10. **Always remind yourself why you are writing each cover letter and be sure to ask for the interview!** Remember, securing an interview is your number-one objective for each cover letter that you write.

In the following cover letter, we show how each of these top 10 tips is employed to create a letter that captures the reader's attention and "sells" the candidate for the Operations Management positions she is pursuing. The notated numbers (1–10) illustrate where each of the 10 tips is used in the cover letter.

2

**Meredith Rockwell**
759 Harbor Court, Unit 5A, Baltimore, MD 21229

(301) 745-7299
rockwell@yahoo.com

April 30, 2010

Daniel Chang
Executive Vice President
Chang Automotive Systems, Inc.
7525 Industrial Parkway
Wilmington, DE 19810

Dear Mr. Chang:

More than ever, good companies need proven performers who can get results in competitive industries and a tough economy. My record as an operations manager speaks for itself: 1

4

- ❑ For BigBox, in just over a year I cut hundreds of thousands of dollars from operating costs, improved productivity 12%, reduced costly order-picking errors, and contributed to the company's first profitable quarter ever.
- ❑ For automotive-supplier Klein Auto Systems, I twice took responsibility for struggling manufacturing operations and brought them to double-digit profitability, primarily through the introduction of Lean Manufacturing and Six Sigma methodologies.

I'm confident I can deliver similar results for Chang Automotive, adding to your company's exceptional reputation for quality products and satisfied customers. 6

3 In brief, I am an experienced operations manager, program manager, and Black Belt project leader. I understand and apply state-of-the-art methodologies for continuous improvement of manufacturing and distribution processes; yet I realize that it is people who ultimately deliver results, and I am strongly focused on building relationships with employees, managers, suppliers, and customers as a primary tool for business success.

10 May we set up a time to talk? I would like to explore how I can help your company tackle its profitability, productivity, quality, and cost challenges—and win. 5

Sincerely,

Meredith Rockwell

enclosure: resume

7 8 9

# Creating and Distributing Your Cover Letters

Chapter 1

# Cover Letter Formats and Types for Every Situation

Writing cover letters can be one of the most difficult tasks in your job search. Although it might have taken you a while to prepare your resume, and it certainly required a great deal of effort, once it's done, it's done. Although there are exceptions, generally a job seeker will use just one resume throughout a job search. Cover letters, on the other hand, must be individually written to have the most impact and generate the most response. This means that you will have to create a new letter each time you send a resume. Here's why:

- **Cover letters are "situation-dependent."** Are you writing in response to an advertisement, reaching out to a network contact, following up on a past letter and resume you submitted, or just sending a general letter of inquiry? What if you're writing the letter in response to a specific referral from one of your colleagues? What if you're writing to recruiters who specialize in your industry or your profession? The situation dictates the strategy behind the cover letter and the specific information you will include.
- **You need to communicate different information to different people in your cover letter.** Suppose you're a customer service representative in the credit-card industry and you're interested in a similar position in the telecommunications industry. The focus in your letter should be on (1) your years of experience in customer service, and not your industry background. However, if you're seeking to transition into a

human resources position in telecommunications, your letter should focus on (1) your years of experience in the industry and (2) the skills and qualifications you have that are transferable to human resources (for example, employee hiring, training, scheduling, and salary administration). *Remember, paint the picture you want the reader to see while remaining in the realm of reality!*

- **You must be creative in presenting your qualifications in your cover letter.** Cover letters should complement your resume, not repeat it. Do not copy text, word for word, straight out of your resume. This means that you will have to decide how to communicate similar information in different words. Here's a quick example: If you're a sales representative and have highlighted specific sales achievements under each position in your resume, you do not want to repeat that same information in your letter. However, you still want to communicate that you've been successful. Instead of listing your individual sales achievements, you might want to summarize them to span your entire career or categorize them by type (for example, revenue growth, new account development, and new product introduction).
- **Cover letters need to convey information that is meaningful in the particular situation.** For instance, if you're responding to an advertisement, your letter should address all (or most) of the hiring requirements as stated in the ad. Demonstrate that you are the number-one candidate. More information on this point follows later in this chapter.
- **Some employers might require that you provide specific information in your cover letter.** If you are writing in response to an advertisement, the ad might request you to submit information such as salary history (what you have earned in the past and in your current position), salary requirements (what your current salary expectations are), verification of U.S. nationality or residency, or other specific data.

To make cover letter writing easier, faster, and more efficient, we've classified cover letters into nine categories that apply to every situation you will encounter in your job search. Each letter you write will fit into one of these categories. Our list is an instant reference guide and map for you to use in developing your own cover letters.

Here's how to use the list. Simply determine why you are writing a specific letter and to whom. Then review "The Nine Types of Cover Letters" to determine which category your letter fits into. Read the section and follow the key points and recommendations. Then combine the recommendations with the writing suggestions in chapters 2 and 3, and you'll be well on your way to creating cover letters that are appropriate, on target, and powerful.

But before we get into the "Nine Types of Cover Letters," we need to look at the different formats that cover letters can follow.

> *Tip* One of your most valuable tools for writing cover letters is the "copy and paste" function in your word-processing program. Although we talk repeatedly throughout this book about how critical it is that you write letters individually to a specific company, individual, recruiter, venture capitalist, or other contact, you do not have to reinvent the wheel. If you've written a sentence, a paragraph, or a list of bullet points that will work well in various letters, copy it in. Letters must be customized, but you can easily copy them and edit them for another use. Make it easy on yourself!

## Cover Letter Formats

As we've stated, cover letters are business documents, and in most cases they should follow a fairly conservative, professional format. Only in rare circumstances is a wildly original cover letter appropriate. Unless you're in a creative or highly competitive field, we don't recommend unusual cover letter formats such as poetry, "wanted" posters, cover letters used as wrapping paper, advertisements, press releases, treasure hunts, or other innovative, nontraditional ideas. We do recommend a businesslike yet up-to-date and polished format.

Within this general guideline, there are three specific formatting styles you can use in the body of your letters:

- Paragraph style
- Comparison-list style (directly comparing your qualifications to the position requirements)
- Bullet style (with introductory and closing paragraphs surrounding bullet-point statements)

Which style you should select depends on the following:

- Who you are writing to.
- Why you are writing to them.
- The type and amount of information you want to include.
- The tone of the letter.
- The writing style of the letter.

As you review the sample letters in this book, you'll see examples of all three of these formats, with the largest percentage falling into style #3—bullet style. This is often the preferred strategy. It allows you to "talk" to a prospective employer, using the paragraphs to introduce who you are and give some insight into your personality and your professional characteristics. You can then use easily skimmed bullet points to highlight credentials, experiences, special projects, honors, awards, and accomplishments that directly relate to the position for which you are applying.

*Tip* No one style of cover letter is right for every situation. You must closely evaluate why you are writing a specific letter, determine what information is essential to include, and then determine which style works best with the information at hand.

## Paragraph Style

Paragraph-style letters enable you to communicate information in the context of a "story" of what has happened, who you are, and what value you bring to an organization. Your paragraph-style cover letter should be well written, position you as a qualified candidate, and energize your reader to action—an offer for a personal interview.

## Comparison-List Style

Comparison-list-style letters—also known as "T"-style letters—allow you to quickly and assertively respond to the specific requirements of a job as stated in an advertisement. If the advertisement is asking for five specific qualifications, this type of letter enables you to directly compare your specific experiences and accomplishments to those qualifications, demonstrating how they match the company's stated needs. Your comparison-list-style cover letter should be brief, aggressive, and on target.

Example

## Sample Paragraph-Style Letter

# Charles Tobin

*Telephone in Japan:* 81-3-2749-8345 (+14 hours EST)
*E-mail:* charlestobin@hotmail.com

*U.S. Contact:* Mary Tobin, Boston, MA
Telephone (617) 555-8282

August 20, 2010

Mr. Frederick Staples
Crest Hills Country Club
75 Tanager Drive
Newton, MA 01579

Dear Mr. Staples:

At the suggestion of Sam Francis of Nicklaus Design, I am contacting you about the Golf Course Superintendent position at Crest Hills Country Club.

During my 15-year career, I have contributed to the successful construction and development of five courses, including world-class facilities in Thailand and Japan. Having worked closely with Nicklaus Design professionals the last eight years, I know firsthand the care and quality they bring to golf course design, and I am equally committed to maintaining design integrity and delivering the consistently excellent quality that your members expect. The Nicklaus motto—"Get the job done right the first time"—is one that I live by as well, and one that I have successfully communicated to my staff, despite wide cultural differences.

You may not be familiar with the Asian courses I've built and managed. They are of superb quality and cater to very sophisticated clientele. The fact that these courses rank among the best in the world is borne out by the *Golf Digest* rankings they earned recently: Royal Thai was named #6 in Thailand, and Cherry Blossom (where I am currently Superintendent) was named the #2 course in Japan. I have enclosed several photographs of the courses in hopes of conveying their beauty and quality.

My eight years in the Far East have been professionally fulfilling, and it has been extremely satisfying to contribute to the successful development of these fine courses. However, having decided to return to the United States, I was extremely interested to learn about the Crest Hills opportunity. I am confident that your collaboration with Nicklaus Design will result in an immediately successful facility. I'd like to be a part of your organization and believe I have the professional skills and experience to contribute to your success.

May we explore this possibility at greater length? I am most easily reached via e-mail, and with notice I can easily arrange to travel to Boston to meet with you and other members of the management team. I look forward to learning more about your plans for the course and exploring how I can help you to make it successful.

Sincerely,

Charles Tobin

enclosures: Resume; golf course photographs

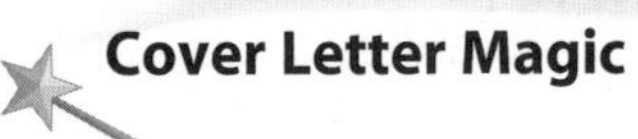

## Sample Comparison-List-Style Letter

# Anna M. Ramirez

452 Broad Street, Englewood, NJ 07053 • 201/555-1208 • ramirez123@worldnet.att.net

August 20, 2010

Box J-7529
Englewood Times
75 Main Street
Englewood, NJ 07053

Re: Job No. SAL-475
Medical Sales

With regard to your current need for a dynamic sales professional, I am confident you will be interested in my relevant accomplishments and experience detailed in the enclosed resume.

You will note that my qualifications closely match your requirements:

| You Require | I Offer |
|---|---|
| ■ 3 years of sales experience | ■ 5 years as a top-performing sales professional—recognized as "number one" in total sales in the region for 5 consecutive years. |
| ■ Medical sales background | ■ 5 years in sales of medical products to physicians, hospitals, long-term-care facilities, and emergency centers. |
| ■ Territory management ability | ■ In my first year with Medi-Quick, I quickly familiarized myself with a new territory and increased sales 200%. Over the past 5 years, I have dedicated myself to new-account development and better coverage of my territory, and these efforts have paid off with significant increases in total territory sales. |
| ■ Relationship-building with health care providers | ■ The key to successful selling lies in customer relationships. I am skilled at developing positive long-term relationships with physicians, medical office staff, and hospital administrators. I provide the support, follow-up, and dependability they need to feel comfortable and confident buying from me, and I rely on strong interpersonal and organizational skills to establish rapport and maintain effective contact. |

I would appreciate the opportunity to discuss your current needs and what I have to offer. With proven sales skills and a superior performance record, I am confident of my ability to help your company achieve important sales goals.

Thank you.

Sincerely,

Anna M. Ramirez

enclosure

Less positively, however, this kind of letter, as its name implies, offers a *direct* comparison of your qualifications with the stated needs. Do not attempt to use this format unless you meet or exceed every qualification listed in the ad; otherwise, you will merely highlight where you are deficient. Further, this letter style does not allow you to "sell" any of your qualities other than through a direct point-by-point comparison. Although this letter style is quite popular among some outplacement firms, in our opinion, it's the least effective of the three. We feel its use will continue to decline, primarily because of its limitations.

If you choose to use this type of letter, follow the example of Anna Ramirez in the preceding sample letter. You will note how clearly she points out that she exceeds every qualification, and she supports her claims with specific accomplishments. She makes as strong a case as possible for herself in this point-by-point comparison.

### Bullet Style

Bullet-style letters enable you to take advantage of the best features of the other two styles. You can begin with an introductory paragraph that communicates who you are and then follow up with a bulleted listing of the top achievements of your career as they relate to a particular company, position, or industry. Then you can go back to the paragraph style for your closing, communicating your interest in the position, detailing any specific information that you feel is appropriate, and asking for the interview. Bullet-style cover letters can often be the most powerful and most compelling style, enticing your reader to closely review your resume and call you to schedule an interview.

## A Word About Electronic Communication

Now, much if not most business correspondence is sent electronically rather than through snail mail. Cover letters are no exception. In fact, although most of the cover letters in this book are presented in traditional print format, we recognize that only rarely will you print and mail your resume and cover letter. In most cases you will send your cover letter by e-mail or paste it into an online application.

## Sample Bullet-Style Letter

Chandra Parker
2357 Carpenters Lane
Cincinnati, OH 45242
chandraparker@fuse.net
(513) 555-0001

August 20, 2010

Mr. David Anderson
Vice President of Administration
Frontline Corporation
725 Walnut Street
Cincinnati, OH 45202

Dear Mr. Anderson:

Reading in today's *Post* about the innovative programs currently underway at Frontline, I was motivated to forward my resume to see if my qualifications might be a good fit for current needs in your Sourcing Department. In particular, Frontline's focus on cost-improvement strategies mirrors my interests and contributions at AMC Packing, where I was instrumental in identifying and implementing significant cost-saving programs. These include the following:

- Saving more than $1 million a year through distribution center reorganization.
- Reducing transportation expenses $330,000 annually through implementation of a highly effective outsourcing program.
- Negotiating contracts for services that delivered cost savings, reduced corporate obligations, and improved customer service.

My management experience includes identifying opportunities company-wide, developing implementation strategies, and executing plans to achieve results. I am an effective communicator across the organization and have a track record of developing positive relationships both within and outside the organization.

Frontline's potential for continued growth is exciting, and I feel confident that my strong bottom-line focus and leadership skills can benefit your company. May we meet to explore your needs and what I have to offer?

Thank you for your consideration.

Sincerely,

Chandra Parker

enclosure: resume

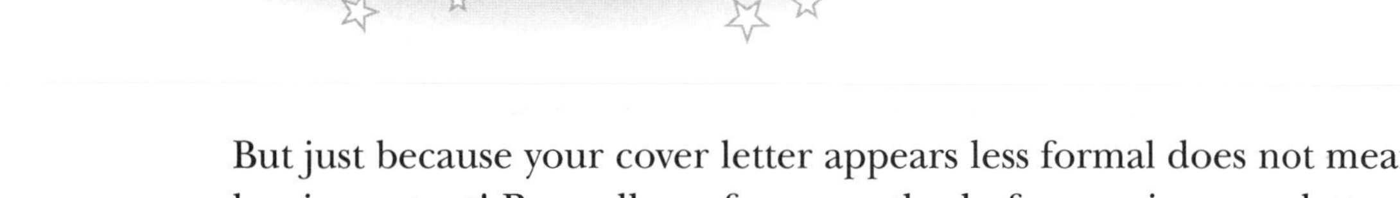


But just because your cover letter appears less formal does not mean it is less important! Regardless of your method of conveying your letter, it is still essential to create a polished, professional, persuasive letter that sells you for the opportunities you are seeking.

The guidelines and examples in the following section, "The Nine Types of Cover Letters," apply to all of your communications, no matter how they are sent. However, we have written an entire chapter (chapter 4) to address specific issues related to electronic communication. Be sure to review it before sending your cover letters by e-mail or through a job-posting site. The information we provide will help you avoid common formatting and content errors that can damage the great impression you are trying to make.

## The Nine Types of Cover Letters

Now let's look at the nine types of cover letters. Remember, these categories are *situation-specific*—your reason for writing a specific letter will dictate the type of letter you choose. Simply skim through the following list for the situation that applies to your present circumstance, and then use that type of letter. To illustrate each concept, we've included sample letters for each of the nine types, and we've recommended the most appropriate of the three styles (paragraph, comparison-list, or bullet) for each type of letter.

### 1. Ad-Response Letter to a Company

***Recommended formats: Comparison-list style; bullet style***

Writing letters in response to specific job advertisements will most likely be an ongoing part of your job search campaign. When you see an advertisement or job posting seeking a candidate with your qualifications, you'll want to respond quickly with a resume and cover letter. The only problem is that these letters are best written individually so that you can highlight how your experience and qualifications match the specific requirements for the job. So, instead of simply using a standard cover letter, you're faced with having to write a separate letter each time. Now, all of a sudden, getting out that quick resume and cover letter is not so quick.

Don't panic! There are ways to get around this and to make the process much easier. We recommend using a comparison-list or bullet style for ad-response letters. The items that you highlight in the bullets or columns—experience, positions, achievements, educational credentials, and so on—should directly match the hiring company's needs. This type of cover letter is easier to write than a paragraph-style letter, because you're writing bulleted, stand-alone items and not a document in which each sentence and paragraph must flow with the next. What's more, these letters are easy to edit, so you can change an item or two and quickly create multiple versions of your letter within minutes.

> *Tip* Compile a comprehensive list of bullet-point statements about your career, employment history, positions, achievements, educational credentials, leadership performance, and so on as ammunition for your cover letters. Then all you'll need to do is select the bullets from the list that match the requirements for each position for which you are applying. See "Step 1: Identify Your Key Selling Points" in chapter 2 for a detailed discussion of preparing these bullet points.

Be sure to reference the position title or number when writing an ad-response letter. You can do this best in one of three ways:

- Include a "position reference line" at the beginning of your cover letter. Type this between the inside address and the salutation. For example:

    Mr. Harry Jones
    President
    ABC Manufacturing Company
    123 Main Street
    Elm, WI 39393

    RE: Purchasing Manager Position–Posting #34837-12

    Dear Mr. Jones:

- Reference the position in the last paragraph of your cover letter with text such as "I would welcome the opportunity to interview for the position of Purchasing Manager (#34837-12) and look forward to speaking with you." With this approach, however, you run the risk of not capturing the reader's attention immediately by appealing to the advertised need.
- Reference the position in the first sentence of your cover letter with a sentence such as "I am writing in response to your advertisement for a Purchasing Manager (#34837-12)." This is our least-favorite way of

**Award-Winning Animator**
**Meticulous Researcher**
**Innovative Educator**
**Skilled Designer**

**SANDRA T. RODRIGUEZ**
2345 Green Ct., Corte Madera, CA 94925 ■ 415-290-0090 ■ sandratee@hotmail.com

August 20, 2010

Van Gogh Entertainment, Inc.
1628 Alta Vista Parkway, Suite 91432
Los Angeles, CA 45103

Re: **Cinematic Artist—Job Posting #CA-9245**

Creating exciting, energetic, realistic 3D environments is what I do best. Whether working on corporate projects—visualizing airport terminals of the future—or creating museum-quality streetscapes, I bring to each project a strong artistic vision complemented by the technical knowledge, project-management skills, and work ethic to deliver high-quality work on schedule.

Your current need for a Cinematic Artist is an excellent match for my experience and abilities. Relevant to your needs, I offer

- Master's degree in design and nearly 3 years of professional experience in 3D visualization, producing small- and large-scale media productions.
- Four years of experience working with 3D Studio Max—I am experienced and prolific in turning clients' architectural design ideas into digital reality.
- Proven abilities in managing design projects from concept to completion and in working collaboratively with other members of the business team (as a team member or team leader).
- Artistic innovation and creativity enhanced by strong research abilities, attention to detail, and willingness to do whatever it takes to "get it right."

Once you have had the opportunity to review my resume and demo reel, I am confident you will agree that my skills, experience, educational background, creativity, and ambition can be valuable to Van Gogh.

Thank you for your consideration. I look forward to your reply.

Sincerely,

Sandra T. Rodriguez

enclosures: resume, demo reel

referencing the position, however, because we prefer that cover letters start with a more dynamic and positive introduction.

### Characteristics

Company ad-response letters are characterized by the following:

- **Targeted nature.** Because these letters are written directly in response to known hiring criteria and requirements, they closely target a specific position.
- **Bullet style.** Your objective when writing in response to an advertisement is to quickly and easily bring your qualifications to the forefront as they directly relate to the position requirements. Using bullet points is the easiest and "cleanest" way to accomplish this.
- **Comparison-list style.** You might choose to use the direct-comparison style in responding to ads; however, remember that this is effective only if you meet or exceed every single one of the stated requirements.

### Sample Ad-Response Letter to a Company

The company ad-response on the preceding page was written in response to an advertisement for a Cinematic Artist. Through a combination of paragraphs and bullet points, it addresses both the specific requirements (Master's degree, experience with StudioMax software, and project management abilities) and the less-tangible skills (creativity, teamwork, and work ethic) listed in the advertisement.

## 2. Ad-Response Letter to a Recruiter

***Recommended formats: Comparison-list style; bullet style***

Writing to recruiters in response to advertisements for specific positions requires exactly the same process as developing company ad-response letters, as detailed in section 1. You already know that

- These letters are best written individually so that you can highlight your experience in direct relation to the requirements of the position as outlined in the advertisement.
- Bullet-style letters are usually the most effective for this situation and are the easiest to edit for use from one position to the next.
- If you choose the comparison-list style, be absolutely certain that your qualifications are a perfect match for the position requirements.

**Gil Nanakara**
gilnan@yahoo.com

2752 Florence Drive
Portland, OR 97219
(503) 555-0454

August 23, 2010

Alice J. Stanton
Management Recruiters, Inc.
235 Belvedere Drive, Suite 125
Portland, OR 97219

Re: **Manufacturing Manager** Position — 8/22/10 *Portland Tribune*

Dear Ms. Stanton:

My passion is to make manufacturing facilities work better: to accelerate workforce productivity, reduce costs, improve quality, maximize capital investments, and increase competitiveness.

Can I make these kinds of contributions to your client's organization? I offer 15 years of progressively responsible engineering and plant management experience and a solid record of results:

- **Cost Savings:** In an increasingly competitive global economy, we shaved 23% from operating costs at Acme Manufacturing—enabling us to compete head-to-head with Asian imports and retain our market share.
- **Operating Efficiency:** Through the implementation of Lean Manufacturing methodologies, we improved throughput and productivity to world-class levels.
- **Team Culture:** In both union and non-union environments, I have successfully instilled an organizational culture of teamwork, cooperation, and shared mission. This results in smoother resolution of *all* operating challenges and enables us to retain our best people while keeping compensation in line with industry standards.

My expertise in consumer products manufacturing is well-balanced and comprehensive, with accomplishments that display a record of sound, efficient, and profitable management of domestic and overseas manufacturing facilities.

Currently, I am earning compensation in the low six figures and am available for relocation within the Pacific Northwest.

I am eager to speak with you about this opportunity and will follow up with a phone call on Friday.

Sincerely,

Gil Nanakara

*resume enclosed*

- It is important to reference the position title and number in your letter.

There are two principal differences between letters you write to recruiters and those you write to companies. First, rather than refer to "you" or "your company," you should refer to "your client" or "your client's organization." This demonstrates that you understand that the recruiter acts as an agent for the hiring company. Second, it is common practice to include salary information, location preferences, and other inclinations that you would not mention in a letter directed to a company. In chapter 3 we elaborate on the additional information that you should include in recruiter letters and also give you suggested wordings.

#### Characteristics

Recruiter ad-response letters are characterized by the following:

- **Straightforwardness.** Don't mess around with recruiters! They know their craft and they know their business—to find a candidate who matches a company's hiring criteria to a "T" and nothing less.
- **Bullet style.** Generally speaking, you have even less time to catch a recruiter's attention than you do a company's. The bullet-style cover letter becomes even more important when you are writing to recruiters. Be honest, be quick, and get to the point.

#### Sample Ad-Response Letter to a Recruiter

The recruiter ad-response letter on the preceding page was written in response to an advertisement for a Manufacturing Manager. The bullet points correspond to the specific requirements of the position; the paragraphs highlight additional "selling points" this candidate has to offer.

### 3. Cold-Call Letter to a Company

***Recommended formats: Paragraph style; bullet style***

You might choose to write cold-call letters to companies to express your interest in employment opportunities, without knowledge of specific advertisements or opportunities. Your challenge in writing this type of cover letter is to give your reader a broad introduction to your skills, qualifications, employment experience, achievements, credentials, and other notable traits that you anticipate will trigger their interest in you and make them offer you the opportunity for an interview.

When writing this type of letter, it is critical that you clearly identify who you are. Are you a sales professional, an accountant, a retail manager, a production operations manager, or a chemical engineer? A Java programmer, a health-care administrator, a management executive, an advertising director, or a graphic designer? Who are you, and how do you want to be perceived?

Just as important, you must communicate what type of position you are seeking. No one is going to take the time to figure this out. Do you want to continue to work as a purchasing agent, or is your objective a purchasing management position? If you're a technology project leader, are you looking to make a lateral move, or are you interested in an IT management position, perhaps as CIO or CTO?

*Tip* When writing a cold-call letter, it is critical to quickly identify *who* you are, what *value* you bring to the company, and what *type* of positions you are interested in. No one is going to take the time to read between the lines and make assumptions. Spell it out!

### Characteristics

Cold-call letters to companies are characterized by the following:

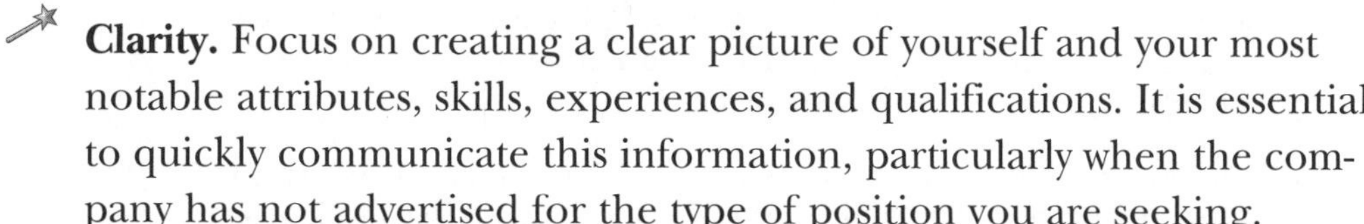

- **Clarity.** Focus on creating a clear picture of yourself and your most notable attributes, skills, experiences, and qualifications. It is essential to quickly communicate this information, particularly when the company has not advertised for the type of position you are seeking.
- **Impact.** Again, because these letters are not in response to a specific opportunity, it is critical that they immediately and powerfully connect with the reader and move him to action to pick up the phone and call you. An effective way to motivate a response is to identify yourself as the solution to the company's problems or needs.

### Sample Cold-Call Letter to a Company

The company cold-call letter that follows was used by a technical writer to approach software companies. She identifies with the company needs, clearly states her expertise, and highlights her key selling points: her successful projects for other software producers.

*Sharyn Walters*

**97 Liberty Street, Apt. 7-B • Philadelphia, PA 19103**
**(215) 555-6767 • sharynw@one.net**

August 20, 2010

Patricia Randall
Director, Technical Communications
Quaker Technical Solutions
57 Broad Street
Philadelphia, PA 19101

Dear Ms. Randall:

Good technical writing involves both science and art: understanding user needs, comprehending software functions, structuring content… then applying strong writing skills and creativity to develop documentation that is elegant, coherent, and, most importantly, useful.

As an experienced technical writer, I have consistently demonstrated strong skills in all of these essential areas. You may be interested in my track record:

- With XYZ, I created several versions of the manuals for the company's primary product line (manufacturing software) just as factory-floor computers were entering the mainstream. This experience provided a strong foundation for the clear, well-organized, sensibly structured manuals that have become my trademark.

- Subsequently, I took on the challenge of writing manuals for software still in development. Through close collaboration with the development team, we consistently produced accurate documentation almost in concert with the software release.

I believe that strong software documentation is essential for customer satisfaction and directly contributes to business success. If you share this commitment and could benefit from my proven skills, we should schedule a time to explore your needs and what I have to offer. When would it be convenient to meet for an interview?

Sincerely,

Sharyn Walters

enclosure

## 4. Cold-Call Letter to a Recruiter

***Recommended formats: Paragraph style; bullet style***

Cold-call letters to recruiters are strategically identical to cold-call letters to companies. In essence, you are writing to the recruiting firm to introduce yourself (the *who* and the *value*) and explore your potential fit for current search assignments (the *type* of position).

Two features distinguish recruiter cold-call letters from company cold-call letters. First and foremost, it is important to disclose information about your job preferences—specifically, your preferences for type of position, type of company, and geographic location. If you are willing to consider only management opportunities, share that information with the recruiter. If you are interested in opportunities with only high-growth technology companies or medical device R&D firms, state that in your letter. If you know that you are not willing to relocate, say so. Or, if you are willing to relocate but only in the Southeastern U.S., communicate that. Be as specific as you can, and don't waste anybody's time—yours or the recruiter's.

The other unique feature of a recruiter cold-call letter is the straightforwardness with which you present information about your salary and compensation objectives. We recommend that you provide some information to give the recruiter an idea of the level of salary or type of compensation you are seeking. You can do this in several different ways, generally in the last paragraph of your cover letter. The most common strategies for disclosing this information without giving away too much information include the following:

- **"Most recently, my salary has averaged $50,000 annually."** This is the best strategy if your salary has varied over the years.
- **"My current salary objectives are in the $100,000 to $150,000 range."** This clearly defines the range without stating a specific figure. If you state a specific number, it can potentially work to your disadvantage—either by taking you out of consideration because your expectations are too high, or short-changing you with a salary that is lower than the company had expected to pay. And don't assume that a low figure will make you an attractive candidate. Both the recruiter and the company might assume that you lack the level of experience they're seeking.

- **"My salary requirements are negotiable and can be discussed at the time of an interview."** This is our least-favorite alternative because you have not disclosed any information. Use this type of response only when, for whatever reason, you do not want to provide any details.
- **"My salary history can be discussed at the time of an interview."** Again, our least-favorite for the same reasons as above.

Note that you can use these same types of statements when writing in response to a company or recruiter advertisement that asks for your salary history or current salary requirements.

Mentioning salary in cover letters is a controversial topic. In fact, discussing compensation at this point in the job search process with any recruiter or company is an issue of constant debate. For a much more comprehensive discussion of this topic, refer to "Step 5: Write the Closing," in chapter 3.

### Characteristics

Cold-call letters to recruiters are uniquely characterized by the following:

- **Disclosure of job, company, and geographic preferences.** Lay your cards on the table, and be specific about your job preferences.
- **Disclosure of salary and compensation information.** Unlike cold-call letters to companies, where you should never discuss compensation, it is a good policy to at least "define the ballpark" when writing to a recruiter.

### Sample Cold-Call Letter to a Recruiter

The recruiter cold-call letter that follows was written for a senior executive looking for a new top-level opportunity. Pay close attention to both section 1 (the opening paragraphs and first set of bullet points, which highlight his general management competencies) and section 2 (the second set of bullet points, which highlight his most significant career achievements). By demonstrating strong experience across a broad range of functions and combining that with tangible achievements, this letter positions Joseph for a variety of senior-level opportunities.

**JOSEPH R. GRANNSON**
**jrg@inmind.com**

13876 Wilson Park South #1403
Memphis, TN 38134

Phone: (901) 555-3726
Fax: (901) 555-3683

August 20, 2010

Don Pardo
Managing Partner
SES Search, Inc.
8888 N. 154th Street, Suite 1212
New York, NY 10024

Dear Mr. Pardo:

Building corporate value is my expertise. Whether challenged to launch a start-up venture, orchestrate a turnaround, or accelerate growth within an established corporation, I have consistently delivered strong financial results. Now I'm looking for a new executive opportunity with a company poised for solid growth and performance.

The value I bring to an organization can best be summarized as follows:

- More than 10 years of direct P&L responsibility across diverse industries and market sectors.
- Strong, decisive, and profitable leadership of global sales and marketing organizations.
- Keen financial, negotiating, and strategic planning performance.
- Consistent and measurable gains in operations, quality, efficiency, and productivity.

To each organization, my teams and I have delivered strong and sustainable operating, market, and financial advantages critical to long-term growth, profitability, and competitive performance. Most notably, I

- Increased sales 19.6%, reduced staff 32%, shortened lead times 50%, and improved quality performance 300%.
- Orchestrated successful turnaround and return to profitability of a $54 million corporation. Cost reductions surpassed $2 million, account base increased 15%, and annualized cash flow improved $1.2 million.
- Accelerated growth of a well-established market leader in a highly competitive and volatile industry, increasing revenues 45% and delivering equally significant reductions in operating costs and corporate debt.
- Advanced rapidly during tenure with the Raffert Corporation, becoming the youngest corporate executive in the 52-year history of the company.

My goal is a top-level management position with an organization seeking to achieve market dominance as well as aggressive revenue and profit projections. I am open to relocate nationwide and would anticipate an annual compensation package of $200,000+.

I look forward to the opportunity to speak with you regarding any current search assignments appropriate for a candidate with my qualifications.

Sincerely,

Joseph R. Grannson

Enclosure

## 5. Referral Letter

***Recommended formats: Paragraph style; bullet style***

When you are writing a referral letter, you are writing to a particular individual at a company or recruiting firm at the recommendation of someone else. These letters can be very similar in style and strategy to cold-call letters. You're not sure whether the company has a specific need for someone with your talents. You don't necessarily know the company's situation. Is it on a growth track? Is it downsizing? Does it have new products to introduce? Is it making money? Is it losing money? So, just as with the cold-call letter discussed earlier, these letters are often more "general" in their presentation and not necessarily focused on a particular position. As mentioned previously, you want to give your reader a broad-based introduction to who you are, what expertise and qualifications you have, and why you would be valuable to the organization.

Although referral letters are very similar in style to cold-call letters, the one major exception is the introduction, in which you immediately reference the individual who referred you to that person, company, or recruiter. To ensure that the recipient will read on, it is critical that you mention the referring person's name and, if appropriate, his or her company or professional affiliation, as the very first item in your cover letter.

> *Tip* For a referral letter to be effective, the person who referred you must be immediately recognizable to the reader because of name, company affiliation, or status within the business community or industry. If not, the impact of your letter is negated, and its value is nonexistent.

Referral letters can work for individuals at all levels. For the senior executive, a referral letter can highlight contributions to revenue and profit growth, strategic leadership, organizational development, turnaround, and other senior-level functions. For the college graduate, a referral letter can focus on academic performance, internships, leadership, enthusiasm, and interest in the organization. The message might change, but the strategy remains the same: "Sell" who you are in a broad-brush fashion in the hope that something within the breadth of your experience will capture your reader's attention.

### Characteristics

Referral letters are characterized by the following:

- **Introduction.** All referral letters begin with an immediate reference to the person who referred you to that organization. This is the single distinguishing qualification of referral letters.
- **General in composition.** Because you do not know whether the company is hiring, or for what types of positions, it is best to sell as much about yourself, your experience, and your career as possible in an attempt to find "common ground" with the company.

### Sample Referral Letter

The referral letter that follows was written by a CFO looking for a similar type of position. He referenced the name of the president of his current company to capture the reader's immediate attention, and then followed with a brief yet hard-hitting summary of his expertise. This letter positioned him as an incredibly qualified candidate.

## 6. Networking Letter

***Recommended format: Paragraph style***

Networking letters are written to your personal and professional network of contacts and are one of the single most vital components of your search campaign. No matter who you are, what you do for a living, or where you do it, you have developed a network of contacts over time, whether deliberately or not. Networking is a natural process that you almost can't avoid. Now, you can use those network contacts to your advantage in identifying employment opportunities, getting interviews, and shortening your job search cycle.

Who are your networking contacts? They can be divided into several categories:

- **Professional network.** This network includes coworkers, colleagues, supervisors, and managers from both past and current employers. If you are a senior executive, this network might also include bankers, investors, business partners, vendors, and others within your professional community.
- **Community network.** Business professionals from your local community—bankers, lawyers, real estate brokers, and others you

**ARNOLD L. LEBERSTEIN**

P.O. Box 38283
Worcester, MA 01605

aleberstein@verizon.net

Home (508) 555-3372
Fax (508) 555-3777

---

August 20, 2010

Michael R. Mannley
President & CEO
LRL Products Manufacturing, Inc.
89 Leister Road
York, PA 18763

Dear Mr. Mannley:

John Johnson recommended I contact you directly. I know that you and John see each other often at the regional CEO meeting each month. I've worked for John for the past six years but will be leaving the company as they shift their operations to Mexico later this year. John knew that you were looking for a new CFO and thought our timing might be perfect.

For the past 20 years, I have served as Chief Financial Officer for two billion-dollar-plus corporations (John's company and Rubbermaid). The scope of my responsibility has been extensive, including the entire finance, tax, internal audit, transactions, information systems, and administrative functions for both corporations. In fact, I am one of a small number of executives credited with leading both of these corporations through dramatic growth and financial success.

Equally notable is my significant experience in corporate transactions—IPOs, LBOs, acquisitions, divestitures, public financings, investment financings, and more. I have earned a reputation for my ability to identify opportunities, and then structure and negotiate complex transactions to achieve growth, expand market presence, and deliver strong bottom-line results. This experience includes transactions in the U.S. as well as major international markets in Europe and Asia.

Now that the time has come to look for new executive opportunities, I would welcome the chance to meet with you. John believes that we are definitely a good match, and I look forward to exploring that potential. I'll phone next week to schedule a convenient time for a meeting. Thank you.

Sincerely,

Arnold L. Leberstein

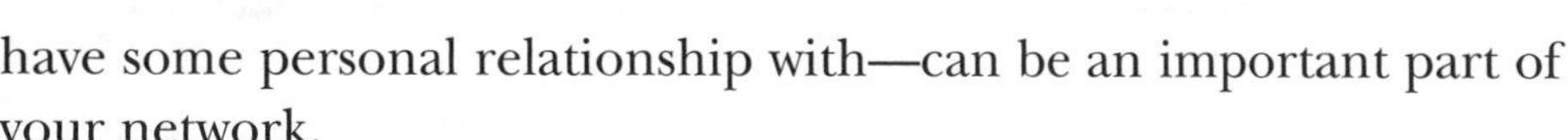



have some personal relationship with—can be an important part of your network.

- **College/university network.** College alumni, professors, and administrators can be a priceless source of leads and contacts for your campaign. And don't forget the college career center—most provide free services to alumni as well as to current students.
- **Association network.** Professional and community associations to which you belong are an extremely valuable networking source.
- **Personal network.** This network includes friends, neighbors, and relatives.

Networking letters can often be the most creative missives you write. Because you are writing to individuals whom you know—either personally or professionally—you can "let your hair down" and develop a letter that is a bit more informal than you would write to a stranger. In turn, you can be more creative in your presentation, tone, language, and style.

The message you want to communicate in your networking letter is, "I need your help." You're writing to these individuals for their assistance, guidance, referrals, and recommendations—not for a job. (If they happen to have a job opening themselves, however, they'll be sure to mention it as a natural response to reading your letter.) If you approach your contacts in this manner, you're very likely to receive a positive response. The key to successful networking is to ask only for what your contact can give you. Everyone can give advice, and most people enjoy helping friends and associates. But if you ask for a job, and it's not in your contact's power to give one to you, you'll create a "dead end" with that networking contact.

> *Tip* You want at least one of three things from each of your network contacts: (1) a recommendation or referral for a specific employment opportunity; (2) information about specific companies; or (3) additional contacts you can add to your network. The whole trick to networking is to expand your contact base by getting new names from your existing network. Leverage their contacts to your advantage.

Just as with cold-call letters, your networking letter should give a strong summary of your skills, experiences, achievements, and credentials. You have no idea what opportunities a particular contact might know about, so you want to be sure to highlight a broad range of qualifications.

This letter is easier to write than most in that you can often use the same letter for all your network contacts. In some instances you will want to change it a bit, particularly at the beginning, where you might want to start with something a bit more personal; for example:

> It's been a while since you and I have seen each other. In fact, I think the last time was at the AMA meeting several months ago in Chicago. I've been meaning to catch up with you since then, but we've been immersed in a new company acquisition, plus Jenny just had our second child. I can hardly keep up with it all!

### Characteristics

Networking letters are characterized by the following:

- **Familiar tone.** Because you are writing to individuals whom you know, your letters should be hard-hitting, powerful, and results-oriented, yet written in a less formal manner than you would write to a stranger.
- **Request for help and contact information.** Remember, the two most valuable results of your networking efforts are (1) specific leads that you will receive from the network and (2) contact information for people and companies you can then add to your network.

### Sample Networking Letter

The networking letter that follows was written for a financial executive looking to make a transition from the restaurant industry. It uses a conversational yet not-too-informal tone. Note the request for an in-person meeting.

## 7. Follow-Up Letter

***Recommended formats: Paragraph style; bullet style***

Follow-up letters are just that—letters that you write to follow up on previous correspondence (your resume and cover letter) that you sent but from which you have had no response. When writing follow-up letters, you have three primary objectives:

- To reiterate your interest in the advertised position or the other purpose of your original letter.
- To highlight your most relevant experience, skills, and qualifications.
- To ask for an interview.

# Robin Madison

4723 Plantation Place, San Diego, CA 92138 ▪ 619-555-0008 ▪ robinmadison@aol.com

---

August 20, 2010

Stanley Prince
Principal
Tyson Consulting
129 Brookline Avenue
Boston, MA 02142

Dear Stan:

May I ask your advice and assistance?

Having completed a turnaround of the financial operation at Le Jardin (a 5-restaurant chain with $14 million in anticipated revenue this year), I have assessed my career options and decided to launch a search for a new position. Whether in a new industry or with a larger organization, I'm ready for new challenges and feel that my track record will be meaningful to any company interested in business growth and tight financial controls.

In the past 15 years, I've had the good fortune to be associated with rapidly growing organizations, and to be in on the ground floor of the accounting/finance operation. Many times, I learned "on my feet"—how to implement accounting systems, negotiate financing, prepare reports and analyses for venture capitalists, and meet a wide array of both accounting/finance and general operating challenges. The results have been satisfying—as you'll note from the accomplishments highlighted in my resume.

Now, I'm eager to transfer my skills and experience to an organization where I can continue to make a difference—and where I'll also continue to learn and expand my professional capabilities.

My expertise and interest are in service industries, and my financial experience has encompassed businesses from start-up to $20 million.

Since I value your experience and perspective, I would greatly appreciate a few minutes of your time to discuss my career options and glean any suggestions you can offer. I'll phone you in the next few days to see if we can get together for a brief meeting.

Thanks very much.

Best regards,

*Robin*

enclosure: resume

For these letters, you will use the same letter category that you used for the first letter you sent. If your first letter was a letter in response to a company advertisement, you will send that same type of letter again. The only difference is that you will change the text and not send the exact same letter. Just as you want your letters to be complementary to your resume, you want your follow-up letters to be complementary to, not repetitive of, the first letter that you sent. Communicate similar achievements of your career using different language, examples, and highlights.

Follow-up letters generally begin with a reference to your previous correspondence and the reason for your contact; for example:

> Several weeks ago I forwarded a letter and resume in response to your advertisement for an Insurance Agent, and I would like to reiterate my interest in the position. My six years of experience in insurance sales and brokerage services have provided me with precisely the skills and qualifications highlighted in your advertisement.

With that introductory paragraph, you've immediately communicated

- Why you're writing to that company.
- The fact that you've previously contacted them.
- That your experience is identical to their requirements.

Always be certain to include another copy of your resume with your follow-up letter, even though you sent one previously. If you are fortunate enough to capture your reader's attention with the letter, you want them to be able to quickly review your resume instead of spending an hour searching through a pile of resumes collected over the past month (because they probably won't take the time to make such a search).

Here's a typical scenario of when you would send a follow-up letter. You see an advertisement in your local newspaper for a Production Scheduler with a large manufacturing company and immediately forward your resume and cover letter. Three weeks pass with no response from the company. You might even see the position advertised again in the Sunday paper. Because your qualifications are so perfectly suited to what the company asked for in its advertisement, you send a follow-up letter with another resume.

### When Is It Appropriate to Send a Follow-Up Letter?

- When you have recently (two to four weeks ago) forwarded your resume and cover letter in response to a specific advertisement and you fit the hiring criteria almost to a "T."
- When you have not heard back from an individual who said he would contact you within a specific period of time. Often, based on the situation and your relationship with that individual, a phone call is a more appropriate and certainly more proactive method of follow-up contact. After your conversation, you can determine whether another letter would be of value—such as a letter highlighting and responding to specific points from your phone discussion.
- When an individual said that she would provide you with some information or contact names, forward your resume to a contact, or initiate some other action on your behalf. Again, determine whether a letter or phone call would be most appropriate based on the specific situation.
- When you sent a cold-call cover letter to a company and now see an advertisement for a position with that company that closely matches your qualifications. This is one instance when the style of letter you send will change based on the circumstances; now you'll send an ad-response letter (being certain to communicate how your qualifications match their specific requirements) rather than a general-interest letter.

### When Is It Not Appropriate to Send a Follow-Up Letter?

- To a targeted direct-mail or e-mail campaign that you've sent out within the last month. Whether your mailing was to the 100 fastest-growing technology companies or to 1,000 recruiters who specialize in your profession, you must remember the strategy behind targeted mailings. It is not wise or thrifty to send a follow-up letter to all these contacts after just a few weeks. However, if several months have passed and you're still in the market, you might think about targeting the same list of contacts again. In this instance, however, your letter will be more like a cold-call letter and less like a follow-up letter, although you might briefly mention that you have contacted them previously. In chapter 6 you can read more about direct-mail campaigns and how to use the power of your word-processing program's mail-merge feature to prepare these quickly and easily.

- If you have received a "rejection" letter from the company or a letter stating that they will keep your information on file. Unfortunately, that's just a nice way of saying, "Thanks, but no thanks. We're not interested."
- To a recruiter with whom you have spoken about a particular position for which you believe you are precisely qualified, but for which the recruiter does not think you are an appropriate candidate. We have seen so many job seekers invest time and effort in trying to convince recruiters that they are the right candidate when, for whatever reason, the recruiter has determined that they are not. You are never going to change the recruiter's mind, so don't waste your energy. Once a recruiter has made up his mind about a candidate, there is no way to change that perception. By sending follow-up letters or making follow-up calls, you are accomplishing nothing. The only appropriate correspondence at this time would be a quick letter of thanks that requests you be kept in mind for other opportunities.
- To the recipients of a broadcast letter mailing. (A broadcast letter is a detailed career-summary letter that you send without an accompanying resume to senior executives at your target companies. It is described more fully in letter type #8, discussed next.) If you could not capture the reader's attention the first time, chances are that the company does not have a need for someone with your qualifications. Save your time and energy for more productive activities.

### Characteristics

Follow-up letters are characterized by the following:

- **Introductory paragraph.** Follow-up letters begin with three essential elements: why you're writing, that you've contacted them before, and that your experience closely matches their requirements.
- **Creativity.** When writing follow-up letters, you must think of new words and phrases to describe your experience, highlight your accomplishments, and capture your reader's attention. These letters must not repeat word for word what you've already said in your resume and your first cover letter.

Example

### Sample Follow-Up Letter

The sample follow-up letter on the following page is a prime example of how to reference your initial contact, reiterate your interest in the position, and highlight your qualifications. As you can see, it is formatted as an e-mail letter.

## 8. Broadcast Letter

***Recommended format: Paragraph style***

Broadcast letters are an unusual hybrid job search strategy and can best be summarized as merging your resume and cover letter into one document. The one distinct advantage that broadcast letters offer is that these letters avoid the knee-jerk reactions employers have to many resume and cover letter packages. These "preprogrammed" actions might include: (1) forwarding it to the human resources department; (2) setting it aside to review later; or (3) depositing it in the "circular file." With a broadcast letter, you are delivering a personal piece of correspondence with no visual cues as to its purpose. Therefore, an individual must read (or at least skim) your letter in order to determine its content. This, then, allows you the opportunity to communicate your message without being immediately "dismissed" as you might have been by using the more traditional approach of a cover letter with a resume.

Broadcast letters are extremely controversial. Some people praise their effectiveness, believing that they generate more interest because they eliminate the visual cues. Others deplore them, believing that they attempt to manipulate the truth, changing the reader's perception of who you are. This, indeed, might be true. The greatest value of a broadcast letter is its ability to create a "different" picture of who you are.

Another point of controversy relating to broadcast letters is that they clearly try to circumvent the traditional human resources resume-screening process. After all, a broadcast letter is a personal letter sent directly to a senior executive. If that executive is interested in you, she will pick up the phone and call you, or perhaps route your letter to a lower-level manager who is the hiring authority for your functional area. Although it's true that one important function of the HR department is to recruit, screen, and recommend candidates, our job-seeking clients have told us time and time again that they have benefited tremendously from conducting a "guerrilla" campaign, working around HR.

Subject: Software Engineer—Monster.com posting SW-43902

Three weeks ago I contacted you, sending a general-inquiry letter about technical job opportunities. When I saw the above-referenced posting on Monster.com, I knew that I had to resubmit my credentials... because I am a near-perfect fit for your needs, and I want to put my skills to work in the atmosphere of exploration that characterizes the Jet Propulsion Laboratory.

In brief, my qualifications include

== Exceptional programming and scripting skills in Java, JavaScript, Perl, and C.

== Extensive development experience in multiple environments and methodologies.

== Leadership roles in the development of secure content managers.

But it is my passionate interest in near-space exploration that sets me apart from other candidates with similar skills and experience.

I can easily schedule a phone interview at your convenience and would be very willing to travel to Pasadena for further discussions. I am confident I will convince you that I have the technical skills you're looking for as well as the intangible qualities—enthusiasm, energy, dedication, sense of mission, and intellectual curiosity—that characterize your best employees.

Thank you.

Sincerely,

Tyler Ott

==================
As specified, I have pasted my resume below in text format. A formatted MS Word version may also be accessed at www.tylerott.com.
==================

Our belief is that, in very select circumstances, broadcast letters written to companies can result in a decisive competitive advantage over the traditional cover letter and resume package. Some of the situations in which you might want to consider using a broadcast letter are the following:

- **When you are transitioning from one industry to another.** The sample letter at the end of this section is a prime example of this situation. The individual portrayed was attempting to transition into the corporate market after more than 20 years in the nonprofit sector. Undeniably, the broadcast letter was by far his most effective marketing tool, allowing him to demonstrate his senior management performance without immediately eliminating him from consideration for lack of corporate experience.
- **When you are not quite right for a particular position, but are well qualified.** Here's the situation. You see an advertisement for a Health Care Administrator. The ad states that you must have experience in six core management functions. Well, you've got five of the six and, in fact, a tremendous amount of experience in the first three. Use your broadcast letter to aggressively "sell" your qualifications, with particular emphasis on the skill sets in which you are most qualified. By focusing on your assets and never mentioning your liabilities, you are positioning yourself as a well-qualified candidate who has "the right stuff."
- **When you acquired your relevant experience years ago.** Consider the following scenario. For 12 years, you worked in training and development for a large corporation. You then took a promotion to the operations management team, where you have worked for 11 years. Your goal is to return to training and development. If you prepared a traditional chronological resume, your relevant experience would be near the end of your resume. With a broadcast letter, however, you can bring all your training and development experience to the forefront to capture your reader's immediate attention.
- **When your age is a liability.** Unfortunately, for all too many job seekers, age is a discriminating factor, particularly when you're over 50. With the traditional resume, a prospective employer can glance at your resume, see that you were working in the 1970s or early 1980s, and ascertain instantly that you are over 50 years of age. To avoid being immediately eliminated from consideration, develop a

broadcast letter that sells your experience, qualifications, skills, and most notable career achievements but does not include specific dates for employment and education as your resume does. This, then, gives a prospective employer the opportunity to be impressed with your career track first, before finding out that you are over 50.

- **When you have not worked for years.** For various reasons, such as child care, elder care, or health or personal issues, you might have been absent from the workforce for a while and are now ready to return. If you send a resume, as soon as someone glances at the dates of your employment experience, it will be obvious that you have not worked for quite a while. However, with a broadcast letter, you can highlight your experience, qualifications, and achievements without ever mentioning dates. This type of letter might end with a paragraph briefly explaining why you have not been working recently, how your situation has changed so that you are now able to return to the workforce, and, of course, the type of position you are seeking.
- **When you want to bring to the forefront something that has been only a sideline in your career.** Suppose you have worked in field service management for 15 years, in which your primary responsibilities included directing a regional PC field service operation. On the side, as time permitted, you also worked with the product R&D team to create new technology products and applications. Now your objective is a position in technology development. The broadcast letter gives you the opportunity to bring those aspects of your career to the forefront while simply acknowledging your responsibilities for field service.
- **When you are at an extremely senior level in your career track.** A broadcast letter is an exclusive, high-end marketing tool for introducing yourself as the first step in an executive job search process. Further, it is a more confidential process than traditional resume distribution. You're writing a personal letter to another top executive, instead of sending along a resume, which (1) immediately communicates you're looking for a job and (2) allows word to get out that you're in the market. You never know how many people might see your resume and mention it to others, thus destroying confidentiality. For example, if you are the CEO of a Fortune 500 company, secure in your position yet interested in other executive opportunities,

consider a broadcast letter as a high-level and confidential communication that you can use to "test the waters" and see what type of initial response you receive.

Unfortunately, we cannot list each situation for which broadcast letters would be appropriate. It's a judgment call each time. Ask yourself this question: "Am I trying to draw significant attention away from what I have done principally throughout my career and focus on a smaller aspect?" Or: "Am I trying to draw significant attention away from the industry or type of organization in which I have worked and position my skills for a different industry?" If your answer is yes, you might consider the value a broadcast letter would bring to your campaign.

One final point about broadcast letters: Although there are select circumstances when you might write a broadcast letter to a company, we do not recommend sending them to recruiters. Recruiters want chronological facts and figures, which the broadcast letter does not provide. Recruiters want to be able to quickly peruse your resume and see where you have worked, what positions you have had, and how long you held them. They want to glance under "Education" to see your credentials. They'll spend only 5 to 10 seconds. That's it. Broadcast letters are not designed to provide such a quick review of factual information. Rather, broadcast letters "tell a story" that one has to read to understand. Recruiters, as a whole, are not willing to invest the time to interpret these letters and extrapolate relevant facts. It's not their job!

#### Characteristics

Broadcast letters are characterized by the following:

- **Depth and quantity of information,** which is greater than a traditional cover letter, as outlined in any of the other categories in this chapter.
- **Number of pages.** It is more than acceptable for a broadcast letter to run two or even three pages, as appropriate for a particular situation.
- **Traditional mail format.** Although most cover letters today are sent by e-mail rather than printed and mailed, the broadcast letter is one exception to this trend. Remember, it is a personal outreach to a hiring authority or senior executive; as such, it is most appropriately sent by traditional mail.

**RONALD R. JOHNSON**
12 St. Paul Street
Baltimore, MD 21098
Home: (410) 555-0876 rjj2@mindspring.com Mobile: (410) 555-6549

August 30, 2010

Gary Meyerson
President
Marteenson Partners, Inc.
55 Greenbelt Parkway
Washington, DC 20056

Dear Mr. Meyerson:

As one of the top three executives in a national organization, I am recognized for my expertise in building strong, efficient, cost-effective, and productive operations responsive to our customers' needs. My efforts, and those of the two other members of the executive management team, were the foundation for our tremendous financial and operational success.

When we started years ago, the organization was an unknown entity. Through our efforts in building a strong business culture, developing sound financial policies, introducing advanced technology, and driving business development, we now boast of a national reputation and strong bottom line. My contributions to that organization and the value I bring to Marteenson Partners are best summarized as follows:

**Financial Leadership**

I built the entire financial, accounting, internal auditing, and budgeting infrastructure from the ground floor. This included developing a progressive cash-management program, managing payroll and related tax affairs, negotiating lines of credit, and managing investments valued in excess of $3 million. Further, I launched a series of aggressive cost-reduction initiatives that reduced overhead costs within specific categories by as much as 40%. Through my efforts, we ended 2000 with a solid 22% net profit and cash reserves equivalent to one full year's operating expenses.

**Revenue & Profit Performance**

During my tenure, annual revenues grew from $18 million to more than $50 million, with annual profits averaging 18% for 10+ consecutive years. My specific contributions focused on creating new sources of revenue through both product and service development. In addition, I personally negotiated several key contracts that have been instrumental to our sustained growth.

**Organizational & Administrative Leadership**

My contributions to the Board of Directors, Executive Committee and Finance Committee, were strong and active. Perhaps most notable were my efforts in relationship development—with legal counsel, bankers, investors, insurance managers, government officials, and others—all critical to the long-term development and viability of the organization. I am a strong communicator with keen negotiation and interpersonal relationship-management skills.

**Human Resources Leadership**

When I joined NBEO, there was no HR function. Under my leadership, we developed a complete HR function, recruitment and benefit programs, retirement plans, training programs, job descriptions, employee manuals, and more. Today, we have a fully integrated HR department able to support the organization as it continues to grow, expand, and strengthen its operations.

**Information Technology**

In an attempt to keep pace with the rapid emergence of new technologies, I spearheaded the acquisition and implementation of a host of computer systems. Further, I led the acquisition of several generations of telephone/telecommunication systems. As such, I bring to Marteenson a good working knowledge of the technology and telecommunication tools available to meet the needs of our industry and enhance our productivity.

Please also note that I have an MBA in Finance and Administration and a BS in Business, both from New York University.

I have been characterized by others as a strong and decisive leader, able to make difficult decisions. Just as vital, however, is my ability to be flexible and respond to constantly changing organizational, financial, and market demands.

Currently, I am confidentially pursuing new senior management opportunities. My goal is to transition my experience into a new, faster-paced and higher-growth organization where I can contribute to the organization while advancing my professional skills.

I would welcome a personal interview to discuss your current executive staffing requirements and would be pleased to provide any additional information you require. Thank you.

Sincerely,

Ronald R. Johnson

### Sample Broadcast Letter

The broadcast letter on the preceding two pages is an excellent example of transitioning your skills from one industry to another. This individual worked as an executive in association management for more than 20 years and really did have a distinguished career. However, his new goal was to transition that experience from the nonprofit sector into "corporate America." What he wanted his readers to focus on was his experience, not the environment in which it was acquired. Had he sent a traditional cover letter and resume, the very first thing someone would have seen would be a list of his employment experience, all in association management. Most likely, they would have gone no further. Using his broadcast letter, he was immediately called for an interview.

## 10. Sponsor Letter

***Recommended format: Paragraph style***

Sponsor letters can be best described as letters written by other individuals to their network of contacts on your behalf. In theory, it's John Smith writing to his colleague, Jane Doe, to tell her about Sam Wilson (the job seeker) and what a valuable employee he would be. Sponsor letters leverage someone else's network on your behalf. These letters are appropriate for only a small percentage of job seekers, because the sponsor letter has one essential requirement: someone who is willing to be your sponsor.

For sponsor letters to be effective, you must have the "right" sponsor. It must be an individual who has a strong network of personal contacts, has an excellent reputation, has impeccable credentials, and is willing to "go the extra mile" for you. The impact of the sponsor letter rests almost entirely on the credibility of your sponsor. If you select a sponsor who does not possess these qualifications, the letters will ultimately be of little or no value to you.

When deciding who you might approach to be your sponsor, consider the following three critical criteria:

- **Your sponsor must be appropriate.** Your sponsor must be at a high-enough career level to have contacts at the level you are seeking—individuals who can get you in the door for an interview and make hiring decisions. Most likely, your sponsor is more senior-level than yourself, with a higher level of management responsibility.

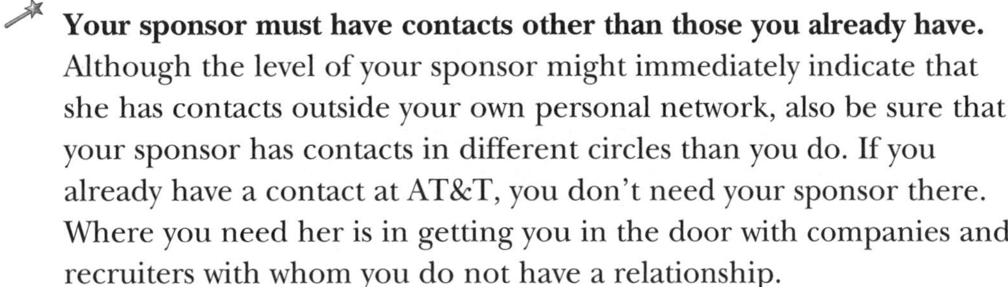

- **Your sponsor must have contacts other than those you already have.** Although the level of your sponsor might immediately indicate that she has contacts outside your own personal network, also be sure that your sponsor has contacts in different circles than you do. If you already have a contact at AT&T, you don't need your sponsor there. Where you need her is in getting you in the door with companies and recruiters with whom you do not have a relationship.
- **Your sponsor must be willing to leverage his network of contacts on your behalf.** When you ask someone to be your sponsor, you're asking a great deal of him. You want him to dedicate time and effort to this project and "stick his neck out" for you. That's right. When John Smith contacts Jane Doe about you, it's his reputation and credibility that he risks. If you ask someone to be your sponsor, you'd better be sure that you can live up to his expectations and your promises.

A good strategy for managing a sponsor letter campaign is to ask your sponsor to write to 10 of his most senior-level contacts. The letter should serve to introduce you, praise your performance, highlight your accomplishments, and communicate the value you bring to that organization. Your sponsor can write the letter, or you can offer to write a draft, making the process easier for your sponsor and faster for you.

### Characteristics

Sponsor letters are characterized by the following:

- **Authorship.** Sponsor letters are written about you by a third person. They are not written by you, the job seeker.
- **Impact.** These letters generally have tremendous impact because of the reputation and credibility of the individual writing the letter.

### Sample Sponsor Letter

The sponsor letter that follows is a prime example of how someone else's contacts can work to your benefit. This individual is currently working as a general manager in the telecommunications industry. His company has just been sold, and he is now interested in applying for several national-sales-management positions with other industry leaders. One of this individual's closest friends is a college friend from more than 20 years ago, now the mayor of a small Northeastern town. Because of his high-profile political career, he knows everyone, including several presidents of some prominent telecommunications companies.

## JOHN S. JOHNSTON, MAYOR

Leicester Town Square • 1 Main Street • Leicester, NY 14890
(716) 555-3766

August 20, 2010

Mr. John E. Taylor, Jr., President
Dreamport, Inc.
301 The Plaza
5355 Town Center Road
Boca Raton, FL 33486

Dear Mr. Taylor:

Can I tell you about Bart Brogan's professional career? No. Can I tell you how many millions of dollars in profits he has helped to generate? No. Can I tell you how tremendously effective he is in reengineering, streamlining, and optimizing business and finance operations? No.

What I can tell you is about Bart Brogan, the man—an individual with strong character, impeccable ethics, and keen business insight. He is a man who has earned the respect of other business, civic, and political leaders.

I met Bart back in college at Brown University, where we both participated in competitive athletics. It was then that I first realized that Bart really was someone unique and talented. I watched him at the competitions and saw his intensity and drive to succeed. What I also witnessed was his innate leadership skill and the camaraderie he elicited. I was impressed.

After graduation, Bart and I went our separate ways, but we have always stayed in touch with one another. He's had a tremendously strong corporate career; mine has focused in the political arena. Nonetheless, we have maintained a personal connection for years, supporting one another in whatever ways possible and challenging each other to achieve our personal best.

What I do know about Bart's professional career is that he is an astute businessman with excellent credentials in strategic planning, finance, general management, and information systems/technology. I am also aware that he has negotiated and structured several significant mergers, acquisitions, and other corporate initiatives.

If you are considering adding to your executive management team, I guarantee you can't go wrong with Bart. Not only would you be hiring an individual who is well respected within the professional community, you would also be acquiring an individual whose liaison, networking, and relationship-management skills will be of certain value to Dreamport.

If there is any additional information I can provide, please contact me directly at (716) 555-3766.

Sincerely,

John S. Johnston
Mayor

Chapter 2

# Preparing to Write

We are making a few assumptions about you, our reader. We're assuming that you've already invested a great deal of time, effort, and energy in writing and designing your resume. If you've hired a professional resume writer, you also have made a financial investment. Now that your resume is complete, you need to use it!

We're also assuming that because you've purchased this book, you have hit a stumbling block in writing your cover letters that, in turn, is preventing you from sending out your resumes. Maybe you've already drafted a letter and are a bit uncertain about the language you've used. Perhaps you've written cover letter notes to yourself but just can't seem to tie them all together into a cohesive structure. Possibly you were pleased with the letter you wrote, but it isn't getting any response. Or maybe you can't get any further than a blank piece of paper or computer screen. Never fear—this chapter will help you get started.

## Six Steps to Better Cover Letters

To improve the ease and confidence with which you write cover letters, we've created a step-by-step process and structure that will allow you to quickly and easily write your cover letters and get your resumes out—*now!* Although you might admire the prowess with which you typed and formatted your resume, love the color of paper you selected, or are thrilled about the quality of your resume, if it is just sitting on your desk or computer hard drive, it is not working for you. Your resume is of no value to you or anyone else if it is not in circulation.

To get your resumes out, all you need to do is follow this six-step action plan to produce a cover letter from start to finish:

**Step 1:** Identify Your Key Selling Points

**Step 2:** Pre-Plan

**Step 3:** Write the Opening Paragraph

**Step 4:** Write the Body

**Step 5:** Write the Closing

**Step 6:** Polish, Proofread, and Finalize

The most time-consuming of these is step 1, identifying your key selling points. To make that process easier, we've devoted this entire chapter to helping you collect an arsenal of information about yourself and your career that will be available for you to consider for *every* letter you write. By investing time and effort now, you'll make the process of producing each unique cover letter practically painless! When you begin the actual writing process with step 2 (in chapter 3), you'll see how your advance work really pays off.

## Step 1: Identify Your Key Selling Points

What qualifications, experiences, achievements, and skills do you bring to a company? It's time to evaluate and quantify what it is that makes you unique, valuable, and interesting to potential employers.

### Know Your Objective

The best place to start is by clearly identifying *who* you are and what your job objective is. Are you an accountant, realtor, or construction project manager? A sales professional, customer service representative, teacher, or nurse? An advertising specialist, social worker, architect, or librarian? A CFO, CIO, COO, or CEO? It is critical that you be able to clearly and accurately define who you are in an instant. Remember, an instant is all that you have to capture your reader's attention, encouraging him not only to read your cover letter in full, but to read your resume and contact you for a personal interview.

What if you are pursuing more than one career goal and can identify yourself with more than one "WHO" statement? If your options are quite different (for instance, programmer and project manager), it's best if you repeat the Action Item exercises at the end of this section for each of your professions. Why? It's quite likely that what is highly significant for one profession will be less important for the other—and remember, you are focusing on why employers would be interested in you, so it's important to convey your experience, skills, and accomplishments that are most directly related to that particular position. On the other hand, if your professions are closely related (marketing manager and product manager), you can create a hybrid job title ("Marketing/Product Manager") and encompass the key points of both.

### Summarize Your Experience

Just as important, you must be able to clearly identify why a company or recruiter would be interested in you. Is it because of the companies you've worked for? The industries in which you've been employed? The positions you've held? The promotions you've earned? The financial impact you've had? What you accomplished? Your specific skills and qualifications? Your licenses and educational credentials? Your patents? Your technical expertise? Your leadership skills? Your foreign-language skills and international experience? Why would someone be interested in you?

These are critical questions to ask yourself. What's more, the answers to these questions will directly impact what you write in your cover letter and how you present that information. You must determine what you have to offer that relates to that company's needs, what will be of interest to that company's managers, and what will entice them to read your resume and offer you the opportunity for an interview.

When you have determined your strongest selling points, you should condense them into strong summary sentences that detail all of your job responsibilities from your current and past positions. Obviously, if you've been working for 15, 20, or more years, you can eliminate some details of your earlier positions, but only if they are not relevant to your current objectives.

Remember that your cover letter is not designed to be a listing of job responsibilities and functions. Rather, it is designed to point out the most notable experiences and highlights of your career as they relate to the needs and interests of the prospective employer. After you've invested the effort in preparing a complete list of summary sentences, you can use it over and over, hundreds of times, as the foundation for virtually every cover letter you write. In theory, it will be your "cheat sheet," a single reference source that contains all the different items, qualifications, highlights, responsibilities, and other bits of information you might include in a cover letter.

Your resume is a good place to start in preparing this list. In fact, your "prep work" for creating your resume can also be the foundation for the material you'll develop for your cover letters. You'll save time and effort in this exercise if you can use your notes, old resumes, and other career summary materials you used to develop your resume.

### What Is a Summary Sentence?

To best demonstrate what a summary sentence is and its value to you in writing your cover letters, here's a quick example:

> Managed daily and monthly accounting operations for a $200 million company with 11 operating locations throughout the Midwestern U.S.

With that summary sentence, you've immediately communicated to your reader that not only did you manage accounting, but you managed accounting for a large and diverse operation. This probably included accounts payable and receivable, general ledger, payroll, financial reporting, bank reconciliations, month-end account reconciliations, staffing and training, and all related computer operations.

So, with just one little sentence, you were able to tell your reader what you were responsible for and the level of that responsibility. Remember, your cover letter should be relatively brief and not repeat all the information that is in your resume. Your only objective with the letter is to pique someone's interest to read your resume and invite you for an interview.

## Sample Summary Sentences

To help you create your list of responsibilities, we've compiled a sample portfolio of 45 summary sentences for various professions. This list is by no means comprehensive; it was created to give you ideas and help get your own creative juices flowing.

Check off all the areas that apply to you and your career, and then read the sample summary sentences under each. Those sentences will give you an idea of the type of information you might want to highlight, depending on your particular career experience.

It would be nice to think that you could just take a summary sentence we've provided and drop it right into your cover letter. Unfortunately, chances are slim that the following samples will be precisely accurate for your career track. These are simply provided as a tool to help you come up with your own summary sentences.

☐ **Accounting and Auditing**

Supervise a six-employee accounts payable, accounts receivable, and internal audit operation for one of the area's largest commercial heating and air-conditioning companies.

☐ **Administration**

As Administrative Manager for a large health-care practice, directed budgeting, equipment acquisition, financial reporting, regulatory reporting, and all departmental staffing and training functions.

☐ **Advertising**

Designed and produced a portfolio of multimedia advertising, marketing, and promotional materials to increase Amazon.com's market image and consumer awareness.

☐ **Association and Not-for-Profit Management**

Member of six-person management team directing fund-raising, community outreach, member development, member services, and all administrative affairs for the American Medical Association's Specialty Practices Division.

☐ **Banking**

Participated in the start-up, staffing, and sales of First National's first Private Banking Program, one of their nationwide initiatives designed to increase market reach and build long-term customer relationships.

☐ **Clerical/Administrative Support**

As assistant to one partner and six managers in a Big Five consulting firm, prepared presentations, proposals, project documentation, and final reports to present a consistently professional image to clients.

☐ **Communications**

Worked with a team of 22 in-house professionals responsible for the conceptualization, design, development, and production of a portfolio of print, video, and multimedia communications to support IBM's new-product rollout programs.

☐ **Computer Programming**

Designed new computer programs for the Finance, Accounting, Administration, Purchasing, and Vendor Management departments of Ford Motor Company's $200 million parts division.

☐ **Construction**

Construction Manager for the $40 million renovation of Park City Plaza Hotel, including full responsibility for architectural design, contractor selection, competitive bidding, field supervision, and regulatory affairs.

☐ **Consulting**

Launched entrepreneurial consulting venture specializing in strategic planning, market planning, new product development, and joint venture negotiations for electronics companies expanding into the Asian marketplace.

☐ **Corporate Finance**

As Senior Finance Executive for Merck's $2 billion international sales division, held full decision-making responsibility for banking, tax, treasury, financial analysis, financial reporting, contract negotiations, mergers, acquisitions, and capital funding programs.

☐ **Customer Service**

Responded to customer calls, faxes, and e-mails, independently addressing a wide range of product, quality, billing, and general customer satisfaction issues for $1 million industrial supplies company.

☐ **Education and Educational Administration**

Advanced rapidly from Classroom Teacher to Grade Chairperson to Assistant Principal to Principal with full leadership responsibility for a 1,000-student high school.

☐ **Energy and Environmental**

Member of the Environmental Engineering Task Force traveling to Mobil locations nationwide to evaluate site conditions, assess potential hazards, negotiate with local regulators, and manage field remediation teams.

☐ **Engineering**

Joined four-person Engineering Task Force leading the redesign and optimization of all product engineering systems for Quaker's entire U.S. operation (six manufacturing plants, 2000+ employees, and close to $2 billion in annual revenues).

☐ **Food and Beverage/Food Service Operations**

Held a fast-paced customer service position in one of the area's largest restaurants, serving up to 500 customers per day.

☐ **Government**

Acted as Chief Operating Officer of a federal government agency responsible for the administration of all educational grant and foundation funds to nonprofit teaching institutions throughout the U.S.

☐ **Health Care**

One of six nurses in a 350-bed teaching hospital selected to participate on a new coordinated health-care team providing care to neonatal and pediatric ICU clients.

☐ **Hospitality**

Held a series of progressively responsible positions in Reservations, Front Office Operations, Guest Services, and Special Events for a 1,000-room Hilton hotel.

☐ **Human Resources**

Earned promotion to Senior HR Director with full responsibility for staffing, training, leadership development, benefits, compensation, employee relations, labor relations, and HRIS for a $45 million retail sales company.

☐ **Human Services**

Provided comprehensive counseling support, interagency referrals, and program development for a caseload of 32 juvenile offenders on probation through a joint court/community outreach program.

☐ **Insurance**

Earned recognition as the top-producing insurance sales agent with the highest revenue and lowest loss ratio out of 200+ agents in a five-state territory.

☐ **International Business Development**

Independently planned and directed all marketing, new business development, new product launch, and joint-venture programs for Ericsson throughout Central and South America.

☐ **Investment Finance**

Sold/marketed a portfolio of mutual funds, stocks, bonds, and low-interest, mortgage-backed securities to private investors and small-business investors throughout the New York metro area.

☐ **Law Enforcement**

Completed a distinguished 20-year career with the Los Angeles Police Department, earning 12 promotions, six honorable decorations, and regional media coverage for personal success in resolving a potentially life-threatening hostage situation on the UCLA campus.

☐ **Legal Affairs**

As a general-practice attorney, specialized in civil matters, personal injury, real estate law, personal tax law, and family law.

☐ **Logistics**

Led business development teams in analyzing, proposing, and implementing logistics programs that focus on value-added service and cost savings for clients around the country.

☐ **Manufacturing**

Independently directed the production of over 2,000 SKUs each year, from the initial stages of production planning and materials acquisition through floor production, quality testing, and final customer distribution.

☐ **Marketing**

Conceived the campaign and directed the production team responsible for introducing Kellogg's newest breakfast product into the national market, building it into a $2 million well-known consumer brand.

☐ **Operations Management**

Held P&L responsibility and oversaw all branch activities in support of contracted accounts for national delivery service; supervised clerical, administrative, and customer-service staff.

☐ **Product Development**

Held full leadership responsibility for all new product development and commercialization projects for the $28 million Internet Systems Division of ABC.

☐ **Project Management**

Brought on board as first project manager for a rapidly growing technology consulting company to oversee its largest-ever contract, a $4+ million software installation for a major national retailer.

☐ **Public Relations**

Launched high-profile nationwide public relations campaigns to support Independent Presidential candidate Chris Towers.

☐ **Purchasing**

Directed the purchase of more than $50,000 annually in office supplies and materials to support the operations of a prestigious civil engineering firm.

☐ **Real Estate**

Managed advertising, leasing, maintenance, and tenant relations for a 332-unit garden apartment complex catering specifically to senior citizens.

☐ **Research and Development**

As Team Leader, directed all technology R&D programs funded by a $2 million grant awarded from the Department of Energy for the design of alternative residential heating systems.

☐ **Retail**

Train and supervise a staff of six retail associates responsible for product merchandising and display, sales, customer service, and loss prevention.

☐ **Sales**

Maintain consistently high sales volume in retail sales of jewelry to both established and walk-in clientele of a six-store jewelry chain's flagship downtown location.

☐ **Scientific Research**

Pioneered the theoretical research of genetic anomalies associated with the aging process and physical deterioration.

☐ **Security**

Member of a six-person industrial security team working to introduce new security standards, technologies, and systems to guard against further corporate espionage activities.

☐ **Senior Management**

Senior Management Executive with full strategic planning, operating, marketing, and P&L responsibility for a $20 million emerging telecommunications company anticipating an IPO within the next 16 months.

☐ **Technology**

Acquired, customized, and implemented emerging database, client/server, Internet, and e-mail technologies to transform a small fabric-design company into a technologically advanced industry leader.

- ☐ **Training**

  Selected for newly created 100% training position, serving as primary operations and applications trainer for all new hires of $7 million hardware/software reseller firm.

- ☐ **Transportation**

  Recruited to Ryder Integrated Logistics to redesign its business model, restaff key positions, and revitalize field marketing in an effort to regain #1 market position in the industry.

- ☐ **Travel and Tourism**

  Planned, scheduled, and managed all corporate travel programs for the executive management team of Macy's and its 22 operating subsidiaries.

### Where Did You Get Your Experience?

One final note regarding your key selling points relates to the type, or types, of organization with which you have been employed. Do you have experience with any of the following types of companies?

- ☐ Start-up venture or new enterprise
- ☐ Turnaround company
- ☐ High-growth company
- ☐ Fortune 10, 50, 100, 500, or 1000 company

You can use this information to further strengthen your qualifications and sharpen the impact of your cover letters. For example, if you have experience in turning around poorly performing companies and you're writing to an organization in need of an aggressive turnaround, sell your experience in reorganizing, revitalizing, and redesigning businesses to improve operations and financial performance. By doing so, you clearly communicate that you've met the same types of challenges that the company is currently facing. Be sure to "talk the right talk" to each audience.

## Action Items

We designed this book to give you both theory and practical exercises to guide you in creating your own winning cover letters. The "Action Items" you see here and in later chapters will lead you step by step through the process. You might prefer to hand-write your responses or type them on your PC. Either way, take the time to complete each Action Item carefully and thoroughly, and you'll create valuable resources and tools that you can use for every cover letter you write.

### 1. Know Your Career Goal

**Fill in the following blank with your job title or profession.** The more brief and concise your answer is, the better. Clarity is the key to effectively communicating who you are to a prospective employer.

I am a ______________________________ .

### 2. Write Responsibility Summaries

**Write strong summary sentences that detail all of your job responsibilities from each of your current and past positions.** Be as detailed as possible, and try to remember everything you did in each position. We recommend using a separate page for each position so that you can easily add other items as they come to mind.

______________________________________________________________________

______________________________________________________________________

______________________________________________________________________

______________________________________________________________________

______________________________________________________________________

______________________________________________________________________

______________________________________________________________________

______________________________________________________________________

______________________________________________________________________

## Let Your Achievements Sell for You

Your achievements are what set you apart from others with a similar background. They answer the reader's all-important question—"What can you do for me?"—because they tell precisely what you have done for someone else. Cover letters and resumes without achievements are simply dry compilations of position titles and responsibilities. They don't sell your unique attributes, and they don't compel readers to pick up the phone and invite you in for an interview.

In thinking about your achievements, ask yourself how you've benefited the organizations where you've worked. In general terms, you can help an organization by doing any of the following:

- **Making money** (revenues, profits, earnings, ROI/ROA/ROE increases, new customers)
- **Saving money** (cost reductions, streamlining, automating)
- **Creating new things** (systems, processes, products, technologies, operations, companies)
- **Improving existing things** (reengineering, redesigning, developing new processes, consolidating)
- **Improving performance** (productivity, efficiency, quality, delivery, customer service)
- **Winning honors, awards, and commendations**

In writing your achievements, think about the two key pieces of information you want to convey: what you did and how it benefited the company. Without either of these components, an achievement is incomplete. Compare these two achievement statements:

- Spearheaded project team that designed, developed, and launched ATP's next-generation software systems.

That's fine, but it's incomplete. When writing about your achievements, make sure you include bottom-line results—with numbers, whenever possible—to make those results tangible.

- Spearheaded project team that designed, developed, and launched ATP's next-generation software systems, which **generated $8.5 million in first-year sales.**

This one sentence—this one achievement—communicates not only success and financial contribution, but a great deal of information about the individual's specific skills. We would surmise from reading it that her qualifications include software engineering, cross-functional team leadership, quality assurance, product testing, product documentation, manufacturing, and product commercialization. We might also assume that she has experience in project budgeting, costing, purchasing, scheduling, and reporting. We got all that information from just one sentence—one achievement.

The specific achievements you include in your cover letters will depend entirely on your professional career, skills, experiences, qualifications, and competencies. Achievements can vary widely—from installing new word-processing software in your office to launching a new business venture that generated $100 million in revenues—and everything in between.

## Identify Your Achievements

The following list will help you identify your achievements. Just as you did in the preceding section, check off every item on this list that applies to you. Then, in the Action Item section at the end of this chapter, write specific achievement statements for every example you can think of from your career. To create a consistent record of accomplishment, you'll need to do this for each of your positions.

To get you started, here's a quick example: If you checked off the first item ("Increased sales revenues"), you might then reword it as "Increased district sales by 22% in just one year for Myers-Baker-Anderson." For another position, you might write, "Grew territory by 27%, nearly twice the regional average of 14%." And if your revenue accomplishments weren't quite so stellar, you can still find a positive way to state your contribution: "Met 100% of performance goals for revenue growth, new business, and customer retention."

Here's the list. Ask yourself whether you have managed, participated in, helped with, or contributed to any of the following:

- ☐ Increased sales revenues
- ☐ Improved profitability
- ☐ Improved customer service

- ☐ Improved customer satisfaction ratings
- ☐ Improved market-share ratings
- ☐ Captured new customer accounts
- ☐ Penetrated new business markets
- ☐ Increased sales within existing accounts
- ☐ Penetrated new geographic markets
- ☐ Identified new market opportunities
- ☐ Reduced operating costs
- ☐ Reduced overhead costs
- ☐ Developed new technology
- ☐ Implemented new hardware, software, or other systems
- ☐ Coordinated team-building and team-leadership efforts
- ☐ Designed new training programs or educational curricula
- ☐ Developed new products or expanded product lines
- ☐ Built new facilities or expanded existing facilities
- ☐ Sourced new vendors
- ☐ Reduced annual purchasing costs
- ☐ Negotiated contracts
- ☐ Improved productivity
- ☐ Improved the quality of operations or products
- ☐ Improved efficiency
- ☐ Introduced new performance standards
- ☐ Streamlined operations, functions, or support activities
- ☐ Exceeded specific performance expectations
- ☐ Simplified business processes
- ☐ Eliminated redundant work activities
- ☐ Realigned staffing to meet business demand
- ☐ Structured or negotiated strategic alliances, joint ventures, or partnerships

- ☐ Structured or negotiated mergers or acquisitions
- ☐ Directed IPOs, private placements, or other corporate financings
- ☐ Appeared on local, regional, national, or international media
- ☐ Coordinated special-event programs
- ☐ Improved the company's image
- ☐ Managed fund-raising programs
- ☐ Solved persistent problems that affected any area of business operations

Other achievements that you can highlight, as appropriate to the type of position you are seeking or company to which you are writing, might include the following. Check those that apply to you, transfer them to your list of achievements, and write a powerful statement of achievement.

- ☐ International experience
- ☐ Public-speaking experience
- ☐ Print and online publishing experience (books, articles, newsletters)
- ☐ Industry honors, awards, or credentials
- ☐ Academic honors, awards, or credentials
- ☐ Industry licenses and registrations

> *Tip* If your list of achievements is particularly long, divide it into "functional" sections such as Sales & Profit Achievements, Technology Achievements, Human Resource & Leadership Achievements, Major Projects, New Products, Marketing Campaigns, Organizational & Productivity Improvements, New Clients, Cost Savings, Start-Ups, Turnarounds, and so on. Each time you sit down to write a cover letter, refer to your list and select the achievements that are most appropriate to the position for which you are applying. You'll be amazed at how much faster you'll be able to write your letters.

*Example*

### Sample Achievement Statements

To help you get started, we've compiled a list of thought-provoking ideas for achievement statements related to 45 different professions and industries. Find your profession, review the list of achievement ideas for it, determine which are appropriate to your specific experience, and incorporate those concepts into your own unique achievement list.

**Accounting and Auditing**

- Identifying misappropriated or uncollected monies
- Implementing integrated computerized systems to link different business units
- Contributing to revenue growth, cost reduction, and profit improvement

**Advertising**

- Capturing or managing major clients, contracts, and campaigns
- Demonstrating a combination of creative talent and business skills
- Earning honors, awards, media coverage, and other "reputation-building" recognition

**Association and Not-for-Profit Management**

- Increasing membership, geographic expanse, and prominence
- Increasing membership fees, revenues, and funding
- Influencing favorable legislative policies

**Banking**

- Growing lending volume, deposits, and customer base
- Expanding into new markets, new products, and new services
- Reducing A/R, write-offs, and risk and asset exposure

**Clerical/Administrative Support**

- Streamlining work processes and improving work flow
- Eliminating redundant or repetitive tasks
- Automating previously manual office functions

**Communications**

- Writing marketing, advertising, and customer communications
- Designing multimedia systems for conventions and trade shows
- Crafting speeches and investor presentations

**Computer Programming**

- Writing new programs for new applications
- Improving user-friendly software capabilities and support
- Enhancing system productivity and performance

**Construction**

- Securing or managing major projects, clients, and contracts
- Delivering projects on time
- Achieving cost savings and avoidance

**Consulting**

- Capturing prominent clients and accounts
- Delivering quantifiable revenue increases, profit contributions, and cost reductions
- Participating in new product/technology development, new market development, and other innovations

**Corporate Finance**

- Contributing to revenue and profit growth, cost reduction, and/or ROI, ROA, or ROE gains
- Negotiating major corporate deals—mergers, acquisitions, financings, private placements, IPOs, and so on
- Managing collateral operating, strategic planning, HR, information technology, and administrative functions

**Customer Service**

- Improving customer-service performance and customer-satisfaction ratings
- Introducing new customer-service and support programs
- Retaining customer accounts in highly competitive markets and industries

**Education or Educational Administration**

- Increasing student test scores and academic rankings
- Expanding educational programs and improving course curricula
- Influencing favorable public policy and legislation

**Energy and Environmental**

- Completing major remediation, haz-mat, or regulatory projects
- Discovering or implementing product and technology innovations
- Making financial contributions

**Engineering**

- Developing and commercializing new products
- Delivering process, design, and performance improvements
- Contributing to new revenues or cost reduction

**Food and Beverage/Food-Service Operations**

- Improving front-of-the-house and back-of-the-house operations
- Increasing revenues and reducing operating and labor costs
- Earning industry recognition and ratings

**Government**

- Implementing new programs, policies, and initiatives
- Delivering budget, deficit, and cost reductions
- Negotiating or managing public/private partnerships

**Graduating Student**

- Achieving academic or athletic honors
- Demonstrating leadership skills
- Acquiring professional skills through "nonprofessional" employment, internships, and so on

**Health Care**

- Improving quality of care, utilization, and health-care policy
- Participating in emerging health-care markets—managed care, PPOs, and so on
- Contributing to improved financial performance and regulatory ratings

**Hospitality**

- Improving guest services and guest satisfaction ratings
- Increasing revenues and bookings
- Upgrading facilities and amenities

**Human Resources**

- Leading organizational, cultural, and productivity improvements
- Capturing cost savings
- Developing and implementing new HR programs, services, and technologies

**Human Services**

- Delivering new programs and services
- Amassing a record of client, program, and project successes
- Contributing to funding, budgeting, regulations, and legislative affairs

**Insurance**

- Growing premium volume and number of insureds
- Reducing risk and volume of claims
- Introducing new products and expanding into new markets

**International Business Development**

- Achieving revenue and profit growth

- Developing and expanding new markets
- Negotiating international deals, joint ventures, acquisitions, and alliances

**Investment Finance**

- Delivering growth in investment yields and portfolio performance
- Expanding range of investment product expertise
- Demonstrating successes in new-product development and client-relationship management

**Law Enforcement**

- Apprehending more criminals than any other officer
- Achieving the highest arrest-to-conviction percentage
- Promoting public education and community outreach programs

**Legal Affairs**

- Handling high-profile cases
- Demonstrating diversity of corporate, industry, and legal expertise
- Improving compliance and reducing risk

**Logistics**

- Improving purchasing, warehousing, inventory, distribution, and transportation operations
- Reducing overhead and operating costs
- Negotiating innovative vendor partnerships and strategic alliances

**Manufacturing**

- Delivering measurable improvements in productivity, efficiency, workflow, process, and product yield
- Reducing labor, material, equipment, and overhead operating costs
- Introducing innovative technologies and systems

**Marketing**

- Managing notable new-product launch campaigns and quantifying financial performance
- Contributing to revenue, market share, earnings, and company growth
- Demonstrating a combination of strategic and tactical marketing expertise

**Operations Management**

- Streamlining, consolidating, and improving operations
- Reducing costs and improving net profit margins
- Introducing advanced systems, technologies, and processes

**Product Development**

- Developing and commercializing new products, with subsequent revenue performance
- Coordinating cross-functional design, engineering, manufacturing, and sales teams
- Developing notable co-development alliances, partnerships, and joint ventures

**Project Management**

- Completing projects ahead of schedule or under budget
- Managing cross-functional project teams and personnel
- Negotiating with third-party vendors, contractors, and business partners

**Public Relations**

- Increasing visibility and market recognition
- Managing PR, special events, and other media-targeted programs
- Coordinating executive liaison affairs

**Purchasing**

- Managing significant purchasing volume and commodities
- Developing U.S. and international vendor sourcing and contracts
- Achieving quantifiable cost reductions and inventory improvements

**Real Estate**

- Developing new projects and properties
- Selling large numbers of properties or generating large dollars
- Managing high-profile properties, resorts, complexes, and buildings

**Research and Development**

- Developing and commercializing new products
- Creating new techniques, processes, and procedures
- Generating new revenue and profit streams

**Retail**

- Increasing sales revenues
- Improving customer service and repeat clientele
- Managing loss prevention and merchandise control

**Sales**

- Increasing sales and growing market share
- Developing new accounts and new markets
- Introducing new products

**Scientific Research**

- Pioneering new research methods and techniques
- Making new scientific discoveries
- Increasing funding and appropriation

**Security**

- Managing sensitive corporate or institutional security programs
- Thwarting potentially hazardous events and emergencies
- Managing relationships with law-enforcement agencies

**Senior Management**

- Increasing revenues, reducing costs, and improving bottom-line profits
- Outperforming the competition and dominating the marketplace
- Leading performance, process, organizational, and technological improvements

**Technology**

- Developing new technologies
- Commercializing existing technologies
- Implementing major projects

**Training**

- Developing and delivering new training programs
- Creating training manuals, curricula, trainer guides, and other instructional materials
- Training other trainers

**Transportation**

- Capturing cost savings
- Achieving productivity and efficiency improvements
- Reducing operating costs

**Travel and Tourism**

- Booking large events, excursions, and corporate programs
- Increasing agency revenues
- Upgrading computer technology

## Action Item

**3. Write Your Achievements**

**Write your achievements for all of your positions.** Just as in Action Item #2 (responsibilities), create a single resource—your cheat sheet—that lists all of your career achievements, accomplishments, and contributions. Again, the more comprehensive your list, the more usable a resource it will be in developing your cover letters. Remember, achievements sell, and cover letter writing is selling—selling you!

There! You've completed the most time-intensive preparation for writing your cover letters. With these comprehensive lists of *responsibilities* and *accomplishments* in your toolkit, you're ready to move quickly through the remaining steps to get your cover letters off the drawing board and into circulation.

Chapter 3

# Writing Your Cover Letters

Remember the six steps to creating your cover letters start-to-finish that you read about in chapter 2?

**Step 1:** Identify Your Key Selling Points

**Step 2:** Pre-Plan

**Step 3:** Write the Opening Paragraph

**Step 4:** Write the Body

**Step 5:** Write the Closing

**Step 6:** Polish, Proofread, and Finalize

If you're working your way through this book step-by-step, you devoted a great deal of time to identifying your key selling points in chapter 2 and creating two resource documents—one highlighting overall skills and responsibilities from each of your positions (summary sentences) and the other highlighting all of your successes, contributions, accomplishments, and special projects (achievements). Now that you've done all your preparation work, let's write a cover letter!

The process of writing your cover letters starts with a brief pre-planning session to identify the specific purpose of that particular letter. Then you can move into the actual writing of each of the three distinct parts of the cover letter: the opening, the body, and the closing.

The easiest way to master this approach is to work on an actual letter. Instead of having you complete exercises and write samples that, although educational, leave you with no final product, let's work on the real thing—you and your career.

To begin, find an advertisement you want to respond to, a network contact you want to reach, a recruiter you'd like to introduce yourself to, or any other situation for which you'd like to write a cover letter. Use that letter as we go through each step of the process. When you complete step 5, you'll be done, and you'll have a letter that's ready to go! We call this a "practical" learning exercise because it has practical application—a finished product.

Just as in the preceding chapter, there are Action Items for you to complete at the end of each step. You can do this either manually (on paper) or electronically (on your PC). Whichever way you choose, be sure to complete the Action Items in their entirety. The notes you take will become the foundation for—and, in some instances, the actual wording of—your cover letter.

## Step 2: Pre-Plan

Before you begin writing a single word of your cover letter, you must determine the appropriate strategy for that particular letter. You're not ready to write until you can clearly answer the following questions:

- **Why am I writing this letter?** Am I writing in response to a print or online advertisement, sending a cold-call letter to recruiters or companies, contacting someone in my network, writing to a company at the recommendation of someone else, or writing a follow-up letter to a company to which I already sent a resume? The answer to this question will significantly impact the content of your cover letter—the introduction in particular. After you've answered that question, review "The Nine Types of Cover Letters" (in chapter 1) and select the type that fits your particular situation.
- **Have I researched the company and the position?** In some instances you know, or can find, information about a company you are writing to, the products it sells, the services it offers, the positions that are open, the types of candidates it hires, its key hiring requirements, and

much more. Do your research! The more you know about the company and the position, the more on-target you can write your letters, relating your experience to their identified needs. If you know the company sells electronic components and you've worked in that industry, sell your related experience! If you know the company is on a growth track and you've worked for two other growth companies, highlight it! If you are an expert in multimedia communications and the cable company you are writing to has just bought a broadcast company, tell them you know the industry! Your goal is to find common ground between you and the company and then leverage that to your advantage.

> *Tip* By researching a company and finding out all that you can, you will be able to write a cover letter that directly relates your experience to that company's needs. The company will see your immediate value to them, and you will have a remarkably solid advantage over your competition.

- **Do I have a contact name?** Have I double-checked the correct spelling of the name and the person's job title? Do I have the full mailing address or e-mail address? The fact is that if you write to the Human Resources department of a company, you'll never quite know where your letter and resume have landed. However, if you write to a particular individual, you not only know who has your resume, you also know who to follow up with. This is critical!

## Action Items

**1. Choose a Type**

Write down the type of cover letter you are writing from the list of "The Nine Types of Cover Letters" (in chapter 1) that best fits your reason for writing this letter. Then, carefully review the section that describes that type of letter in detail.

*continued*

*continued*

**2. Compile Information About the Company**

Write down everything that you know or have learned about the company—industry, products, services, number of employees, annual sales revenues, and more.

______________________________________________

______________________________________________

______________________________________________

**3. Compile Information About the Position**

Write down everything that you know or have learned about the position—the specific job duties, minimum requirements, supervisor's name and title, "inside" information from a source within the company, and anything else that is pertinent.

______________________________________________

______________________________________________

______________________________________________

**4. Write Down Contact Information**

Write down the name, title, and full mailing address of the individual you will be contacting. If you are sending an online letter, also note that individual's e-mail address.

______________________________________________

______________________________________________

______________________________________________

*Example*

## An Example: Chris Matthews

To make the process of cover letter writing easier and faster for you, we've created a fictitious job seeker, Chris Matthews. Chris is an experienced construction project manager who wants to relocate to Florida. He is preparing a cover letter to respond to ads in Florida newspapers.

Work along with Chris as you both progress through steps 2 through 6, creating a cover letter from start to finish.

Here are Chris's completed Action Items for "Step 2: Pre-Plan":

1. **Choose a type.** To begin his job search, Chris will use letter type 1: Ad-Response Letter to a Company. Browsing online, he peruses the newspaper classifieds in all of the major cities in Florida. He finds a listing seeking a Licensed Contractor for Tedesco Construction in Fort Myers.
2. **Compile information about the company.** Through research, Chris learns that Tedesco is a medium-sized commercial construction firm with an excellent reputation for quality. It has a healthy business with corporate clients and also regularly wins bids from municipalities—in fact, it recently won a bid from the city of Fort Myers to build a new safety center.
3. **Compile information about the position.** The ad is very brief, simply specifying "Licensed Contractor." But Chris knows what kinds of skills and achievements will be of value: the ability to finish projects on schedule and on budget, a knack for working with subcontractors, and the broad experience needed to erect a complex structure.
4. **Write down contact information.** Because the company is not technologically advanced, Chris will use a traditional mailed letter (rather than e-mail). He plans to write to the president of the company, whose title was included in the ad. He has gone the extra mile to find out her name.

   Cynthia Mars, President
   Tedesco Construction, Inc.
   1230 Seaside Boulevard
   Fort Myers, FL 33907

## Step 3: Write the Opening Paragraph

The opening paragraph of your cover letter is your hook—your "sales pitch" of who you are and why you would be of value to that specific organization. You should write it to entice the recipient to read your letter in its entirety and then take the time to closely review your resume. Because it is so critical, the opening paragraph is often the section that will take you the longest to write.

> *Tip* If you're having trouble writing the opening paragraph of your cover letter, leave it for the time being and move on to the body of the letter. After you've written the rest, the opening paragraph usually flows much more smoothly and quickly.

You must address three specific questions in the opening paragraph of your cover letter:

1. Who are you?
2. Why are you writing?
3. What message are you communicating?

There are literally hundreds of opening paragraphs you can use that differ in style, wording, impact, tone, and presentation. The type of opening to choose depends on two key criteria:

1. **What is appropriate for the specific situation?** Are you writing in response to an advertisement or following up with a network referral? Are you writing to Fortune 100 companies to explore potential opportunities, or are you responding to a posting from an Internet job site? The specific situation almost always dictates the type of opening you select.
2. **What feels right?** When you read the following samples, you'll really like a few of them, feel lukewarm about others, and definitely not like some of them at all. That's okay. People differ; cover letter styles differ. Select one that not only fits the situation, but one that you feel good about, like its tone, and believe will work for you.

## Sample Opening Paragraphs

We've chosen 41 of our favorite opening paragraphs to share with you. Some are aggressive; some are mild-mannered and conservative. A number are typical in style; others are vastly different from anything you've probably ever seen. Read them all and select the ones that you are most comfortable with.

### Sample 1: Ad-Response Letter to a Company or Recruiter

> I am writing in response to your advertisement for a (NAME OF POSITION) and have enclosed my resume for your review.

**Advantages:**

- Direct, clear, and concise.
- Immediately identifies the position for which the candidate is applying.

**Disadvantages:**

- Passive and a bit passé.
- Reads the same as hundreds of other cover letters the company or recruiter has read before.

## Sample 2: Ad-Response Letter to a Company or Recruiter

You will want to interview me for the Administrative Director position with Pfizer because I

- Managed all administrative and business support functions for Merck's four-person senior executive management team for 12 years.
- Implemented the full suite of Microsoft Office programs and coordinated on-site training for 200+ administrative personnel.
- Saved $10,000 in annual purchasing costs.

**Advantages:**

- Immediately asks for the interview.
- Highlights experience in the same industry (both companies are large pharmaceutical manufacturers).
- Quick and easy-to-read style.

**Disadvantage:**

- Can be interpreted as too aggressive (but we don't think so).

## Sample 3: Ad-Response Letter to a Company or Recruiter

Born and educated in Australia, I have lived and worked around the globe—from Asia to Latin America, from the U.S. to the Philippines. The strength of my cross-cultural experience, combined with 15+ years of senior management experience, places me in a uniquely qualified position for your search for a **Director of International Business Development.**

**Advantages:**

- Interesting, informative, and fun introduction.
- Communicates the candidate's overall expertise.
- Clearly highlights the position for which the candidate is applying.

**Disadvantages:**

- Candidate could be perceived as "older" due to 15+ years and such extensive global experience.
- Conversational rather than hard-hitting—requires reading the full paragraph to determine the specific reason for writing, although the bold type certainly helps make this information more noticeable.

## Sample 4: Ad-Response Letter to a Company or Recruiter

Your recent advertisement for an Operations Manager calls for skills and experience I have demonstrated throughout my career—most recently as Director of Operations for Office Depot's Corporate Accounts Warehouse.

**Advantages:**

- Clearly identifies why the candidate is writing.
- Appeals to the company's interests by referring to its advertised needs.
- Immediately communicates that the candidate held a highly relevant position with a well-known organization.
- Links the candidate's experience to the specific position.

**Disadvantages:**

- Appropriate only if the candidate's experience is directly relevant to the advertised position.
- Rather bland.

## Sample 5: Ad-Response Letter to a Company or Recruiter

There is nothing that I have found that offers more challenge than "closing the deal." The strategy, the partners, and the money involved can be complex. But when the deal closes, the personal satisfaction is tremendous. It is this expertise that I bring to the position of Venture Funding Manager.

**Advantages:**

- Unique, interesting introduction.
- Immediately identifies the candidate's number-one qualification.
- Links the candidate's experience to the specific position.

**Disadvantage:**

- Appropriate only if the candidate's number-one qualification is what the hiring company is focused on.

## Sample 6: Ad-Response Letter to a Company or Recruiter

When I was 7, like many others, I seriously planned to become a professional baseball player. Unlike so many others, however, I found a way to stay involved in sports despite not making it to the major leagues. Playing baseball through high school and college, and then becoming involved as Clubhouse Manager for a AAA baseball club, were natural outlets for my interest and ambition. I then "fell" into a sales position, where I've excelled for three years. Now I see an ideal opportunity to combine my deep interest with my proven professional skills and would be delighted to interview for your Sports Sales Associate position.

**Advantages:**

- Unique and interesting introduction that, in the right circumstances, can really captivate the reader.
- Gives a quick but comprehensive "life" summary.
- Clearly states the position for which the candidate is applying.

**Disadvantages:**

- Applicable only for a candidate seeking to transition from one industry to another.
- Could be interpreted as too "homey."
- Requires that the reader complete an entire lengthy paragraph before finding out why this individual is writing.

## Sample 7: Ad-Response Letter to a Company or Recruiter

I would like to submit my name for consideration for your advertised Warehouse Manager position. My qualifications follow.

**Advantages:**

- Clear and concise.
- Immediately communicates the position the candidate is applying for.

**Disadvantage:**

- Boring, with no "hook" to grab the reader's attention.

## Sample 8: Ad-Response Letter to a Company or Recruiter

> Success. I believe that it lies in one's ability to merge the strategic with the tactical, to understand the market and the competition, to effectively control a company's finances, and to build a strong and committed workforce. No one function is accountable for performance. It is the integration of all functions and the combined strength of the management team that makes things happen. This knowledge and hands-on approach to executive management are what distinguish me from other candidates for the position of CEO.

**Advantages:**

- Communicates that this candidate understands business and executive management.
- Uses a unique style and executive-level presentation.

**Disadvantages:**

- Style is appropriate only for a mid- to senior-level position.
- Can be interpreted as too vague, theoretical, or obscure.
- Rather wordy, without immediate impact.

## Sample 9: Ad-Response Letter to a Company or Recruiter

> Please accept this letter and enclosed resume as application for the position of City Manager. You will find that not only do I have the specific qualifications you are seeking, I am a strong business leader, a graduate of McAllen Leadership Conference, and a current resident of the city with a wide network of personal, professional, and political contacts.

**Advantages:**

- Immediately identifies the position for which the candidate is applying.
- Highlights what the candidate considers to be her three most significant selling points.
- Combines a traditional introduction ("Please accept...") with a proactive style ("...strong business leader...").

**Disadvantages:**

- Might not be addressing the "hot buttons" of the hiring committee.
- Language might be viewed as stodgy or old-fashioned.

## Sample 10: Ad-Response Letter to a Company

> A start-up company is only as good as the people behind it, and when you're in the Internet arena, you need people who are experienced and knowledgeable in this ever-changing medium. I believe your search for the newest addition to your team is over if you seek an entrepreneurial-minded sales professional with expertise in formulating, managing, and marketing emerging Internet services.

**Advantages:**

- Distinctive introduction that will stand out from the crowd of competitors.
- Makes an immediate industry connection between the candidate and the hiring company.
- Alludes to the specific position for which the candidate is applying.

**Disadvantages:**

- Might be telling people what they already know ("A start-up company is only as good...") and, therefore, might be considered somewhat condescending.
- The recipient must read the whole paragraph to "get it" and to identify the position for which the candidate is applying.

## Sample 11: Ad-Response Letter to a Company

> Your search for a Retail Sales Manager is over if you are interested in someone who can ignite sales, reduce losses, and build a top-performing sales and customer-service team. I have done it in the past and will continue to do it in the future—ideally with Macy's Retail Management. I present to you my resume for your consideration for a position on your management team.

**Advantages:**

- Powerful and confident introduction that is most appropriate for candidates in sales, marketing, and business development (demonstrates that you really can sell).
- Highlights overall areas of expertise and achievement.

**Disadvantage:**

- Could be interpreted as a bit too boisterous for some organizations.

## Sample 12: Ad-Response Letter to a Recruiter

I meet all the hiring criteria for your search for an Administrative Director. Briefly summarized, my qualifications include the following:

**Advantages:**

- Clean, clear, and concise.
- Briefly addresses hiring criteria as stated in the advertisement.

**Disadvantage:**

- Passive approach that is similar to hundreds, maybe thousands, of letters the recruiter has previously seen.

## Sample 13: Online Letter to a Company or Recruiter

I submit my qualifications in response to your job posting for a Nurse Manager and have attached my resume at the bottom of this letter.

**Advantages:**

- Clear and concise opening suitable for an abbreviated online letter format.
- Immediately identifies the position for which the candidate is applying.

**Disadvantage:**

- Boring, but appropriate for "quick-read" e-mail letters.

## Sample 14: Online Letter to a Company or Recruiter

With 12 years of experience as a high school teacher, I more than meet your hiring requirements for the Teacher Training Specialist position. My resume is available for your review at www.onlineresume/lrosen.html.

**Advantages:**

- This concise and straightforward introduction is ideal for an online cover letter.

- Connects the candidate's experience with the advertised position and its specific requirements.
- Demonstrates technological proficiency (by including the Web site address).

**Disadvantage:**

- Does not provide any captivating information or entice the recipient to read.

## Sample 15: Cold-Call Letter to a Company or Recruiter

> Are you in need of a top-producing sales professional? An individual who has built new sales territories, delivered double-digit revenue growth, and consistently outperformed the competition? Someone who excels in transitioning customer relationships into profitable partnerships?

**Advantages:**

- Can be a powerful introduction if the reader answers "yes."
- Can entice readers if the candidate has used the right keywords to grab their attention.
- Demonstrates that the candidate knows how to sell (the letter itself is a sales pitch).

**Disadvantage:**

- Is virtually worthless if the reader answers "no."

## Sample 16: Cold-Call Letter to a Company or Recruiter

> Recruited to RAP Technology in 1989, I am one of five executives responsible for the dramatic growth of the company, from a $7 million privately held government contractor into a $200+ million NYSE high-tech systems provider with operating subsidiaries worldwide. My contributions have been diverse, with dual roles as Senior Vice President of Operations and Chief Technology Officer.

**Advantages:**

- Immediately communicates that the candidate has value. RAP recruited him, so others must want him as well.
- Demonstrates significant achievement and outstanding financial performance.

**Disadvantages:**

- Is appropriate only if the candidate was recruited for his last position.
- Is appropriate only if the candidate has one very significant achievement to highlight.
- Does not immediately communicate the type or level of position the candidate is interested in.

## Sample 17: Cold-Call Letter to a Company or Recruiter

> As one of the top three executives in a national nonprofit organization, I have been recognized for my expertise in building strong, efficient, cost-effective, and productive operations that are responsive to our members' needs. When we started three years ago, the organization was an unknown entity. Today, we have increased our membership 400%, increased our funding 200%, and are recognized as one of the top 500 nonprofits in the country.

**Advantages:**

- Immediately identifies who the candidate is and his level of experience.
- Highlights quantifiable achievements that are quite significant.

**Disadvantage:**

- Appropriate only if the candidate is writing to an individual in the same industry (in this instance, nonprofit).

## Sample 18: Cold-Call Letter to a Company or Recruiter

> Beginning my professional career as one of the first female engineers ever hired into MCI, I progressed rapidly through a series of increasingly responsible technical, product development, marketing, and sales management positions with MCI, Sprint, and AT&T. And to each, I delivered financial results.

**Advantages:**

- Demonstrates innovation and fast-track promotion.
- Communicates significant industry expertise.
- Vaguely highlights success and achievement.

**Disadvantages:**

- Unclear as to what this candidate's current objective is.
- Niches this candidate into one specific industry—telecommunications (fine if that's where her search is strictly focused).

## Sample 19: Cold-Call Letter to a Company

> Building corporate value is my expertise. Whether challenged to launch a start-up venture, orchestrate an aggressive turnaround, or lead an organization through accelerated growth and expansion, I have consistently delivered strong financial results.

**Advantages:**

- Aggressive, powerful, and high-performance.
- Most appropriate for a senior management or executive-level position.

**Disadvantages:**

- Can be interpreted as too aggressive (although we don't think so).
- Not focused on any particular type of company (start-up, turnaround, or growth) that the candidate is interested in—is "all over the place."

*Tip* You can use countless variations on the "building corporate value is my expertise" strategy. For example, if your expertise is in managing turnaround businesses, you might start with "Leading organizations through massive change and reorganization is my expertise." Obviously, you'll need to also modify the second sentence in the paragraph to highlight achievements that are directly related to turnaround, reorganization, revitalization, process improvement, performance improvement, change management, and other related functions.

Or, if your success has been in developing new products, you could begin your cover letter with, "Developing new products that have generated millions of dollars in new sales revenues is what I do best." Then continue with your next sentence that highlights relevant achievements, functions, and keywords.

These types of letters aren't restricted for use at just the senior management or executive level. Suppose you're an office manager whose expertise is creating order from chaos. You might consider writing "Creating efficient, productive, and well-organized business support operations is the value I bring to your company."

If you like this strategy, first identify your number-one qualification or area of expertise, and then work on developing a strong and powerful two- to three-sentence introductory paragraph. You will find numerous variations of this opening in the sample letters in chapters 7 through 13.

## Sample 20: Cold-Call Letter to a Company

I am writing and forwarding my resume in anticipation that you may be "in the market" for a well-qualified President and CEO. Highlights of my professional career that may be of particular interest to you include the following:

**Advantages:**

- A "toned-down" version of sample 19.
- Immediately identifies who the candidate is, level of experience, and type of position being sought.

**Disadvantage:**

- If the reader is *not* "in the market," the letter is of little value.

## Sample 21: Cold-Call Letter to a Company

Never in the history of industrial automation has the pace been faster, the competition stiffer, or the economic factors more complex. With the rapid emergence of the information technology marketplace, every company is faced with tremendous challenges and unlimited opportunities.

Are you prepared to compete and win?

I can make a positive impact. With 20+ years of experience in the information technology industry, most recently in data warehousing, digital communications, and e-commerce, I bring a wealth of technical and managerial expertise to Blue Ridge New Media Partners.

**Advantages:**

- Quickly communicates that this is a senior-level candidate.
- Demonstrates industry knowledge and expertise.
- Is unique in style and presentation.
- Does not communicate an immediate message of "I want a job."

**Disadvantage:**

- Does not quickly communicate why the candidate is writing; therefore, might lose the reader's attention.

## Sample 22: Cold-Call Letter to a Company

> During my ten-year career with Westinghouse, I earned seven merit promotions, advancing from Management Trainee through a series of increasingly responsible production assignments to my current position as Manager of Production Scheduling. Now my goal is to transition my experience into a smaller, higher-growth organization such as Excelsior Technology.

**Advantages:**

- Communicates promotion, achievement, and success.
- Quickly and effortlessly explains the reason for leaving her current position.

**Disadvantages:**

- Does not state a particular position in which the candidate is interested.
- Highlights experience with a large corporation when the candidate is currently looking for opportunities with small companies.
- Communicates a focus on the candidate's career and goals rather than the company's needs; an employer's knee-jerk reaction could be, "So what?"

## Sample 23: Cold-Call Letter to a Company

> Twenty years ago, consumer electronics virtually sold themselves. With just a bit of advertising, a company was set to launch a new product. Today, things have changed dramatically, and marketing has become one of the most vital components for any successful company. With both global competition and new product rollouts at an all-time high, it is no longer enough just to develop a great product. You need an astute marketer, and that is precisely what I am.

**Advantages:**

- Clearly communicates who the candidate is (albeit at the end of the paragraph).
- Demonstrates substantial industry experience.
- Captures interest and should command immediate agreement with the philosophy expressed.

**Disadvantage:**

- Can be interpreted as condescending (doesn't everyone already know this information?).

## Sample 24: Cold-Call Letter to a Company

> I am currently employed as the Hotel Manager with The Emerald Suites in San Diego. After eight years, I have decided to confidentially explore new opportunities and am contacting a select group of hotels that would be most interested in a candidate with my qualifications.

**Advantages:**

- Immediately communicates who the candidate is.
- Highlights years of experience in the hotel industry.
- Drops the "right" name (assuming that The Emerald Suites is a prestigious property).

**Disadvantages:**

- Not particularly exciting or captivating.
- Unclear as to what type of position the candidate is seeking (although we can guess).
- May convey an impression of self-importance—and there's definitely more focus on the candidate's interests than the employer's needs.

## Sample 25: Cold-Call Letter to a Company

> If you are looking for an experienced Pharmaceutical Sales Representative who can increase market share, build strong physician relationships, deliver effective presentations, and capture competitive business, then you will be interested in the experience and accomplishments highlighted in the enclosed resume.

**Advantages:**

- Immediately communicates who the candidate is.
- Identifies with the company's needs and promises the ability to deliver results.
- Immediately communicates why the candidate is writing.

**Disadvantage:**

- If the company is not looking for someone with these qualifications, the first paragraph will not capture interest.

## Sample 26: Cold-Call Letter to a Company

> If you ask any one of my colleagues, employers, or clients, they will all tell you the same thing about me: I am a unique combination of **Technical Expert** and **Customer Service Specialist.** It's what I have done for years, it's what I enjoy, and it's the value I bring to TXT Systems, Inc.

**Advantages:**

- Unique letter style and tone.
- Who the candidate is stands out boldly.

**Disadvantages:**

- Does not state the specific type of position the candidate is seeking.
- Might be considered somewhat pompous (although we don't think so).

## Sample 27: Cold-Call Letter to a Company

> I am a well-qualified Bank Manager seeking a new and more challenging career opportunity with a financial institution in need of strong strategic, operating, and management leadership.

**Advantage:**

- Clearly and immediately communicates who the candidate is.

**Disadvantages:**

- Vague in terms of what type of position the candidate is currently seeking.
- Not particularly exciting, interesting, or captivating.

## Sample 28: Cold-Call Letter to a Company

> When I joined the investment management team at USF&G, I knew I was in for an exciting opportunity. Little did I know that during my five-year tenure, the company would be acquired twice and experience better than 200% market growth. In response to the dramatic changes within the organization, not only was I retained during each of these transitions, I was promoted three times to my current position as Director of Retail Investor Services, the exact type of position I am now seeking with your financial institution.

**Advantages:**

- Interesting and informative introduction.
- Communicates the candidate's fast-track career, promotion, and value to his current employer.
- Communicates the type of position the candidate currently holds and relates it directly to the position being sought.

**Disadvantage:**

- Leaves the reader wondering why this individual is seeking new employment opportunities if his career with USF&G has been so phenomenal.

## Sample 29: Cold-Call Letter to a Company

> I am a well-qualified marketing professional with 15+ years of experience. Most notable have been my achievements in new market development, new business development, market research, service/product line expansion, and customer management. Now, after a long and successful career with ABC, I am seeking to relocate to Atlanta and am quite interested in opportunities with your local network affiliate.

**Advantages:**

- Clearly communicates this candidate's expertise and core skill sets.
- Communicates the candidate's generalized achievements.
- Highlights that the candidate is (or will be) available in the local market; therefore, no relocation is required.

**Disadvantages:**

- 15+ years of experience can be interpreted as maybe 20, 30, or more years and, therefore, makes this look like an older candidate.
- Candidate appears to be moving downward in the career cycle.

## Sample 30: Cold-Call Letter to a Company

> Do you seek the missing link to connect your U.S. operations with your expansion into Latin America? If so, we should meet. You will be particularly interested in the past five years of my career, during which I have provided the knowledge and experience to build Allied Signal's presence throughout the entire Latin American region. Starting with virtually nothing, I built a multimillion-dollar market that continues to grow at better than 25% annually.

**Advantages:**

- Captures immediate attention if the reader is interested in expanding into Latin America.
- Clearly communicates the candidate's experience and success.
- Highlights a very tangible achievement.

**Disadvantage:**

- Potential exists that the recipient could answer "no" to the introductory sentence, making the letter virtually powerless and a waste of time.

## Sample 31: Cold-Call Letter to a Company

As I begin to launch my new career, I am looking for a company with a reputation for continual growth and achievement. From its beginning in 1899 as Brown Telephone Company, Sprint has grown tremendously and positioned itself as one of the industry's leaders. Sprint has precisely the spirit and drive that I seek as I near graduation and begin my career in human resources.

**Advantages:**

- Demonstrates that the candidate has devoted time to researching the company and its history.
- Communicates the specific type of position the candidate is seeking.

**Disadvantages:**

- Immediately identifies that this candidate (a graduating student) has no relevant experience.
- May be interpreted as manipulative and pandering to the company.
- Gives no reason why the company should be interested in this candidate.
- Communicates what the candidate is looking for rather than what he or she can offer the company.

## Sample 32: Cold-Call Letter to a Company

FOR IMMEDIATE RELEASE

Lew Johnson, Sports Information Director at Maine State University, recently announced his desire to contribute his three years of experience in sports and

> public relations to a Division I school. Johnson's contract with MSU expires in May, and he sees this as an opportunity to meet bigger challenges. Johnson's performance at MSU has brought a great deal of attention to the athletic department, from athletes, students, parents, and the general public. He knows he can do the same for a larger athletic department at a larger school.

**Advantages:**

- Unique press-release format that is particularly enticing for a public relations or marketing communications position.
- Demonstrates creativity, innovation, and the ability to capture the reader's interest.
- Clearly identifies who the candidate is, his experience, and his current employment objectives.

**Disadvantages:**

- Could be interpreted as a traditional press release and either forwarded to the PR department or discarded.
- May be too creative for a traditional or conservative university.
- Written in the third person, which is generally not advisable.

## Sample 33: Cold-Call Letter to a Recruiter

> I am writing in anticipation that you might be working with a client company seeking a well-qualified candidate for a position in Technology R&D. Highlights of my career that might be of particular interest to you include the following:

**Advantages:**

- One of the preferred methods when writing to a recruiter.
- Clear and concise as to the type of position the candidate is seeking.
- Immediately identifies the candidate's industry preference.

**Disadvantages:**

- Passive and passé.
- Similar in tone and presentation to thousands of letters the recruiter has previously received.
- Nothing distinguishing to immediately capture the reader's attention.

## Sample 34: Referral Letter

Walter Clark recently described your broker-training program to me, and it certainly caught my attention as I seek to start a new career in the financial services industry. Mr. Clark is familiar with my extensive professional experience and recommended I submit my resume directly to you for consideration for one of your vacant investment professional positions.

**Advantages:**

- Highlights the name of the referring individual, who is someone the recipient knows.
- Communicates that it was Mr. Clark's recommendation that this candidate contact the company, because Mr. Clark believes there might be a match between the company and the candidate.
- Identifies the type of position the candidate is most suited for.

**Disadvantages:**

- The letter could potentially be passed on to someone who is not familiar with Mr. Clark, therefore negating the impact of the letter.
- Does not highlight any particulars about the candidate's experience.

## Sample 35: Referral Letter

John Greene of CIO Enterprises suggested I contact you regarding your search for a Corporate Counsel. I've worked closely with John and his executive team for the past 18 months to facilitate their private placement and subsequent IPO. With the successful conclusion of that assignment, I'm now interested in other corporate funding and development projects, so John thought we might be a good fit for one another.

**Advantages:**

- Highlights the name of the referring individual, who is someone the recipient knows.
- Clearly communicates the value the candidate can bring to the company through the example of what she has done for CIO Enterprises.
- Is clear about the type of position the candidate is seeking.

**Disadvantages:**

- If the company has no corporate funding and development projects on the horizon, the candidate's experience will not capture the reader's interest.

- The letter could potentially be passed on to someone who is not familiar with Mr. Greene, therefore negating the impact of the letter.

## Sample 36: Networking Letter

> As a fellow CEO, I've most likely dealt with many of the same issues that you have—issues related to reducing costs, optimizing operations, improving staff competencies, and, ultimately, strengthening bottom-line financial performance. My particular achievements have been in the transportation industry, but the skill sets I demonstrated are easily transferable to another industry.

**Advantages:**

- Immediately communicates the level of this candidate's expertise.
- Best used when approaching network contacts for their assistance and recommendations.
- Builds camaraderie with the reader.

**Disadvantages:**

- Clearly communicates that the candidate does not have experience related to the recipient's industry and, therefore, might immediately exclude him from consideration.
- Not focused on any particular opportunity.

## Sample 37: Networking Letter

> Your name came to my attention recently as I began researching the pharmaceutical and medical research industries. I am interested in a career in sales and am looking to gain further insight into these industries and major players like yourself. I hope that you will help me in this pursuit of information by meeting with me to answer a few questions. Please understand that I am not asking for a job, but rather for some of your time to increase my knowledge.

**Advantages:**

- Excellent introduction for a letter requesting an informational interview (as opposed to a job interview).
- Alerts the recipient to the fact that her name is well known and well respected in the industry.
- Not asking for a job—just for information and time.

**Disadvantages:**

- Appears as a novice in the industry with no relevant experience.
- Might be interpreted by the reader as a waste of her time.
- Might be construed by the reader as an indirect attempt to secure employment.
- There is no personal reference; the writer is essentially "cold-calling" the recipient.

## Sample 38: Follow-Up Letter to a Company or Recruiter

Three weeks ago I forwarded my resume for consideration for the position of Advertising Specialist with WRKR Broadcasting. I'm sure you received quite a response and have had to devote time to reviewing the qualifications of each of the candidates. At this time, I would like to reiterate my interest in the position and assure you that my qualifications not only meet, but exceed, your hiring requirements.

**Advantages:**

- Connects the candidate's experience to the company's specific hiring requirements.
- Demonstrates that the candidate follows up on a task that he has initiated.
- Reconfirms the candidate's interest in the position.

**Disadvantages:**

- Might be a waste of time if the hiring manager did not respond to the first inquiry.
- Might be interpreted as "pushing" the hiring manager too hard to follow up (we don't think so).
- Is probably less effective, and certainly less direct, than a follow-up phone call.

## Sample 39: Follow-Up Letter to a Company or Recruiter

After we met last month at the AMA meeting, you asked that I forward my resume to you. Assuming that you've received it by now, I wanted to follow up to schedule an interview with you. During our conversation, you mentioned that you were interested in a candidate with an extensive background in the insurance and risk-management industries. That is precisely my background and the value I bring to AAA.

**Advantages:**

- Brings to the reader's immediate attention that she has already met the candidate and, at that point, asked the candidate to forward his resume.
- Clearly communicates who the candidate is.
- Clearly communicates the experience the candidate brings to the company.

**Disadvantages:**

- Might be a waste of time if the hiring manager or recruiter did not respond to the first inquiry.
- Might be interpreted as "pushing" too hard to follow up (we don't think so).
- Might be less effective than a follow-up phone call.

## Sample 40: Sponsor Letter

After our leadership conference last week and our discussion about your search for a new Director of Procurement, I think I've found just the right candidate for you. Jonas Viens has been an employee with our organization for eight years and currently serves as Assistant Director of Purchasing and Vendor Relations. His level of expertise in vendor sourcing, price negotiations, and contract administration is outstanding and a valuable asset to our organization. However, Jonas has decided to relocate to Miami, a real loss for us but a potentially outstanding opportunity for you.

**Advantages:**

- Excellent example of a sponsor letter introduction.
- Clearly communicates who the candidate is and his value to the hiring organization.
- Immediately connects the candidate with the hiring company's needs.

**Disadvantages:**

- Can be used only if written by a third party—a candidate's sponsor.
- Appropriate only if this senior executive is writing to a colleague—another senior executive.

## Sample 41: Sponsor Letter

> Mary Morton is a winner. I know from experience. Mary worked for me for 14 years, first as Sales Manager and then as VP of Sales and Marketing during my tenure as CEO of Ryder Dedicated Logistics. Her performance was top-of-the-line, consistently exceeding revenue and profit objectives and winning major accounts. What's more, she knows our industry, how the marketplace works, and what it takes to win. If you're looking for a VP of Sales to replace Roger, you can't go wrong with Mary.

**Advantages:**

- Powerful introduction and testimonial from a third party.
- Clearly communicates who the candidate is.
- Clearly communicates the need the candidate fills.

**Disadvantages:**

- Can be used only if written by a third party—a candidate's sponsor.
- Appropriate only if this senior executive is writing to a colleague—another senior executive.

### Action Item

**Write Your Opening Paragraph**

Write the opening paragraph for the cover letter you have selected to write for this exercise. You can select one of the preceding samples and edit it to your experience, qualifications, achievements, and the specific situation at hand. Or, if you prefer, you can write an entirely different introduction that is appropriate and that "feels good" to you.

## Chris Starts His Letter

Remember Chris Matthews? He's about to start his letter to Tedesco Construction to see whether he can "sell" his qualifications as a Licensed Contractor for the company.

Chris wants to appeal to the main concern of construction companies everywhere: getting the job done on time. Here's how he starts his letter:

> With in-depth construction management experience and a 20-year record of never missing a project-completion date, I have proven skills and a track record of performance that can benefit your company as a Licensed Contractor.

## Step 4: Write the Body

After reading and progressing through step 3, "Write the Opening Paragraph," you're now ready to tackle the real task at hand. You're ready to write the body of your cover letter—the substance, key qualifications, accomplishments, successes, and whatever other information you can highlight that will entice the reader to closely review your resume and offer you the opportunity for a personal interview.

> *Tip* Before you begin writing, again consider why you're writing the letter you have chosen for this exercise. Regardless of your profession, the type of position you are interested in, your industry experience, your professional skill set, your technical proficiency, or any other variable, you have just one purpose in writing the letter:
>
> **To sell the product—and the product is you!**

### Highlight Your Features and Benefits

To sell any product, you must highlight the attractive *features* and *benefits* of that product. Put yourself in the buyer's shoes and ask yourself:

- What will catch my attention?
- What's interesting about this candidate?
- What's innovative or unique about this candidate?
- Why is this candidate different from (or better than) other competitive candidates?
- Do I understand the value I'll get from this candidate?
- Do I need this candidate?
- Do I want this candidate?

Whether or not you're conscious of it, every time you buy something, you ask yourself these questions and others. It's the typical process that everyone goes through when they're deciding whether to make a purchase. It is imperative that you remember this as you begin to write your cover letters. Understand that you must clearly communicate the answers to these questions in order to get people to want to "buy" your skills, expertise, and value.

> *Tip* Your cover letter *should not* be written as "Here I am; give me a job." Instead, it should be written as, "Here I am; this is why I am so valuable; *now* give me a job." Focusing on the value and benefits you have to offer is a good way to capture the reader's attention. Remember, the employer's most compelling question is "What can you do for me?", not "What do you want?"
>
> Your challenge is to convey that value in a short and concise document—your cover letter.

## Refer to Your Key Selling Points Lists

Refer to the lists of responsibilities and achievements you developed in "Step 1: Identify Your Key Selling Points" in chapter 2. Your lists include information from both your current position (if you are currently employed) and all of your past positions. The sole reason that you completed this task was to prepare for what you are going to do now: write the "meat" of your cover letter.

Unfortunately, there are no rules to guide you in selecting what to include from your lists and what to omit. It is entirely a judgment call based on the specific situation at hand. Consider the following scenario:

You're currently employed as a customer service manager with a large telemarketing company. If you're applying for a similar position in the credit-card industry, the responsibilities and accomplishments you will highlight in your cover letter are those related to customer service, problem resolution, team building, and business unit management. You will *not* highlight your years of experience in the telemarketing industry.

If, on the other hand, you're applying for a position in sales in the same industry, the responsibilities and achievements you will highlight are those related to customer relationship management, account management, and product/service support, as well as your extensive experience in the telemarketing industry.

So, as you can see, what you highlight in your cover letter is determined exclusively by the specific situation at hand—the position, the company, the industry, and the required qualifications and experience. It is not necessarily based on what you consider to be your most significant responsibilities and achievements from throughout your career, but rather what is *most relevant to the hiring company and its needs.*

Achievements, accomplishments, contributions, and successes are the cornerstone of any effective cover letter. It goes without saying that you want to demonstrate that you have the right skills, qualifications, and experience for a particular job. However, you do not want your letter to be a "job description"—merely a listing of job responsibilities. First of all, you've addressed a great deal of that information in the resume that you'll be sending along with your cover letter. Remember, you do not want your letter to simply reiterate what's in your resume. The challenge is to write a cover letter that complements the resume and brings the most notable information to the forefront, as related to the particular position or situation.

Secondly, when you write in your cover letter that you have "Seven years of experience managing electronics purchasing for GE," you've immediately communicated a whole set of implied skills (such as vendor sourcing, contract negotiations, inventory planning, competitive bidding, product review, and knowledge of electronic products). To keep your cover letter short and succinct, do not waste space simply listing all of your skills and competencies as they are noted on your resume. Instead, highlight the notable achievements that will set you apart from the crowd and give readers a good idea of what you can do for them.

Depending on the format of your letter, you can convey this information in paragraph style, in comparison-list style, or in bullet points. If you're writing full paragraphs, make sure they are fairly short to promote readability. Edit and tighten your copy so that every word and phrase conveys information that relates to the employer's needs and your most relevant qualifications.

Your lists of responsibilities and achievements are your tools. First review what you know about the company and the position (your action items from "Step 2: Pre-Plan"). Then carefully review your lists to determine which responsibilities and achievements are most appropriate to this particular situation, and incorporate them into your letter. Sometimes you'll use them exactly as you have written them; sometimes you'll edit them to integrate them into the flow of your cover letter; and other times you might consolidate several of them into one statement or achievement. However you elect to use these lists, use them wisely. You have gone to the effort to prepare them. Now let them work for you as the foundation for every letter you write.

**Write the Body**

Write the core section of the cover letter you have selected to write for this exercise. You can use the paragraph style, comparison-list style, or bullet style, depending on the particular reason you are writing this letter. Be sure to focus on your achievements so that you can quickly and accurately communicate your value and strength in performance. Use the samples in chapters 8 through 13 to give you ideas on how to write powerful text that communicates a positive message of performance.

### Chris Writes the Body of His Letter

Chris Matthews continues his letter to Tedesco Construction with a brief list of qualifications and accomplishments followed by a paragraph expanding just a bit on how he is able to do what he does. He carefully communicates key strengths in the areas that he believes are *most important* to his reader.

> In brief, I offer:
>
> - In-depth expertise in all facets of commercial/industrial construction
> - Florida General Contractor license (fully up to date with annual CEUs)
> - Record of 100% on-time, on-budget project completion
> - High quality standards and the ability to get top results from contractor crews
> - Proven dependability, integrity, and dedication to customer satisfaction
>
> As a partner in a small construction company, I have managed every stage of a project, from preparing bids to handing over keys to new owners. Through team-building, clear communication, and careful progress tracking, I resolve small problems before they escalate and routinely deliver successful, profitable projects.

## Step 5: Write the Closing

Now that you've written your introductory paragraph and the balance of your cover letter, all you have left to write is the closing paragraph. Simple enough—and, in fact, this is generally the easiest section of your letter to write. To get started, ask yourself these two simple questions:

1. What style of closing paragraph do I want to use?
2. Is there any specific personal or salary information I want to include that was requested in the advertisement to which I am responding?

When it comes to choosing style, closing paragraphs are easy. There are only two styles—*passive* and *assertive.* There are, obviously, various options within each of these styles, and we explore these later in this section. The distinction between the two styles is evident:

- **Passive style.** A passive letter ends with a statement such as "I look forward to hearing from you." With this sentence, you are taking a passive approach, waiting for the hiring company or recruiter to contact you. This is not the strategy we recommend.
- **Assertive style.** An assertive letter ends with a statement such as "I look forward to interviewing with you and will follow up next week to schedule a convenient appointment." In this sentence, you are asserting yourself, telling the recipient that you will follow up and asking for the interview!

We strongly recommend that you always end your cover letters with an assertive closing paragraph. Remember that the number-one objective of your cover letter is to get an interview. Ask for it!

Furthermore, we also advise that you outline an agenda that communicates that you will be expecting their call and, if you don't hear from them, you will follow up. This puts you in the driver's seat and in control of your job search. It also demonstrates to a prospective employer that once you've initiated something, you follow it through to completion. This is a valuable trait for any professional.

Inevitably, there will be instances in your job search when you will not be able to follow up:

- If you are responding to a blind advertisement with a P.O. box, you won't know who to call.
- If you are responding to an advertisement that states "No phone calls," don't call.

- If you are sending out 1,000 letters to recruiters across the nation, don't waste your time trying to follow up on each of them. If a recruiter is interested or has an opportunity for which you are suited, he or she will call you.
- If you know that you'll never get the individual you want to speak with on the phone, don't waste your time or money trying.

*Tip* Follow up with a phone call after forwarding a resume and cover letter only when the situation is appropriate. You do not need to follow up every single contact with a phone call.

The closing paragraph of your cover letter is also the preferred placement for any personal or salary information you will include. There are generally only two times you will want to include this type of information:

- **When the advertisement asks for it.** Common requests include such things as salary history (what you have made in the past and are currently earning if you are employed), salary requirements (what your current salary objectives are), citizenship status, or geographic preference.

> I look forward to interviewing for the Sales Manager position and can assure you that the strength of my sales production, sales training, and account management experience will bring measurable value to Centric's sales organization. In response to your specific requests, my salary requirements are in the $50,000 to $70,000 range. I am a U.S. citizen and am open to relocation anywhere in the Southwestern U.S. Thank you.

*Tip* You will have already addressed the skill and qualification requirements of the position earlier in your letter—in your opening paragraph and in the body of the text. Save the closing paragraph for the "extras" that you might need to include.

- **When you are writing "cold-call" letters to recruiters.** When you are contacting recruiters, it is appropriate to address salary requirements (a range is fine) and any geographic preferences in the closing paragraph of your cover letter.

*Example*

> If you currently have an open search for a Logistics and Distribution Manager, I would welcome the opportunity to interview for the position. Be advised that my current salary is $65,000 annually and I would anticipate a 10% to 15% increase in my next position. Thank you for your consideration. I look forward to speaking with you.

## The Salary Question

Before we present the various sample closing paragraphs we've developed for your use, let's take a few minutes to discuss salary and how you can best deal with divulging salary information when it is requested.

First, keep in mind that it is never to your advantage to volunteer salary information. If you do so, you give employers a reason for screening you in or out of consideration, and you place yourself at a disadvantage in later salary negotiations. On some occasions, however, such information might be specifically requested. What do you do in those cases?

If an employer or recruiter asks you to provide a salary history (what you have made in your past and current positions), you have four basic options:

1. You can provide brief information in your cover letter, such as "My salary history has averaged $100,000 to $125,000 over the past five years." This defines the "ballpark" of your salary range and is usually quite adequate for the first contact you'll have with a recruiter or hiring company. If you choose to disclose salary information, we recommend this type of response.
2. You can provide more detailed information in your cover letter, such as

   *Example*

   > My salary history is as follows: Retail Sales Manager—JCPenney ($75,000/year); Retail Sales Manager—Kmart ($62,000/year); Sales Department Manager—Kmart ($45,000/year); Sales Associate—Kmart (progression from $18,000 to $35,000/year).

   In this example, you've still been brief but managed to include a great deal of information while demonstrating consistent growth in your compensation.
3. You can prepare a separate page—titled "Salary History"—that lists your employers, job titles, and both beginning and ending salaries. The following is a sample format:

*Example*

Customer Service Representative
Beginning Salary—$22,000/year

Sir Speedy Printing Company
Ending Salary—$35,000/year

Here's another format that might be appropriate if you've held several positions with the same company:

*Example*

**IBM—NEW VENTURES DIVISION**

| | |
|---|---|
| General Manager | $137,000/year |
| National Sales Manager | $102,000/year |
| Regional Sales Manager | $ 85,000/year |
| Key Account Manager | $ 55,000/year |
| Sales Associate | $ 38,000/year |

4. You can choose not to provide this information, either ignoring the request entirely or addressing it without disclosing salary information: "I will be glad to discuss salary once we have determined that I am a good fit for the position, responsibilities, and environment." There is the risk, of course, that the reader will be annoyed that you did not supply the requested information. In our experience, however, the most common response of hiring managers and HR people is, consistently, to *look at the resume anyway.* By not disclosing salary history, you are probably not hurting your chances of being asked for an interview, and you are maintaining a decided advantage in any ultimate salary negotiation. Of course, if the advertisement states "Responses without salary history will not be considered," you must comply. (See the following discussion of salary requirements for the details on the pros and cons of supplying and not supplying this kind of information.)

If an employer or recruiter asks you to provide your salary requirements (what your current salary objectives are), you again have four basic options:

1. You can provide a range, such as "My salary requirements are in the $55,000 to $65,000 range." This "ballpark figure" is generally enough information for this initial stage of contact with a potential employer or recruiter. In fact, this is our preferred method of response.

2. You can provide a specific number in your cover letter, such as "My salary requirements are $90,000 per year." This is not a particularly good strategy because it limits you. The position for which you are applying might be slated for a $100,000 salary. However, you've already agreed to work for $10,000 less a year. What a bargain for the

company! Or, a specific number can hurt you in the other direction. Suppose the company is prepared to pay only $75,000, but it's a great opportunity. You might just consider it, but potentially you've excluded yourself from consideration with an inflated salary expectation. And finally, any salary requirement that is too high *or* too low can effectively "screen you out," particularly in the first stages of resume review. When a recruiter or HR person is flooded with hundreds of resumes, the first response is to weed out anyone who doesn't fit every aspect of the job profile.

3. You can "take the fifth" and reply with, "My salary requirements are negotiable and can be discussed at the time of an interview" or "My salary requirements are flexible and will be discussed when I know more about the position and your company." Either way is really avoiding the question, but at least you are acknowledging that you saw the question. The only time we recommend this strategy is when you have absolutely no idea what a position will pay and don't want to oversell or undersell yourself.

4. You can ignore the request and not divulge your salary requirements. There are definite benefits to this strategy. First, you will not be screened out based on salary. Second, you won't "paint yourself into a corner" with a salary figure that might be much lower than the company is willing to pay or one that is significantly higher than the range for the position. Third, you are able to keep the focus on what's really important: whether you're the right person for the job. As every shopper knows, once you've found an item that you love, you're nearly always willing to pay just a bit more than you budgeted. By avoiding salary discussion until the company is convinced it wants to "buy" you, you give yourself a definite negotiating advantage. And both formal and informal research supports the finding that resume reviewers look at the resume anyway, even when salary requirements are not included.

   This approach can definitely work in your favor—but if you choose not to divulge salary requirements in your letter, you must prepare yourself to answer salary questions when they arise—often at the very first screening interview. The best strategy is to continually steer the conversation back to the matter at hand: whether you're the right person for the job, whether you have skills and experience that can help the company, and so forth. Spend the time to learn salary negotiating techniques (through a book or a coaching session with a career professional) so that you can handle these questions professionally and consistently throughout your search. And finally, this strategy will *not* work with recruiters. As we've stated several times previously, it's important to be up front with salary and personal requirements when dealing with recruiters. They won't take your candidacy any further unless they know you're in tune with their client's needs.

Depending on your level within the management ranks, you might share other information in your cover letters relative to your salary and overall compensation package. This information might include such items as signing bonuses, performance bonuses, equity interest, stock options, profit-sharing plans, deferred contribution plans, deferred compensation plans, and other management and executive incentives. Regardless of your career level, we wholeheartedly recommend that you read *Next-Day Salary Negotiation* by Maryanne L. Wegerbauer (JIST Publishing) for an in-depth exploration of the strategies, tips, and techniques for effective salary and compensation negotiations.

## Sample Closing Paragraphs

The following 35 sample closing paragraphs are quick and easy to review. Note that some closing paragraphs are indeed one paragraph, whereas others are two paragraphs, largely to improve readability. Simply select the samples that you are most comfortable with and adapt them for your use.

### Sample 1: Ideal if responding to a recruiter advertisement

If you are working with a client company seeking a candidate with my qualifications, I would welcome the opportunity to speak with you. Be advised that I am open to relocation and that my current compensation exceeds $85,000 annually. Thank you.

### Sample 2: Solid closing for a company ad-response letter

I think you'll agree I meet and exceed your needs for a Firm Administrator. I would appreciate the opportunity to meet with you and can be reached at (555) 333-2838 to schedule an appointment or for more information. Thank you for your time and consideration. I look forward to meeting you in the near future.

### Sample 3: Aggressive closing for a company ad-response letter

After reviewing the enclosed resume and visiting with me, I think you'll agree I'm the missing piece of your team. My experience in the industry is solid, my knowledge of the technology vast, and my client contacts of tremendous value to IBM. I will follow up next week to schedule an interview. I look forward to meeting you. Thank you.

### Sample 4: Strong closing for a company ad-response letter

Aware that you are currently recruiting for a Quality Engineer, I would welcome the opportunity to interview for the position. I guarantee that the depth and quality of my experience and technical skills are ideally suited and would bring measurable value to your organization. Thank you. I appreciate your confidentiality.

### Sample 5: Ideal closing for an ad-response letter (to recruiters or companies)

My goal is a top-level management position with an organization seeking to achieve market dominance as well as aggressive revenue and profit projections. I am most interested in interviewing for the position of General Manager—Aeronautics Division, where I will provide the strategic and tactical leadership critical to succeed in today's fast-moving environment.

I look forward to interviewing with you and the other principals involved in the hiring process. Thank you.

### Sample 6: Clearly positions the candidate as an asset and highlights qualifications for a specific position

I am confident that I can make a meaningful contribution to Archer Associates as the link between your growing offices. I am willing to travel in the U.S., Canada, Latin America, and Europe, and would be pleased to relocate to Orlando.

I would appreciate the opportunity to meet with you to discuss your growth objectives and how I can help you in achieving them. Please feel free to contact me for further information to support my candidacy for this position. Thank you.

### Sample 7: Closing for a cold-call letter to a recruiter

Currently, I am exploring finance and accounting management opportunities within the medical technology market. As such, I would welcome the opportunity to speak with you regarding any current search assignments. Please note that I prefer to remain in the Miami metro market and that my salary requirements are negotiable. Thank you.

### Sample 8: Concise and versatile closing for ad-response and cold-call letters

I am confident I can deliver similar results for your company. May we meet to explore your needs and how I can contribute to your growth and success?

### Sample 9: Cold-call letter closing

I would appreciate the opportunity to speak with you about how I can help your company live its mission by improving customer service, productivity, and efficiency through information technology. I will call in a few days to arrange a meeting that is convenient for you. In the meantime, if you need more information, please feel free to call me at (555) 555-1234. Thank you.

### Sample 10: Concise and direct closing for a cold-call letter to a company

Currently, I am exploring new engineering and project-management positions within the chemical industry. As such, if you are seeking a decisive, action-driven, and technically astute leader for your engineering organization, I would welcome a personal interview. I'll follow up on Tuesday to arrange a mutually convenient time for our meeting. Thank you.

### Sample 11: Focuses on how to contact the candidate

I am confident I can make a quick and valuable contribution to Robbins & Robbins, and I am sure you'll agree once we've had the opportunity to meet. Because of my travel schedule, it is easiest to reach me via e-mail at sallysmith@gmail.com. I look forward to meeting with you and the rest of the sales and customer-service team.

### Sample 12: Focuses on a relocation requirement

I am willing to relocate for the right opportunity—one that provides a challenge; a way for me to make an ongoing, positive impact; and the potential to grow with the dealership. I would appreciate a personal interview at your earliest convenience and will call to schedule a convenient time. Thank you for your consideration.

### Sample 13: Ideal if the candidate is seeking a position that requires relocation or travel

I would welcome the chance to meet with you to explore international sales opportunities and do appreciate your time and interest. On a personal note, I am single and currently renting my home. Therefore, relocation or travel can be immediate. Thank you.

### Sample 14: Ideal if the candidate is looking to remain in the same geographic area

Currently in the process of leaving Brenview Associates, I am eager to remain in the area and am contacting a select number of companies I believe would be interested in a candidate with my broad general management and operations experience. Can we meet to explore such opportunities? I can be available at your convenience and will follow up in the next ten days to schedule a time.

### Sample 15: Focuses on personal attributes and the reason for wanting to work for a specific company

Characterized by others as creative, intuitive, flexible, and decisive, I believe my strongest value is my broad operational and business perspective. The opportunity that you are offering with Bayer has tremendous potential and unlimited opportunities—thus my interest in meeting with you to further discuss the position, your needs, and my capabilities. Thank you.

### Sample 16: Focuses on personal attributes

The enclosed resume describes my qualifications in some detail. But it is difficult to convey on paper the personal qualities I bring to every challenge: drive, focus, commitment, a high energy level, and a strong work ethic. I am eager to take on new challenges and am confident that I can deliver strong results for Megacorp's Medical Products Division. May we meet to explore your needs and what I have to offer?

### Sample 17: Focuses on professional competencies

My experience lies principally in the product, service, and distribution industries, and my track record clearly demonstrates my ability to deliver strong financial results. I thrive in challenging, fast-paced, and results-driven organizations where teams work cooperatively to achieve aggressive business goals.

May we meet to explore your current and anticipated executive staffing needs? I can guarantee that the quality of my leadership performance will have a significant positive impact on your operations. Thank you. I'll follow up next week.

## Sample 18: Explains past employment experience

Since leaving EDS in 2008 after a long and successful career, I have been engaged in a number of consulting assignments while I've evaluated new opportunities, trying to find just the right fit for someone with my combination of leadership, customer management, and technical expertise. Your advertisement appears to require precisely the qualifications I bring to an organization. As such, I would welcome the opportunity to further explore the position. Thank you in advance for your time and consideration. I'll follow up next week if I haven't yet heard back from you.

## Sample 19: Explains the reason for leaving a company

After two years of success at Miller, the company is now poised for dramatic growth. However, the investor group has decided to pull the funding, and without a strong cash infusion, our growth and development opportunities have been significantly hindered. This has prompted my decision to leave the organization.

Through this experience I've found that I have enjoyed the constant interaction with the investor group and the accountability it demands. Therefore, I am contacting a select group of firms where I believe the opportunities are the strongest and my experience would be of most value. May we meet to explore such an affiliation? I'll call to speak with you, and we can go forward from there. Thank you.

## Sample 20: Explains why the candidate is seeking to return to an industry where he had previous experience

My goal is to return to the financial services industry in a mid-level management capacity. I am open to a number of opportunities that would allow me to use the diversity of my management skills across various disciplines—operations, sales/marketing, finance, and IT. I would also anticipate that the position would have a strong international focus to capitalize on the wealth of my experience abroad and my foreign-language skills.

I would welcome the chance to meet with you, and I look forward to your immediate response. Thank you for both your time and your consideration.

## Sample 21: Explains why the candidate is interested in changing careers and industry focus

At this juncture in my career, I am seeking the opportunity to transition my experience into either an investment or large commercial lending institution where I can continue to plan, strategize, negotiate, and execute favorable transactions—thus my interest in meeting with you to explore such opportunities. Thank you. I'll follow up next week.

## Sample 22: Explains why the candidate wants to work for that particular company

Currently, I am exploring new senior-level sales, marketing, and business development opportunities where I can provide both strategic and tactical leadership. Aware of the quality of your products, your commitment to global expansion, and your focus on customer service, I would be delighted to meet with you to discuss

potential employment. I thank you in advance for your consideration and look forward to speaking with you.

## Sample 23: Explains why the candidate is transitioning from consulting back to a corporate role

Most recently, I have provided operating, strategic, and marketing expertise on a consulting basis to an organization in need of strong hands-on leadership. This assignment has been quite rewarding, but I miss the dynamics of working "on the inside." As such, I would welcome the opportunity to interview for the position of General Manager with Zion Corporation and will phone next week to schedule an interview.

## Sample 24: Explains why the candidate is remaining in the profession, but just changing industry focus

My goal is to continue in association management; however, my direction has changed. Throughout my career, I have been quite interested in the building, construction, and housing industry. In fact, I worked for a $200 million REIT early in my career. Through this experience, I developed a strong foundation and understanding of the industry, its partners, its financial demands, and its operating requirements. Years later, I earned my real estate license, just to keep my "fingers in the pot." Now, I am ready to make a full transition to an association whose mission is to service that industry—thus my interest in your announcement for an Executive Director of BOMI and my request for a personal interview.

## Sample 25: Excellent strategy to explain why the candidate is in the job market

Now that HHXT has been acquired, I am working to facilitate a seamless transition to the new ownership team. Concurrently, I am exploring new executive opportunities and would welcome a personal interview for the CEO position at your earliest convenience. Thank you.

## Sample 26: Explains why the candidate is choosing to leave a company after years of employment

Please note that I am currently employed with Metropolitan and that they are not aware of my decision to leave the corporation. However, after eight years of intense legal, financial, and regulatory issues that have dramatically impacted the company's operations, I am ready to move on to new opportunities and new challenges. As such, I would welcome a personal interview for the advertised position. I guarantee that few Senior Auditors have the breadth of experience and technical qualifications that I bring to your organization.

## Sample 27: Clearly communicates why the candidate wants to remain in a particular industry

I have found the energy industry to be demanding and competitive, yet exciting, with unlimited opportunity. Even though I have been offered positions outside of the industry, my objective is to continue to advance my career in energy distribution and operations management. I look forward to interviewing for the position of VP—Energy Distribution and thank you for your consideration. I'll follow up next week.

## Sample 28: Demonstrates strong leadership and communicates a positive message of performance

These achievements are indicative of the quality and caliber of my entire professional career. Whether challenged to accelerate growth, orchestrate a top-to-bottom turnaround, or position an organization for long-term growth, I have provided strong leadership and even stronger financial results. Now I am seeking a similar professional challenge and would welcome an interview for the position of CEO with KTZ Partners.

## Sample 29: Communicates stability with the current employer

I am slated to return to the U.S. this spring to manage a large domestic production operation for my current employer. It is a tremendous opportunity. However, before accepting, I have decided to confidentially explore other senior management positions within the industry—thus my interest in speaking with you as soon as possible to determine my fit for your Manufacturing VP position. Thank you.

## Sample 30: Communicates performance and accomplishment

Never satisfied with the status quo, I strive to build profitable businesses by clearly understanding the market, the competition, and what needs to be done to retain a competitive lead. This is the strength and track record I bring to QSR.

May we meet to discuss your search for an Operations Manager? I'll call to arrange a mutually convenient time. Thank you.

## Sample 31: Follow-up letter to a recruiter, announcing that the candidate has accepted a new position

More than excited about my new position, I feel honored to be part of Centric's new management team. However, as any astute business professional today will tell you, it's never wise to close yourself off from other potential opportunities. As such, if you ever receive an exciting search assignment for which I fit the bill, I'd appreciate a quick call. Thank you.

## Sample 32: Informal network contact

I would appreciate any ideas, recommendations, or referrals you could offer and will, in the future, be delighted to do the same for you if the situation ever arises. I've enclosed a copy of my resume and will follow up with you shortly to get your feedback. Thanks so much.

## Sample 33: Formal network contact

Now that the time has come to move on, I am anxious to identify new executive opportunities where I can combine my legal and general management skills to provide strong, decisive, and actionable leadership to another technology venture. In anticipation that you might be aware of an organization seeking an individual with my skill set and track record of performance, I have taken the liberty of enclosing my resume.

Any assistance you can offer would be most appreciated. I thank you for this effort and those in the past. If there is ever anything I can do for you, please do not hesitate to contact me.

### Sample 34: Ideal for a network contact with someone the candidate knows quite well

I'll follow up with you in two to three weeks to get your feedback and recommendations. I can't thank you enough for your help. If I can ever return the favor, please do not hesitate to get in touch. My best to you and your family.

### Sample 35: Effective, professional closing for use when writing to a venture capital firm

Currently, I am confidentially exploring new professional challenges and opportunities and would be delighted to speak with you about such positions with one of your portfolio companies. I guarantee that the wealth of my financial expertise, combined with strong strategic, operational, and leadership skills, will add measurable value to your investment. Thank you. I look forward to your call.

*Action Item*

**Write the Closing Paragraph**

**Write the closing paragraph of the cover letter you have selected for this exercise.** You can select one of the preceding samples and edit it as appropriate, or you can write an entirely different closing that is appropriate and that you feel good about.

## Chris Writes His Closing Paragraph

In his closing paragraph, Chris conveys the rationale for seeking a position in Florida (he is currently living in another state). He uses an assertive close and will follow up appropriately. Note how he suggests a meeting during his next trip to Florida.

I have been a regular visitor to Florida for more than 10 years and now plan to make the state my permanent home. Tedesco Construction and this position seem to be an excellent fit for my skills and track record. I will follow up with a phone call next week and would be delighted to meet with you when I am in Florida the week of the 30th. Thank you.

## You're Done with the Writing Part!

Congratulations! By completing all the Action Items in this chapter, you've written a cover letter for a specific job search situation. Now that you've done it once, simply repeat the steps for each cover letter you write. You'll find that the process becomes easier and faster each time you do it, and you'll create a variety of cover letters that will be applicable for many different situations during your search.

Example

### Chris's Cover Letter

Chris has also finished his cover letter. The final product appears on the following page.

## Step 6: Polish, Proofread, and Finalize

The process we've recommended for writing your cover letters suggests that you first craft the opening, then the middle, and then the closing of each letter. Although the step-by-step process makes the task fairly quick and easy, you will probably find that your letters need final polishing, wordsmithing, and tweaking to ensure that each section flows into the next and that you have a cohesive-sounding whole.

Take the time to proofread your letter thoroughly and carefully. Read it for sense and flow; then read it again to check for spelling errors, punctuation mistakes, and grammatical inconsistencies. As we've suggested before, have your spouse or a friend proof your letter—and then read it one more time to be absolutely certain there are no errors. We cannot emphasize this point enough. The people who receive your cover letter and resume *do* judge your professionalism based on the quality and accuracy of these documents. In fact, in a survey of hiring authorities conducted for a prior book, *90 percent of respondents* mentioned quality and appearance factors (typos, misspellings, smudged print, low-quality paper) as reasons for *immediately discarding a resume package.* Don't take a chance that your carefully written letter and resume will end up in the circular file before your qualifications are even considered.

### Things to Watch For

Here are a few things to look out for during the polishing phase:

- **Spelling.** Use your computer's spell-checker, but don't rely on it totally. The spell-checker won't flag an "it's" that should be "its" or a "there" that should be "their." Make triple-certain you've correctly spelled all names: people, organizations, software programs, and so forth.
- **Grammar and punctuation.** If you're not confident about your grammar and punctuation skills, purchase an all-purpose reference guide and use it as often as you need to. Don't let your cover letter be discarded because of basic grammar and punctuation errors. Two good

**Chris Matthews**
123 West Park Avenue, Chicago, IL 60606
312-444-3627— cmatthews42@aol.com

---

August 20, 2010

Cynthia Mars, President
Tedesco Construction, Inc.
1230 Seaside Boulevard
Fort Myers, FL 33907

Re: ***Licensed Contractor Position,*** *The News-Press,* August 17, 2010

Dear Ms. Mars:

With in-depth construction management experience and a 20-year record of never missing a project-completion date, I have proven skills and a track record of performance that can benefit your company as a Licensed Contractor.

In brief, I offer

- In-depth expertise in all facets of commercial/industrial construction
- Florida General Contractor license (fully up to date with annual CEUs)
- Record of 100% on-time, on-budget project completion
- High quality standards and ability to get top results from contractor crews
- Proven dependability, integrity, and dedication to customer satisfaction

As a partner in a small construction company, I have managed every stage of a project, from preparing bids to handing over keys to new owners. Through team-building, clear communication, and careful progress tracking, I resolve small problems before they escalate and routinely deliver successful, profitable projects.

I have been a regular visitor to Florida for more than 10 years and now plan to make the state my permanent home. Tedesco Construction and this position seem to be an excellent fit for my skills and track record. I will follow up with a phone call next week and would be delighted to meet with you when I am in Florida the week of the 30th. Thank you.

Sincerely,

Chris Matthews

*Resume enclosed*

resources are *Woe Is I: The Grammarphobe's Guide to Better English in Plain English,* by Patricia T. O'Connor, and Strunk and White's classic, *The Elements of Style.*

- **Interesting language.** As much as possible, avoid clichés and outdated language (for example, "Enclosed please find my resume."). It's difficult to find new ways to express familiar sentiments (such as "I would appreciate the opportunity for an interview"), and it's certainly not necessary to come up with unique language for every phrase. But make sure that your cover letter doesn't sound like a cookie-cutter, one-size-fits-all letter that could have been written by any job seeker.

Before sending your cover letter, be sure to review chapter 5, "Cover Letter Presentation," for tips on making your letter look its best.

## Tips and Tricks from the Top

Here are some of our favorite tips for writing effective cover letters as painlessly as possible.

### Don't Reinvent the Wheel

Much of our discussion has focused on the fact that you should write your cover letters individually based on the specific situation. And that is quite true. The more focused your letters, the greater the impact and the more likely you are to get a response and an opportunity to interview. However, you *do not* have to reinvent the wheel with each and every cover letter you write. If you're a sales representative writing in response to advertisements for other sales positions, you can very often use the same letter with just a few minor editorial changes to match each opportunity.

Remember your word-processing program's copy and paste feature. It's a great tool!

### Specialist Versus Generalist Letters

This is a difficult concept to grasp, so pay very close attention. In today's competitive job search market, companies hire specialists to solve specific problems, manage specific operations, or perform specific functions. The "general management" layer that existed for so many decades has been obliterated as the entire world becomes more specialized. This has permeated virtually every industry, including technology. Think about it.

We don't have just programmers now. We have C++ programmers, Java scripters, and Web designers!

Consider this concept as you begin to write your cover letters and market yourself. It is to your advantage to be a specialist—regardless of your profession or industry. People can immediately understand the value you bring to their organization when you specialize in one or a group of related functions. Of course, the general manager will always exist, but the opportunities are much tighter and the positions much harder to find. It is our opinion that if you position yourself as a specialist, you will find that your job search moves along much faster and more positively.

Of course, you might position yourself as a specialist in several different (though usually related) careers. Let's say your career has been in sales. You started as a field sales representative, moved up to a sales-management role, and most recently have been the director of sales training for your organization. As you contemplate a career move, you're considering a wide range of positions under the general "sales" umbrella. If you try to sell yourself as a "jack of all trades," you might not find many takers. But you can position yourself as a specialist in sales, sales training, or sales management—and promote your related strengths as added value you bring to the organization.

### Sell It to Me; Don't Tell It to Me

Cover letter writing is sales–pure and simple. You have a commodity to sell—yourself—and your challenge is to write a marketing communication that is powerful and pushes the reader to action. (You want him to call you for an interview!) Therefore, it is essential that you "sell" your achievements and don't just "tell" your responsibilities. Here's a quick example. If you are an engineer, you could "tell" your reader that you've worked on developing new products. It doesn's sound very exciting, does it? you could "sell" the fact that you've participated in the design, development, testing, and market launch of 12 new products that now generate over $2 million in sales each year. Which letter would capture your interest?

### Getting Over Writer's Block

Very often, the most difficult part of writing a cover letter is getting started. You can sit and look at that blank piece of paper or computer screen for hours, frustrated and wondering whether the whole world has such a hard time writing cover letters. If you are in a profession that requires you to write—such as advertising, marketing, communications, or public relations—the process can be much easier. (However, both of us have had plenty of clients from these "writing" professions who have told us they found writing their own career marketing materials the most difficult writing tasks they've ever attempted.) If you are in finance, engineering, purchasing, quality, production, or another "non-writing" career track, cover letters can be an especially formidable task. That's why it's so important to follow the step-by-step process we have created. It is guaranteed to make cover letter writing faster, easier, and much less painful!

If you're still having trouble, consider this simple thought: *You do not have to start at the beginning!* Even after writing thousands and thousands of cover letters, we occasionally still sit stumped, unable to come up with just the right opening paragraph. Instead of wasting time and brain power, and getting frustrated, we just leave it alone and move on to another section in the letter that we feel more confident writing. You'll find that after you get going, new ideas will pop into your head and the more difficult sections will come much more easily and confidently.

## Answer the Employer's Most Important Question: "What Can You Do for Me?"

A powerful cover letter can help you get what you want: a new—perhaps more advanced, more convenient, more satisfying—position. And it is certainly important that you understand what you want to do, the kind of company you'd like to work for, and the environment in which you'll be most productive. Yet you must remember that employers aren't really interested in you. They're interested in *what you can do for them.* If you do not keep this thought in the forefront of your mind when writing your cover letters, you're likely to produce a self-centered "here I am—now give me a job!" letter that probably won't do much to advance your job search.

When writing your cover letters, consider the employer's needs, and make sure that you communicate that you can add value, solve problems, and deliver benefits for that employer. You can do this through a strong focus on accomplishments (making the employer think "Ah, she did that for Acme Widgets; she can do the same for me.") and through careful attention to the wording and tone of your letter so that you appear to be more interested in contributing to the company than in satisfying your own personal needs.

## Cover Letter Checklist

Before mailing, faxing, or e-mailing each cover letter you prepare, complete the following checklist to be sure that you have met all the rules for cover letter writing. If you cannot answer "yes" to *all* of the questions, go back and edit your letter as necessary before mailing it.

The only questions for which a "no" answer is acceptable are questions #5 and #6, which relate specifically to the company to which you are writing. As we have stated previously, in some instances you can find this information, but in others (such as when writing to a P.O. box) you cannot.

| | Yes | No |
|---|---|---|
| 1. Do I convey an immediate understanding of "who" I am within the first two sentences of my cover letter? | ☐ | ☐ |
| 2. Is my cover letter format unique, and does my letter stand out? | ☐ | ☐ |
| 3. Have I highlighted my most relevant qualifications? | ☐ | ☐ |
| 4. Have I highlighted my most relevant achievements? | ☐ | ☐ |
| 5. Have I included information I know about the company or the specific position for which I am applying? | ☐ | ☐ |
| 6. Have I highlighted why I want to work for *this* company? | ☐ | ☐ |
| 7. Is my letter neat, clean, and well-presented without being over-designed? | ☐ | ☐ |
| 8. Is my letter error-free? | ☐ | ☐ |
| 9. Did I have someone else proof my letter? | ☐ | ☐ |
| 10. Is my cover letter short and succinct, preferably no longer than one page? | ☐ | ☐ |
| 11. Do I ask for an interview in the letter? | ☐ | ☐ |

Chapter 4

# The Anatomy of a Winning Electronic Cover Letter

## (Plus Electronic Resume Tips)

This chapter is short, succinct, and to the point.

*Why?*

Because electronic (e-mail) cover letters are short, succinct, and to the point.

*So why do electronic cover letters get a chapter all their own?*

Because the way we communicate has been forever altered by the rapid emergence of e-mail as a primary channel of communication in today's fast-paced business world. Consider how letter writing has changed over the past century:

- In 1900, when a gentleman wrote a letter to his associates, it was elegantly composed and beautifully handwritten. Magnificent imagery and symbolism virtually jumped off the page.
- In 1942, when Winston Churchill wrote to his advisors, his letters were a bit less grandiose, but still detailed, informative, and well-executed.

- In 1987, when Frank Barnes (MBA and CFO) wrote to Xerox for a position on its executive management team, he prepared a comprehensive, one-page letter on his PC summarizing his career track and highlighting his most notable achievements. Then he printed his letter and mailed it to the company.
- Today, when Julie Jones, Esq., wrote to Microsoft for a position on its corporate legal team, she e-mailed her materials—a six-sentence cover letter with her resume. The letter was extremely brief, highlighting her two most notable career successes and asking for the interview. No fluff, no flowery language, no imagery, and no real detail. There was just enough to whet her reader's appetite and get him to read her resume and offer her the opportunity for a personal interview.

Julie's letter is typical of most e-mail cover letters. They are characterized by their brevity and impact. There are no wasted words. There is no grand introduction or career overview. They are hard-hitting, concise, and on target for the particular position.

## Electronic Cover Letters

What characterizes an electronic cover letter?

- Brevity
- To-the-point style and tone
- Written in brief paragraphs or a bullet-style format
- Generally written in response to a specific advertisement or online posting or to a network contact
- Most similar in style to the "company ad-response," "recruiter ad-response," and "networking" letters outlined in chapter 1

Just like other ad-response letters, e-mail cover letters *must* highlight the specific qualifications, experiences, skills, and accomplishments you offer as they relate to the requirements of the position. However, your challenge with electronic letters is to do this as quickly as you can. You have even less time than with the traditional "paper" resume and cover letter to catch someone's attention and interest. Therefore, your electronic letters must immediately present your unique qualifications, highlight your most significant achievements, and ask for the interview.

In a networking context, you have a bit more leeway because you are writing at the suggestion of a trusted referral. But it's best to be brief and to the point in these e-mail letters as well. Give your reader just enough information to understand who you are, why you're writing, and what to expect… most likely, a follow-up phone call from you to set up a meeting.

## Electronic Cover Letter Hints

To make your e-mail cover letter most effective, follow these simple suggestions related to the unique needs of this format:

- Use the e-mail subject line to alert recipients to your reason for contacting them, thus improving your chances that they will open your e-mail. If you're applying for a specific position, mention it in your subject line. If you're writing at the suggestion of a networking contact, mention that person's name.
- *Do not* include the recipient's full mailing address as you would structure a typical "paper" cover letter. Use only the salutation line (Dear Ms. Brown:).
- As with other ad-response letters, be sure to address any additional requests for information stated in the advertisement (such as salary history, salary requirements, ability to relocate, citizenship or residency status, foreign-language skills, and technology proficiency).

## Sample Electronic Cover Letters

The following are three examples of our preferred style for e-mail cover letters.

## The Preferred Electronic Cover Letter Style for Companies

This is a classic ad-response letter highlighting key qualifications that closely match the position requirements. It is brief and to the point. Note the footnote describing how the resume is being sent. Later in this chapter we discuss a variety of options for sending your resume with your electronic cover letter.

From: "Seth Sefert" <ssefsdf@yahoo.com>
To: "Shanna Miller" <s.miller@co.com>
Subject: Newcastle Plant Manager
Date: Fri, 20 Aug 2010 15:42:43

Dear Ms. Miller:

My strong qualifications for your Plant Manager position have prompted me to contact you. They include

* 10 years of experience in Plant and Operations Management (consumer goods and food industries).

* Management of a 220-person manufacturing operation and a $145 million annual operating budget.

* Annual productivity gains averaging 18% and cost reductions totaling over $2.8 million.

* Implementation of SPC, MRP, SAP, and other automated technologies.

I would like to meet with you to discuss my ideas for productivity improvements within your Newcastle facility. Thank you.

Seth Sefert

*******************
My resume is attached in Word format.

## *Example* The Preferred Electronic Cover Letter Style for Network Contacts

In the sample below, the friendly tone and summary (rather than specific) information distinguish this networking letter from a job-application letter. But like the previous sample, this letter is crisp and to the point.

From: "Seth Sefert" <ssefsdf@yahoo.com.>
To: "Chris Diamond" <chris.diamond@globalcorp.com>
Subject: Referred by Dale Howard
Date: Fri, 20 Aug 2010 15:50:42

Dear Chris,

At the suggestion of Dale Howard, I am contacting you to see if you would be willing to share a few minutes of your time with me next week.

Dale knows me well from our work together at Megafood. While Dale was COO, I served as Plant Manager of the Yorktown facility, where we achieved annual productivity gains averaging 18% and cost reductions exceeding $2.8 million.

As you may know, we have recently been acquired by Kraft, and I am in the market for a new manufacturing management position. Because you are so well connected, both at Global and in the Philadelphia community, your advice and suggestions will be invaluable.

I will call you on Friday to see when it might be convenient for us to get together. I look forward to speaking with you and truly appreciate your time and advice.

Seth Sefert

**********************
I have attached my resume to give you a more complete picture of my background.

## The Preferred Electronic Cover Letter Style for Recruiters

Now, let's take that same letter and modify it for sending to a recruiter. The main difference is the closing. We have added appropriate personal and salary information relevant to a recruiter while still keeping the letter brief and crisp.

From: "Seth Sefert" <ssefsdf@yahoo.com>
To: "Richard Hanson" <r.hanson@recruiter.com>
Subject: Newcastle Plant Manager
Date: Fri, 20 Aug 2010 15:44:43

Dear Mr. Hanson:

My strong qualifications for the available Plant Manager position have prompted me to contact you. They include

* 10 years of experience in Plant and Operations Management (consumer goods and food industries).

* Management of a 220-person manufacturing operation and a $145 million annual operating budget.

* Annual productivity gains averaging 18% and cost reductions totaling over $2.8 million.

* Implementation of SPC, MRP, SAP, and other automated technologies.

The Megafood plant in Yorktown, Pennsylvania, where I am currently plant manager, has been acquired by Kraft Foods, and production will be moved out of state this fall. I am available for immediate relocation to the Toledo area and would anticipate a salary of $125,000 to $150,000 per year.

I look forward to learning more about this interesting opportunity.

Seth Sefert

*******************
My resume is attached as a Word document.

### Final Thoughts on Electronic Cover Letters

When writing electronic cover letters, be sure to pay close attention to spelling, grammar, and tone, just as you would with a traditional cover letter. Perfection and accuracy are vital, as always.

The greatest advantage of e-mail communications is immediacy. If you send cover letters and resumes to 500 recruiters, you'll receive e-mail and telephone responses within a day or two, compared to a week or longer delay for responses to your mailed letters. In our experience of helping job seekers at all levels, we find that e-mailed resumes are very effective when used in broad campaigns to recruiters, responses to online postings, outreach to new network contacts, and as a method of immediate communication with people you've already spoken with.

But do be wary of the impersonal nature of e-mails and the ease with which they can be ignored. When sending a follow-up to an e-mail letter, you can again communicate via e-mail, but it is usually preferable to make a phone call and attempt to establish "live" communication. It's very easy for the recipient to overlook your letter in a sea of e-mails received daily. By telephoning, you can set yourself apart and build a more personal relationship.

Finally, bear in mind that any of the letters included in this book can be sent by e-mail even if they appear as traditional printed letters. Although many of the traditional letter samples are a bit longer than we prefer for e-mail communications, as long as your message is clear and your letter is presented in easily viewable chunks and not as one mass of text, you should feel free to send most of your job search correspondence by e-mail. It is the preferred communication channel for most business correspondence today.

## Electronic and Scannable Resumes

Your electronic and scannable resumes are simply different formats for your formatted, printable resume. The content is the same. To be sure your resume is seen and read, it is important that you choose the right format for the circumstances. This section discusses your options.

## Electronic Resume Hints

Of course, you will always want to send your resume along with your electronic cover letter. You have five distinct options for transmitting your resume electronically:

- **Paste your resume into the e-mail message itself.** This is by far the most efficient method of transmitting your resume electronically. Unfortunately, although this is the easiest method, it's also the least attractive. When you paste your resume into an e-mail message, all the effort you invested in making it look good is virtually gone. Your resume is now just words on a page with a minor bit of formatting that you can add back in.
- **Send your resume as an attached word-processing file.** In many instances, this is the best solution. Recipients—especially recruiters and Human Resources departments—are quite accustomed to receiving resumes in this form and often prefer them because of their readability. Just be certain you are using Microsoft Word, the industry standard word-processing program. And if you are sending unsolicited resumes, be aware that some people will not open e-mail attachments for fear of picking up a virus. And finally, be sure you are carefully following any instructions in the ad or posting. Are attachments welcomed? Are word-processing formats specified? Are you instructed to cut and paste? Don't damage your chances by ignoring instructions.
- **Attach your resume as a PDF file.** PDF (portable document format) is a popular format for sending documents via the Web. A key advantage is that all formatting is retained, but the recipient does not need to have Microsoft Word or any other specific piece of software to be able to open and read your resume. A downside is that your resume exists as a graphic, rather than text, and cannot easily be entered into a resume-tracking system. This is our preferred option only when your resume is highly designed and that design is an important part of the overall image you wish to convey. Otherwise, we recommend that you send your resume as a Word file.
- **Send your resume as an attached text file.** We don't see much advantage to using this option. It makes work for your recipients and does not give them a reader-friendly format. Unless this option is specified, we recommend you opt for one of the first two choices.

- **Include your resume as part of a complete Web portfolio and reference the URL in your e-mail cover letter.** This solution combines the ease of e-mail transmission with the impact of a sharp visual presentation. If you choose this option, we recommend that you also include the text version of your resume in the e-mail message (see the first item in this list), thereby giving readers immediate access to your resume and then the option of obtaining a fully formatted version to view and download if they want.

  If you choose to post your resume on a Web site or Web portfolio, it's best to get a stand-alone site just for your resume rather than include it on a personal or family site. Don't distract the employer or embarrass yourself by including your resume on a site with family updates, children's cute sayings, or a scanned-in picture of your spouse doing the limbo on your Caribbean vacation. In a job search, it's to your advantage to keep your communication professional at all times.

## A Word About Scannable Resumes

Electronic scanning of resumes—and sometimes cover letters—has become common practice at large companies. Resumes that are scanned or downloaded become "searchable" documents that are stored in a central database and can be accessed quickly through an electronic keyword search.

Although many modern scanning systems can accommodate type enhancements such as bold, italics, and underlining, to be certain all of your text is entered correctly, it's best to prepare a plain-vanilla version of your resume that can be scanned by any type of scanning system. Remove all type enhancements, vertical and horizontal lines, and fancy bullets. Choose a clean sans serif font such as Arial for maximum readability, and make certain that you haven't condensed the font or reduced the letter spacing such that letters touch each other—this is likely to cause scanning errors.

Of course, you can avoid the scanning controversy altogether by sending your resume electronically, either as an e-mail or via or the company's online Web application form if they have one.

# Cover Letter Presentation

You've been working for hours, maybe longer, to develop a high-impact, attention-grabbing cover letter. You probably thought that you were done and your letter is ready to go. Not just yet! Writing is only the first step in preparing your letter. Now that you've written the words, we'll focus on the visual presentation of a winning cover letter.

As we discussed in chapter 4, you are likely to send most of your cover letters by e-mail. In those instances, the content of the letter is all important and the visual presentation should be kept quite simple. Even if you can add background designs, borders, or other visual enhancements to your e-mail message, we recommend that you do not do so for your cover letters. Such enhancements can be hard to read and even annoying for recipients. Instead, keep the background plain white and use the standard font that you use for your e-mails—perhaps Arial, Verdana, or Times New Roman.

But on occasion you will want to print and mail or hand-deliver your cover letter and resume. In fact, this approach can give you a decided advantage now that most other candidates will be sending their materials by e-mail. For those special circumstances when you want to make an extra effort, or when you are bringing your printed materials to an in-person meeting, be certain to follow the guidelines in this chapter to create a visually distinctive and impressive cover letter and resume that will enhance your image and advance your candidacy.

## Developing Winning Visual Presentations

What makes a winning cover letter different in presentation from other cover letters? Isn't one letter just the same as another? Quite clearly, the answer is "no."

Winning cover letters are distinguished by the following:

- **Professionalism.** Take just a quick glance at any cover letter in this book, and you'll notice that these letters look extremely professional. Each was originally produced and offers a sharp, high-impact presentation. Remember, the quality of your cover letter is a direct indication of the quality of work you will produce for an employer!
- **Clean, neat, and easy-to-read presentation.** Take another look at some of the sample letters in this book. They are neat, with even margins and equal spacing throughout. The size of type is easy to read without being too large or looking too "elementary." They are quick to read because they are so well presented.
- **Perfection.** Every winning cover letter is perfect and totally error-free. We recommend that you proofread each cover letter a minimum of three times and then have a friend, relative, or coworker proofread it again. Your objective—your only objective—is 100 percent accuracy. Nothing short of that is ever acceptable.

## Design Considerations

Many of the issues in this section—cover letter format, font, type of paper, and color of paper—might be decisions you already made when you prepared your resume. We recommend that you use those same specifications when preparing your cover letters. Through consistent presentation, you will create a top-notch, professional presentation. A consistent image demonstrates thought and planning in preparation—another great message to communicate to a prospective employer!

Many of these design considerations are really just personal preferences. The format that you chose for your resume, for example, is most likely one that you liked (as well as one that "worked" to present your qualifications as you would like them to be perceived). The same thing is true about cover letters. Pick a style that you like, that is appropriate, and that is consistent with your resume.

If you really like ivory-colored paper, for instance, use it for everything—your resume, cover letters, thank-you letters, and any other job search correspondence. If you really like purple paper, use it for the invitations for your next party, and select something that is more professional, more conservative, and more appropriate for your career correspondence.

What do we mean by appropriate? Consider this. You're the manager of an accounting department interviewing candidates for a bookkeeping position. The first resume and cover letter you receive are neat and conservative, typed in a sans serif (without the little curlycues) typestyle such as Arial, and on bright white paper. The presentation is precise, neat, and clean, visually demonstrating exactly the qualifications you are seeking in a bookkeeper. Then you pick up the next resume. It's also neat and clean, but it's "loud." Both the resume and cover letter are typed in italics, they're difficult to read, and the gold paper is, well, interesting. Now, remember, you're hiring a bookkeeper. Which candidate would you be most interested in? The answer is obvious! Let your visual presentation match what you do for a living and how you want to be perceived by a prospective employer.

Although the resume in italics on gold paper is not appropriate for a bookkeeper, it can be appropriate in other situations. What about a young graphic artist? Or a theatrical stage designer? Those professions require creativity, flair, and the ability to visually capture an audience's attention. Now italics on gold doesn't seem quite so unusual. Again, it's a question of matching your visual presentation with the image you are working to create. The following sections explore some specific design considerations.

## What Format Should I Use?

There are two basic cover letter formats—block style and modified block style. Which style you select depends entirely on your personal preference. There is no right way; there is no wrong way. Our only recommendation is that when you have selected the style you prefer, stick with that style for *all* of your correspondence so that the presentation of all your materials is consistent.

Here are examples of both:

**Block-Style Letter: Everything Is Flush Left**

August 20, 2010

John Doe
President
ABC Manufacturing Company
123 Main Street
Greensburg, PA 15601

Dear Mr. Doe:

Building top-performing sales territories is what I do best. Whether challenged to build a new sales region, accelerate growth within an established market, or launch the introduction of a new portfolio of products, I have consistently delivered strong revenue results.

[rest of letter continues here]

Sincerely,

Greg LaMontica

Enclosure

Example **Modified Block-Style Letter: Indented Date, First Lines of Paragraphs, and Closings**

August 20, 2010

John Doe
President
ABC Manufacturing Company
123 Main Street
Greensburg, PA 15601

Dear Mr. Doe:

Building top-performing sales territories is what I do best. Whether challenged to build a new sales region, accelerate growth within an established market, or launch the introduction of a new portfolio of products, I have consistently delivered strong revenue results.

[rest of letter continues here]

Sincerely,

Greg LaMontica

Enclosure

## What Font Should I Use?

Twenty-five years ago there were two fonts for resumes and cover letters—Courier and Elite. These two typestyles came in two sizes (10-point and 12-point). That was it. Your choice of font and size depended on what kind of typewriter you were using. Today, your choices run in the hundreds. If you're like most of us, your PC came with more fonts than you can count, most of which you've never even looked at. You've chosen a few that you like, and you use them for just about everything.

The following list includes fonts that are commonly used for cover letters and resumes. You'll note that the list is divided into "Serif" and "Sans Serif" categories. A quick glance at each font will tell you that serif fonts contain tiny header and footer strokes on each letter; sans serif fonts are cleaner

looking, without extraneous strokes. Which is better? It's simply a matter of personal preference. Conventional wisdom says that serif fonts are easier to read; we don't necessarily agree or disagree—it really depends on the individual font. Some fonts look better than others in larger sizes; others lose readability at small sizes.

One area where sans serif fonts might have an advantage is in documents meant for computer scanning. Letters without extraneous strokes are easier for the scanner to read and leave less room for misinterpretation. For that reason, we recommend sans serif fonts for scannable resumes and cover letters.

| Sans Serif | Serif |
|---|---|
| Tahoma | Times New Roman |
| Arial | Bookman |
| Century Gothic | Book Antiqua |
| Gill Sans | Garamond |
| Lucinda Sans | Century Schoolbook |
| Veranda | |

**Exercise: Experiment with Typestyles**

If you're uncertain about what typestyle to use for your materials, take a few minutes and do the following exercise.

Type the following resume excerpt exactly as it is typed here using bold, italics, and underlining just as we have. Note that we've used a resume in this instance (as opposed to a cover letter) because of the many different type enhancements resumes contain. Then copy and paste the paragraph 10 or 20 times, changing the typestyle each time. Print your test pages, and you'll see what each typestyle looks like and whether it's appropriate for your job search materials.

Sales Manager—*Veterinary Products Division* 2008 to Present

SMART PETS, INC. *(Division of AAA Veterinary, Inc.)*, Portland, Oregon

Independently plan and manage all sales, marketing, customer service, and business development programs through a four-state region in the Western U.S. Challenged to increase sales revenues, expand market penetration, and improve competitive industry ratings.

- Built regional sales from **$2.8 million to $6.4 million** in 12 months.
- Launched the introduction of **18 new products generating $1.2 million** in new sales revenues.

## What Type Enhancements Should I Use?

If you're unfamiliar with the terminology of type enhancements, these simply are **bold,** *italics,* Small Caps, ALL CAPS, and underlining—things you can do to a typestyle to make its presentation more noticeable. In the preceding exercise, you can easily see what type enhancements can do to make things stand out in a document.

Just as in the preceding excerpt, we're sure that you have many type enhancements in your resume. And you should. But cover letters are not resumes. They are letters—fairly formal and conservative business documents. As such, you should severely limit your use of these type enhancements. In fact, you might not use any of them in your letter. If you do, you should use them quite sparingly, and only to highlight really important things that you want your reader to see quickly.

What types of things might you choose to highlight visually in your cover letters?

- Notable achievements (particularly numbers and percentages)
- Notable educational or professional credentials
- Notable company names (employers, partners, vendors, customers)
- Notable honors and awards (academic and professional)
- The position for which you are applying

Do not format an entire letter in italics or bold. You might think it looks different. You're right. You might think it looks distinctive. You're right. You might think it looks sharp and professional. Not necessarily! Unless you are looking for a position in a creative industry such as graphic design,

theater, art, film production, media, or something related, keep your cover letters clean and conservative—and, most importantly, *readable.*

## What Paper Color Should I Use?

Ah, the infamous paper color question! We've responded to questions about this for decades now. Is plain white paper the best? Sometimes. Is ivory paper an acceptable standard? Yes. Is light-gray paper recommended? Sometimes. What about papers with borders? Sometimes. Paper with logos and graphic designs? Occasionally. Parchment paper? Perhaps. What about really distinctive colors such as blue, pink, brown, or gold? These are appropriate only in certain instances.

As you can see, there are no rules for color selection. Just as with all of your other design considerations, the paper color you select is based largely on your own personal preferences and the appropriateness to your career. To make your selection process a bit easier, here are a few of our standards for paper selection:

- White and ivory papers are always appropriate for virtually any job seeker in virtually any situation.
- Light-gray paper offers a conservative presentation with a degree of sophistication and visual distinction. This color is particularly recommended for people in accounting, finance, insurance, general management, and executive management.
- Papers with borders can also offer a conservative yet distinctive presentation, as long as the papers are nicely designed and not flamboyant.
- Papers with logos and graphic designs are a relatively new addition over the past 10 years. Have you ever seen a teacher's resume with an apple logo in the corner? What about a sports marketing director's resume with basketballs, soccer balls, and baseballs on the bottom? These papers can be unique. Yet there is controversy. In fact, our opinions differ. One of us believes that papers like these are distinctive and eye-catching. The other thinks that they are generally too cute. You be the judge, but wisdom would say that if you have any reservations, do not select this type of paper. And if you do choose to include graphics, make certain they are appropriate to your profession and were not chosen simply because you like cats, for example.

- If you're unfamiliar with parchment paper, it's two-toned with a look that's often described as marbleized. In decades past, parchment paper was a common selection for job search materials. Over the years, it has become much less frequently used, for no particular reason that we could identify. Our only reason for not using it is our personal preference. We don't like it, but you might, and that's fine as long as the presentation is conservative.
- Our final category is colored paper—blue, pink, brown, tan, gold, green, yellow, or any of a number of other distinctive colors. For the average job seeker, these papers are not recommended. Remember, your objective is to create neat, clean, conservative, and visually distinctive resumes and cover letters, not advertisements!

There are exceptions to this rule, however. Consider the graphic artist with her resume on a blush-colored paper. It can be sharp! What about the geologist preparing his resume on rusty-brown paper? Or the nurse who uses a light-blue paper? Certain colors "match" certain professions and, when appropriate, can be a unique presentation that will quickly grab your reader's attention.

Suppose you're a manager hiring a landscape designer. You're looking through a pile of 50 or more resumes that you've received, most of them on white and ivory, with an occasional gray one. Then, all of a sudden, you come across a resume on a great green paper. It immediately communicates landscaping, doesn't it? Colored paper can work in certain circumstances, but *only* in certain circumstances.

### What Type of Paper Should I Use?

Your options here include bond, linen, cotton, and parchment papers. This decision is strictly personal preference, because all of these types of paper are acceptable and widely used. One of us definitely prefers linen papers because they feel so nice, whereas the other uses only cotton papers because they feel heavier than linen. Before stocking up, run a few test prints on your printer with your chosen paper. Most modern-day papers are formulated to be used with laser printers, inkjet printers, or both. But some papers smudge a bit, or absorb too much ink, or look better with one type of printer or the other. Find one you like that works well with your equipment, and use it for all of your job search communications.

*Tip* Consistency in design and presentation will distinguish you from others competing for the same position *and* communicate that you are a professional concerned about the quality and image of your work product—a great message to send to a prospective employer!

Chapter 6

# Answers to Common Cover Letter Questions—and Tips to Help You Beat the Odds

If job search were an exact science, life would be so much easier!

When you add 82 + 11, it always equals 93. When you add 2 parts hydrogen to 1 part oxygen, you always get water. When the earth revolves around the sun, you know that on June 20th or 21st, the summer solstice will always occur. These are not questions. They are facts. There is no discussion; there are no surprises. Each is measurable, predictable, and consistent. Each is an exact science with an exact answer to an exact question. There is no room for personal interpretation.

Unfortunately, there is nothing measurable, predictable, or consistent about any aspect of job search, including cover letter writing. Job search is not an exact science, and there are no exact answers. In fact, the answer to almost every question is, *"It depends"*—on the situation, the job seeker, the position, the industry, the economy, the location, and a number of other factors. Thus the challenge of your entire job search campaign: It all depends!

In this chapter we examine frequently asked questions and dilemmas faced by job seekers, relating to such issues as the length of your cover letter, when and how (and if) to include salary information, how to transmit your cover letter and resume, printing and paper options, and how you should go about conducting your search. We give you our opinions—sometimes more than one!—and provide information that will help you make the best decision for your unique circumstances.

## Frequently Asked Cover Letter and Resume Questions

Ask yourself this question: "Should a resume always be just one page?" Keep your answer a secret, and ask that same question of five other people. How many different answers did you get? Several, we would assume. No one ever agrees on job search issues. There is constant conversation and disagreement about virtually everything—from the number of pages to the color of paper; from providing salary information to selecting envelope size; from how to address the letter to when to follow up. The list goes on and on.

With more than 25 years of combined experience in resume and cover letter writing, career coaching, and job search marketing, we've heard just about every question imaginable, and then some. Following are what we have found to be the most frequently asked questions—along with our professional opinions and recommendations. But bear in mind that these are not *facts.* Your own circumstances could dictate a different action than we recommend.

### How Long Should My Cover Letter Be?

Should your cover letter always be one page? It depends.

Generally, cover letters should be one page in length. This is true for approximately 90 percent of all cover letters. Remember that your cover letter has three main purposes:

- To tell your readers why you are writing.
- To highlight your most relevant experiences, skills, qualifications, and achievements.
- To ask for the interview.

Your goal is to whet the reader's appetite, intrigue him, and get him to closely read the information you have submitted. In the vast majority of circumstances, you can accomplish this on one page.

### Exceptions to the One-Page Rule

There may be instances, however, when one page is just not enough. If you believe that the information you are including in your letter is essential information that is not communicated in your resume, go ahead and prepare a two-page letter. But be sure that everything you've included is vital to favorably presenting yourself to a company or recruiter.

Two-page letters are most frequently used by the following types of job seekers:

- **Career changers.** When you're faced with positioning yourself for a new career path, it might take more than one page to communicate relevant experiences, skills, and accomplishments that are not highlighted on your resume. It is critical that these cover letters clearly emphasize your transferable skills and qualifications to demonstrate your eligibility.
- **Industry changers.** If you are attempting to change industries, you might also find that your cover letter is longer than the traditional one page. In this situation, you must focus your letter on your skills and qualifications that are transferable from one industry to the next.
- **Senior executives.** These individuals must communicate a wide range of expertise and accomplishments across a broad spectrum of disciplines (such as management, leadership, products, industries, technologies, countries, customer markets, operations, finance, human resources, administration, sales, marketing, advertising, public relations, and investor relations). Because the information is so extensive, it might require a second page. And with senior-level candidates, hiring authorities are usually looking at more than "what" you've done. They want to know "how" and "why" you've done it so that they can assess your style and strengths with regard to their existing management team and organizational needs.
- **Scientists and technologists.** Often, due to the complexity of your technical qualifications and associated management and business

skills, a two-page letter is necessary to communicate all of the relevant information.

- **People seeking government jobs.** What do we all know about government? Paper counts! Even though we often hear about a government's shift to a paperless environment, trust us: There are still volumes of paper in virtually every government office. When writing a cover letter for a position with a state, local, or national government agency, if you have a great deal of valuable information that you believe is essential to communicate, you do not have to be as concerned about keeping it all on one page.
- **People seeking university and academic appointments.** Academia is much like the government in its unique relationship with paper and documents. Again, if you believe the information is important and will favorably position you, be sure to include it, even if it takes two pages.

*Tip* We recommend that, if possible, you keep your cover letter to one page. If appropriate and warranted, two pages are acceptable. But your cover letter should *never* be longer than two pages.

### Broadcast Letters

One specific type of cover letter is almost always two to three pages in length—the *broadcast letter*. You'll remember from chapter 1 that broadcast letters are used in place of the more traditional resume and cover letter package and can best be described as a combination of both documents.

When you send a broadcast letter, you do not include a resume. Therefore, it is critical that you communicate more information about your career history, qualifications, accomplishments, educational credentials, and other related skills and experiences than you would in a "regular" cover letter. For broadcast letters to be effective, exciting, and enticing, you must include specifics to capture your reader's attention. These specifics might include employment experience, college degrees, technology skills, professional affiliations, publications, and other information that clearly demonstrates your knowledge and expertise. As such, these letters are longer than traditional cover letters.

## Should I Include Salary Information in My Cover Letter?

It depends. We are of two minds. We offer dual recommendations in two situations but agree with one another on the other two situations. See which rationale feels most comfortable to you.

- **If you are responding to an advertisement that has requested your salary history or salary requirements:**

  **Supply the information.** If you do not provide this information when requested, certain companies and recruiters will not look at your materials.

  **Don't supply the information.** Repeated surveys show that nearly 100 percent of readers admitted that they will look at your resume and call you for an interview even if your salary information is not included. Why give them ammunition to screen you out?

- **If a personal contact or source you've uncovered during your search has requested your resume and salary information:**

  **Supply the information.** To do otherwise would seem unresponsive and impolite.

  **Consider addressing the issue without providing numbers that can be detrimental in a future salary negotiation.** Say something such as "I'd be glad to discuss salary when we meet, once I learn more about the position and you have the chance to assess my fit for your needs."

- **When contacting companies either as a cold call or in response to an ad where salary information has not been requested:**

  **Do not supply the information.** It is much better to have this conversation in person and not on paper. Always try to defer any discussion of salary until you have been offered the position.

- **When writing "cold" to recruiters:**

  **Always offer salary information.** It helps them determine your "proper fit" within a hiring organization. A recruiter will not work with you without knowing whether you match the requirements (including salary) for the specific position she is attempting to fill.

## How Can I Best Communicate Salary History or Salary Requirements?

Review the suggestions presented in "Step 5: Write the Closing" in chapter 3. Multiple examples are given; choose the one that feels most comfortable to you.

## Should I Send My Resume to the Human Resources Department?

If you are writing "cold" to a company (not in response to a specific advertisement), should you address your resume to the Human Resources department? The answer to this question is a resounding "NO!" HR departments "process" and evaluate resumes. They generally do not make hiring decisions (except for HR positions). Instead, send your resume to the President, CEO, COO, CFO, Vice President of Sales, Director of Customer Service, Accounting Manager—whoever is the decision-maker for the department or function in which you are interested. These individuals have the authority to schedule an interview and make a hiring decision. It is much more efficient to work "down from the top" than for your resume to get out of the HR department.

## Should I Follow Up a Faxed or E-mailed Resume?

If you've faxed or e-mailed your resume and cover letter to a company or recruiter, should you follow up with a paper copy in the mail? No! Times have changed. If you had faxed your resume and cover letter 10 years ago, the answer would have been "yes." If you had e-mailed your resume and cover letter five years ago, the answer again would have been "yes."

Today, however, we recommend that you do not mail a hard copy if you have already transmitted your information electronically. Electronic communication is now a totally acceptable method of communication in virtually any business, industry, and market sector. The only time you should follow up with hard copy is when it has been requested. Try to control the paper flow!

## What Size Paper Should I Use?

Should you use Letter-size or Monarch-size paper for your cover letters? It depends. Which do you like better? That's what we recommend that you use. We have never found that the size of paper made any difference in whether an individual job seeker was offered the opportunity for a personal interview.

Here are the pros and cons of both:

- **Monarch-size paper** (7 x 9 inches) does stand out from the more traditional letter-size paper and visually presents itself more like a piece of personal correspondence. However, it can easily be misplaced and lost in the daily shuffle.
- **Letter-size paper** (8½ x 11 inches) is the standard, is an acceptable presentation in any circumstance, is easy to file, and is less likely to be misplaced.

## Should I Use the Same Paper for Everything?

Should your cover letter be on the same paper as your resume? It depends. Generally we do recommend that you be consistent. If you've chosen ivory paper, you should use it for everything—your resume, cover letters, thank-you letters, and any other job search correspondence. This kind of coordinated presentation is quite professional.

However, in some instances you might choose to use a paper that is different but complementary. Consider the following circumstances:

- You're a business professional or executive and have printed your resume on a light-gray paper with a surrounding white border. It's really sharp! You might elect to print your letters on a high-quality white paper as a unique enhancement to your presentation.
- You're a talented graphic artist competing for a position in metropolitan New York. You want someone to immediately notice you and your artistic talent. In this instance, you might select a blue-and-white pinstripe paper with your personal logo design in the background for your resume, and matching plain blue paper with logo for your cover letters. In fact, graphic artists and other creative professionals should use their resumes and cover letters to demonstrate their visual creativity. For those individuals, the resume does not communicate just words. It should also communicate a powerful visual image.
- If you have printed personal stationery that complements your resume, feel free to use it. It presents a professional, high-quality image.
- Do not make the mistake of using your business stationery for your job search. It is unprofessional and sends a message that you use your employer's resources for your own benefit.

## Do My Communications Need a Consistent Look?

Should your resume, cover letter, and other job search communications "look" the same? Yes!

Pick a standard presentation (font style, font size, heading, format, and paper) for your documents, and stick with it. Consistency breeds familiarity, and familiarity can breed confidence in your ability. Furthermore, it creates a more professional, elegant, and high-quality presentation.

## What Size Envelope Should I Use?

When you choose to mail or deliver your resume and cover letter, should you use a large envelope (9 x 12 inches) or a regular #10 business envelope? Just like the size of paper, this decision is really based on your personal preferences. The vast majority of recipients really don't care—and even if they do have a preference, they will not discriminate against you because your presentation is different. Here are our recommendations:

- Use regular #10 business envelopes for most of your mailings and communications. The savings in postage will add up quickly.
- Use larger envelopes if you're trying to make a really top-flight impression. Large envelopes are most appropriate for high-level network contacts, direct mail to executives, and responses to senior-level advertisements.
- Use larger envelopes if you are sending more than three sheets of paper or if your paper is extremely heavy. Thick stacks of heavy paper do not fold well. And if, for instance, you are a graphic designer sending design samples, by all means send them flat in a larger envelope for the best possible appearance.
- Consider using larger envelopes to mail resumes and cover letters that are intended to be scanned. Creasing and folding laser-printed pages sometimes causes laser toner to smudge, flake, or create "ghost" impressions that could reduce the scannability of your resume.

*Tip* No one has ever made a hiring decision based on the size of an envelope. And there's always the chance that the hiring manager might never actually see the envelope itself—just the contents. Use what you like, and don't fret!

## What If I Don't Know the Addressee's Name?

How do you address a letter when you don't have a specific name? Here it doesn't depend. It's personal choice. Take a look at a few possible salutations:

- **Dear Sir/Madam.** All-purpose and inoffensive, although it might be perceived as stodgy and old-fashioned.
- **To Whom It May Concern.** Another standard; has the downside of being impersonal and old-fashioned.
- **Dear Hiring Executive (or Hiring Committee).** Formal, but appropriate.
- **Dear Human Resources (or Human Resources Representative).** Acceptable only if you're writing to a "blind ad" that lists only a P.O. box and you cannot call to get a specific individual's name.
- **Dear Hiring Authority.** Acceptable only if, despite your best efforts, you have been unable to uncover the name of the non-HR person to whom you're sending your resume.
- **Good Morning (or Good Day).** A bit more up-to-date, but it reminds us of junk-mail greetings that try (unsuccessfully) to be personal.
- **Re: Job Title You're Applying For** (leaving off a specific salutation). A useful method for replying to want ads, when you truly don't know to whom you are sending your resume. We think it's preferable to the "Dear Human Resources" greeting.
- **No Salutation** (begin your letter immediately after the inside address). Again, perfectly acceptable for want-ad replies. Might be considered an improvement over old-fashioned, nonspecific greetings.

Here are a few that we *do not* recommend:

- **Dear Sir.** Because this is not accurate about half the time, we do not recommend it.
- **Gentlemen.** Again, not necessarily accurate and very old-fashioned.
- **Dear Gentleperson.** Great for a 19th-century romance novel, but not particularly appropriate for today's job search market.

## What If I Am Unsure of the Addressee's Gender?

How do you address a letter when you have a name but don't know whether it's a man or a woman? It doesn't depend here, either. Simple answer—Dear R. Smith (assuming that "R. Smith" is the contact name listed in the ad). But do make an effort to find out the person's gender so that you can address your letter to "Dear Mr." or "Dear Ms."

## Should I Follow Up with a Phone Call After Each Resume and Cover Letter I Send?

It depends. Telephone follow-up can be quite costly and time-consuming, and it is often difficult to get the person you want to speak with on the phone. You can try calling at off-hours (such as 7 to 9 a.m. or 5 to 8 p.m.) when an individual is most likely to answer the phone himself. If you call during the day, be sure to make an effort to establish some rapport with the gatekeeper (for example, the administrator, secretary, assistant, or receptionist). That individual can have tremendous power, making the difference in whether you get through or are blocked.

We do not recommend that you call after every resume and cover letter you've sent. It would be a poor investment of your time to spend your entire day leaving phone messages, not to mention the frustration it will cause.

### Exceptions to the Rule

The situations in which we do recommend that you call are the following:

- When you have a top-level contact at a company.
- When you consider yourself an ideal candidate for a position (and we mean *ideal*).
- When you have been referred by someone to a specific person.

## Do I Need to Mention Why I'm in the Job Market?

It depends. There's certainly no requirement that you do so, but if your reason is particularly legitimate (such as a plant closing or a management change due to the successful IPO you were instrumental in negotiating), you might send a positive message by mentioning this information. In any event, be prepared for the question "Why are you leaving your current

job?" or "Why are you looking?" to come up early in your search, and practice a concise, positive, and believable response. Never "badmouth" your company, boss, or coworkers.

### Do I Need to Make My Cover Letter "Scannable"?

What does "scannable" mean, anyway? Scannable simply means machine-readable. Many companies now scan resumes into a database and then search by keywords for candidates who match specific requirements. To be scannable, your resume should not contain italics, underlining, or graphics, and the font should be clear, readable, and at least 11 points.

Some companies scan cover letters along with resumes; others do not. It certainly could not hurt to check your cover letter format for scannability. It should not be difficult to change any nonconforming elements to make sure that every valuable word is correctly entered into the database.

Of course, you can avoid the issue altogether by sending your cover letter and resume electronically.

*Tip* For a great deal more information on computer scanning and keyword inclusion in your career marketing documents, see the "Scannable Résumés" section in chapter 9 of this book's companion, *Résumé Magic,* by Susan Britton Whitcomb, PCC, CCMC, MRW, NCRW.

## Using Your PC in Your Job Search

The vast majority of job seekers manage their job search campaigns using a PC. You might be using your PC for a variety of applications, including the uses detailed in the following sections.

### Word Processing and Desktop Publishing

You can use word-processing and desktop-publishing programs to prepare resumes, cover letters, thank-you letters, and other job search correspondence.

To take full advantage of your computer's capability, learn to use features such as envelope and label printing and mail merge. Word-processing programs offer advanced formatting features such as variable line spacing,

font width and spacing adjustments, bullet-shape variations, and paragraph boxes and rules (lines) that can enhance your visual presentation quite nicely. The samples in this book use many of these features—particularly in the headings. Skim through the samples, select a few you like, and see if you can replicate them on your PC.

### Quick Typesetting Rules

To give your documents a truly polished appearance, follow these typesetting rules:

- Use only one space after a period (instead of the two you were taught when you learned to type).
- Avoid underlining; instead, to create a border above or below a line of text such as a heading or company name, use the "borders" or "paragraph rules" feature of your word-processing program.
- Adjust the margins of your document so that your letter is nicely centered left to right.
- Center your letter top to bottom by spacing down a few lines before you begin typing. Double-space between paragraphs, and add one or two extra blank lines after the date at the top and before your typed name at the bottom (this is where you will add your signature).
- Because this is a business letter, follow your salutation with a colon, not a comma.

### Mail Merge

Mail merge is an advanced word-processing feature that allows you to type a cover letter in one file, type a list of names and addresses in another file, and then merge them to create individualized letters for e-mail messages. Mail merge is a tremendously powerful application that lets you produce dozens or hundreds of individualized cover (letters and envelopes, if you are using snail mail) with just a few simple commands.

The most frequent use of mail merge is for bulk mailings (for example, sending your resume and cover letter to 200 sales recruiters in the Northeastern U.S.). Although we have focused, and will continue to focus, on the fact that you should write your cover letter individually to address a

specific opportunity, company, or situation at hand, there are times when individual letters are not necessary. Direct mail is one of those times. When you are writing "cold" to a group of recruiters or companies, all in the same profession or industry, you can often use the same letter word for word. Mail merge now allows you to produce those letters quickly and easily with minimal cost. You can merge your letters into new documents and then print and mail each letter. Or, for an e-mail campaign, you can merge your letters into e-mail messages that automatically appear in your e-mail program's "out" box.

## Database Management

Many job seekers use their database and contact-management programs (such as Access, ACT!, and FileMaker Pro) to manage their contact lists and information. As your job search proceeds, you will begin to accumulate more and more contact information—advertisements, referrals, network follow-ups, and so on. Keeping track of this information can be a daunting task. Some job seekers prefer the index-card method, others prefer the notebook method, and others now turn to their PCs and take advantage of the database method of contact management. Choose whichever method works best for you, but choose one. If you think that you can manage all this information "in your head" or on scraps of paper, you're wrong. We guarantee you'll get lost in the process, misplace some vital contact information, or lose the name of the hiring manager at the company you really want to work for!

> *Tip* Managing your contacts is one of the most critical aspects of your job search. The more contacts you develop, the more new contacts you'll get, and the more opportunities that will be open to you. Keeping track of all that information—whether on paper or with your PC—is vital to a quick and successful job search.

## PC-Based Calendars and Appointment Books

You might also find that your PC offers an easy-to-use calendar and appointment book for scheduling interviews, follow-up phone calls, follow-up correspondence, and all of the other commitments that will arise as part of your job search. Most PCs have built-in appointment/calendar

programs. Probably the best-known is Microsoft Outlook Express. Use it to your advantage. Or, if you prefer, use a paper calendar. But just as with your contact information, write it all down and do not rely on your memory. A missed appointment is a lost opportunity.

## The Internet

The Internet offers vast, powerful, and readily accessible information sources. It's also an inexpensive and immediate method of communication. Use it wisely and you can accelerate your job search, gain access to wonderful opportunities, and gather the information you need to make good decisions about jobs, pay, relocation, and other career issues.

With the proliferation of job sites, resume-posting sites, and career information available online, the Internet has become an important element in every job search. The following online job search activities enable you to take full advantage of this enormous resource.

### Create a Text (ASCII) Version of Your Resume

You can do this easily by using your word-processing program's Save As feature. Save the file in a text-only or ASCII file format with a new file name; then close and reopen the newly saved file. You'll see that your resume has been transformed to plain-vanilla formatting in Courier type. Relax! You still have the fully formatted version of your resume under its original file name. Your new version is perfect for transmitting via the Internet, with full readability guaranteed for any recipient. You can go through this version and add extra blank spaces and keyboard symbols to improve readability.

Here's an example of a text resume, using the resume excerpt we worked with in chapter 5:

= = = = = = = = = = = = = = = = = = = = = = = = = = =

2008 to Present

Sales Manager—Veterinary Products Division

---

SMART PETS, INC. (Division of AAA Veterinary, Inc.), Portland, Oregon

Independently plan and manage all sales, marketing, customer-service, and business-development programs through a four-state region in the Western U.S. Challenged to increase sales revenues, expand market penetration, and improve competitive industry ratings.

=== Built regional sales from $2.8 million to $6.4 million in 12 months.

=== Launched the introduction of 18 new products generating $1.2 million in new sales revenues.

With this version of your resume, you're ready to post your resume on the Internet, reply to online job postings and advertisements, and apply for jobs directly at company Web sites.

### Post Your Resume on Resume Web Sites

Resume sites, or resume banks, are enormous repositories of resumes that are "searchable" by employers and recruiters—sometimes for free and sometimes for a fee. If your resume has the right keywords for a particular search, you will be contacted by the hiring company or recruiter. Disadvantages of posting your resume include a lack of confidentiality (your current employer just might come across your resume while searching for new additions to the staff) and the inability, in most cases, to remove your resume after you post it. You also leave yourself open to contact from candidate-hungry recruiting and placement firms that might not screen your resume thoroughly and call you for totally irrelevant jobs. And you can be sure you'll start receiving "junk" e-mails and perhaps even phone calls from companies that want to sell you some fantastic product or service to help you in your job search.

### Visit Job-Posting Sites

By entering your own keywords on the hundreds of job sites available (such as Monster and CareerBuilder), you can look for positions that are a good match for your current career goals. You can find both general and specialized sites. Some of these sites are free, and some require you to become a subscriber. But be careful not to spend too much time on these seductive sites! You can burn up hours perusing sites and responding with cover letters and resumes, but your chances of earning a response are quite low (less than 5 percent) because of the huge numbers of respondents. Instead, focus on more productive search methods such as personal networking.

### Visit Professional Association Sites in Your Field

Check the professional associations of which you're a member to see whether they have a Web site with a career section; quite often, you'll find highly relevant job postings for which you can apply.

### Explore the Sites of Companies That Interest You

Many companies post their available jobs on their Web sites, either instead of or in addition to their traditional (and much more expensive) methods of advertising for help or engaging the services of a recruiting firm. In addition to job postings, you'll find a wealth of information about the company's culture, mission, and operations that you can incorporate into your cover letters and use to your advantage during interviews.

### Research Companies, Industries, Business Trends, and Salaries

As a research tool, the Internet is immensely valuable. You can find great quantities of detailed information about almost any topic—including specific companies, industry trends, business activity, and so forth.

Knowledge is power—and never more so than when you're negotiating your salary. On the Internet, you can research salary information to find out industry averages and other information. And you can compare the cost of living in various cities to see how much a move will affect your financial situation.

## Distributing Your Resumes and Cover Letters

Picture this. It's 1980 and you've just prepared your resume and 25 individual cover letters to launch your job search campaign. How did you distribute your resumes back then? The answer is simple, because there was only one answer—via the U.S. Mail.

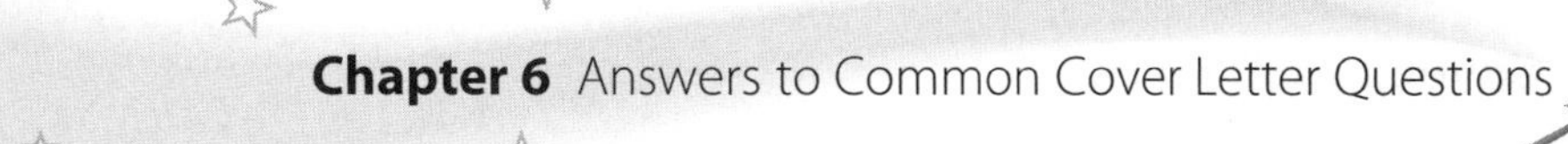



Ten years later, in 1990, you're ready to launch another search. Now you have a decision to make. Should you send your resumes and cover letters via mail, or should you use the latest and greatest technology—fax machines?

Today, the process for resume and cover letter distribution has become even more complex. Not only can you mail or fax, you now have e-mail at your disposal. Undeniably, e-mail is the quickest, easiest, and lowest-cost method of distribution. But which method is right for you? Do you have to select just one method, or can you use a combination of all three? How do you know what works, for whom, and when?

Recently, in an informal survey of some of the nation's top resume writers and career coaches, the decision was split 50/50 between mail and e-mail, with few advocating the use of fax campaigns. Mail campaigns were preferred because of their strong visual presentation. E-mail campaigns were chosen because of their ease, efficiency, and immediacy.

To best determine which distribution method is right for you and your campaign, let's evaluate the pros and cons of all three:

| Method | Pros | Cons |
|---|---|---|
| **Paper Campaigns** | Paper resumes and cover letters retain their formatting and sharp visual presentation of you and your qualifications.<br><br>People can "touch" and "feel" your paper resume, making a stronger and more immediate impression. | It is the most expensive method of distribution.<br><br>It is the slowest method of distribution.<br><br>Resumes and cover letters can be entered into a database (for retention) only if the recipient is willing and able to scan them. |

*(continued)*

*(continued)*

| Method | Pros | Cons |
|---|---|---|
| **E-mail Campaigns** | E-mail campaigns are immediate.<br><br>E-mail campaigns are the lowest-cost method of distribution.<br><br>E-mail messages can be saved in a database for future use and retrieval. | E-mail messages can be easily ignored and deleted.<br><br>The sharp visual presentation of a paper resume may be lost.<br><br>It is extremely difficult to get all the e-mail addresses you need, particularly if your search campaign is targeted to companies (versus recruiters).<br><br>Not everyone has an e-mail address; therefore, some of your potential contacts will be eliminated. |
| **Fax Campaigns** | Faxed resumes and cover letters retain their formatting and sharp visual presentation.<br><br>Faxing is immediate.<br><br>Faxed documents are much harder to ignore than e-mailed documents.<br><br>They are slightly less costly than paper campaigns. | Fax campaigns are more costly than e-mail campaigns.<br><br>It is extremely difficult to get all the fax numbers you need, particularly if your search campaign is targeted to companies (versus recruiters).<br><br>Not everyone has a fax; therefore, many of your potential contacts will be eliminated.<br><br>There is a higher rate of transmission failures as compared with the U.S. Mail.<br><br>Some visual appeal is lost, and clarity of transmission may be affected by both the sending and the receiving fax machine. |

Whether you choose to do your campaigns yourself or hire a professional who specializes in the preparation of job search campaigns is entirely up to you. If you have the technical expertise and the data you need, producing your own job search campaign might be the best and lowest-cost strategy. However, if you do not have access to the right data, if you are technologically challenged, or if your time is at a premium, you might want to consider contracting with a company that can provide these services. Remember, do what you do best and let other experts do what they do best!

## Managing the Paperwork and the Job Search Process

One of the greatest challenges you will face in your job search is managing the paperwork process. If you're not careful, it will overtake you and you'll find yourself buried in a pile of faxes, e-mails, notes, and scraps of paper. You must devise—and *stick to*—a structured process to manage it all. If you don't, your job search will be disorganized, you'll misplace important contact information, you'll forget interviews and scheduled follow-ups, and you'll be forever lost in the process.

You have basically two choices as to how you will manage your search campaign. You can do it either on paper or on your PC. The choice is yours. Whatever is easier for you to manage and control is the method you should select.

### Managing Your Campaign on Paper

If you choose to manage your search campaign on paper, you'll need a good supply of index cards and a notebook. We recommend that you write on an index card the full name and contact information (company name, address, phone number, fax number, e-mail address, URL) of every job search contact you have. Include the date that you forwarded a resume and cover letter, the specific advertisement you responded to (if applicable), and the date you received a response. If the response is not positive, simply note it on the index card, and you're finished (at least for the time being) with that contact.

If the response is favorable, create a notebook page for the company and transfer all relevant information from the index card onto the page. Use the notebook to continue to document all of your communications, meetings, interviews, and contact names with that company or recruiter. Be sure to write down everything that transpires between you and that company or recruiter. If, after the interview process and other communications, you are not offered the position, simply move that piece of paper to an inactive section in the back of your notebook.

One of the greatest advantages of managing your search on paper is that the information is always at your fingertips. No matter who calls or when, you can quickly pull an index card or open your notebook to have immediate access to information about the position, the company, the requirements, the salary, the location, and much more.

You'll obviously also need a calendar or day planner to keep track of appointments, follow-up calls, interviews, and your other commitments. Spend the extra few dollars and buy a calendar that is 8½ x 11 or 5 x 8 so that you have plenty of room to write down everything.

Even if you elect to manage your search campaign on paper, you will still need your PC for word-processing and e-mail applications.

### Managing Your Campaign with Your PC

If you choose to manage your search campaign on a PC, you'll need a database or contact-management program and a calendar. You will do precisely the same as we outlined in the previous section. The only difference is that you will maintain all of your documents electronically.

On one hand, this appears to make your job search much more efficient, and in many instances this is true. However, the one downside is that you are entirely dependent on your PC for all of your information. If you're standing in the kitchen one evening at 8 p.m. and a prospective employer calls, you don't have the information at your fingertips. Was this a sales position or a marketing position? Is it the company calling, or a recruiter? What were the specific requirements of the job? What were they looking for in an ideal candidate?

With a paper system, you have all of this information at your disposal. If you're dependent on technology, you'll have to

1. Wing it.
2. Ask them to hold for a minute while you run to your office and turn on your PC.
3. Ask them if you can call them back in five minutes.

We do not recommend any of these strategies, but if you are faced with this situation, we recommend either #1 or #2. Don't ever put a prospective employer off by using #3. Their response can quite easily be, "Well, if you're not interested, I'll call someone else." The opportunity can evaporate in an instant.

Perhaps the best approach is to start with #1 (wing it) and, while continuing the conversation on a cordless phone, walk to your office, turn on your computer, and hope that you can access any necessary information before the end of the conversation.

## Helpful Hints

Here are a few other helpful hints for effectively managing your job search process and the flow of information, paper, faxes, and e-mail messages.

### Keep Everything

We like paper. We like to be able to touch it, feel it, and put it somewhere for retention. You never know when that scrap of paper, old business card, or notes on a new company moving into the area will be of value in your job search. To keep track of it all, we suggest a file cabinet or file drawer devoted exclusively to your job search and your career. File cabinets are great inventions and are remarkably more efficient than the old "pile it on the floor" system that we all know so well.

### Touch Everything Only Once!

Part of what consumes such a great deal of our time is shuffling paper. Paper now enters our lives at such a breakneck pace that we can hardly keep up with it! The key to improving your organizational skills is to try to touch everything only once. When you receive a fax, an e-mail message, or a piece of mail, look at it, do what needs to be done, and then put it away finished. This simple task alone will dramatically improve your efficiency and is much more effective than the traditional "throw it in the pile and look at it later" method.

### Write Down Everything!

As basic as it might sound, write down everything–appointments, networking luncheons, interviews, follow-up calls—everything! Don't rely on your memory. This is particularly true for those of us who have "senior moments" when we know that we know something, but just can't

remember it! And don't think for a minute that you have to be a senior citizen to have a senior moment. It happens to all of us.

### Checklists Are Great Things

Checklists are some of our favorite things! Why? It's not because they make us more organized. It's not because they make us more efficient. It's because we get to cross things off! That, in and of itself, is really motivating and rewarding.

If you live by the "Post-it Note management strategy," give checklists a try. It's not a huge leap from piles of little pink notes to a single sheet of paper, so the transition is relatively easy. You'll be amazed by (1) how much neater your desk is when there are not 100 Post-it Notes on it, and (2) the thrill and exhilaration of crossing things off your list.

### Develop a Schedule and Stick to It

Flexibility is one of the keys to success for any job seeker. You can "roll with the punches" and quickly respond to changes and opportunities. That's great. But just as critical is your ability to manage and control your time.

The only vehicle that will provide you with such control is a definite schedule—a schedule that you stick to 100 percent of the time (barring situations that you consider emergencies). No matter how many times you might be tempted to make an exception, don't, unless it's an opportunity for an interview or a networking contact. When you developed your schedule, we assume you devoted the time to create a job search management tool that fits your life. Stick to it!

Use this schedule as a model for developing your own:

| | |
|---|---|
| 8:00 a.m.–10:00 a.m. | Follow-up phone calls and networking contacts. |
| 10:00 a.m.–Noon | Preparing resumes and cover letters for distribution. |
| Noon–12:30 p.m. | Lunch. |
| 12:30–4:00 p.m. | Interviews. |
| 4:00 p.m.–6:00 p.m. | Follow-up phone calls and networking contacts. |

*Tip* If you're sharper in the morning, you might want to schedule your interviews for the morning and your writing time for the afternoon.

Now, doesn't all that sound great? The problem is, it won't work nearly that efficiently. On Monday, you'll have an interview scheduled for 9 a.m., and on Wednesday, you'll have interviews the entire day. Therefore, you must juggle your schedule to accommodate someone else's interviewing schedule. In a job search, this is essential.

And if you're employed, obviously you can't spend 8 or 9 hours daily on your job search. So it's even more critically important that you structure times in your already overcrowded day for your job search. Unless you make the search a priority, it will not be successful. Here's a sample schedule you can adapt for your use if you're currently working:

| | |
|---|---|
| 7 a.m.–8 a.m. | Follow-up phone calls and networking contacts. |
| Noon–1 p.m. | Working lunch: Get out of the office to a secure, private location. You can schedule initial (brief) interviews for this time, as well as continue your networking activities. |
| 5 p.m.–7 p.m. | Interviews, follow-up phone calls, and networking contacts. |

For more lengthy interviews, you will need to arrange for time off from work.

Part II

# Sample Cover Letters

Chapter 7

# Before-and-After Cover Letter Transformations

This chapter and the six that follow it contain examples of excellent and successful cover letters written by career professionals for their clients. You can use these examples to help compose your own winning cover letters.

A tremendous amount of thought and effort went into selecting the letters included in this book. It was our objective to assemble a "user-friendly" collection of the very best cover letters written by top professionals in the careers and employment industry. To find such a source of qualified talent, we turned to our colleagues—professional resume writers, career coaches, career counselors, recruiters, outplacement consultants, military and government transition specialists, and others worldwide.

All cover letter submissions were carefully reviewed against stringent standards for quality, writing style, tone, visual presentation, impact, creativity, and diversity. Only those letters that met our requirements have been included. At the top of each cover letter page is the name of the professional who wrote it. We list contact information for each writer in appendix D, in case you'd like to get in touch with him or her for help with your cover letters and resume.

> *Note* Nearly all of the contributing writers have earned one or more professional credentials. These credentials are highly regarded in the careers and employment industry and are indicative of the writer's expertise and commitment to professional development. Appendix D (where you'll also find contact information for each contributor) explains each of these professional credentials.

Note that there is a special section at the end of each of the next seven chapters that includes "A Magic Example"—a cover letter written by Susan Britton Whitcomb, PCC, CCMC, NCRW, MRW; author of this book's companions, *Résumé Magic, Interview Magic,* and *Job Search Magic.* These letters are some of the best we've ever seen. Be sure to pay close attention to their style, tone, and presentation.

## How to Use the Samples

Among these samples you might find a cover letter that is almost identical to your needs and that is written for someone with a background similar to yours. Great! Take that letter, edit it as necessary, and you're ready to go. More likely, however, you'll find bits and pieces from a letter here and a letter there that are in line with your particular situation.

Even if you have to start writing from scratch, reviewing these letters will get the wheels turning in your head and give you ideas for strategies, formats, opening paragraphs, presentation of accomplishments, closing paragraphs, and more—in fact, every element of your cover letter.

# 1–Before

101 Queen Street
Centreville, Ontario
A2A 3B3
(905) 555-6000

January 27, 2010

Mr. Amol Sandhu
Manager
Human Resources
OmniTech Services Inc.
555 Valley Drive
Centreville, Ontario
B3C 4D5

Dear Mr. Sandhu,

I would like to apply for the position of Electronics Technician (Job # 555) you have advertised.

I have been repairing and servicing electronics equipment for the past 22 years. I have experience with the C460 series printers, colour printers, inkjet and laser printers, and audiovisual equipment. In addition, I have excellent customer service and troubleshooting skills.

I am available for interviews. Please contact me at the above phone number and I look forward to hearing from you.

Sincerely,

James Muirfield

This "before" sample is a straightforward response to an advertised position. It lacks visual appeal and only briefly mentions qualifications.

# 1–After

*Writer: Ross Macpherson, MA, CPRW, CJST, CEIP; Whitby, Ontario*

James Muirfield

101 Queen Street ◇ Centreville, Ontario A2A 3B3 ◇ (905) 555-6000

January 27, 2010

Mr. Amol Sandhu
Manager, Human Resources
OmniTech Services, Inc.
555 Valley Drive
Centreville, Ontario
B3C 4D5

**Re: Job #555 "Electronics Technician"**

Dear Mr. Sandhu,

It is with great interest that I respond to your advertisement for an Electronics Technician. I believe that both my experience and skills are a perfect match for the position, and I would appreciate your careful consideration of my credentials as presented below and in my attached résumé.

As my résumé indicates, I have **22 years of solid experience** as a service and repair technician. Over the course of my career, I have consistently proven my ability to provide outstanding customer service and solve the most difficult of technical issues.

I have been recognized by past employers for the following personal strengths, and it is these same qualities and results that I would bring as a technician with OmniTech Services:

- **Outstanding technical proficiency and expertise**
- **Proven ability and perseverance to solve the toughest technical issues**
- **Highest level of customer service and client relations**
- **Friendly, punctual, and willing to take the extra step to ensure customer satisfaction**

I am very excited about this position and would appreciate the opportunity to meet and discuss my qualifications. Thank you for your consideration, and I look forward to hearing from you soon.

Sincerely,

James Muirfield

*Résumé attached*

This version of James Muirfield's cover letter highlights his strong qualifications—both technical skills and personal attributes such as customer service skill and punctuality. This letter also effectively communicates his enthusiasm for the position.

## 2–Before

To Whom It May Concern:

I have worked for Galt Grocery Outlet from October of 1998 until the present time. I am looking for stable job that will better my experience in the construction or fencing business.

While working for Galt Grocery Outlet, I was a manager assisting in running the store and managing the employees. Experience learned: Driving a forklift at Galt Grocery Outlet and the Pear Shed during the summer and I also learned communication skills from working with customers and employees.

I have received my diploma from Galt High School graduating with a 3.0 GPA and also had a year and a half of college studying the Administration of Justice.

My hobbies include weight lifting, hiking and fishing in my spare time.

Throughout my years working with Galt Grocery Outlet I have received Employee of the Year, and employee of the month three times.

Richard Carpenter

92743 Rich Road
Galt, California 95632
(209) 555-4092

This candidate tried unsuccessfully to combine a resume and cover letter. With formatting errors, both first- and third-person writing, inclusion of high school G.P.A., a hard-to-find address, and hobbies not directly related to the career objective, it's easy to see why this document was relegated to the round file.

# 2–After

*Writer: Nancy Karvonen, CPRW, JCTC, CCM, CEIP, CJST*

## RICHARD CARPENTER

92743 Rich Road
Galt, CA 95632
(209) 555-4092 / rc@aol.com

January 28, 2010

Mark Morgan
Director
California Warehouse Distributors
7388 Murieta Drive
Rancho Murieta, CA 95683

Dear Mr. Morgan:

Are you looking for an experienced warehouse manager or heavy-equipment operator? I'm certain that you occasionally come across a safety-oriented candidate with excellent people skills who stands out from the crowd, and I fit that description. You will find my résumé enclosed.

- ✓ Throughout my career, I have consistently delivered solid, quantifiable results for my employer, through productive and cost-effective methods.
- ✓ In reviewing my background, you will find that I have succeeded in providing effective leadership, direction, and management; and skillfully operated a variety of forklifts in fruit packing and warehouse environments.
- ✓ I have been instrumental in generating long-term benefits for the firms that I have served—benefits that can best be summarized as the following:
  1. Increased financial support
  2. Increased public support
  3. Increased organizational efficiency and safety

At this point in my career, I am seeking new challenges and opportunities to continue to provide strong and decisive leadership and improve financial results. If you could benefit from a dedicated and goal-directed employee with proven skills and abilities, I would welcome a personal interview where we might establish a mutual interest. Thank you for your time and consideration.

Sincerely,

Richard Carpenter

Enclosure: Résumé

Richard's revised cover letter, which emphasizes relevant experience and results, helped him land a job within one week.

# 3–Before

Eleanor Sandoval
75 Netherlands Court, Apt. 6-C
New York, NY 10021
(212) 555-8765
elsan@aol.com

October 22, 2010

Peter Rockhouse, Esq.
Evans, Rockhouse & Stanford, LLP
725 Avenue of the Americas
New York, NY 10027

Dear Mr. Rockhouse:

Given your mission to curb the tide of attrition among the ranks of your Associates and provide a more harmonious environmetn, I feel confidnet that I could make a substantial contribution as Director of Associate Relations. For the past twenty-one years, I have been a successful legal recruiter from all sides of the recruitment spectrum – business, school and law firm. Four of those years were spent as Director of Legal Recruiting for Abrams, Howe & Castor. It was my charge to upgrade the level of legal talent and to aid and abet in providing a more congenial atmosphere at the firm. To every task set by the Partners, I achieved well beyond their expectations.

What I have disdovered after an eighteen month return to headhunting is that while monetarily successful, I miss the day to day operation of a law firm and quite frankly, I miss the atmosphere. My experience, creative approach and personality combined to create a job I not only excelled in but loved. It has always been a tenet of my professional faith that if a person loves the job, it is done superbly.

After reading yesterday's New York Law Journal, I felt strongly that this positon literally had my name on it. Therefore, I have takent he liberty of submitting myr esume to you as Managing Partner of Evans, Rockhouse & Stanford. I eager await word from you.

Sincerely,

Eleanor Sandoval

This version of the cover letter is obviously a rough draft, with no attempt made to polish the formatting or even spell-check for typographical errors. Much of the information included is relevant and interesting, however.

# 3–After

*Writer: Linsey Levine, MS, MCDP, LMHC; Ossining, NY*

**ELEANOR SANDOVAL**

**75 Netherlands Court, Apt. 6-C**
**New York, NY 10021**
**(212) 555-8765 elsan@aol.com**

October 22, 2010

Peter Rockhouse, Esq.
Managing Partner
Evans, Rockhouse & Stanford, LLP
725 Avenue of the Americas
New York, NY 10010

Dear Mr. Rockhouse:

After reading yesterday's *New York Law Journal,* I felt strongly that the position of Director of Associate Relations literally had my name on it.

For the past 21 years, I have been a successful legal recruiter from all sides of the recruitment spectrum—business, school, and law firm. Four of those years were spent as Director of Legal Recruiting for Abrams, Howe & Castor, where it was my charge to upgrade the level of legal talent and provide a more congenial atmosphere among Partners and Associates at the firm. To every task set by the Partners, I achieved well beyond their expectations.

What I have discovered after an 18-month return to headhunting is that although I am financially successful, I miss the day-to-day interaction and operation of a law firm, and, quite frankly, I miss the atmosphere. My business experience, creative approach, and service-oriented personality combined to create a job I not only excelled in, but loved. It has always been a tenet of my professional faith that if a person loves the job, it is done superbly.

Given your mission to curb the tide of attrition among the ranks of your Associates and provide a more harmonious and productive environment, I feel confident that I could make a significant contribution to Evans, Rockhouse & Stanford and have enclosed my resume for your consideration.

I would appreciate the opportunity to meet and speak with you directly regarding some of my ideas for attorney recruitment and retention that would complement your firm's goals. I will call your office next week to see if we can arrange a mutually convenient time to meet.

Sincerely,

Eleanor Sandoval

enclosure

This letter opens with a strong statement that was buried in the previous version. The writer did an excellent job of reorganizing the information and improving the professional tone. Note the appeal to the reader's interests in the last paragraph.

134 Merrick Road, Apt. 5D
St. Albans, NY 11135
Telephone (718) 555-9001

March 3, 2010

Philip Barnes
Parkway Elementary School
320 E. 241 Street
New York, NY 10000

Dear Mr. Barnes:

Thank you for taking a moment to review my attached resume. I am submitting it to you for employment consideration for your recent opening for a teacher.

For the past four years, I have dedicated myself in helping children grow academically as well as socially. Working with children has been and is a wonderful adventure to me.

I trust you find my academic and employment experience suitable in qualifying for employment with your organization. Please feel free to contact me should you need more information.

I look forward to speaking with you.

Sincerely,

Cameron Anderson

This "before" sample is a classic example of a "transmittal letter"—a letter that merely announces a resume and does little to sell the candidate.

# 4–After

*Writer: Christine Ferguson, CPRW*

## Cameron Anderson

134 Merrick Road, Apt. 5D, St. Albans, NY 11135
(718) 555-9001 • c.anderson@verizon.com

---

March 3, 2010

Philip Barnes
Parkway Elementary School
320 E. 241 Street
New York, NY 10000

Dear Mr. Barnes:

A rewarding and successful teaching experience motivates me to bring my commitment to the Parkway School. I offer four years of experience, dedication, and a talent for motivating students to achieve academic excellence.

As a substitute teacher at Holy Trinity, I developed a homework assistance program that significantly improved students' academic performance. My determination in bringing the program to reality was fueled by my desire to help students succeed.

My determination and commitment have also allowed me to do the following:

- Help students overcome problems affecting their academic performance.
- Deliver lessons in a creative and meaningful manner to facilitate comprehension of subjects.
- Empower students and increase their levels of academic performance.

Is it possible to meet with you to discuss how my skills can help your students? If you have any questions or require additional information, please contact me at (718) 555-9001.

Sincerely,

Cameron Anderson

---

***"I highly recommend Cameron. She is a self-motivated person who takes the initiative and follows through."***

*Tina Foxworth*
*Principal*
*Holy Trinity School*

This dynamic and effective "after" version of the letter is enhanced by a quote from a very credible source: the principal of a school where this candidate worked.

## 5–Before

September 23, 2010

Mr. Jerome Skinner
Manager, Human Resources
Canada Pharmaceuticals
1000 Central Street North
Augusta, Ontario
A5B 5C5

Dear Mr. Skinner,

I am graduating from the Augusta Institute of Pharmaceutical Technology and am interested in a position in your Research & Development department.

I am a very hard working student and have received excellent grades on my lab projects.

For example, I successfully created a formulation matrix for IR tablets and determined its strength by copying penicillin V potassium tablets. In another project, my group examined confounding, standard order, experimental error, significance testing via ANOVA, polynomial equations, and optimization in pharmaceutical application of $2^{4-1}$ fractional factorial design.

I am very interested in a position at Canada Pharmaceuticals in the Research and Development department. You are welcome to review my attached resume. Thank you for your consideration.

Sincerely,

Catherine Westbrook
31 Masters Road
Augusta, Ontario
A2B 2C2
(905) 555-4455

The formatting and language of this letter convey a less-than-professional message, and the information highlighted is only a small part of what this candidate has to offer.

# 5–After

*Writer: Ross Macpherson, MA, CPRW, CJST, CEIP; Whitby, Ontario*

## CATHERINE WESTBROOK

31 Masters Road
Augusta, Ontario A2B 2C2

Phone: (905) 555-4455
Email: cwestbrook@mail.com

September 23, 2010

Mr. Jerome Skinner
Manager, Human Resources
CANADA PHARMACEUTICALS
1000 Central Street North
Augusta, Ontario
A5B 5C5

Dear Mr. Skinner:

As a graduating student from the **Augusta Institute of Pharmaceutical Technology,** I am particularly attracted to Canada Pharmaceuticals as a progressive leader in pharmaceutical research and development, and as an employer that can provide both the challenge and opportunity I am seeking.

Pharmaceutical research and development offers the opportunity to work on the cutting edge of medicinal innovation and discovery, and it is for this reason that I pursued it as a field of study. My academic experience has exposed me to the challenges and excitement of working in a team toward a common goal, and it is within this dynamic environment of teamwork, innovation, and a collective desire to succeed that I particularly thrive. It is exactly Canada Pharmaceuticals' dedication to these very principles that makes me confident that I would be a valuable contributor and that excites me about opportunities within your company.

In addition to my academic qualifications, I would bring the following personal strengths to a position in Canada Pharmaceuticals:

- **An enthusiasm for challenges, especially those that require new ways of thinking and collaborative input across scientific specialties.**
- **Outstanding teamwork and leadership skills, where I have demonstrated my ability to both contribute and motivate.**
- **A dedicated work ethic and desire to make a difference, which is reflected in my academic, work, and volunteer experience.**

I would appreciate the opportunity to meet and further share with you my qualifications and enthusiasm for joining the Research and Development team at Canada Pharmaceuticals. Thank you for your consideration, and I look forward to hearing from you soon.

Sincerely,

Catherine Westbrook

Enclosure

Although it contains a great deal more information, this letter retains its readability through effective formatting. The first two paragraphs compliment the company and give the candidate's strong reasons for wanting to work there.

## 6–Before

October 25, 2010

Box W0XX1
24 Heber Plaza,
Miami, FL 33132

Dear Sir or Madam:

I am responding to the position, International Regional Sales Manager, advertised in The Miami Newspaper, October 24, 2010.

My academic credentials include a Masters in Business Administration, which has provided the foundation for my extensive international professional experience. This international work includes experience in various markets including Latin America and the United States.

I have been a Marketing Manager and Deputy General Manager at Swiss Watch Corporation in Panama, where I successfully met the challenge of introducing Swiss Brands to the Central American market and South American market. In addition, in my capacity as an International Account Executive for Video Services, I have been marketing 3D model home simulation services to foreign construction companies. Furthermore, I have worked in the area of Customer Relations with non-linear editing systems manufactured by Avis Technology. All of my international experience has been enhanced by the fact that I speak various languages proficiently, including Spanish, French, English, Hebrew and have a working knowledge of Portuguese.

I would like the opportunity to further discuss my experience and qualifications with you. Please feel free to call me at (305) 999-0624. Thank you for your consideration.

Sincerely,

Gabriel Hamda

This letter is full of "I" statements and shows very little knowledge of or relevance to the employer's needs. Further, it is not written in a style and format that are commensurate with the midlevel management position the candidate is pursuing.

# 6–After

*Writer: Lisa LeVerrier Stein, CPRW, CEIP, JCTC; Deerfield Beach, FL*

**GABRIEL HAMDA**

142 E. Ocean Club Drive
Aventura, FL 33180

(305) 999-0624
gabrielhamda@mindspring.com

October 25, 2010

Box W0XX1
24 Heber Plaza
Miami, FL 33132

RE: International Regional Sales Manager

Dear Hiring Professional:

Building corporate value and delivering sustained revenue growth is my expertise. For the past eight years, I have proven my ability to lead aggressive market expansion into international markets. Highlights of my professional career include the following:

- Introduced innovative simulation technology into international territories, including Brazil, Mexico, Venezuela, Costa Rica, and Colombia
- Increased Swiss Watch sales by 35%, resulting in $2 million in additional annual revenue
- Negotiated successful corporate partnership with Kodak in El Salvador, resulting in 56 new distribution channels with more than $200,000 in annual sales
- Spearheaded successful launch of *Watch* products in Panama, Colombia, and Bolivia, resulting in huge mass-media campaigns

My strengths lie in my ability to conceive and implement strategic action plans to identify new market opportunities, introduce state-of-the-art technologies/products, and negotiate strategic partnerships to drive Latin American market expansion and revenue/profit growth. Equally notable are my strong qualifications in public relations and promotion, recruiting and training, customer relations, and cross-cultural communication (fluent in English, Spanish, French, and Hebrew).

Currently, I am seeking a mid-level management position where I can continue to provide strong and decisive sales and marketing leadership. If my experience and abilities are a match for your goals, I would welcome the opportunity for a personal interview. I can assure you that my international sales and marketing expertise will be of value to your organization.

Sincerely,

Gabriel Hamda

Enclosure: résumé

Opening with a strong statement that conveys value to the organization, the "after" version of this letter goes on to emphasize specific accomplishments that are relevant to the hiring company's needs. The closing is assertive and professional.

# 7–Before

Tammy Eaton
555 Wonder Valley Road
Vicksburg, OR 95555
(555) 555-5555
tmeaton@or.aha.org

May 19, 2010

Search Committee
American Heart Association, Middletown Chapter
555 East Main Street
St. City, OR 55555

Attn: Search Committee

Please accept this letter in application for the Middletown Chapter Manager position. Enclosed please find my resume and letters of recommendation. I am available for relocation.

My resume outlines my 19 years of experience with American Heart Association. I am a "people person" and enjoy working with staff, contributors, volunteers, healthcare professionals, and the community at-large. I also have strong management experience as an Acting Chapter Manager with the Downtown Chapter and as a National Projects Coordinator with the national level. As an Acting Chapter Manager, I maintain excellent communications between the chapter and it's constituencies, oversee budgets and control expenditures, update the Vice President of Community Services on activities of the chapter, make management recommendations as appropriate, and provide supervisory oversight and support to my staff.

I am confident this experience would enable me to build internal and external relationships, maximizing limiting operating resources, with enhancement of the delivery of services to ensure that the mission and goals of the American Heart Association continue.

Thank you. I look forward to hearing from you.

Very truly yours,

Tammy M. Eaton

Enclosure

This "before" letter fails the first rule of referral letter writing: Immediately name your referral source in the first sentence of your letter. The letter is also vague, short on measurable results, and contains a serious grammatical error ("it's" should be "its") that in and of itself might torpedo this candidate's chance for an interview.

## A Magic Example

# 7–After

*Writer: Susan Britton Whitcomb, PCC, CCMC, MRW, NCRW; Fresno, CA*

**Tammy M. Eaton**

555 Wonder Valley Road
Vicksburg, OR 95555
(555) 555-5555
tmeaton@or.aha.org

May 19, 2010

Jennifer Marks
Search Committee Chair
American Heart Association, Middletown Chapter
555 East Main Street
St. City, OR 55555

Dear Ms. Marks:

Jack Hennesey, Terry Carver, and Joe Piceda have urged me to apply for the American Heart Association's Middletown Chapter Manager position. As an ardent and long-time supporter of Heart, I am pleased to submit my résumé for the position.

Qualifications I can deliver to the chapter stem from my 19 years with Heart. Included in this tenure is significant management experience at the national and chapter levels. Specific contributions in the disciplines of operations, corporate relations, fund development, finance and accounting, human resources, and technology are outlined on the enclosed résumé.

Most recently, under my direction as Acting Chapter Manager, the Downtown Chapter enjoyed a 21% increase in fund development, operated in the black for the first time in four years, partnered with Saint Joseph's Medical Center to implement "Healthy Hearts" in K–12 schools, and resurrected an advisory panel made up of committed and talented business and community leaders.

In an era when societal and economic influences have yielded a decline in volunteer services and financial resources, your committee no doubt wants an individual with proven leadership experience in the not-for-profit sector. I believe my track record is indicative of my ability to build internal and external relationships, maximize limited operating resources, and enhance the delivery of services to ensure that this chapter of the American Heart Association continues to thrive.

I look forward to learning more about how I can assist in meeting the chapter's immediate needs and long-term goals.

Sincerely,

Tammy M. Eaton

Enclosure

Starting strongly with multiple referrals, the "after" version of the letter goes on to state verifiable accomplishments along with general qualifications. And, very importantly, it identifies with the non-profit organization's mission.

# Winning Cover Letters for Blue-Collar and Trades Positions

## Top 5 Cover Letter Writing Tips for Blue-Collar and Trades Positions

1. Be certain to highlight your technical qualifications as they relate to the position. Often these specific technical requirements—such as a cosmetologist's license, heavy-equipment operator's certificate, or welding certification—are bona fide job requirements, and without them you cannot be considered for the job.
2. Turnover is often high in blue-collar professions. If you can stress traits such as work ethic and a strong performance record, you will be a strong candidate.
3. Use language that is comfortable for your educational level and vocabulary, but be certain that your letter sounds professional and is absolutely correct in grammar, spelling, and punctuation.
4. Mention any recent education, training, or other evidence of continuing professional development; this shows you are serious about your profession and dedicated to improving your skills.
5. Just as with any other type of profession, consider the needs of the employer and sell yourself as the solution to those needs.

# 8

*Writer: Susan Guarneri, MS, NCC, NCCC, LPC, CPRW, CEIP, IJCTC, MCC, CERW; Wausau, WI*

**Timothy O'Neill**
**37 Paramount Drive, Lawrenceville, NJ 08648**
**(609) 555-5555**
**ton@aol.com**

January 18, 2010

Mr. John Hogan
Main Street Manufacturing
17 Main Street
Lawrenceville, NJ 08648

Re: **Machinist or Maintenance Machinist** position

Dear Mr. Hogan:

If you believe that properly maintained equipment and machinery are vital to manufacturing production deadlines, we think alike.

If you need customized parts, equipment, and machinery to meet rush orders, we should talk.

If you are looking for a dependable and conscientious machinist, maintenance machinist, or industrial machinery repairer, please consider my qualifications:

- **18 years of experience as a Machinist** producing or repairing parts and equipment for major industrial manufacturers, pharmaceutical companies, and research organizations.
- Completed rush order projects on time and with **quality results.**
- Experienced with a wide variety of equipment, tools, fixtures, and materials, which means I can bring **immediate value** to your operation.
- Loyal, dedicated, and **dependable** hard worker.
- Quick learner with a knack for **solving problems.**

To help you learn more about my qualifications, I have enclosed my résumé. Throughout my work history I have been successful as a machinist because I have acquired excellent skills, planned carefully for projects, and kept on good terms with people at all levels.

It would be a pleasure to meet with you at your convenience to discuss the contributions I would make to your team. I am ready to put my energy and experience to work for you. May I hear from you soon?

Sincerely,

Timothy O'Neill

Enc.

Opening with interest-generating statements and continuing with bullet points that highlight key qualifications, this cover letter grabs and keeps the reader's attention from beginning to end.

*Writer: Rhoda Kopy, BS, CPRW, JCTC, CEIP*

**9**

**JOHN A. KEARNEY**
**1812 Diamond Drive • Toms River, NJ 08753**
**732-555-3132 • j.kearney@gmail.com**

May 15, 2010

David Carlisle
Piedmont Properties
1866 Bradley Boulevard
Eatontown, NJ 07724

Dear Mr. Carlisle:

I am interested in securing a position as a Maintenance Technician / Supervisor, with full responsibility for overseeing the maintenance of a large apartment complex or housing development. My resume is enclosed for your review.

With more than 10 years of experience in all aspects of building maintenance, I can be a valuable addition to your staff. My expertise in the areas of carpentry, plumbing, electrical work, painting, landscaping, and pool maintenance has led to the present occupancy rate of 98% in the apartment complex I presently oversee.

I was specifically selected to rectify serious safety and health hazards and initiate extensive repairs and renovations at two apartment complexes. The ability to accurately assess needs and promptly implement solutions has contributed to my success. Through effective planning and scheduling, I have consistently demonstrated the ability to keep complexes in tip-top shape with minimal manpower. While other complexes of comparable size require a work force of four, I get the job done with a work force of two.

If you are searching for a maintenance professional who is committed to high standards of workmanship, relates well with residents, and is used to being on call around-the-clock, please contact me to arrange an interview.

Thank you for your consideration.

Sincerely,

John A. Kearney

Enclosure

By addressing such key issues as occupancy rate, safety, economy, and tenant relationship-building, this letter strongly appeals to the interests of its primary audience: property owners.

# 10

*Writer: Meg Montford, MCCC, CMF; Kansas City, MO*

## John W. Bridges

525 W. Harrison
Olathe, KS 66061
913-555-9999

jackbridges@aol.com

2860 Fast Street
Santa Ana, CA 92703
714-555-8888

November 30, 2010

Human Resources Manager
City Hall
105 Central Street, Room 120
Santa Ana, CA 92701

Position: **STREET SUPERINTENDENT**

My 20 years of experience in all facets of public works make me well qualified to be your next Street Superintendent. Having the longevity with one city employer speaks to my dedication and strong work ethic. Supervisors have applauded my dependability, punctuality, and ability to meet established project deadlines. My current manager has commented, "Last winter John never missed a call out for snow. This is the type of leadership this shop needs if we are to be successful."

The city of Olathe is the fastest-growing city in Kansas. Classified the third-largest city in the state by area, Olathe has 1,500 lane miles and continues to add 10–12 lane miles per year. It is a suburb of Greater Kansas City. I have worked for this city during its rapid growth and have conquered the challenges this growth process has provided its city workers.

Training and technical development are very important to me, and I take advantage of every opportunity to acquire the knowledge that will advance my skills. As a crew leader, I have directed many workers on the job sites and am confident of my ability to oversee your staff of 27. Work zone safety is a critical issue in our field, and I take pride in my proactive approach to using safety equipment, meeting safety requirements, and following procedures.

In January 2010, I will be relocating to your city for family reasons, but can be available for an interview before then. Please contact me at my Olathe telephone number to schedule a meeting. Thank you for your consideration of my application.

Sincerely,

John W. Bridges

This letter packs a lot of information. The candidate reinforces his qualifications with a very effective quote, gives enough information about his current employer to show relevance to the city in which he's applying, and informs the reader that he will be relocating to that city in just a few months.

# 11

*Writer: Carole S. Barns*

**HAROLD S. MILLER**

**1341 Pinehurst Avenue NE ■ Boston, MA 02266 ■ (617) 555-1144**

February 6, 2010

Douglas Turkell, District Secretary
Fire Protection District 101
145 NW Lester Lane
Boston, MA 02266

Dear Mr. Turkell:

Enclosed is a résumé in application for testing for promotion to Career Lieutenant in Fire Protection District 101. As a current Firefighter in the District who has served as an Acting Lieutenant for the past 5 years, I have the skill, the knowledge, and—most importantly—the dedication and commitment to ensure that citizens and businesses are provided with safe, efficient, and quality fire prevention, education, and management. Let me highlight a few of the areas where I believe I am exceptionally qualified to fulfill the requirements of the position:

| YOUR REQUIREMENTS | MY QUALIFICATIONS |
|---|---|
| ■ First Class Firefighter for 1 year. Training in up to 276 hours of specialized firefighting programs. Possess valid EMT certification. | ■ I have been a Firefighter since 2000 and achieved my First Class Firefighter status in April 2001. A graduate of the University of Massachusetts, I also have a degree in Fire Command and Administration from Bunker Hill Community College. All of the required courses—from Supervision to Time Systems—have been taken. I completed my formal studies with a GPA of 3.8. I am a certified EMT. |
| ■ Supervise strategic and tactical emergency operations and/or Command System (ICS). | ■ I have completed 28 hours of instruction on ICS and have an excellent working knowledge of the system. Tactics are among my strongest skills. I achieved the District's highest score on the most recent tactical exercise. |
| ■ Be able to effectively use personnel and resources in both emergency and non-emergency situations. | ■ As Acting Lieutenant for the District for the past 5 years for up to 75% of my shifts, I am frequently responsible for the day-to-day operations of the crew. My leadership skills generate trust because I believe in fair and equal treatment of others and that all leaders are more effective if they lead with a team mentality. |
| ■ Excellent communications and public relations skills. | ■ With strong written and verbal communications abilities, I am particularly effective in dealing with the public. I am an enthusiastic provider of public education programs and enjoy going the extra step to promote a positive, helpful image of the Fire Protection District among our "customers." |

I look forward to the examination and evaluation process and the opportunity to demonstrate before the Review Committee my abilities to handle tactical, personnel, and citizen issues.

Sincerely,

Harold S. Miller (hsmiller@comcast.net)

Enclosure: Résumé

This letter expands on a simple comparison-list style with some strong selling points for each qualification. Although he is applying for a promotion within the fire department where he works, the job seeker still "sells himself" just as if he were an outside candidate. Don't assume those who know you are fully aware of your accomplishments and capabilities!

# 12

*Writer: Janet Beckstrom, CPRW, ACRW; Flint, MI*

## Samantha T. Coles

258 DeMarl Avenue
Mt. Morris, MI 48458
810-555-2391
samcoles@aol.com

June 4, 2010

Mount Hope Community College
Attention: Employment Office
3300 Selmer Avenue
Mt. Hope, MI 48654

Dear Employment Director:

I understand that Mount Hope Community College has an opening for a professional cosmetologist to teach in your Cosmetology program. As a graduate of the Mr. David's School of Cosmetology and a soon-to-be graduate of the Cosmetology Management program at Mount Hope, I hope you will consider me for this position. My resume is enclosed.

As you can see from my resume, I am a licensed cosmetology instructor in addition to being a licensed cosmetologist. I currently run an 11-chair salon I opened in 2001. In addition, I maintain my own clientele as a hairdresser.

My skills as a cosmetologist have been recognized by Mount Hope's *On the Town Magazine,* which named me the "Most Creative Stylist." Also, Her Products (a beauty supply wholesaler) asked me to work as a platform artist at several beauty shows across the country. I even demonstrated the use of their products in an instructional video they produced.

I'm sure I have the right combination of education and experience to make an excellent cosmetology instructor. I hope you will call me to arrange a personal interview. I can be reached at the above number or in my salon at 810-555-1212. Thank you for your consideration.

Sincerely,

Samantha T. Coles

Enclosure

This letter is a straightforward presentation of the candidate's qualifications for the job. The third paragraph highlights some notable and highly relevant achievements.

*Writer: Janet Beckstrom, CPRW, ACRW; Flint, MI*

**13**

**Jonathan P. Franklin**

1854 Broadway Street
Vassar, MI 48555

517-555-0935
jfranklin@hotmail.com

Dear Hiring Manager:

I have worked in a manufacturing environment for more than 15 years, in positions ranging from die setter to production supervisor. Because I have had experience from both the hourly and supervisory viewpoints, I believe I can be an effective supervisor for your company. I hope you will consider my interest for an appropriate position on your supervisory team.

The enclosed resume describes my employment background. One area that I am particularly knowledgeable about is ISO9002/QS9000. I have worked in several companies that have undergone inspections and eventual certification. In fact, I was placed in my current position at GM Flint Assembly because of this experience. At Flint, I was significantly involved in preparing several internal departments of the Paint Department for inspection. I developed manuals, trained employees, and generally coordinated the preparations. We expect to be certified by the end of this year.

I don't think you will find a supervisor who is more hardworking or dependable. I know what needs to be done, and I work to that end. What I don't know how to do, I teach myself with help from someone who does know. I am constantly looking for new challenges and ways to improve myself. I'm a hands-on leader who creates a friendly environment for my employees, which invariably translates into a more loyal crew.

After reading this letter, I hope you agree that I have what it takes to be the kind of supervisor you are looking for. Please give me a call to arrange a convenient meeting time. Thank you for your consideration.

Sincerely,

Jonathan P. Franklin

Enclosure

This cold-call letter is intended for use as-is, without personalization. Although this approach is less desirable than personalizing each letter, it is extremely practical for job seekers who don't have access to a PC to address and modify each letter. In the third paragraph, the candidate communicates important "intangibles" that will set him apart from other applicants.

## A Magic Example

# 14

*Writer: Susan Britton Whitcomb, PCC, CCMC, MRW, NCRW; Fresno, CA*


**Roger Shamblin**

55555 Plains Drive
Denton, TX 75555
(940) 581-5559 rshamblin@aol.com


March 4, 2010

Manson Manufacturing Company
P. O. Box 12345
Denton, TX 75555

Attn: Welding Department Supervisor

Please consider my résumé for the position of welder advertised in *The Denton Times*. I have recently completed a Certificated Welding Program at Denton Community College that included more than 1,000 hours of hands-on training in the following areas:

- **Basic Welding:** Oxy-acetylene fusion welding on plate, pipe, and tubing of mild steel, stainless steel, and cast iron; soft and hard soldering on ferrous and nonferrous materials; use of hand torch, straight-line cutter, and dupli-cutter; and electric arc welding on mild steel plate and pipe.
- **Mig-Tig Welding:** Basic mig and tig welding on mild steel, stainless steel, and aluminum; basic plasma cutting systems; and welding in flat, horizontal, vertical, and overhead positions with emphasis on working towards A.W.S. plate certification.
- **Welding Fabrication:** Advanced shop welding practices on mild steel plate and pipe; advanced mig welding on mild steel; advanced tig welding on mild steel, stainless steel, and aluminum plate; inner shield, flux core; test and inspection of welds; and project design, including flowcharting and project construction.
- **Metals:** Metal process applications, including working with bench metals, forming wrought iron, laying out and forming sheet metals, casting, and forging.
- **Related Courses:** Electricity, blueprint reading, machine shop (turning), CNC milling, and CADD.

Welding instructors at Denton Community College gave me some of the highest grades in the program for my quality workmanship and study habits. In addition, my internship supervisor, Joe Brown at Upright Harvester, was very happy with my performance and asked that potential employers call him directly for a reference (Mr. Brown's number is 555-5555).

Thank you for your time. I look forward to hearing from you.

Sincerely,

Roger Shamblin

Enclosure (Résumé)

In addition to addressing, in detail, all the specific skills and qualifications needed for this job, the job seeker uses the second-to-last paragraph to communicate a few intangibles (excellent academic record and strong personal recommendation) to further sell himself as a strong candidate for the advertised position.

Chapter 9

# Winning Cover Letters for Young Professionals/ New Graduates

## Top 5 Cover Letter Writing Tips for Young Professionals/ New Graduates

1. Highlight "professional" skills that you have developed through both professional and nonprofessional experiences. For example, if you have worked on important team projects while at school, communicate that you know how to get results in a team environment.
2. If technology skills are important in your chosen field, be sure to emphasize your skills in this area.
3. Mine your academic experiences for evidence of leadership skills. These are important in a work environment and are evidence of your potential.
4. Highlight your academic achievements. They indicate your intelligence and competitiveness.
5. Relate your skills, experience, and interests to the employer's needs. Show that you understand business priorities and are ready to make a contribution; don't simply state, "I've graduated! Now I need a job!"

# 15

*Writer: Laura DeCarlo, MCD, CCM, CERW, JCTC, CECC, CCMC, CEIC; Melbourne, FL*

YVONNE P. SMITH
15 Caribbean Isle Lane, #8
Orlando, FL 32808
(407) 555-8790 • yvonnesmith@gmail.com

July 6, 2010

Attn: Ms. Denise Seatl
District Manager
Eckerd Drugs
22 Lake Buena Vista Road
Orlando, FL 32808

Dear Ms. Seatl:

Think of all the things that make a Manager with Eckerd Drugs GREAT....

Drive, dedication, and a willingness to learn and achieve. Exposure to different levels of the sales process. Current knowledge of Eckerd Drugs' store policies and procedures as an Assistant Manager. A competitive, professional personality. Skills and talents to exceed goals and set records. Excellent results. *I believe I have what you are looking for!*

Realizing that this summary, as well as my resume, cannot adequately communicate my qualifications in-depth, I would appreciate having the opportunity to discuss with you how I can continue to be an asset to your firm. I look forward to speaking with you.

Thank you for your time and consideration.

Sincerely,

Yvonne P. Smith

enclosure: resume

This letter starts off with an irresistible "hook," followed by a paragraph that details precisely those qualities that will be of most interest to the reader. For new graduates, experience is not usually the strongest selling point. Rather, the candidate's potential and personal attributes are usually of most interest to prospective employers.

*Writer: Kathryn Bourne, CPRW, JCTC*

**16**

**SAMANTHA CROSS**

117 Greenbriar Way, #214 ❖ Denver, CO 48210 ❖ 312-555-6794 ❖ scross@mac.com

December 4, 2010

Mr. Kent Laverly, Principal
LW Design
505 West Broadway Avenue
Denver, CO 48232

Dear Mr. Laverly:

Isn't it important to LW Design that

❖ Clients feel their project is important to the firm?
❖ All projects are handled with the utmost professionalism?
❖ Employee creativity is in a constant state of development?

Of course it is. Superior corporate goals and objectives will ensure that LW Design will remain a premier Denver firm for decades to come.

These values are also core to my developing career. As you will see in the enclosed résumé, I recently graduated from the Art Institute of Seattle with a 9-month internship at Newton Architecture. Under their mentoring I gained hands-on experience in space planning, material and finish selections, color board assembly, writing specifications, and compiling architectural finish books.

Another strength I bring to LW Design is the ability to build confidence with existing customers, as well as establish rapport and trust with prospective clients. In addition, holding a degree in Business Administration and Marketing, I fully understand the importance of adhering to budgets, maintaining positive vendor relationships, managing day-to-day marketing activities, and applying innovative ideas to capture new projects.

I would appreciate the opportunity to further explore the needs of LW Design and how my strengths could have a positive impact on the company's bottom line. I will be contacting you next week to arrange for a meeting time that is convenient for you.

Sincerely,

Samantha Cross

Enclosure

This letter appeals to its audience in two ways: First, with an interesting design and font selection, it demonstrates strong graphic skills—communicating an important attribute by showing rather than telling. Second, it leads off with questions that demonstrate knowledge of the company's values.

# 17

*Writer: Vivian VanLier, CPRW, JCTC, CEIP, CCMC, CPRC; Valley Glen, CA*

**NOREEN BERGMAN**

**5555 Magnolia Court • Valley Glen, CA 91405 • (818) 555-6565 • noreen555@ucla.edu**

March 27, 2010

Sarah Hartford
Director of Human Resources
Pacific Enterprises, Inc.
2745 Topanga Boulevard
Los Angeles, CA 94005

Dear Ms. Hartford:

In June I will graduate from UCLA with a degree in Business Economics. My willingness to work hard is evident from the fact that I hold part-time professional positions concurrent with my studies. These experiences have enabled me to gain a realistic view of the demands and challenges of the business world.

I would welcome the chance to discuss opportunities with your firm. I believe that my energy, analytic skills, organizational abilities, and creativity in tackling problems can make a positive contribution to your company. I am equally comfortable working independently to meet company goals as well as collaboratively as part of a team. I have always been able to establish and maintain excellent relationships with clients and co-workers at all levels. My professional skills include the following:

- Client relations, research, and account management strengths gained as a Finance Assistant at a brokerage firm.
- Experience in managing client records, preparing financial statements, and completing tax returns for a CPA firm.
- Assisting low-income clients and students with income-tax preparation as a volunteer.
- Serving as a group leader—planning and implementing activities as a camp counselor for four summers.

Please consider me a serious candidate for a position with your firm. I look forward to a personal meeting so that I can provide you with additional information to supplement what appears on my enclosed resume.

Sincerely,

Noreen Bergman

encl: resume

Using a combination of paragraphs and bullets, this candidate conveys important qualifications—academic history, experience, and personal qualities that communicate her potential to become a valuable asset to the firm.

# 18

*Writer: Don Orlando, MBA, CPRW, JCTC, CCM, CCMC, CJSS; Montgomery, AL*

**Mark Morstad**
1440 Norton Avenue
Montgomery, Alabama 36100
[334] 555-5555—morstad1@aol.com

February 23, 2010

Ms. Nora W. Morgan
Comptroller
Topline, Inc.
1200 Ventura Avenue
Suite 1000
Montgomery, Alabama 36100

Dear Ms. Morgan:

Where do you look, in your organization, for the person who does the "nitty-gritty" work to build Topline's future success? Where is the person who frees senior decision-makers for the work only they can do? If you need those profit-enhancing capabilities, I would like to join your team as your newest, entry-level project analyst.

Even before I earned my degree, I got great satisfaction from helping businesses succeed. Naturally, when I attended school I majored in the field that seemed just right for me: commerce and business administration.

However, I wanted more practical, hands-on knowledge than I saw in my college courses. And so I took the jobs others might have shunned to get practical, hands-on experience. None of the job titles were impressive. But helping pay my way through school as a bartender, doorman (you may read that as "bouncer"), laborer, and assembly worker taught me a lot about how to work with people to get the job done and serve the customers—sometimes very tough customers.

Now I want to put all that I've learned to work. Perhaps a good next step is to hear about your specific needs. May I call in a few days to arrange a meeting?

Sincerely,

Mark Morstad

Enclosure: Résumé

This letter is an excellent demonstration of how a new graduate can relate seemingly irrelevant experience to a company's needs. Sprinkled throughout the letter are terms that clearly show an understanding of what's important to businesses—terms such as "profit-enhancing," working with people "to get the job done," and "build future success."

# 19

*Writer: Lisa LeVerrier Stein, CPRW, CEIP, JCTC; Deerfield Beach, FL*

## Carol Hobesound

2460 Country Club Boulevard, Deerfield Beach, FL 33442 • (954) 444-8617 • carolh@gmail.com

September 27, 2010

Shanna Detwiler
VP Human Resources
General Media Corporation
75 High Ridge Road
Stamford, CT 09602

RE: Marketing Assistant

Dear Ms. Detwiler:

"If you wish to reach the highest, begin at the lowest." –Pubilius Syrus

I know my quoting Pubilius Syrus is a sign of youthful idealism. However, I know it takes hard work and proven dedication to move up within an industry. I'd like to reach the highest by starting at the beginning within the PR/Marketing industry.

I recently graduated with a BA in Communications from Wake Forest University in North Carolina. I am seeking an entry-level position with a dynamic PR/Marketing firm in Connecticut, offering opportunity for upward mobility based on performance. I realize it takes hard work and proven dedication to move up within a firm–I'm willing to start at the beginning and prove my skills and dedication along the way.

As my résumé indicates, I have excellent customer service skills. This is demonstrated by my proven ability to quickly establish rapport with a diverse range of customers and suppliers. My strong written communication skills are demonstrated by several writing samples prepared during college, which can be furnished upon request. I am also proficient with both PC and Macintosh software, including Windows applications, Microsoft Word, WordPerfect, electronic mail, and Internet browsers. Finally, my excellent work ethic and positive attitude are contagious.

Temporarily, I am residing in Florida to care for an elderly family member. However, I am seeking to relocate to Connecticut by November 2010 and am seeking employment to begin at that time.

I look forward to discussing possibilities to grow within your firm and am very excited about the opportunity to capitalize on my communications background and assist your company in the PR/Marketing arena. Thank you for your time and consideration–I can assure you that I will make a positive contribution to your organization.

Sincerely,

Carol Hobesound

Enclosure: résumé

The technique of beginning with a quote is a surefire attention-getter. This candidate continues by relating the quote to her career goals and interest in joining the firm. As in the preceding example, the letter contains ample evidence that the candidate knows what is important to businesses.

*Writer: Kirsten Dixson, CPBS, JCTC; Exeter, NH*

# 20

## Heather Jones

(212) 555-1111
100 East 75th Street #2A, New York, NY 10020
hjones@hotmail.com

April 23, 2010

Ms. Julie McCafrey
DesignPros International
123 Avenue of the Americas, Suite 999
New York, NY 10035

Dear Ms. McCafrey:

Ms. Jane Smith suggested that I contact you to discuss the contribution that I could make to DesignPros in a Contract Design Internship this summer. I am currently a student at The Interior Design Institute and am anxious to begin my professional design career. Unlike many of my peers whose only experience is academic, I offer not only strong educational credentials, but also practical, "hands-on" business experience.

My strength is being able to work with people to generate ideas that work. My career has been focused in the areas of advertising project coordination, customer relations management, and events planning. Former managers would describe me as capable, motivated, and detail-oriented.

The most rewarding work for me has always centered on creativity and design. As a child, I made barrettes, boxes, and dolls and sold them to local stores. In high school, I took every art and photography course that I could and even won a tri-state photography contest. Then I earned a degree in business administration and began working in marketing. Once I made the decision to make a career change, I began to create again. I made and sold pillows, blankets, painted furniture, pictures with beads, mosaics on tables and mirrors, water-colored lampshades, etc. Friends suggested that I should do it for a living. I agreed and quickly commenced my formal design training. I have excelled in my coursework and am looking forward to bringing my creativity and business acumen to this profession.

I have enclosed my resume to provide more information on my strengths and career achievements. I'm also prepared to show you a preliminary portfolio of my work. I look forward to speaking with you to further pursue this opportunity. Thank you for your consideration.

Sincerely,

Heather Jones

Enclosure

This candidate provides evidence that sets her apart from her peers who might also be applying to this company. The story of her lifelong interest in design is interesting and highly relevant.

# 21

*Writer: Maria Hebda, CPRW, CCMC; Trenton, MI*

**Thomas N. Jones**

424 Columbia Avenue • Trenton, Michigan 48183
tomjones@yahoo.com • (734) 555-8205

January 15, 2010

Recruitment Center
P.O. Box 2945
Arlington, Virginia 22209

**RE: Central Intelligence Agency Employment**

I am interested in exploring employment opportunities with the Central Intelligence Agency (CIA). The enclosed résumé is in accordance with the instructions stated in the CIA's *Job Kit and Resume Preparation Guide*. I would like to be considered for all possible positions. An acceptable salary would be in the mid-$20K range.

***Qualifications I bring to your agency include the following:***

- Proven performance in fast-paced and high-stress working environments
- Strong analytical skills with exceptional attention to detail
- Highly motivated and aggressively take on great responsibility
- Planned and implemented more than 100 strategic missions with a 100% success rate
- Hands-on experience with classified documentation
- Experienced in intelligence report writing, including in-depth reports on high-interest areas of operation

My record is one of great responsibility, dedication, and solid accomplishments. I am confident that my experience and abilities can make a valuable contribution to the CIA. I am available for immediate employment and willing to relocate.

Should any questions arise regarding the information on my résumé, please do not hesitate to contact me. I look forward to hearing from you in the near future.

Sincerely,

Thomas N. Jones

Enclosure

With six highly relevant bullet-point qualifications, this letter clearly communicates that the candidate has what the CIA is looking for. The first paragraph reinforces this message by showing compliance with the standard operating procedures that the CIA expects.

# 22

*Writer: Rhoda Kopy, BS, CPRW, JCTC, CEIP*

**Heather T. Alberts, R.N., B.S.N.**
**18 Porter Avenue • Lakehurst, NJ 08733 • 732-555-3378**
**heatheralberts@mac.com**
***— Willing to Relocate —***

January 8, 2010

Daniel R. Farrantino
Northeast Regional Sales Manager
Omni Pharmaceutical Products
Jackson Lane
Princeton, NJ 08540

Dear Mr. Farrantino:

I am a well-spoken, assertive nursing professional with the motivation, medical knowledge, and ability to promote pharmaceuticals to health care professionals. My resume is enclosed for your review.

Throughout my career, I have interacted extensively with pharmaceutical representatives; I know how important it is for them to be knowledgeable about the efficacy, benefits, contra-indications, and potential side effects of drugs. As health care professionals, we expect them to know the answers; if they don't, they lose credibility.

Having administered and monitored the effects of a wide range of pharmaceuticals, I am confident of my ability to promote these products to medical professionals. My associates refer to me as "Ms. PDR" because of my extensive knowledge of and interest in medications. On a daily basis, I had to clearly present medical information to patients, and frequently had to use skills of persuasion with patients, nurses, and physicians.

With more than 15 years of experience in emergency nursing, I have a talent for being focused and decisive in the most challenging of situations. Strong organizational and time-management skills are imperative in handling medical crises; I firmly believe I can handle any situation as a result of my background.

If you are searching for an energetic health care professional with the knowledge and determination to succeed as a Pharmaceutical Representative, please contact me to arrange an interview. Thank you for your consideration.

Sincerely,

Heather T. Alberts, R.N., B.S.N.

Enclosure

This letter makes a strong case for the candidate's transition from nursing to pharmaceutical sales. In any kind of career transition, it's important to relate past experience and demonstrated skills to the needs of the new profession.

# 23

*Writer: Lorie Lebert, CPRW, IJCTC, CCMC*

## ALLISON S. THORNWEBER

**1061 HOLLYBERRY ROAD — ROYAL OAK, MI 48067**
**248.555.1061**
*e-mail: athornweb@hotmail.com*

July 17, 2010

Thomas Kent, Ph.D.
Directory, Library Services
University of Michigan
Ann Arbor, MI 49109

Dear Dr. Kent:

I am writing in anticipation of a position in Library/Information Sciences, Archival Administration, or related fields/divisions. Highlights of my employment and academic experience include the following:

- ***Strong Project Management Skills.*** With extensive experience working in libraries, museums, and nonprofit corporations, I have been involved in planning, research, exhibits, and public service that resulted in significant accomplishments.
- ***Excellent Academic Record.*** Since entering universities at the Master's and Bachelor's levels, I have consistently maintained above-average grades while holding outside employment and volunteering.
- ***Communications and Public Relations Skills.*** In each of my positions I have dealt cooperatively with the general public, co-workers, and superiors. My skills in interpersonal relations and cross-cultural communications are excellent.
- ***Analytical and Organizational Skills.*** Practical employment in areas of my concentration allowed me to demonstrate my strengths in data research and analysis, project organization, and computer proficiency.

I am anxious to launch my career in a full-time, permanent position and would welcome the opportunity to meet with you to discuss your specific requirements. I can make myself available at your earliest convenience for a meeting/interview.

Thank you for your time reviewing my credentials. I look forward to speaking with you.

Sincerely,

Allison S. Thornweber

Enclosure: Résumé

The attractive formatting and easily skimmed bullet points do a good job of communicating this entry-level candidate's professionalism and potential.

# 24

*Writer: Cheryl Ann Harland, CPRW, JCTC; The Woodlands, TX*

## Susan Russell

20 Victory Road ◆ Dallas, Texas 75007 ◆ (972) 555-9870 ◆ E-mail: srussell@gateway.net

February 21, 2010

Human Resources Director
Dell Computers
31 Pasadena Avenue
Phoenix, Arizona 99841

Dear Human Resources Director:

Building cooperative relationships between multi-disciplinary groups is my expertise. As a project manager for Texas Instruments, I have been responsible for coordinating, organizing, and facilitating multimillion-dollar IT projects impacting the entire organization (45,000 employees worldwide). It is my project-management experience, coupled with my supervisory, training, and development background, that I wish to integrate into an HR/Organizational Development role.

Over the years, I have been successful in building trust and cooperation between employees and management, creating environments that support and reward individual accomplishment and contribution.

Having just completed my BBA in Organizational Behavior, I am ready to combine my 20-year technical/supervisory career into a training and development and/or instructional design position, where I can be instrumental in creating training programs that will be responsive to your company's ever-changing organizational needs.

Thank you for reviewing the enclosed qualifications. I look forward to a personal interview at your convenience.

Sincerely,

Susan Russell

Enclosure

Having recently completed a degree, this candidate presents both education and 20 years of experience as key selling points. Note the effective use of the "building corporate value is my expertise" opening strategy (described in sample 19 in chapter 3).

# 25

*Writer: Lynn Andenoro, CPRW*

**Jeffrey A. Anderson**
3605 South 2800 West
West Valley City, Utah 84119
(801) 555-4678
janderson@verizon.net

October 17, 2010

KUTV Channel 2 News
2185 South 3600 West
Salt Lake City, Utah 84119

Attention: News Operations Manager

It is with great interest that I respond to your job posting for the News Editor/Engineering Controller position with Channel 2 News in Salt Lake City. I believe I have the qualifications and enthusiasm you are looking for. My résumé is enclosed for your review.

During my senior year of high school I worked as a video editor for a local cable TV station in Garden Grove, California. I gained considerable hands-on experience, a wealth of practical knowledge, and a determination to pursue TV and film production as a career. Concurrent to my work at Channel 3A, I also studied TV Production in an occupational studies program in my community.

I quickly learned the technical skills of the trade, injected creativity and energy, and was soon filming breaking news stories in the community, covering local meetings and sporting events, editing news footage for weekly broadcasts, and assisting with studio productions and community-access programming.

I would like the opportunity to meet with you and discuss how I might become a beneficial part of your team at Channel 2 News. I will call to follow up with you next week. Before then, I can be reached at 555-4678. Thank you for your consideration.

Sincerely,

Jeffrey A. Anderson

Enclosures: résumé and tape

The appealing (and relevant) graphic at the top of this letter is an effective enhancement to its traditional formatting.

*Writer: Donna Farrise, JCTC; Hauppauge, NY*

**26**

**DIANE M. WILSON**
555 Meadow Brook Street
Westbury, NY 12345
(631) 555-5555
e-mail: diane@yahoo.com

April 17, 2010

McGraw-Hill
1221 Avenue of the Americas
New York, NY 10020

Dear Sir/Madam:

With innate reading/proofreading ability, and demonstrated skills in editing grammatical, typographical, and composition errors, I am actively seeking a challenging **freelance reader/proofreader/editor** position. My work has been recognized for theoretical sophistication and rhetorical clarity. Highlighted qualifications and contributions I would bring to your organization include the following:

- Aptitude to read/proofread complex novels and diverse subject matter/disciplines; i.e., instruction manuals, college textbooks, education manuals, math textbooks, journals, etc.

- Ability to edit into abstract frame, produce plausible and innovative interpretation, and provide written and oral commentary. Mastered skills through the reading of scholarly texts and diverse disciplines, editing press releases, and teaching experience.

- Conspicuously well-reasoned, possessing solid research ingenuity, progressive text development, and comprehensive results meeting deadlines.

- Experience working with a cross-section of individuals, developed through performance as an educator/counselor.

I have been characterized as a top-quality reader, proofreader, and editor, with a remarkable sense of humor. I would welcome the opportunity to meet with you and discuss the possible merging of my talent, experience, and enthusiasm with your **freelance reading/proofreading** needs.

Very truly yours,

DIANE M. WILSON

Enclosure

A simple yet striking page border, combined with a clean format and easily skimmed bullet points, makes this a very attractive letter.

# 27

*Writer: Salome A. Farraro, CPRW*

**MARYBETH LONG**

**48 Lake Avenue ⌘ Buffalo NY 14202**
**716/555-0909 ⌘ *E-mail:* marybeth@myemail.com**

February 8, 2010

Mr. Edward P. Murphy
Deputy Superintendent
Mayfield Central School District
19 Main Street
Mayfield, NY 14623

Dear Mr. Murphy:

I am interested in being considered for a position within your Guidance Department and have enclosed a completed application and my resume for your review.

During my three years with Brunswick Junior/Senior High School, I have had the opportunity to work with a diverse student population at the middle and high school grade levels. Currently, I manage a caseload of 200 students in the middle school, where individual and group counseling—as well as crisis intervention and peer mediation—occupy a large portion of my time. In addition to academic and future planning, I assist teens with self-esteem, anger management, social skills training, drug abuse, and sexual abuse issues. I view primary prevention as a critical aspect in assisting young people through the stages of their lives, balanced with a focus on student development and academic excellence.

I have benefited professionally from the experiences and knowledge gained at Brunswick and am confident I can share that effectively with your school district. Additionally, I believe that my excellent work ethic; strong interpersonal, organizational, and communication skills; and ability to establish a solid rapport with students, families, and peers alike would make me an effective member of your Guidance team. I have taken the liberty to enclose letters of reference that reflect the quality of work for which I strive.

I would appreciate the opportunity to interview for a Guidance Department position at Mayfield. Please feel free to contact me at the above telephone number or e-mail address.

Thank you for your time and consideration.

Sincerely,

Marybeth Long

Enclosures

Primarily a straightforward presentation of qualifications, this letter is enhanced by the last sentence in paragraph 2, where the candidate communicates her educational philosophy.

**28**

*Writer: Shanna Kemp, M.Ed., JCTC*

# DANIELLE ALBRIGHT

972-455-8383 HOME
922 LAKEVIEW LANE, #4122 972-678-3483 MOBILE
LEWISVILLE, TEXAS 75067 danielle_albright@yahoo.com

Dear Personnel Manager:

Are you searching for a dynamic, goal-oriented individual with a strong desire to succeed and lead others to success? Are you searching for an enthusiastic, proactive team member with strong interpersonal skills and a desire to work with people? Look no further.

I am a driven and focused individual who knows how to set goals and work to achieve them. This is clearly exemplified by my time in college. When I started my degree program, I set my sights on finishing early and doing well in all my courses. Since I also needed to earn the money to pay for my schooling, I knew I had set a demanding goal for myself. I persevered, however, and expect to graduate in December from the University of North Texas in just 3½ years with a 3.0 GPA while working 20+ hours per week and taking course loads of 18 hours per semester.

Aren't I the type of person you want working for you?

My degree is in psychology. I have always enjoyed working with and helping people. It has become my desire to work with people in a business atmosphere—to assist others with the professional side of their needs and work in a company where I can set long-term goals for success.

I have enclosed my resume for your consideration. I would appreciate the opportunity to meet with you in person to discuss how I may further the goals of your company. I look forward to your call.

Sincerely,

Danielle Albright

Enclosure

Capturing the reader's attention with interest-generating questions makes for a strong opening paragraph. The information the candidate shares about her personal qualities and school experience is interesting, relevant, and powerful. The attractive letterhead design enhances the total presentation.

# 29

*Writer: Michele Haffner, CCMC, CPRW, JCTC; Glendale, WI*

**MARIE GILMAN**
2110 East Kane Avenue
Shorewood, WI 53211
Cellular: (414) 555-6025 – Home: (414) 555-0619
E-mail: mgilman@aol.com

---

January 14, 2010

Dr. Robert Deahl, Dean, College of Professional Studies
Marquette University
P.O. Box 1881
Milwaukee, WI 53201-1881

Dear Dr. Deahl:

As a single, working mother who recently completed undergraduate and graduate degrees, I can certainly empathize with the students who are enrolled in your Professional Studies program. At times while working on my own degree, I recall feeling overwhelmed. Fortunately, community resources such as yours help adult, working students thrive in their environments. I emerged from the experience motivated, ready to assist others in the spirit of your mission statement: "…providing service that expresses the highest degree of understanding, respect, honesty, compassion, and guidance."

Therefore, I would like to be considered for the position of Adult Student Advisor. You will see from the enclosed resume that my background and education closely match your requirements for the job. As a community counselor, my work has included assisting single mothers and their children as the family adjusts to major life changes such as returning to school or work. In addition, my recent graduate training has included course work in career counseling and career development within four-year colleges. The needs of special groups (delayed entrants, mid-life changers, displaced home workers, etc.) were covered thoroughly.

I can arrange to be available for an interview at your earliest convenience and look forward to meeting with you.

Sincerely,

Marie Gilman

Enclosure: Resume

This candidate effectively relates her personal situation to the needs of the job for which she is applying. This is entirely appropriate because these personal experiences give her an appreciation of the needs of students and the demands of college life.

**30**

*Writer: Deborah Wile Dib, CPBS, CCM, NCRW, CPRW, CEIP, JCTC, CCMC; metro NY*

# Anjelique Tarakas

**Freedom Quad, P.O. Box 0021**
**University at Albany, Albany, NY 12222**
**518-555-0101 • anta@cnsvax.albany.edu**

**Permanent Residence**
**45 Sloane Drive, Great Neck, NY 11702**
**516-555-0303 • anjel@mindspring.com**

---

April 21, 2010

Mr. William Cousins
Director of Human Resources
Chase
25 Park Avenue
New York, NY 11010

Dear Mr. Cousins:

You advertised for an entry-level Financial Analyst in Sunday's *New York Times.* As a soon-to-graduate university senior majoring in Business Administration with a concentration in Information Systems Management, my qualifications should meet your requirements.

Taking initiative has always been my academic and career focus. I certainly understand responsibility, hold an intense work ethic, and strive to do my best in any situation. During four years of work and internship experiences, I have enthusiastically sought challenging projects and have made strong contributions not normally expected of an intern. Highlights include the following:

- The development of an Access-to-Excel migration spreadsheet that organized a company-wide PC inventory system for MedFlo instruments.
- The creation of an Excel spreadsheet that permitted MedFlo to implement more rapid vendor payment.
- The successful learning and selling of high-profit liability coverage while an intern at Budget Rent-a-Car (normally done only by experienced sales force).
- The planning and implementation of a large warehouse document relocation project for Symbol Technologies.
- The fulfillment of positions as Vice President of Finance and Community Service Coordinator for Pi Sigma Epsilon, Professional Sales and Marketing Fraternity.
- The attainment and successful performance of Teacher Assistant positions for two educators.

A demanding course load, multiple campus leadership positions, challenging internships, and a variety of work experiences have prepared me for the rigors of an entry-level Financial Analyst's position at Chase. My technical and business background is balanced by courses in art and the humanities, creating the ability to grasp business and technology needs as well as the skills to think past the obvious aspects of a situation. I have an intense interest in pursuing and overcoming difficult challenges, I work hard, and I have the drive to make a difference.

I'd like to meet and discuss the ways in which I can contribute my experience and energy to Chase. I can be reached at my academic address via phone or e-mail and look forward to speaking with you.

Sincerely,

Anjelique Tarakas

This candidate presents both quantifiable qualifications (in a bulleted list) and intangible qualities that show she is very well suited for the job for which she is applying.

# 31

*Writer: Christine Ferguson, CPRW; Bronx, NY*

## Christina A. Thomas

120 Fifth Avenue, New York, NY 10250
(212) 555-1023 ❖ CAT@juno.com

---

February 3, 2010

Yvonne Harris
Metropolitan Children's Therapies
123 Maple Way
New York, NY 10002

Dear Ms. Harris:

Over the last three years I have become familiar with all aspects of service delivery for speech-impaired clients. Since 2007, I have been instrumental in overseeing/coordinating service delivery for a speech-impaired child...my son.

Since his birth, I have participated in every facet of his care, from recruiting qualified service providers to administering therapy. This experience has inspired me to embark on a career as a Speech Therapist or Special Education Teacher. My hard work and tireless efforts to facilitate his progress have resulted in marked improvements.

The areas in which I have made considerable contributions are Diagnostic Planning, Case Management, and Speech Therapy. My résumé provides an overview of my role and achievements in each of these areas. Additionally, I am pursuing a degree in Speech Therapy / Special Education at Westchester Community College. I am confident that the knowledge and experience I have acquired to date will help your clients achieve their goals.

I would like to schedule a personal interview where we can discuss my strong enthusiasm and qualifications for a position in your organization. I can be reached at the address and phone number listed above. Thanks in advance for your time and consideration. I look forward to your response.

Sincerely,

Christina Thomas

This letter is another example of relating personal experiences to the needs and demands of a specific job. The diamond-shaped graphic under the candidate's name is a striking and attractive enhancement.

**32**

*Writer: Ross Macpherson, MA, CPRW, CJST, CEIP; Whitby, Ontario*

# DANIELLE GREEN

1999 Port Smith Road
Pinehurst, Alberta N5L 5M5

(905) 555-6789
dgreen@mail.com

***Goal: Pharmaceutical Sales***

January 23, 2010

Mr. Bryan Hodgins
PharmLab Canada
44 Industry Way
Pinehurst, Alberta
N5N 7M7

Dear Mr. Hodgins:

I understand that PharmLab Canada is introducing a new cardiovascular medication, Milocaid, and that you are looking for salespeople within the Pinehurst area.

Throughout my professional and academic careers, I have consistently driven myself to meet challenges and achieve goals, and it is within this type of challenging and results-oriented environment that I particularly thrive. Likewise, it is exactly these qualities that attract me to a highly competitive and exciting career in pharmaceutical sales, and in particular to PharmLab Canada as an industry leader that can provide both the challenge and opportunity I am seeking.

With both professional experience in a technical lab environment and an honours degree in Biomedical Science, I have an excellent background in health and biomedical settings and am both comfortable and proficient with highly technical terminology and communication. This advantage, combined with my demonstrated sales and marketing accomplishments, makes me confident that I would be a valuable contributor to the PharmLab Canada sales team.

Success in sales is measured in ***results,*** and I can bring the following results-oriented qualities to PharmLab Canada:

- **Demonstrated proficiency in selling to customer needs, fostering client relationships, and managing key accounts to maximize revenue and retention.**
- **Outstanding teamwork and leadership skills, where I have demonstrated my ability to both contribute and motivate.**
- **A goal-driven work ethic and dedicated approach to all tasks and undertakings.**

I would appreciate the opportunity to meet and further share with you my qualifications and enthusiasm for joining the sales team at PharmLab Canada. I invite you to review my attached résumé and thank you for your consideration.

Sincerely,

Danielle Green

*Enclosure*

The attention-getting bullet points in this letter relate potential (what the candidate *can* do) rather than specific qualifications—these are covered in the earlier paragraphs.

# 33

*Writer: Janet Beckstrom, CPRW, ACRW; Flint, MI*

**Jeremy S. Yale**

2384 Sparrow Road • Kingston, MI 48534 • 810-555-3449 • jeremyyale@yahoo.com

Dear Employment Director:

*You are the master of your own destiny.*

That's what I tell other sales representatives when I am trying to help them understand how a successful career in sales is within their reach. Within a short three-year period, I have developed strong sales skills that have enabled me to build a record of sustained sales increases. I enjoy helping others improve their sales skills by using some of the methods that have been successful for me. The enclosed resume highlights some of my specific accomplishments. It supports my interest in a position with your organization.

My experience demonstrates that I have the ability to transition into selling diverse products and services. After all, sales is sales. My strongest sales tool, I believe, is that I am willing to truly listen to my customers. Since I hear what they are saying, I am prepared to identify and offer the product or service they need at a price they cannot turn down. It's a win-win situation.

After reviewing my material, I hope you will agree that I am the kind of highly motivated, successful sales professional that you are looking for. Please contact me at the above number to arrange a convenient meeting time so that I can elaborate on how my track record in sales can benefit your organization. Thank you for your time and consideration.

Sincerely,

Jeremy S. Yale

Enclosure

The compelling philosophy stated in the first sentence of this letter should grab the attention of every reader. The letter becomes even more effective when the candidate goes on to relate the importance of that philosophy to his career success to date.

A Magic Example

34

*Writer: Susan Britton Whitcomb, PCC, CCMC, CCM, MRW, NCRW; Fresno, CA*

**CHARLES MARTIN EDWARDS III**
555 South Fairfield
San Francisco, CA 95555
(415) 555-5555
cme3@comcast.net

June 23, 2010

Hudson Parker, Hiring Partner
Jones, Marriott & Parker, Attorneys at Law
555 West Kennowith
San Francisco, CA 95555

Dear Mr. Parker:

Having graduated with honors from Hastings School of Law and recently passed the Bar, I am seeking interviews with civil litigation firms that devote a portion of their practices to international law. The enclosed résumé details my education, experience, skills, and legal interests. Among my qualifications are the following:

- Scholarship developed as an extern for California Supreme Court Justice Louis Madigian and as a staff writer for *The Hastings Law Review*;
- Courtroom skills learned while conducting preliminary hearings as an intern with the Alameda County District Attorney's Office;
- Leadership gained as a college quarterback and volunteer team leader with Habitat for Humanity; and
- International experience acquired while studying law in London, England, and traveling extensively throughout Europe, Mexico, and Central America.

Given the combination of these experiences, I am confident I have developed a professional resourcefulness and personal diversity that will enable me to become a capable member of your firm. Your consideration of my qualifications for associate attorney positions will be appreciated.

Sincerely,

Charles Martin Edwards III

Enclosure

The four bullet points in this letter convey the job seeker's key qualifications–so a quick skim of the letter would quickly convey his most important information.

Chapter 10

# Winning Cover Letters for Mid-Career Professionals

## Top 5 Cover Letter Writing Tips for Mid-Career Professionals

1. Focus on your career accomplishments. By describing what you have done for other employers, you will demonstrate your potential to make similar contributions for this employer.
2. If you have managed staff, be sure to communicate team and managerial accomplishments as well as individual achievements.
3. Relate your accomplishments to the overall goals of the organization as well as your unique sphere of influence.
4. Emphasize career progression. Your advancement indicates reward for past achievement and shows your readiness to continue to move upward.
5. Don't take up valuable space by including details of college or early career experiences; in most instances, your most recent positions will be most relevant.

# 35

*Writer: Debra O'Reilly, CPRW, IJCTC, CEIP; Brandon, FL*

**Jayne Smyth**
101 Main Street
Friendship, CT 06000
**203-555-1010**
**jsmith@mac.com**

February 10, 2010

Hallmark Cards, Inc.
ATTN: Human Resources Director
P.O. Box 100000001
Kansas City, MO 64141

Re: Positions for **Sales Professionals**

Dear Human Resources Director:

When you care enough to send the very best...send me!

The opportunity to represent Hallmark Cards, the perennial industry leader, would be a dream come true. Because I share your philosophy that only my best is good enough to offer, I have consistently been a top-producing sales representative for my current employer, constantly exceeding sales quotas and earning recognition from clients, peers, and supervisors. Accomplishments have included the following:

- ☑ Among 50 sales representatives, rank in the top three for the past two years, supporting the achievement of departmental sales goals averaging $500,000 per month.
- ☑ Regularly produce 30% or more over daily sales goals.
- ☑ Selected to manage key national accounts.
- ☑ Commended by peers for providing sales assistance/support with accounts in a competitive environment.
- ☑ Chosen to mentor new hires.

I offer you solid sales experience, a strong customer focus, and effective leadership skills, in combination with an "only the best will do" work ethic. I eagerly anticipate the opportunity to discuss your goals for your new territory and the ways in which I might help Hallmark achieve and exceed them. Thank you for considering my qualifications.

Sincerely,

Jayne Smyth

Enclosure

The opening line of this cover letter is perfectly tailored for its recipient. After capturing the reader's attention, the letter follows up with strong accomplishments that support this candidate's claim to be "the best."

# 36

*Writer: Michele Haffner, CCMC, CPRW, JCTC; Glendale, WI*

## George E. Brown

3265 North Bartelt Street
Milwaukee, Wisconsin 53211

E-mail: geb3@earthlink.net
Telephone/Message: (414) 555-3081

---

November 30, 2010

Mr. Daniel Tilman
Roadway Express, Inc.
6880 South Howard Avenue
Oak Creek, Wisconsin 53154

Dear Mr. Tilman:

Having visited your company's Web site, my impressions were of an organization that is forward thinking and always looking for new ways to improve. An open-door type of relationship appears to be prevalent between you and your customers. Therefore, it would seem necessary for your sales representatives and management personnel to possess strong communication abilities in order to effectively carry out your mission.

As you can see from the enclosed résumé, my educational concentration in communications has been balanced by actual work experience. I have been required to conduct financial analysis, solve technical difficulties (sometimes remotely), and give the highest possible levels of customer service. I am certainly willing to learn all about the industry and your organization so that I can be a productive team member.

My promise is that a meeting will not be a waste of time, yours or mine. In addition, I can make myself available at your convenience to discuss your needs in detail. Thank you for your consideration of my qualifications, and I look forward to hearing from you.

Sincerely,

George E. Brown

Enclosure: Résumé

In this letter, the job seeker creates rapport by identifying with the target company's mission. Mentioning that he has researched the company by visiting its Web site is another way to communicate that he knows the company he's approaching and can indeed be a "productive team member."

# 37

*Writer: G. William Amme, JCTC*

**John H. Libby, Ph.D., N.C.C., L.M.H.C.**
**2400 Germantown Avenue**
**Philadelphia, PA 19004**
**(215) 798-2018**
**jlib007@aol.com**

Job Posting L-1711
*Mental Health* magazine
PO Box 10007
Philadelphia, PA 19001

Dear Sir or Madam:

I am very interested in your position of Clinical Supervisor as advertised in the July issue of *Mental Health* magazine.

My enclosed résumé reflects both my 15 years of counseling and psychotherapy experience and my outstanding educational credentials. I am now seeking additional challenges and opportunities in the mental health counseling field. If you can use a well-trained and highly competent professional with exceptional real-world experience, *I am your ideal candidate*. The following highlights how my background meets your stated position requirements.

| *You Require:* | *My Qualifications:* |
|---|---|
| Master's degree. | *A Doctorate in Psychology and a Master's in Health Services, as well as a post-Master's degree as Specialist in Mental Health Counseling.* |
| 24 graduate semester hours in Psychology. | *More than 115 graduate semester hours in Psychology and Neuro-Linguistic Programming.* |
| Experience teaching at the college level. | *Experience teaching at both the junior college and university graduate levels.* |
| Background as Licensed Therapist or Mental Health Counselor. | *More than 15 years of successful practice as a Licensed Therapist and Mental Health Counselor.* |
| The ability to teach both day and evening classes. | *The ability to teach day and evening classes as demonstrated by my current employment schedules.* |

You may note that along with my educational and college-level teaching credentials, I have had substantial success in working with Mood Disorders, including Major Depression and Anxiety Disorders in both individual and group therapy. In addition, my experience in rehabilitation and career counseling may provide collateral benefits to your institution.

Letters and résumés help you sort out the probable from the possible, but they are no way to judge the caliber of an individual. I would like to meet with you and demonstrate that along with my credentials, I have the personality and skills that make for a successful counselor, instructor, and supporting team member. Recognizing the demands of your schedule, I will call you soon after you receive this letter. I would appreciate my application being treated as confidential as I am currently employed.

Sincerely,

John H. Libby, Ph.D., N.C.C., L.M.H.C.

encl: Résumé

In addition to a close match between specific requirements and his qualifications—as demonstrated in a well-organized table—this candidate sells himself by providing additional, highly relevant qualifications and describing himself as the "ideal candidate."

*Writer: Georgia Adamson, MRW, ACRW, CCM, CEIP, JCTC, CCMC; Campbell, CA*

**38**

**ROGER ARNOLD**

466 Geneva Street
San Rafael, CA 90000

(555) 555-5555
rarnold@isp.com

---

February 28, 2010

Ms. Deborah Jacobsen
Vice President, Corporate Security
Megacorp Enterprises
1111 Allen Road
San Francisco, CA 94000

Dear Ms. Jacobsen:

Could you use a law enforcement management professional with a successful track record in security program planning, implementation, and operation, as well as a reputation for effective leadership and exceptional team-building? If so, I believe you will find the enclosed résumé worth a close look.

Throughout my law enforcement / security career, I have focused on empowering my subordinates to succeed by encouraging them to develop their strengths and grow professionally. In many cases in which individuals were dissatisfied, I resolved the underlying problems and turned their attitudes around. This approach consistently produces highly effective, supportive teams under my command.

Prior to my current work in the executive protection field, I managed up to 250 police officers and 50–100 civilians as a Watch Commander, Division Commander, and SWAT Team leader with the Haslett County Sheriff's Department. I also managed custodial facilities that housed more than 3,000 inmates and dealt frequently with operational issues that included budgets, staffing, and scheduling. As president of the Deputy Sheriffs' Association, I successfully negotiated several union contracts and resolved a variety of personnel problems.

In addition to becoming a Certified Executive Protection Specialist, I ensure my continuing ability to handle demanding responsibilities by maintaining excellent physical condition. For example, I compete as an amateur boxer and recently won a World Title in this sport.

Based on my experience and strong commitment, I am confident that I can add significant value to your security function. If appropriate, I would like to schedule a meeting to discuss your needs and the contribution I can make to the success of your organization. I look forward to speaking with you soon.

Sincerely,

Roger Arnold

Encl.

The opening question in this cold-call letter should capture the reader's attention. It is followed up by well-written and well-organized paragraphs that communicate strong qualifications.

# 39

*Writer: Deborah Wile Dib, CPBS, CCM, NCRW, CPRW, CEIP, JCTC, CCMC; metro NY*

Martina Marchesi

42 Laurel Road
Aquebogue, NY 11732
631-555-1010

Specialty Foods Consultant ♦ Fresh Produce Authority ♦ Organics Specialist

June 14, 2010

Mr. Tim Mathesion
Vice President of Operations
The Greenery
2523 Links Road
Chicago, IL 12543

RE: The Greenery Regional Produce Coordinator: Southwest Region

Dear Mr. Mathesion:

You are looking for a dynamic marketer and manager with broad industry experience and the skills needed to bring in the margins necessary for profitable operations and long-term growth. My accomplishments with The Greenery and other well-known industry leaders clearly demonstrate my ability to creatively react to today's rapidly changing natural-foods marketplace while retaining a keen focus on the bottom line.

Mr. Mathesion, although you are probably aware of my work as manager of The Greenery's Southampton location, I'd like to review the highlights of my tenure with The Greenery:

- Converted a negative 6-point contribution margin to a positive 3-point contribution in the Southampton produce department.
- Created a better price image by walking the competition weekly to select "meet or beat price" items, resulting in a stabilized market share from a downtrending market share.
- Improved the bottom line by increasing quality standards, establishing proper receiving and stocking methods, and improving team members' morale and pride in their stores.
- Mentored a team member, Thomas DeMatia, into a successful Southampton produce team leader.
- Selected by Alesia Reynolds to write the new Southwest regional produce training manual.

In more than 10 years in the natural-foods business, I have held positions in all areas of the industry—Produce Manager and Buyer, Store and Display Designer, Store Opening Manager, Specialty and Organics Food Consultant, and Wholesale Produce Distributor. I am accustomed to maximizing productivity and increasing corporate profits through expert cost and inventory control, forecasting, planning, trend spotting, spoilage reduction, display creation, vendor relations, and employee development. In addition, I have a strong understanding of what it takes to get the product from the field to the table.

In an unusual and attractive two-page format, this candidate presents her qualifications for a significant promotion with her current employer. When applying for internal promotions, it's important

**Martina Marchesi** page two

The following accomplishments demonstrate previous experience that I will bring to the position of Regional Produce Coordinator:

- Opened five stores in the past nine years, from a 1,000-square-foot organic produce store to a 20,000-square-foot full-service natural-foods store.
- Learned to recognize, create, and uphold the highest standards through work in the Bay Area, New York City, and the Hamptons, all among the most competitive and discriminating regions in the United States.
- Worked with some of the best distributors in the world through two years of employment in the Seattle Produce Terminal.
- Developed an appreciation for the freshest food and the art of selling into the customers' hands through several summers running farmers' markets and farm stands in San Francisco and Southampton.
- Continually trained staff in leading-edge and classic whole-foods marketing, display, and operations styles and techniques.
- Consistently built loyal customer base by hands-on sales techniques, impeccable standards and quality, enticing displays, fair pricing, educational events, and personal service.

Mr. Mathesion, as an industry veteran, I have long respected The Greenery for its market leadership, sound operations, value orientation, and presentation standards. Now that I work with The Greenery, I'm continually excited by the company and its goals. I very much enjoy my current position but feel strongly that I am ready to make a more substantial contribution by bringing my industry expertise and my commitment to excellence to the Southwest Regional Produce Coordinator's position. If you feel that my experience and drive can benefit The Greenery in this or other positions, let's talk!

Sincerely,

Martina Marchesi

not to assume that senior managers know everything you've done for the company; spell it out just as you would in a letter to a stranger.

# 40

*Writer: Shanna Kemp, M.Ed., JCTC*

## BRETT KINCAID

421 East Washington
Carrollton, TX 75006
Home: (972) 555-3099
Fax: (972) 555-2561
E-mail: bkin@aol.com

"First, you've got to get the best possible people to work with you." —Norman Brinker

April 27, 2010

Charles Durham
Vice President, Human Resources
Brinker International
725 Ranch Parkway
Dallas, TX 75001

Dear Mr. Durham:

While it would be an exaggeration to say that I can leap tall buildings in a single bound, or restore the safety of humanity with a "mighty heigh-ho Silver," it would be perfectly accurate to say that I am the best possible person to add to Brinker's research and development team.

Mr. Brinker's philosophies on hiring the best people and creating strong teams of employees have resulted in repeated success. He has discovered that it is imperative that the people you work with are inwardly motivated, have a "can-do" attitude, and are enthusiastic and energetic. Using those words to describe me would not be an exaggeration.

As you can see from my enclosed resume, I have a strong history of successfully building new business and developing new products. My success stems from my love for the work and my ability to create strong teams of employees and develop personal relationships with my business allies.

Like Mr. Brinker, I believe a job should be challenging and fun. I am ready for a new challenge and would like to find it at Brinker International. As you read my enclosed resume, you will not find a superhero, but you will find an outstanding employee and leader, ready to take the next step, work hard, have fun, and make superhuman efforts toward success.

It will be a pleasure to meet with you at your convenience to discuss my credentials in detail. I can be reached at the above numbers when you are ready to set up a time to meet. I look forward to your call.

Sincerely,

Brett Kincaid

Enclosure

The quote that starts this letter is particularly effective because the person being quoted is the founder of the company to which the job seeker is applying. The "superhero" theme mentioned in the first paragraph is used effectively in the closing.

**41**

*Writer: Kirsten Dixson, CPBS, JCTC; Exeter, NH*

**Julie H. May**

411 Meadow Lane
Yonkers, NY 10709
914-555-6666 res./msg.
914-555-7777 fax
bestteacher@aol.com

June 28, 2010

Dr. William Lewis
Principal
P.S. 42
Tuckahoe, NY 10707

Dear Dr. Lewis:

I noted with interest your June 13, 2010, advertisement in the *New York Times* for a **Grade 2 Teacher** for a leave replacement. As a certified teacher with experience teaching this grade level and firsthand knowledge of P.S. 42 through extensive volunteer activities, I believe that I am an excellent candidate for this position.

I understand that you need someone who is self-directed and who possesses the necessary qualities for managing another teacher's class—flexibility, good humor, rapport with parents, familiarity with the school culture, and the ability to go beyond the lesson plans in accordance with meeting the current needs. At this point, I welcome the challenge of making a positive impact on the minds of elementary-school–aged children. I am committed to achieving this goal through ongoing professional development to learn the latest effective teaching methods.

I have enclosed my resume to provide more information on my strengths and career achievements. I am also open to other opportunities in the school. If, after reviewing my material, you believe that there is a match, please call me. Thank you for your consideration.

Sincerely,

Julie H. May

Enclosure

In an attractive format, this letter does an excellent job of responding to the specific qualifications listed in the job advertisement.

# 42

*Writer: Christine Ferguson, CPRW*

**SHARON A. ROBINSON**

10 Hone Street
Bronx, NY 10452

sharonrob@hotmail.com

Telephone/Fax
(718) 555-8382

April 17, 2010

Michael Thomas
Human Resource Director
National Insurance Company
18 Madison Avenue
New York, NY 10022

Dear Mr. Thomas:

As a longstanding member of the 49th District Community Committee, I have had the distinct pleasure of communicating with you in the course of conducting business with Cable Company.

I am writing to you because, after many years serving the community, I have decided to use some of my capabilities in a corporate setting. Following is an overview of my skills and background:

- **Administration.** More than 12 years of experience as CEO of the Community Affairs Organization—reduced operational costs, raised funds, and administered daily activities.
- **Sales and Marketing.** Successfully procured donations for scholarships; sold advertising space; generated ticket sales for numerous events. Developed ministry's mailing list from nil to virtually 900 names.
- **Staff Training and Supervision.** Supervised corporate and volunteer staff.
- **Program Development.** Crafted well-received events; workshops; and financial, social, and recreational programs.

I have watched Cable Company become a leader in the telecommunications industry and would be honored to contribute to its growth and success. I am confident my skills and background can help achieve this. I genuinely appreciate your time and help and look forward to hearing from you.

Sincerely,

Sharon A. Robinson

To make a connection with the person to whom she's writing, this job seeker uses a "self-referral" technique—she mentions a prior association and then relates that experience to the job she is seeking. Her qualifications, well highlighted in bold, lead off a concise list of bullet points.

*Writer: Jean West, CPRW, JCTC*

# 43

*Anna Smith*

***17 Pomeroy Road***
***North Reading, MA 01867***
***978-555-9393 • Fax: 978-555-3834 • E-mail: asmith@email.com***

---

July 17, 2010

Conversent Communications
Attn: Human Resources
90 Maple Street
Stoneham, MA 02180

Re: Sales Careers with Conversent Communications

Would a person with 15 years of sales, marketing, training, and management experience for three Fortune 500 companies interest you? What if that person could couple her experience with the ability to build productive business relationships and effectively interface with all levels of management, staff, and customers? If this describes the professional you want to represent your company, please give me your valued consideration.

I am a consistent, "hands-on" manager who contributes to and supports corporate merchandising programs. I have built strong, effective, and loyal teams who take pride in being the best in the company. A sense of urgency characterizes my management style. I take great pride in getting things done right the first time around.

My résumé provides more details, but some highlights of my experience include the following:

- Launching new products and programs to increase market share, consistently exceeding sales quotas.
- Start-up operations and management of retail sales and service centers.
- Strong management, team building, motivation, and training experience.

My objective is to obtain a position where I can apply my talents, energy, and problem-solving expertise to positively impact a company's growth. I am willing to travel and am fluent in Spanish.

I feel confident that my 15 years of experience in the telecommunications field will be an important asset for your company. I look forward to talking with you soon.

Sincerely,

Anna Smith

Enclosure: Résumé

This cold-call letter leads off with some thought-provoking questions. Then it summarizes qualifications in both paragraph and bullet formats.

# 44

*Writer: Elizabeth Axnix, CPRW, JCTC, CEIP; Riverside, IA*

**Matthew Kincaid**
110 North Knisel Street
Riverside, Iowa 52327
319.354.7822
mkincaid@earthlink.net

February 18, 2010

Xena Marketing Corp.
Attn: Susan Quinn, Director
179 Executive Park Drive
Iowa City, Iowa 52240

Dear Ms. Quinn:

*"According to Darwin's* Origin of the Species... *the species that survives is the one that is able best to adapt and adjust to the changing environment in which it finds itself."*
—Dr. Leon C. Megginson

Fast, fluid, and flexible—isn't that what Darwin *really* meant?

Marketing certainly can be viewed as a survival of the fittest, and I:

**Thrive** on managing the myriad details necessary to propel the ordinary to excellence;

**Relish** the opportunity, and responsibility, to motivate and coach my staff to achieve their potential; and,

**Embrace** the challenges key to demonstrating pride of mastery in marketing quality products to dominance.

My salary requirements are realistic and, given the strengths and attributes I possess, make me an excellent value for your company's compensation dollar. I also realize flexibility is essential and am therefore open to discussing your company's salary range for a professional with my background and business acumen.

Would your organization benefit from these attributes? Please call me at your earliest convenience to discuss my focus on bringing a fresh perspective to the marketing arena.

Very truly yours,

Matthew Kincaid

*Enclosure*

This letter is attention-getting and easy to read, with its short, punchy sentences and paragraphs, an interesting quote, and bold type highlighting key attributes.

# 45

*Writer: Laurie Smith, CPRW, JCTC; Charlotte area, NC*

## Patricia Bates

4983 CLEAR BROOK COURT
FALLS CHURCH, VA 22043
(703) 534-8945
BATES3498@EARTHLINK.NET

June 17, 2010

Mr. James Ryan
Cooper & Associates
1400 Peachtree Lane
Atlanta, GA 30330

Dear Mr. Ryan:

Is your organization looking for a customer service manager who is

- An effective communicator, able to talk to and write effectively for audiences at all levels;
- Determined and persistent...does not back off when the situation gets tough;
- A team player, not easily rattled, confident without self-importance;
- Ever-vigilant for wasted time, effort, resources, or money; and
- Able to develop/implement processes and procedures to keep your company profitable?

If so, I believe my qualifications will interest you. Throughout my 15 years in the direct mail order/telemarketing business, I have consistently created environments, processes, and procedures that spurred my teams to increased productivity, sales, and camaraderie. Serving in diverse roles spanning Credit, Distribution, Customer Service/Telemarketing, and Operations, I played an important part in the growth of a family of companies over 10 years from $1 million to $35+ million in revenues.

I look forward to the opportunity to discuss how I might contribute to your company's growth and increased profitability through excellence in customer service. You may reach me during business hours at (301) 845-2308, or evenings at (703) 534-8945. Thank you for your consideration.

Sincerely,

Patricia Bates

Starting off with a bulleted list of key attributes, this letter captures immediate attention. Then it goes on to summarize experience and accomplishments.

# 46

*Writer: Cindy Kraft, CCMC, CCM, CPRW, JCTC; Valrico, FL*

**SALLY SUE SMITH**
813-555-8765
sallysmith@aol.com

1384 Stone Hill Way, Brandon, FL 33511

February 18, 2010

Mr. Robert Jones
Kline Pharmaceuticals
1803 Lois Avenue
Tampa, FL 33619

Dear Mr. Jones:

A successful consultative salesperson has the ability to develop and nurture long-term relationships. My success in this area is well-documented. My customers will tell you I am . . . efficient and organized . . . a helpful people person with superior follow-through . . . and excellent at building rapport and fostering mutually beneficial relationships. My supervisors look at the bottom line and acknowledge my overall contributions to the company.

Although my résumé is practical in nature, it cannot convey the full level of my eagerness to undertake new challenges. I would like to continue my successful growth in the field of pharmaceutical sales. You will find that I am a rapid learner with a great deal of excitement and enthusiasm in all my endeavors.

I believe that I can make a positive contribution to Kline Pharmaceuticals and look forward to discussing my capabilities in more detail. I am available for a personal interview at your earliest convenience, and will call you next week to arrange a convenient time when we might meet to discuss in detail your objectives and challenges.

Very truly yours,

Sally Sue Smith

Enclosure

Instead of discussing specific accomplishments, this job seeker focuses on core attributes and uses others' opinions to reinforce her statements about herself. Note the aggressive closing—very suitable for someone seeking a sales position.

*Writer: Don Orlando, MBA, CPRW, JCTC, CCM, CCMC, CJSS; Montgomery, AL*

**47**

**WILLIAM CROSS, COLONEL, USAF**
554 Kinchloe Drive
Burleson Air Force Base, Wisconsin 53000
[414] 555-5555 (Office)—[414] 555-6666 (Home)
cross024@aol.com

February 29, 2010

General Marshall Morgan, USAF (ret.)
Chancellor
Gallatin Military Institute
1400 Gallatin Road
Gallatin, Tennessee 37500

Dear General Morgan:

When you look at your organizational chart, where do you find the person responsible for meeting the expectations of your cadets and their families, your instructors and your staff, and admissions officers at leading colleges? Of course, everyone at Gallatin Military Institute contributes to that vital mission. However, I would like to serve as your "expectations multiplier." You call that position Commandant of Cadets. The difference is more than semantic.

For most of my military career, I have been fortunate to pursue my real vocation: molding groups of strangers into capable, confident, educated young people. I love that process because it can be done only by reaching out to individuals. Even today, in my senior position, those people include faculty, staff, students, and even—sometimes—parents.

Today it's fashionable to speak of nearly everyone as a "mentor." And it's politically incorrect to talk about "tough" academic programs. But I have never believed the two were anything but complementary. Instructors at military schools are the best mentors because they hold students to demanding standards—and then provide every means to reach them. It is hugely rewarding to see "unpolished" cadets demonstrate to themselves, and everyone else, that they can guide their education and therefore their lives.

If I could continue molding young minds and bodies into new leaders, I would never leave the Air Force. However, although they have consistently promoted me over some tough competitors, the Air Force must soon send me to positions too far removed from my life's work. That is why I am seeking eagerly to contribute to a private military school. Experience tells me that a good first step might be to explore Gallatin Military Institute's specific needs. May I call in a few days to arrange a time to do that?

Sincerely,

William Cross, Colonel, USAF

Enclosure: Résumé

Transitioning from military to civilian life presents unique challenges. This letter expertly relates the candidate's Air Force experience to the needs of the organization and the position for which he is applying.

# 48

*Writer: Christine Ferguson, CPRW*

**JEREMY N. BROSNAN**

1225 August Road
New York, NY 10100

Phone: (718) 555-1244
Prevent00@aol.com

---

Date

**Proficient Loss-Prevention Expert**
**Committed to Helping You**
**Achieve a Healthier Bottom Line!**

Dear Hiring Manager:

Each year retailers lose an estimated $26 billion in merchandise to shrinkage, primarily through theft and employee error. This means 1 to 2 percent of total sales are lost, and for larger companies, this loss totals in the millions. Some companies find themselves in this predicament because of an ineffective loss prevention program, or lack of one.

**Here's how I can help:**

- Draw on practical experience to readily identify and eliminate unnoticed internal issues and longstanding loss-related problems.
- Introduce profit-enhancing strategies where current system of "checks and balances" fails to catch and reduce employee errors.
- Replace outdated training models with new and effective management techniques to train, build, and lead an improved, intuitive loss-prevention staff.
- Collaborate regularly with internal and outsourced team members to address current problems and anticipate future challenges, thereby decreasing lost revenue year over year.

My background includes four years in loss-prevention management and a meritorious career in law enforcement that spans six years. If you feel your company can benefit from someone with my background and expertise, please feel free to contact me at the telephone number or e-mail address listed above.

Thank you for taking the time to review my qualifications. I look forward to hearing from you soon.

Sincerely,

Jeremy N. Brosnan

Don't be fooled by the brevity of this letter! It is hard-hitting and highly effective. The attention-getting headline and strong first paragraph appeal to the employer's most pressing concern (minimizing financial losses). The bullet points zero in on key qualifications.

**49**

*Writer: Beverly Harvey, CPRW, JCTC, CCM, CCMC, CPBS, CJSS; Pierson, FL*

# JASMINE L. FORESTER

E-mail: jaslforester@gate.net
Fax: (561) 843-2585

Home: (561) 596-7458
Cellular: (561) 362-7519

1518 Rambling Rose Court
Boca Raton, FL 33486

---

October 27, 2010

Frederick Longini
Miami Industries, Inc.
27-A Bayside Avenue
Miami, FL 33160

Dear Mr. Longini:

Dr. Albert Thalheimer recommended that I forward my resume to you in the interest of a sales management position with your company.

Building market share and driving revenues is my main area of expertise. Whether challenged to build presence in new markets, lead sales organizations in highly competitive markets, or create strategic marketing programs to deliver rapid growth, I have consistently delivered strong, innovative results. Most notably my contributions include the following:

- As Pharmaceutical Sales Representative for Pharmacia & Upjohn, I became the top sales performer within 18 months and was promoted to District Manager responsible for eight representatives throughout Southeast Florida.
- As District Manager for Merck & Company, I identified market needs and won support for increased allocations of resources and funding from internal product marketing teams to improve market share in the South Florida area.
- As the top-producing sales representative for Pfizer, I grew the diabetes product line from 33% to 104% of quota and increased three cardiovascular lines 150%.
- As Sales Representative for the *Orlando Sentinel,* I improved revenues and was promoted to Contract Sales Manager within two months, managing its largest national account.

These achievements reflect the core of my career—create strategic market plans, build new markets, negotiate partnerships and strategic alliances, and drive long-term revenue and profit growth. Just as notable are my strengths in organizational development, team building, and leadership.

Although secure in my current position, I am interested in a more challenging opportunity. I would welcome the opportunity to discuss the contributions I can make to your organization.

Thank you for your consideration.

Sincerely,

Jasmine L. Forester

Enclosure

Note how this letter follows the "first rule of referral letter writing"—the name of the referring party is mentioned in the very first sentence. Additionally, the candidate reinforces the referral with strong results that are relevant to the sales position she's seeking.

# 50

*Writer: Meg Montford, MCCC, CMF; Kansas City, MO*

## Ellen E. Palmer

10620 E. 98th Terrace, Kansas City, MO 64134 (816) 555-9999 eep@yahoo.com

March 16, 2010

Mr. U. Zeke
Principal
Alternative Education Center
1000 Harrison
Kansas City, MO 64108

Dear Mr. Zeke:

Although successful in my current position at Franklin High School, the opportunity to contribute to the education of students at an alternative school excites me. My rewards of teaching occur when the light comes on in a student's eyes as he grasps the math concepts I am presenting. Because small groups and individual tutoring situations provide me the most effective teaching arenas, the mathematics instructor position at your institution would offer the perfect medium for my teaching talents.

Traveling and living in other parts of the world have been my good fortune, allowing me to study and interact with other cultures. These life experiences I would like to share with your students. Art history has always been a passion of mine. I have toured the National Archeological Museum in Athens, Greece, as well as the Rijksmuseum and Van Gogh Museum in Amsterdam, The Netherlands. Additionally, I have traveled throughout the United States, visiting museums from coast to coast. With my life experiences, plus the knowledge derived from elective coursework in college, I can develop for your students a cultural course of study. Included in the course would be art history and trips to Kansas City–area museums, plus access to other art-related resources within our community. This could satisfy the culture credit the alternative students need for graduation.

Will you be available next Monday for me to call to discuss my qualifications further? If you wish to contact me sooner, please call me at home any evening at 816-555-9999.

Thank you for your consideration.

Sincerely,

Ellen E. Palmer

Some professions are more "quantifiable" than others; for some, less-tangible qualities are extremely important. Teaching is a good example. In this letter, the job seeker communicates what she would bring to the position—not in terms of results, but in terms of life experiences and teaching philosophy.

**51**

*Writer: Kristie Cook, CPRW, JCTC*

**SHANE J. BAKER**
6741 E. Summit
Pittstown, NJ 08867
908-555-0098 – sjbaker@earthlink.net

---

**GROWTH-DRIVEN DIRECTOR WILL TAKE YOUR DEALERSHIP TO THE NEXT LEVEL**

Your search for a top-flight director is over if you seek someone who can ignite sales, increase OSI/CSI objectives, and commit to your dealership's success. I present to you my resume for your consideration for a position on your management team.

I bring to you and your team:

- More than 15 years of award-winning experience in automotive management
- Dynamic career of consistently increasing sales and improving customer service and quality
- Energy, enthusiasm, perseverance, and motivation
- Proven record in sales, leadership, and management that shines with superior achievements

My key strength is initiating and implementing changes to turn departments around into profit machines. This process starts with building rapport with my employees and colleagues at the onset, motivating others to exceed expectations, and delivering the extra effort necessary to achieve the goals of the department and dealership. I have been commended many times for outstanding performance as both a team player and individual contributor. The awards mentioned on my resume provide evidence of my dedication to succeed.

I am confident that I can make similar contributions to your dealership. My goal is to help you meet your overall objectives in any way I can. I am determined, motivated and excited to make a difference at your store.

I am willing to relocate for the right opportunity—one that provides a challenge; a way for me to make an ongoing, positive impact; and the potential to grow with the dealership. I would appreciate the chance to talk with you to further discuss your needs and goals. Please call me at (908) 555-0098 to schedule a meeting at your convenience.

I look forward to meeting with you in the near future. Thank you for your time and consideration.

Respectfully,

Shane J. Baker

The headline is used very effectively in this cold-call letter written for a specific niche industry. Numerous relevant accomplishments in the body of the letter support the "brag" in the headline.

# 52

*Writer: Mark Berkowitz, MS, NCC, NCCC, CPRW, IJCTC, CEIP*


## Nicole Savarino

P.O. Box 626, Katonah, NY 10536
(914) 767-5555
nsavarino@mac.com

To teach is to touch a life forever!

June 17, 2010

Ms. Helene Kane, Principal
Furnace Woods Elementary School
25 Schoolhouse Road
Chappaqua, NY 10514

Dear Ms. Kane:

I am contacting you at the suggestion of Tony Savastano, a guidance counselor at Blue Mountain Middle School, who felt that my background and experience would be an excellent match for the Kindergarten vacancy at your school. I am well aware that in today's job market, you will find teachers with more years of experience than I have had, although ***you won't find anyone willing to work harder.*** My record is one of solid accomplishments in my teaching assignments.

Review of the accompanying resume will show how well my qualifications match those of the position. Among my qualifications are the following:

- ☒ ***Enthusiastic, high-energy educator*** with proven track record in fostering academic learning and enhancing student creativity. I believe in making learning as much fun as possible.
- ☒ ***Recognized*** by both ***parents*** and ***administration alike*** for ***classroom effectiveness.***
- ☒ ***Proven expertise*** in taking academic subject matter and ***"making it come alive"*** for students through well-planned, hands-on activities that foster development of creative and critical-thinking skills.
- ☒ ***Acknowledged for raising the bar*** in elevating students' standards and ***igniting*** their ***curiosity.***
- ☒ ***Demonstrated ability*** to ***consistently individualize instruction,*** based on students' interests and needs, at the most appropriate level.

I am confident that this background provides the skills you require for this position and that an interview would demonstrate that my expertise would be an excellent addition to Furnace Woods' educational program. I look forward to the opportunity to discuss in greater detail how my experience would benefit Furnace Woods Elementary School. In the interim, thank you for your consideration, attention, and forthcoming response.

Very truly yours,

Nicole Savarino

Enclosure: Resume

Clever graphic elements are attractive and appropriate for this teacher's cover letter. Note how the referring person's name is "dropped" right away to make sure that this letter is not passed over.

# 53

*Writer: Arthur I. Frank, MBA; Flatrock, NC*

## ROY H. HAMILTON

**1513 Lakes Trail, Indianapolis, IN 46234 (317) 555-2254 (317) 221-8907 E-mail: hamil@aol.com**

August 15, 2010

Gloria Baker
VP Sales and Marketing
Regal Worldwide Traders
2575 Carmel Boulevard
Indianapolis, IN 46240

Dear Ms. Baker:

After contributing to the rapid growth and success of several fast-track organizations for 14 years, I am seeking new challenges with an enterprising group in need of someone with exceptional planning, leadership, sales, and marketing management qualities. **Taking command of a sales force... then training, motivating, and driving it to become an industry leader, is my greatest strength.**

As evidenced in the enclosed resume, my experience encompasses all aspects of corporate business development, including strategic planning, systems integration, internal management consulting, resource utilization, and human resource management. My ability to analyze needs and develop unique programs designed to yield a profitable outcome has proven to be one of my greatest assets.

Credited with significantly impacting bottom-line profitability wherever I have worked, I excel at streamlining less-than-efficient or stagnant sales operations. My record of achievements is exemplary, as I have successfully directed and managed a wide variety of assignments while meeting or exceeding projections. **Proactive management enabled me to boost revenues from $2 million in annual sales to $54 million within 5 years,** while serving as the top sales and marketing executive at Crown Marketing Group.

Characterized by others as visionary and decisive, I possess keen instincts and intelligence, am results driven, and have an aptitude for solving business problems. The essence of what I have done for others and what I can do for you as well is best summed up by a thread running through all of my performance evaluations, namely that *"Roy's attitude and aggressive style motivate his fellow workers. He has the desire and drive to be the best at whatever he does."*

Weighing the combination of these factors, I am certain I can be a high-impact player in almost any area of sales management, marketing, and administration.

I know that resumes help you sort out the probables from the possibles; however, I would like to meet with you and demonstrate that, along with my credentials, I have the personality and horsepower suitable for your organization. Be assured your investment of time will be amply repaid.

Sincerely,

Roy H. Hamilton

Enclosure

P.S. ... I would be delighted to share with you a few of the techniques I've applied to boost sales and improve closing ratios irrespective of economic conditions, if you feel your current selling staff needs a shot in the arm.

For sales professionals, measurable results are the most important thing to communicate in both the resume and cover letter. In this letter, boldfacing and underlining make the results stand out. The "P.S." is a highly effective attention-getter in both printed and e-mailed letters.

# 54

*Writers: Jane Roqueplot, CPBA, CWDP, CECC, and Chris Palmer; Sharon, PA*

## Steven A. Daniels

254 State Line Road
Martin's Corners, MD 16133

(724) 555-7223
sdaniels@aol.com

May 15, 2010

District Church of Zion
District Office
Attn: Reverend Howard S. Templeton, *District Superintendent*
884 Northern Pike
Zelienople, PA 16001-8326

Dear Reverend Templeton:

The prospect of working as the Director of the **District Church of Zion Camp** would be the fulfillment of a major goal and vision since my rebirth in Christ. I am submitting my résumé as a statement of my intense interest in achieving this objective.

My past relationship with the camp has been positive and rewarding, and I trust that my energy and enthusiasm for the camp's operation can contribute to the continued success and expansion of the facility. Since a need has been expressed for a proactive director, I am confident I can answer that call and apply my considerable skill and spirit to the future success of the operation, ensuring that this valuable resource will be available for the benefit of future generations. I envision groups of all ages using the camp as a setting for meetings and events founded in and perpetuating Christian doctrine.

My professional experience and skill as a business owner and contractor will allow me to address every physical need of the camp. My administrative experience will allow me to plan and oversee its smooth daily, weekly, monthly, and yearly budgeting and operation. My unfaltering faith will allow me to recognize, protect, and further the most important interest involved—the spiritual.

A personal meeting is an excellent opportunity for us to have a detailed discussion about the benefits I can bring to the camp as Director. I will be happy to provide you further documentation of my background at that time. Please contact me at your earliest convenience to schedule a time and place to meet.

Respectfully,

Steven A. Daniels

Enclosure

Personal qualities can be strong selling points. In this letter to a Christian camp, the writer's faith is relevant and important to highlight, but note that he goes further by including important accomplishments and experience that qualify him for the position.

# 55

*Writer: Loretta Heck; Prospect Heights, IL*

**ROBERT P. BIRNARD**
402 East Maude Avenue
Arlington Heights, IL 60004
(847) 555-7035
rpbirnard@hotmail.com

June 23, 2010

Schneider Lock Company
Human Resources Department
1915 Jamie Drive, Suite 165
Colorado Springs, CO 80920

Dear Sir or Madam:

Creating successful sales programs is more of a challenge than ever before. With the advent of multiple electronic technologies, in tandem with the existing marketing channels, a Sales Manager is faced with unlimited options for business development. My success lies in my ability to evaluate each of these channels, determine the most appropriate mix of sales and marketing tools, and create the campaigns that deliver results.

Throughout my professional career, I have facilitated the strategic planning, development, and implementation of marketing programs designed to accelerate base business while launching the introduction of numerous new products, services, and technologies. My ability to build and lead cross-functional teams of creative design, marketing, and management personnel has been critical to my performance.

I am knowledgeable and comfortable selling and managing in various industries. It is with pride that I possess a selling management style that has given me a unique viewpoint for developing innovative selling presentations for tough, demanding customers. This, along with excellent listening and communication skills, has earned me the reputation for creating a profitable bottom-line situation for both parties.

Now, at this point in my career, I am seeking new professional challenges where I can continue to provide strategic, tactical, and creative sales leadership—as such, my interest in meeting with you to explore opportunities with Schneider Lock Co.

Thank you for your consideration.

Sincerely yours,

Robert P. Birnard

enclosure: resume

The first paragraph of this letter establishes rapport by identifying common concerns and then describing solutions.

# 56

*Writer: Karen Wrigley, CPRW, JCTC; Austin, TX*

## JENNIFER P. KNIGHT

6119 West 91st St., #60 • Overland Park, KS 66210
Home: (913) 555-6126 • Mobile: (816) 555-8432

September 30, 2010

HR—SEM
KC Star
9172 Grand Blvd.
Kansas City, MO 64108

Dear HR Authority:

In response to your ad for ***Special Events Manager*** in the September 27th edition of the ***Kansas City Star***, I have enclosed my confidential resume for your review and consideration. The position described sounds like just the kind of new challenge and opportunity I am seeking. As my résumé will indicate, my experience uniquely qualifies me for this position!

| ***You Require:*** | ***My Experience:*** |
|---|---|
| Revenue and expense goal accountability | **Presently leading organization to be first in company history to hit forecasted sales of $50 million while operating within budgeted expenses!** |
| Vendor, sponsorship, exhibitor sales relations | **Successfully manage contract negotiations and independent contractor relations, including monitoring service performance.** |
| Track record of revenue-producing special events | **Conceptualized, planned, and implemented revenue-producing and PR promotions, including a basketball game event that resulted in a daily sales increase of 20%.** |
| Three years sales and staff management/leadership | **More than 12 years managing sales staffs. Appointed Resource Manager to lead very diverse groups of individuals into productive team members and environments.** |
| Detail oriented | **Selected to oversee all aspects of detail-oriented assignment—Physical Inventory for all Kansas stores.** |
| Able to meet deadlines with limited resources | **Decreased payroll deficit by $7,000 during busiest retail season while maintaining excellent customer servicing.** |
| Able to work weekend hours throughout the year | **Twelve years working weekend and "retail hours"!** |

As my résumé is only a brief overview of my qualifications, I would appreciate the opportunity to meet with you personally so that we may further discuss how I can meet the particular needs of the ***Kansas City Star.*** I will contact you this week to verify your receipt of this information and to arrange for an interview.

***Your consideration is greatly appreciated!***

Sincerely,

Jennifer P. Knight

Enclosure: résumé

The attractive formatting of this comparison list makes it easy to skim, yet it provides substantive information to "sell" the candidate.

**57**

*Writer: Jean West, CPRW, JCTC*

# SUSAN JONES

**819 Beach Boulevard**
**Daytona Beach, FL 32153**
**727-555-2534**

---

October 4, 2010

Victor Prince
President
Prince Media Works
73 Seminole Drive
Daytona Beach, FL 32150

Dear Mr. Prince:

As an experienced manager in several facets of the communications industry, I have the reputation for tackling and completing any project with enthusiasm to achieve corporate goals.

As a highly motivated person with tremendous energy, my goal is to find a position with broader responsibilities where I can put my experience and knowledge to work to benefit a company's bottom line. Please note that I am willing and able to travel outside of the U.S. and am fluent in Spanish.

Having the background, experience, and ability to make a strong contribution in a management position with your company, I would welcome the opportunity to talk with you.

Sincerely,

Susan Jones

Enclosure: Résumé

***What People Say . . .***

◈ *"Today (we) are* ***growing beyond expectations based on suggestions by Susan.*** *She has brought a wealth of knowledge in marketing these services.*

*"She handled* ***high-level executives with professionalism and integrity*** *and* ***received many compliments*** *from other Directors and Vice Presidents associated within the organization* ***on her suggestions and marketing strategies."***

James Weston
New Frontiers Technology

◈ ***"Her creativity*** *in introducing new techniques* ***and her ability to coach her team to peak performance have been a motivation to her fellow managers . . .***

*"Susan has the potential and background to handle a number of management jobs within the organization.* ***She should especially be considered for openings requiring organization and motivational skills."***

Frederick Smith, Director
Cellular Communication
Atlanta, GA

◈ ***"Her hard work, dedication, and leadership skills were invaluable. She is one of the key reasons that the office was so successful."***

Roger West
Manager, Bell Telephone

Notice how effectively the quotes sell this candidate! This letter is well designed, making it easy to read both the letter and the testimonials.

*A Magic Example*

# 58

*Writer: Susan Britton Whitcomb, PCC, CCMC, MRW, NCRW; Fresno, CA*

**TERRI HOLLINGSWORTH**

555 North Peach
Dallas, TX 75555

terrih@earthlink.net

Business: (555) 555-5555
Mobile: (555) 544-4444

December 12, 2010

Ms. Jennifer Carter, CEO
Dami, Vasquez & Lindstrom
555 Sunnyside
Dallas, TX 75555

Re: Your Need for a Financial Manager

Dear Ms. Carter:

***Numbers drive business decisions***—without solid data, planning is ineffective and progress is unmeasurable.

Throughout my career in finance, I have implemented systems that captured meaningful data and enhanced decision-making processes. I am equally skilled at general management functions and offer a solid understanding of the business cycle, from marketing and sales through production and distribution. Minimal employee turnover and high productivity evidence my ability to communicate, motivate, and build teams.

Currently, I serve as the senior financial officer for a Dallas-based manufacturing and distribution firm. At the time I joined the company, it was experiencing a number of financial and internal challenges. One of my first initiatives was to create financial performance-monitoring models for virtually every area of the company. This included the development of formalized budgeting and planning processes, credit and collections policies, and monthly variance reports. I also negotiated favorable loan agreements and monitored loan activity against budgeted projections. The combination of these efforts supported significant financial improvements:

- A threefold increase in operating funds
- A 60% increase in annual revenues
- A 36% increase in collection of outstanding receivables (from 62% to 98%)
- A 30–40% increase in individual customer revenues with the introduction of new customer financing programs

I look forward to delivering similar results for your organization. May we talk at your earliest convenience?

Sincerely,

Terri Hollingsworth

Enclosure

This letter is an effective combination of a strong opening paragraph, "meaty" paragraphs describing relevant experience, and brief, hard-hitting bullet points.

Chapter 11

# Winning Cover Letters for Senior Managers and Executives

## Top 5 Cover Letter Writing Tips for Senior Managers and Executives

1. Be sure your letters are sophisticated in their language and presentation.
2. Highlight your major achievements that impacted the entire company or organization.
3. Use dollars, numbers, and percentages to drive home the value of your contributions.
4. Because your ability to achieve organizational goals depends greatly on other people within the organization, be sure to communicate strong leadership skills.
5. Mention any experience you have that relates to key issues and challenges the company is currently facing—such as rapid growth, recovery from Chapter 11, acquisition integration, e-commerce launch, and other significant organizational challenges.

# 59

*Writer: Laurie Smith, CPRW, JCTC; Charlotte area, NC*

**Benjamin R. David**

**230 Oakwood Circle, Savannah, GA 45452**
**(912) 323-4940 bendavid@comcast.com**

February 21, 2010

Mr. James Baker
President
International Telesales, Inc.
460 Concord Parkway
Philadelphia, PA 11663

Dear Mr. Baker:

In today's intensely competitive consumer marketplace, the ultimate success of any telemarketing operation requires management that can

- Organize a call center or fleet of call centers to draw maximum quality and production from available staff, resources, and databases;
- Instill self-confidence and motivation in managers, supervisors, and sales and customer service staff and train them for maximum achievement in sales and customer satisfaction;
- Clarify and strengthen the organization's core values and principles to facilitate dynamic business growth and profitability enhancement, while keeping the people side of the business strong; and
- Take advantage of the latest call center and Internet technologies to make customer communication quick, low cost, rewarding for all parties, and seamless.

I believe my track record as outlined in the enclosed résumé demonstrates that I can ensure all of the above for your organization. In my current position as Vice President of Operations for an industry-leading telecommunications firm, I have led my team to deliver a 40-fold increase in a key business segment, and more than tripled operating margins through a variety of quality, performance, employee incentive, and process reengineering efforts.

During my tenure as Call Center Director for a showcase telemarketing operation, my team produced more than $25 million in profits on $55 million in revenues over ten years (nearly a 50% profit margin), smoothly transitioned operations from manual to fully automated with no decrease in production, and launched a "package savings" program that increased profit per order by 300%. Immensely successful programs in the areas of employee training, dispute resolution, strategic marketing, and organizational transition/ restructuring were adopted as models company-wide. I have been called upon on numerous occasions to consult internally as well as with telemarketing organizations of major telecommunications and financial industry corporations.

I attribute my consistent success in large part to the ability to build and maintain a principle-centered environment that preserves the company's core values while stimulating growth and progress. Equally important is a strong focus on ensuring positive customer contacts at all levels, both internally and externally. You will find that I am very skilled at developing sound action plans, as well as in oversight of and follow-through on those plans.

I welcome the opportunity to explore my potential contributions to your telemarketing operation's quality, revenues, and bottom line. Thank you for your consideration of my qualifications; I look forward to discussing the possibilities.

Sincerely,

Benjamin R. David

Enclosure

After starting with a list of bullet points that capture the reader's attention, this letter goes on to summarize career achievements that are directly related to those points—and to the organization's bottom line.

*Writer: Cindy Kraft, CPBS, CCMC, CCM, CPRW, JCTC; Valrico, FL* **60**

**EDGAR ALFONSO**

813-555-7245
entrepreneur@usa.net
3455 Oceanside Drive, Palm Harbor, FL 34685

February 12, 2010

Stacy Smith, Human Resources Manager
Barney's Gourmet Coffee
3184 Coffee Lane
Denver, CO 80001

Dear Ms. Smith:

The wise Will Rogers said, "Even if you're on the right track, you'll get run over if you just sit there." Barney's has done an outstanding job of implementing change, innovation, and creativity to become a leader in the 21st century.

My career experience has been as a "change agent," implementing forward-thinking ideas, concepts, and programs that motivate highly successful teams, generate strong and sustainable profitability, and ensure customer loyalty. My past experience includes…

- Providing proactive leadership, with the understanding that when my team is successful we are all successful, allowed me to be effective in spearheading innovative projects and programs that established long-term profitability. Eckerd's first-time entry into the Denver market **generated 110% more profitability** than new stores in existing markets.
- Implementing quality customer service programs that foster long-term customer loyalty. By conducting research and analyzing market data, **we gathered extensive information on the nature of our shopper and what she expected and responded to in the marketplace, and then created an environment to enhance her shopping experience.**
- Analyzing market trends and identifying opportunities that provide long-term profitability. I was able to **position the North Florida region as the ONLY region in the company to exceed its bottom-line profit projections.**

Barney's is well positioned for growth. Managing growth requires expertise in driving change, building highly motivated teams, improving performance, and directing operational efficiency. May I offer my expertise?

Sincerely,

Edgar Alfonso

Enclosure

This letter gets off to a strong start with an effective quote and a tie-in to the company. The bullet points, with bold print highlighting strong numbers, support this candidate's ability to deliver results in several important areas.

# 61

*Writer: JoAnn Nix, CPRW; Van Buren, AR*

## CAROLYN BROWN

62 Rosewood Lane
Houston, TX 77702

*Residence:* (713) 555-3891
*E-mail:* cbrown2@hotmail.com

Dear Selection Committee:

As a **Senior Portfolio Manager** with 11 years of experience in the financial service industry, one of my primary goals has been to follow the advice of Henry Kissinger: *"The task of a leader is to get his people from where they are to where they have not been."* As you will soon learn, one of my greatest strengths is mentoring and guiding my colleagues so they may reach great professional heights. I truly believe in empowering my peers; competent professionals deliver results and enhance a corporation's image.

I joined American Capital Corporation in 2001, advanced to Senior Portfolio Manager in 2003, and have been a valuable resource and critical link between clients, management, and interdepartmental team members. Currently I spearhead an $18 million portfolio comprising 16 complex accounts and manage a staff of 7 professionals. My 10-year career has afforded me an opportunity to gain a wealth of financial/accounting knowledge.

In short, I am a leader both by example and through effective management of individuals and provide financial leadership and guidance to my clients. It is essential that I develop very close relationships with each client to know the intimate details of their financial status to help steer the companies toward financial independence.

I have reached a juncture in my career where I am highly interested in moving up the management ladder and feel it is time to examine other career opportunities. I am most interested in a position that offers additional opportunities for advancement, a chance to continue to mentor and guide my peers, and the ability to use my rich mix of skills. I am an extremely strong manager who is vision-driven, intelligent, aggressive, intuitive, and extremely tenacious! I am considered "as sharp as a tack" by those who know me, and I know that, as a manager, I can add tremendous value to an organization.

If you believe that my qualifications and experience would greatly contribute to your organizational goals, I would welcome the opportunity to introduce myself and my credentials to you in a personal interview. I will take the liberty of contacting your office next week to arrange a meeting. I look forward to meeting or speaking with you soon.

Sincerely,

Carolyn Brown

*Enclosure: Résumé*

Starting with a personal philosophy of management, this letter gives compelling evidence of leadership skills. The language is "executive level" from start to finish.

*Writer: Linsey Levine, MS, MCDP, LMHC; Ossining, NY*

**62**

**Robert Brown**
111 Riverside Drive #12B
New York, NY 10025
Home: 212-555-8943 E-mail: robbro@msn.net

---

April 5, 2010

Ms. Alice O'Riley
President, The Riverside Foundation
2573 Central Park West, Suite 8-B
New York, NY 10021

Dear Alice:

I enjoyed speaking with you on the phone and, pursuant to that conversation, have enclosed my resume.

I'm looking for a unique executive opportunity where I can provide critical management functions—vision, leadership, strategic planning, finance, marketing, administration, legal insight, operations control—to enable an organization to accomplish its goals.

My career in the corporate and not-for-profit arenas has been accelerated based on my ability to deliver results despite financial, market, and organizational challenges. The blend of my business, legal, and financial skills, and the ability to translate vision into meaningful action, has proved successful in the following areas:

- Managing businesses and organizations to turn around performance and achieve full potential
- Developing and implementing long-range plans, including marketing, product, operations, financial, and acquisition/divestiture strategies
- Analyzing and controlling all aspects of operations to reduce costs and improve profits
- Organizing, reorganizing, training, and motivating to improve individual and group effectiveness
- Negotiating favorable partnerships, strategic alliances, and joint ventures

At this time, I am interested in exploring new executive challenges and opportunities where I can continue to provide decisive and effective operating leadership. I would appreciate the chance to meet and discuss your ideas and thoughts at your earliest convenience.

I certainly appreciate your time and consideration and will phone next week to speak with you further.

Best regards,

Robert Brown

*Enclosure*

This is an excellent example of an effective networking letter. To give the reader a sense of how she might be helpful in his search, the candidate provides an overview of his capabilities and current goals. Note how he keeps control of the follow-up.

# 63

*Writer: Nina Ebert, CPRW/CC; central NJ*

## VICTOR JOSEPHS

| vjo@verizon.net | 70 Ellen Drive, Marlboro, NJ 07746 | (555) 758-0448 |
|---|---|---|

January 12, 2010

Box VJ234, Wall Street Journal
545 E. John Carpenter Freeway #400
Irving, TX 75062

Re: Sales Manager—January 10 *Wall Street Journal*

Either I am a talented salesperson and smart sales manager, or I have been very lucky throughout my 20+ year career. Personally, I doubt that luck has much to do with anyone's success.

Inherent management and communications skills are my strengths. I have extensive experience in the areas of profit-and-loss responsibilities, staff hiring, training and development, marketing and account development, and sound decision making. Smart business planning and straightforward management practices have propelled my career.

I hire the right people for the right job, implement a strong business plan, make my expectations very clear, provide excellent training, and track the numbers. I do not micromanage. I build strong teams. (I terminated only two employees throughout my career and remain in touch with all of the others.) I travel to meet my customers in person and am recognized by them for initiating innovative solutions to challenging problems.

My résumé provides an overview of my background. I look forward to the opportunity to meet with you in person to provide you with further insight into my professional value. Until we meet, thank you for your consideration.

Yours truly,

Victor Josephs

Enclosure

This is a rather unusual letter for a sales management professional in that it sells with words, not with numbers. The strong opening will be helpful in catching the attention of the readers, who will probably be inundated with resumes in response to their *Wall Street Journal* advertisement.

*Writer: Kathryn Bourne, CPRW, JCTC*

# 64

**JOSÉ L. GONZALES**

4412 East Springfield Road, Havasu, AZ 84132
Res: (520) 555-7323 Fax: (520) 555-7324
E-mail: lane45@sprynet.com

January 31, 2010

Mr. James P. Purdy, Vice President
Lifton, Inc.
310 Center Parkway Drive
San Diego, CA 95612

Dear Mr. Purdy:

We have read the articles, we have seen the news items on television—the growing Hispanic business and consumer markets are the new frontiers. Is your company poised to enter this dynamic environment? Are you eager to move ahead but not quite sure where to begin? Then we should talk. I can get you where you need and want to be!

Developing and increasing international and national market value is my expertise. Whether the challenge originated with a start-up business venture or with an established company, my successful career in marketing management has led companies to profitability and growth. With an established presence in Mexican markets and knowledge of the Latin American area as a whole, I can be the catalyst for your next major expansion.

As you will see in the enclosed résumé, I have consistently designed and implemented strategies, plans, and actions that have delivered strong and sustainable revenues and profit growth. My strengths include the following:

- Proven leadership skills—evidenced by smooth internal reorganizations and transitions.
- Proficiency and success in multicultural business environments—I am bicultural/bilingual in Spanish and English and highly adept at cross-cultural communications.
- Astute analysis and understanding of market surveys—to ensure growth of both revenue and profit.

My goal is to secure a senior management position with an organization in need of strong and decisive leadership to open new markets. I would welcome the opportunity to discuss the needs of Lifton, Inc., and explore how I can significantly benefit the organization. I will contact you next week to arrange a meeting at a mutually convenient time.

Sincerely,

José L. Gonzales

Enclosure

Appealing to a specific market niche (Latin America), this letter opens strongly and then goes on to sell this candidate based on his capabilities and results.

# 65

*Writer: Lorie Lebert, CPRW, IJCTC, CCMC*

**BRIAN C. COOPERSMITH, CPM**

***Senior Real Estate Marketing & Management Executive***

**1061 QUAILS RIDGE DRIVE**
**WEST BLOOMFIELD, MICHIGAN 48322**
E-mail: **bccoopersmith@aol.com**
Residence: **248.555.6101**
Fax: 248.555.1601

September 25, 2010

David Winston
President
Wolverine Properties Ltd.
252 Creek Road
Bloomfield, MI 48320

Dear Mr. Winston:

In the 1990s, a group of like-minded visionaries and I had an idea for a new business venture. That idea developed into a multimillion-dollar conglomerate with operations in five states and more than 120 properties in a variety of interests. With nearly two decades of strong and profitable property management expertise, I bring experience and wisdom that come from extensive general administration.

Implementing hands-on strategies and providing personal contact, I believe, are key to building successful business relationships. I am effective at establishing and maintaining business alliances as well as developing strategic programs that increase revenue and add value.

Throughout my career, I have experienced full responsibility and leadership of entire corporate real estate, property management, and financial functions. The scope of responsibilities has been diverse and included financial and strategic planning, property analysis, corporate management, and internal administration. Concurrent executive management responsibility involved corporate expansion and sales management.

Currently, I am exploring opportunities that would benefit a company's success and serve as a source of new possibilities. I believe my expertise would be of value to a company looking for effective leadership and direction. The enclosed résumé summarizes my achievements, experience, and other information you will find helpful in understanding my background.

If you are seeking leadership from someone with my qualifications, experience, and track record, I would welcome a personal interview. I appreciate you taking time to review my credentials.

Sincerely,

Brian C. Coopersmith, CPM

Enclosure

Telling the story of his early success is an original and effective opening for this letter. Leadership skills are emphasized throughout.

*Writer: Beverly Harvey, CPRW, JCTC, CCM, CCMC, CPBS, CJSS; Pierson, FL*

# 66

RAYMOND PHRAMPUS
560 Mourning Dove Circle
Lake Mary, FL 32746

Cell: (407) 620-9533
E-mail: tronv@aol.com

Home: (407) 322-9543
Office: (407) 322-9587

July 17, 2010

Gordon Smith
CEO
Consolidated Corporation
75 Biscayne Bay Boulevard
Miami, FL 33162

Dear Mr. Smith:

I am a successful entrepreneur who has developed, marketed, and built four new ventures, plus numerous joint ventures, strategic alliances, and partnerships within the consumer products industry. Combined revenues have exceeded $525 million annually, with my most recent project forecasted to generate $275K in its first-year sales. I have met the challenges of start-up, turnarounds, and high-growth expansions while delivering strong revenue and profit growth.

The wealth of experience I bring to a venture is vast, with particular emphasis on the identification and development of new business opportunities, strategic and tactical planning, new product development and launch, marketing, sales force development, distribution channel development, and the maximization of sales potential domestically and internationally. Just as significant are my strengths in general, operations, manufacturing, and administrative management. My leadership style is decisive, yet flexible in responding to the constantly changing market, economic, and business demands.

Based on my achievements, I have been featured in industry-leading publications as well as the local newspaper citing my innovativeness, industry leadership, and expertise in market growth and penetration, business management, and profitability.

At this juncture in my career, I am seeking the opportunity to transition my qualifications into a high-growth corporation in need of strong executive leadership. Therefore, I have enclosed a brief summary of my career. I would welcome the opportunity to meet with you to determine the contributions I could make to one of your portfolio companies. Thank you.

Sincerely,

Raymond Phrampus

Enclosure

Businesslike and to the point, this letter respects the time constraints of the CEO and immediately gives him information he can use. The candidate's career accomplishments are notable, so he uses them as primary attention-getters and selling points.

# 67

*Writer: Ross Macpherson, MA, CPRW, CJST, CEIP; Whitby, Ontario*

*Robert A. Bertram*

100 Pebble Drive
Banff, Alberta A5B 6D7
Home: (403) 555-7600
Cell: (403) 555-2222
bob.bertram@mac.com

February 7, 2010

Brian Talbot
Executive Vice President
eGrocers.com Ltd.
2200 Brock Street, Suite 2000
Toronto, Ontario
M1N 2N1

Brian,

After all of our voicemail exchanges, it was a pleasure to have finally spoken with you in regard to joining your team as CFO. As promised, I am providing a "scribbled account" of my experience and qualifications in the accompanying résumé; I think you will agree they are an excellent match to your specific current and future needs.

As you may have gathered, I am a results-driven financial and operational executive with a strong entrepreneurial spirit. My particular strengths lie in my ability to create solid and cost-effective foundations, focus on both macro and micro issues, apply innovative thinking, and remain adaptive not only to spot opportunities but also to capitalize on them.

I had an opportunity to sample your grocery service this weekend, and also to review Ted's message on the Internet, and I feel we have a strong connection of values, specifically with regard to your focus on family and customer service. Additionally, the type of innovative and fast-paced Internet/service company you describe is precisely the environment in which I will excel.

I will be in touch within the next 24 hours to follow up and discuss matters further. I am looking forward to receiving my groceries "between 7 and 10 pm—*guaranteed.*"

Sincerely,

Robert A. Bertram

Enclosure

Having already networked with an Internet start-up about its CFO position, this candidate specifically did not want to seem to be "applying for the job"—he saw this as a business transaction, not an application process. The casual and personal tone of the letter reflects his desire to let his personality come across.

# 68

*Writer: Vivian VanLier, CPRW, JCTC, CEIP, CCMC, CPRC; Valley Glen, CA*

## KEVIN JONES

**1234 Pacific Shores Place**
**Malibu, CA 95555**

**Mobile (310) 555-6655**
**kjones@gmail.com**

October 27, 2010

Sabine Muller
CEO
Pacific Traders, Inc.
2723 Ocean Parkway
Malibu, CA 95553

Dear Ms. Muller:

In today's global economy, balancing the technical intricacies of international trade with the complex subtleties of working with diverse cultures and international business protocols is essential to achieving profitable results. ***This is the expertise that I bring to the table.***

I have developed the key strategic alliances required to facilitate the most complex projects—whether it is sourcing artisans in remote locations, managing private-label production processes, or negotiating international credit and shipping terms. My background includes

- More than 10 years of successful import/export experience in diverse areas of consumer products
- In-depth knowledge of import regulations, tariffs, duties, and international trade agreements
- Project and product management strengths
- Expertise in vendor sourcing, manufacturing, distribution, and shipping
- Cross-cultural communication skills
- Well-respected international reputation for integrity and reliability

If your organization is seeking expansion in international markets, I would welcome the opportunity for a personal meeting. I appreciate your time in reviewing my qualifications.

Sincerely,

Kevin Jones

enclosure

This relatively brief letter conveys a great deal of information. First, the candidate communicates his expertise and how this can help a company in today's competitive business environment. Second, he provides "quick-read" bullet points that drive home his capabilities.

# 69

*Writer: Kristie Cook, CPRW, JCTC*

***ROBERT MILLER***
4950 Pierce St.
Olathe, KS 66061
(913) 555-0496
rgmiller@comcast.net

March 4, 2010

Kay Curtis
ERI, Inc.
1345 151st St.
Olathe, KS 66061

Dear Ms. Curtis:

Are you looking for an executive-level candidate with strong skills in turning around revenues and profits, and expertise in the agricultural industry? If so, we have good reason to meet, as I can make a significant contribution to one of your clients. Please find my resume enclosed to review and forward to your clients in need of a professional with my qualifications.

My resume demonstrates my fast-track progress to Vice President, the position I have held for more than five years now. When I took over this position temporarily, the Kansas division was making little money and no profits, and had a 100% annual turnover rate. Immediately I turned around the division, proving to the President of the company that I was the right person for the permanent Vice President position.

In the past five years, I have increased revenues to more than $5 million, and they are steadily rising. The annual turnover rate has dropped to 10%. I have made remarkable improvements to the six-state division in every aspect, including marketing, customer service, employee relations, and operations. I am the only division manager with written revenue goals and an action plan to meet those objectives. Unfortunately, there is nowhere to progress in my career with my current employer.

I seek an opportunity where I can make a valuable contribution to the bottom line of an agricultural company and grow professionally with the organization. If you would like to work with a candidate with my qualifications, please call me at (913) 555-0496. I believe I can help you create a win-win-win situation for your clients, you, and myself. Thank you for your time and consideration. I look forward to meeting you in the near future.

Sincerely,

Robert Miller

enclosure

In this letter to a recruiter, the candidate provides a rationale for his job search and does a good job of appealing to the interests of both the recruiter and his client, the hiring company.

# 70

*Writer: Carole S. Barns*

**EMILY K. LANGSETH**

345 Lincoln River Road ♦ Dallas, TX 75275 ♦ 469 / 455-9101 *(Home)* ♦ eklangseth@yahoo.com

February 29, 2010

Leonard Brown, CEO
Children First
25 Sleepy Hollow Lane
Baltimore, MD 21202

Dear Mr. Brown:

- **Leading** sales and marketing organizations to multimillion-dollar status is my experience.
- **Creating** a network of international sourcing channels is my expertise.
- **Inspiring** multidisciplined teams to deliver their best performance is my talent.
- **Understanding** technology and manufacturing processes and how to leverage them for improved growth, service, and quality is my strength.
- **Providing** unparalleled service to customers is my passion.

This experience, expertise, talent, strength, and passion is what I can bring to Children First as its Vice President of Sales & Marketing.

Currently I am an executive with Crescent Clothes, a leading wholesaler of family apparel with international sales of more than $175 million. In recognition of the significant contributions I've made to the company's growth and bottom line during my 15-year sales and marketing career with it, I was promoted two years ago to Executive Vice President of Sales.

While secure in my position, I am confidentially seeking an opportunity to expand my range of leadership and become part of a company that mirrors my commitment to family. My goal is to work in an environment that is grounded in hard work but acknowledges the value of creativity and humor in boosting productivity and profitability. Children First—with its emphasis on quality and service—is an organization where my ability to manage people, projects, and resources to their highest potential can help guide the transition to your next level of success.

Let me highlight some of the achievements that reflect the quality and caliber of my professional career, as well as bottom-line contributions I have made:

- **As Executive Vice President of Sales,** increased overall sales volume by 24% through product diversification, new account development, exclusive manufacturing sourcing, and hiring top-notch personnel.
- **As Sales Executive,** won a 38% market share of core accounts and increased sales in the Children's Division by 27%.
- **As Product Engineer, Children's Division,** led from my Taiwan base the effort to increase sales 19% in one year.
- **As Production Control Manager,** reduced manufacturing costs 14%.

My strengths lie in my ability to recognize new opportunities, conceive and implement the action plans to capture those opportunities, and negotiate strategic partnerships to drive global market expansion and revenue/profit growth. Equally strong are my qualifications in general management, P&L management, and staff selection and training.

I believe I am the candidate who can take the past and present sales/marketing successes of Children First, grow and expand them, and provide a rich future for the organization, its customers, and its employees. I look forward to discussing in greater detail with you the ways in which my experience and expertise can drive that future. I will call you within the next week to schedule a conversation.

Sincerely,

Emily K. Langseth

Enclosure: Résumé

The matching lists of bullet points—one describing general areas of expertise and the other detailing specific accomplishments—begin and end this letter on a strong note.

# 71

*Writer: Don Orlando, MBA, CPRW, JCTC, CCM, CCMC, CJSS; Montgomery, AL*

CONFIDENTIAL

Shinwell Johnson
4114 Burberry Mews
Malton, Alabama 36000
johnn346@aol.com
☎ [334] 555-5555

Tuesday, 07 December, 2010

Mr. Charles W. Morgan
President and CEO
Topline, Inc.
1200 Ventura Avenue
Suite 1000
Montgomery, Alabama 36100

Dear Mr. Morgan:

On the next pages you will find nine documented capabilities that can add to Topline's success. Each one is complete with quantified results that went right to the bottom line. I would like to put every one of them at your disposal by joining your management team.

My company values what I do. Overall, I've led us to a 63% increase in sales since 1996. And, although I love what I do, and we are growing in our limited field, I miss the challenges under which I thrive. That is why I am looking, confidentially, for new opportunities of mutual benefit.

May I call in a few days to explore how well I might match Topline's specific needs?

Sincerely,

Shinwell Johnson

Enclosure: Résumé

CONFIDENTIAL

The brevity of this letter is one of its strengths. It is focused, hard-hitting, and appeals to the reader's interests. By referring to an attachment in terms of benefit to the reader ("nine documented capabilities that can add to Topline's success"), the candidate piques the reader's interest and encourages him to read further.

*Writer: Deborah Wile Dib, CPBS, CCM, NCRW, CPRW, CEIP, JCTC, CCMC; metro NY*

**72**

**Declan McBride**

**35 East 58th Street, New York, NY 10010**

**phone:** 212-555-1010 **cell:** 212-555-0303 **fax:** 212-555-4404 **e-mail:** declanmcb@aol.com

September 17, 2010

Mr. Thomas H. Clemens
Vice Chairman
Citibank
200 Fifth Avenue
New York, NY 10017

Dear Mr. Clemens:

Roger Davidson spoke with you on Wednesday, September 15th, and suggested that you and I meet. Roger feels that my expertise in domestic and international real estate, corporate finance, and business building might benefit Citibank. I'd like to meet with you and find out.

First, some background:

As a true generalist in my field, I have successfully tackled numerous projects that cannot be pigeonholed into a niche-hiring model. I think and act outside the box, and a company that values profitable problem-solving will value me, for that is what I do best. What I can bring to Citibank is a vast knowledge of real estate and corporate finance that spans 15 countries, 4 continents, and multi-billions of dollars in acquisitions, disposals, developments, financing, and joint ventures for major corporations, governments, and privately held firms.

Everything that I have accomplished in my 20 years in business has demonstrated adding value and problem-solving along the length of the real estate value chain. It would be impossible in a brief letter to discuss all the features of my experience that may engage you. I think you will be interested to know that my credentials include achievements in

- Technology—improving efficiency by process and knowledge management
- Operations—adding value at the physical property level
- Finance—creating value through innovative financing
- Strategy—positioning of companies optimally in relation to key constituents

In addition, I've seen, survived, and thrived in the up-and-downswings of two full market cycles, even developing a $150 million project (521 Park Avenue) that sold out at record prices at the bottom of the market. My career itself has been outside the box—a cross-cultural, cross-border journey that took me from work in my native Ireland, to management of a state-owned real estate fund in Saudi Arabia, to an internationally renowned investment bank in New York City, to running my own firm, to acting as international advisor to ABC News and other entities.

Mr. Clemens, the enclosed information illustrates many of my successes—profitable projects that demonstrate the types of abilities I can bring to Citibank. I would very much enjoy an informal meeting to talk over Citibank's needs and how I might make a difference to the company. I'll be in touch with you this week.

Best regards,

Declan McBride

Enclosures

This candidate successfully positioned his "generalist" background into a deal-making selling point rather than the detriment he had found it to be when he looked at lower-level positions requiring specific "niche" expertise. With this letter, he secured numerous interviews for high-level international financial and consulting positions.

# 73

*Writer: Vivian VanLier, CPRW, JCTC, CEIP, CCMC, CPRC; Valley Glen, CA*

## CHRISTINE STONE

**5555 Valley View Drive** **(818) 555-6655**
**Woodland Hills, CA 91555** **chris_stone@gmail.com**

August 20, 2010

Matthew Taylor
Executive Vice President
The Commerce Companies
2755 Brentwood Boulevard
Los Angeles, CA 90024

Dear Mr. Taylor:

Strong human resources leadership can have a tremendous impact on operating results. By building and managing an effective HR infrastructure, and developing successful productivity, efficiency, quality, and performance management, I have consistently made a direct contribution to corporate goals. Highlights of my professional career include the following:

- Fifteen years of senior-level experience as an HR Generalist providing HR planning and leadership in union and non-union environments across diverse industries
- Implementation of HRIS technology and applications to improve information flow and use in strategic planning initiatives
- Strong qualifications in employee relations with the ability to build confidence and trust between employees and management
- Introduction of loss control, safety, and worker's compensation fraud programs
- Authoring employee manuals to provide employee guidelines in compliance with changing regulatory environments

Most significantly, I have positioned myself and the HR function as a partner to senior management to work together toward producing top-performing workforces able to meet operating challenges. I am currently seeking a new opportunity as a senior-level HR professional with an organization seeking talent, drive, enthusiasm, and leadership expertise. As such, I would welcome a personal interview to explore such positions with your organization. Thank you.

Sincerely,

Christine Stone

enclosure

With concise bullet points that capture her most salient qualifications, this candidate conveys her expertise and relevant experience in a fairly brief letter.

# 74

*Writer: Lisa LeVerrier Stein, CPRW, CEIP, JCTC; Deerfield Beach, FL*

## John Glogau

5000 S. 92nd Street
Boca Raton, FL 33496

Phone (561) 982-1109
johnglogau@mcc.com

February 15, 2010

John Brown, CEO
International Telecommunications, Inc.
12900 Riverside Avenue
San Bernardino, CA 98770

Dear Mr. Brown:

As Director of International Development for ABC Freight Systems, I led a start-up international transportation services division through critical start-up, growth, and operations cycles. For the past seven years, I built international market presence, accelerated revenue growth, and outperformed the competition. Notable achievements include the following:

- Expansion into 47 countries within the first year and 160 countries within four years
- Gross margins in excess of 30% after first year of operation
- Consistent annual growth in sales volume resulting in revenue increases of 25% per year

As Director, I also established an International Customer Service Center and Telemarketing Center. I recruited and trained all staff and played a significant role in developing an automated billing, tracing, and accounting system that significantly improved customer response time.

Complementing my ability to produce sales dollars and lead start-up sales organizations are equally strong qualifications in training and leading professional sales teams. While at ABF, I conducted front-end analysis, researched training needs, and implemented a powerful sales and negotiation training program that helped reduce sales force turnover from 18% to 8.5% in five years.

I lead by example and provide strong decision-making, problem-solving, and project-management skills. In fact, I have never missed a project deadline. If decisive and action-driven leadership are your goals, we should meet. I welcome the opportunity for a personal interview and can assure you that my expertise will be of value in your sales and global expansion efforts. Thank you.

Sincerely,

John Glogau

Enclosure: Résumé

This letter is extremely well written, with an executive-level tone, concise language, and a strong focus on bottom-line results. Numbers included are impressive.

# 75

*Writer: Don Orlando, MBA, CPRW, JCTC, CCM, CCMC, CJSS; Montgomery, AL*

CONFIDENTIAL

JOSIAH AMBERLY

444 Ponder Dr. Midlane City, AL 35000 ☎ [256] 555-5555 josiah@aol.com

November 16, 2010

Ms. Nora W. Morgan
President and CEO
Topline, Inc.
1200 Ventura Avenue
Suite 1000
Montgomery, Alabama 36100

Dear Ms. Morgan:

For more than ten years, I've had full profit and loss responsibility for a manufacturing company. My company's business is making wood products; *my* business is making sales. And I like that part of the business so well, I want to devote all my energies and talents to serving as a senior sales professional.

As a first step, I have attached a "research document" designed to illustrate sales-related performance. In it, you will find more than a half dozen sales contributions to my company's bottom line. Behind the numbers is this personal, professional code that guides all I do:

- A positive attitude is a major sales tool. It makes my company come alive for customers, colleagues, and management.
- A good sales record rests on *tomorrow's* numbers. My goal is to have our customers think of us as the sole source they can't do without.
- A corporate reputation for honesty is the best "cold calling" sales tool.

If my approach to business and my track record appeal to Topline, I would like to explore how I can serve your specific needs. May I call in a few days to set up an appointment?

Sincerely,

Josiah Amberly

Enclosure: Résumé

CONFIDENTIAL

Starting off with a compelling rationale for seeking a sales rather than general management position, this job seeker goes on to highlight sales philosophy and strong results that should capture his reader's attention.

# 76

*Writer: Martin Buckland, CPRW, CJST, CEIP, JCTC, CPEC; Oakville, Ontario*

**PHILLIP TROTTER**
2020–444 Water Street, Toronto, Ontario M7R 1K1
(416) 333-3333
pt@gmail.com

18TH February 2010

Mr. Paul Smith
Director of Human Resources
City of Toronto
666 Bay Street
P.O. Box 213
Toronto, Ontario M5R 2V2

Dear Mr Smith:

*"Success is a journey, not a destination"* is my company philosophy, and it applies to this vibrant city also. The City of Toronto is becoming an increasingly popular place to visit. I am proud to live in and serve my home community in a number of ways: through the medium of television by producing and hosting the *Neighbour to Neighbour* show, as a volunteer with a variety of organizations, and by being selected to officiate as the Master of Ceremonies with our municipality at the "Sound of Music Festival" and the "Lakeside a la Carte."

The advertised position, Executive Director of Tourism Toronto, sounds exciting and fits exactly into my realm of community involvement and spirit. My résumé is enclosed. One of my greatest strengths is the ability to motivate and cultivate support for events, which is a quality this position requires. I am also regarded as an effective communicator, another requisite that enhances my feeling that I should be considered for the Executive Director position.

I would welcome a personal interview to discuss how I can continue to promote the City of Toronto. I appreciate your time in reviewing my résumé.

Sincerely,

Phillip Trotter

Enc.

Obviously, this letter was written just for this opportunity as Executive Director of Tourism for Toronto. It conveys passion for the city as well as strong qualifications for the position.

# 77

*Writer: Diane Burns, CCMC, CPRW, CCM, IJCTC, CLTMC, CPCC, FJSTC, CEIP; Boise, ID*

**John P. Michaels**

**4678 Littleton Way • Chicago, IL 60646**
**Tel: (555) 555-5555 • JPM@yahoo.com**

November 26, 2010

Mr. Andrew Seth
Services Corporation
275 Steffens Drive
Chicago, IL 60612

Dear Mr. Seth:

Distinguished executive experience in Logistics and Transportation Management, an exceptional record of complex issue resolution, and numerous deployments throughout Europe and the Middle East with senior oversight for logistics operations and planning qualify me for consideration with your organization. I have enclosed my resume with brief highlights of experience for your consideration.

Over the years I consistently improved and coordinated various logistical operations:

- Managed, programmed, and estimated all logistical accounts; negotiated contracts; processed earnings; and reconciled automated findings reports
- Held complete oversight for petroleum, oils, and lubricants accountability for bulk and coupon issue
- Maintained warehouses in state-of-the-art posture

My expertise is recognized through superior performance ratings, numerous letters of commendation, and prestigious awards. My skills and experience would be a genuine benefit to your operations; I can provide aggressive and attainable results, and streamlined and efficient operations, training, and executive management. These attributes have been highly sought by logistics managers throughout my military career:

*"Magnificent performance from a truly quality officer."*

*"His technical expertise knows no bounds and has resulted in dramatic improvements in the repair parts supply policy."*

*"His outstanding accomplishments…reflected his unquestionable commitment to precision planning, exacting management and quality staff work."*

*"I would fight to have him assigned to any of my future units."*

You may contact me at the above address or phone number to further discuss my qualifications and how I can best serve your requirements, enhance your operations, and increase your posture in logistics and transportation. I will be happy to provide you with additional information or references. Thank you for taking the time to review my qualifications.

Sincerely,

John P. Michaels

Enclosure

There is little to indicate that this letter is from a transitioning military officer; it does a good job of communicating military experiences in "civilian" terms. The quotes definitely help sell this candidate.

**78**

*Writer: John O'Connor, MFA, CRW, CPRW, CCM, CECC, CFRW; Raleigh, NC*

***JANE J. JOHNSON***

***112 American Way***
***Anywhere, NC 27615***
***janejohnson@internet.com***
***(919) 555-5555***

December 13, 2010

Sarah Allen, Esq., Managing Partner
Rudnick & Wolfe
203 North LaSalle Street
Suite 1800
Chicago, IL 60601-1293

Dear Ms. Allen:

Please review and consider my credentials for an Attorney position with Rudnick & Wolfe.

After much personal and professional career analysis, I am very excited about forwarding my credentials for relocation back to the Chicago area. Currently, I serve with the law firm of Manning, Fulton & Skinner in Raleigh, North Carolina, where I have utilized skills in real property and real estate law and mortgage law to develop a large, highly respected practice.

I feel that my background in business analysis and business consultation with insurance and banking industry companies provides your firm with the opportunity to develop and grow business in these industries. Without reservation, I offer you the highest level of professional and personal commitment.

Some of the key areas where my experience is strongest are

- Property Sales and Acquisitions
- Corporate Analyst/Process Liaison
- Business and Holding Entity
- Leasing of New Properties and Renewals
- Real and Personal Property Loans
- Environmental Problems and Problem Resolution
- Strong Representative Client Base/Professional Industry Leadership

My career history emphasizes significant achievements and transferable leadership performance that will allow me to develop new clients and keep current professional relationships. My salary requirements are $120,000+, depending on compensation package.

Thank you for your time and consideration. I look forward to speaking with you soon.

Sincerely,

Jane J. Johnson

Enclosure

Focusing on areas of expertise within the legal field, this letter is a straightforward business communication. Its lack of a "sales pitch" is very appropriate for its conservative law-firm audience.

A Magic Example

## 79

*Writer: Susan Britton Whitcomb, PCC, CCMC, MRW, NCRW; Fresno, CA*

**CAROLE SCHULTZ**

555 Shell Drake Circle
The Woodlands, Texas 75555

cschultz@earthlink.net

Residence: (555) 555-5555
Voice Mail: (555) 544-4444

September 27, 2010

C.J. Olson
Executive Recruiters, Inc.
555 Southside
Houston, Texas 75555

Dear Mr. Olson:

*"Treat employees like partners and they act like partners."*
Fred Allen, CEO, Pitney Bowes

As a business leader, I believe strongly in giving employees ownership of their work. This empowerment model has been key to my success as an engineering manager, global manufacturing manager, and, most recently, vice president of international business development for a multimillion-dollar tech organization. The enclosed résumé outlines my 12 years of senior management experience, highlights of which include the following:

- **Strategic Planning:** Authored strategies for growth management, turnaround, and market contraction for Data-Tech, Inc. Identified profitable acquisition and diversification opportunities and facilitated negotiations for sale of software division to Fortune 500 company.
- **Growth Performance:** Increased unit sales 25% and captured $25+ million in revenue growth per year, despite shrinking price points. Member of sales closing team for contracts with the top five manufacturers of computer equipment.
- **Profit Enhancement:** Cut costs in major expense category by $10 million through design integration and innovative alliance programs with vendor partners such as Lucent and NEC.
- **Human Resources:** Managed diverse, geographically dispersed workforce of 300+ in R&D, manufacturing, and business development. Unified marketing, sales, and engineering on a global scale. Noted for exceptional team-building, motivational, and leadership skills.
- **Manufacturing:** Oversaw technology manufacturing operations in Asia, Europe, and the United States. Persuaded overseas contract manufacturers to invest $50+ million in capital improvements. Brought 20 new products to market with significant commercialization value.

I'd like to put these strengths to work in another strategic/directional role. Should one of your client companies have need of an executive with my track record, I would appreciate an opportunity to talk.

Sincerely,

Carole Schultz

Enclosure

Writing to a recruiter, this executive relates three areas of expertise and supports them with brief summaries of her achievements in these areas. Her leadership philosophy is communicated in the first paragraph and is enhanced by the quote that leads off this letter.

Chapter 12

# Winning Cover Letters for Technical and Scientific Professionals

## Top 5 Cover Letter Writing Tips for Technical and Scientific Professionals

1. Be sure to spotlight your most significant and most "saleable" technical qualifications as they relate to the specific company to which you are writing.
2. Demonstrate how your technical skills have positively impacted the company's operations, productivity, and financial performance.
3. It is beneficial for technical professionals to cite evidence of "people" skills. Tell how you've worked with teams, communicated with nontechnical people, improved morale, or made contributions other than just technical feats.
4. Relate your technical skills to overall business needs; don't try to sell "technology for technology's sake."
5. Show that you are up to date with technology by using it in your job search. Today, it's LinkedIn, Twitter, Facebook, and other social/professional networking and communications tools; along with online portfolios such as VisualCV or your own Web site and personal productivity tools, such as an iPhone or BlackBerry. Tomorrow, who knows? Be sure employers see that you "walk the talk" of technology.

# 80

*Writer: Janet Beckstrom, CPRW, ACRW; Flint, MI*

6539 Bennington Road
Owosso, MI 48867

**ANDREA S. QUINN**

989-555-4521
andreaq@msn.net

February 23, 2010

Charles Martin, Director of IT
Campanella Industries
3525 Industrial Boulevard
Flint, MI 48552

Dear Mr. Martin:

Three years ago I didn't know a proxy server from a proxy voter, or a wire crimper from a hair crimper. But I became interested in the IT field and challenged myself to return to school, earn a degree, and embark on a new career. That's where I am now—I've finished the first two parts of my goal and now I am looking for my first job in my new career. My resume is enclosed for your review.

As you may know, Baker College has a comprehensive program leading to a degree in Computer Networking Technology with a Microsoft Option. Even my internship coordinator commented on how well prepared I am for someone new to the field. Beginning this summer I plan to take the appropriate certification exams until I obtain the Microsoft Certified Systems Administrator (MCSA) credential.

Beyond the education and training I've received is something a little more intangible—my commitment and motivation. For example, my internship coordinator wrote on my evaluation that "[Andrea] is thorough and relentless in getting problems resolved—and yet with a smile on her face!" I can bring that kind of positive attitude to your organization.

I would appreciate it if you would review my credentials and contact me for an interview. I'm confident that given the opportunity, I can be a valued member of your IT team. Thank you for your consideration.

Sincerely,

Andrea S. Quinn

Enclosure

With a recent degree in Computer Networking Technology but no hands-on experience, this individual used her letter to communicate the value of her education and the strength of her motivation.

# 81

*Writer: Ross Macpherson, MA, CPRW, CJST, CEIP; Whitby, Ontario*

**JASMIT KHANDARI**

4 Riverside Avenue ▪ St. Augusta, Ontario L2L 5X5
(905) 333-4567 ▪ jkhandari@hotmail.com

April 7, 2010

Alison Kostic
Manager—System Development
DataStor Systems
33 Pinehurst Avenue, Unit 12
St. Augusta, Ontario M3N 4P5

**Re: Junior Programmer**

Dear Mrs. Kostic:

Let's face it, basic computer-programming skills are a dime a dozen these days. What truly makes the difference, especially in a Junior Programmer, is professional commitment, the drive to excel, and the ability to apply those skills consistently and contribute to a company's ongoing success. It is exactly this difference that I can bring to your development team.

I am a graduate of Computer Programming at St. Augusta College and am currently working to complete my MCSA and A+ Certifications. Among my qualifications, I can offer you the following:

- **Technical expertise in Windows, Linux, Java, Oracle, SQL, Visual Basic, VBScript, HTTP, FTP, and SMTP**
- **Exceptionally strong in team environments with proven team leadership skills**
- **Advanced communication and client relations skills**
- **Mature and highly professional work ethic—consistent promotion through previous career positions demonstrates a commitment to excellence and an understanding of what it takes to excel**
- **Highly motivated and driven to succeed**

While my academic record demonstrates the technical qualifications I can offer you, my professional and personal achievements demonstrate the type of commitment I can bring to the job. With a successful career behind me—one characterized by consistent promotion and recognition for top performance—and a room full of trophies and awards as a 3rd-degree black belt in karate, I know what it takes to face challenges, work hard, and get the job done. Give me the chance and I'll show you what I can do!

I encourage you to review my attached resume to get a better sense of my qualifications; however, it is in a personal interview that I can best communicate all that I can offer. I would appreciate the opportunity to meet with you in person, and am available at your convenience.

Thank you for your time and consideration. I look forward to hearing from you.

Sincerely,

Jasmit Khandari

*Encl.*

To support a career transition from the hospitality industry to computer programming, this letter emphasizes maturity and commitment to position the candidate above much younger and "greener" competition.

**82** *Writer: Louise Garver, MA, CPRW, CEIP, JCTC, CMP, MCDP, CLBF, CPBS, CCMC, CJSS, COIS; Broad Brook, CT*

**Steve Sanders**
48 Mountain View Road
Croton, NY 56788
(914) 858-9980
stevesand@home.com

February 4, 2010

Re: Applications Support Specialist—Memphis News, 2/3/2010

As a proficient computer professional with four years of experience in software applications design, development, testing, and maintenance for clients, I am particularly qualified for the Applications Support Specialist position at your company.

Currently an Applications Consultant with a company specializing in health care software applications, I offer a solid background in system applications, development, customer support, and project management.

In my present role, I manage the implementation of our clients' nursing applications for client/server and other platforms. Client evaluation, product demonstrations, design/development of application solutions, support throughout the implementation cycle, and on-site client training in system customization and use are my primary responsibilities, as well as system audits. With solid project planning, coordinating, and management skills, I have a successful track record in delivering results within tight deadlines.

In addition, my position involves strong analysis, research, and writing/updating technical documentation for applications. I test, troubleshoot, and maintain software applications on a daily basis, working closely with our QA group. An excellent problem solver, I am able to quickly get to the root of an issue and design a solution. In providing technical support, one of my strengths is to treat each customer as a key account that deserves outstanding service and response.

As part of a team-oriented environment, I also mentor new employees, providing ongoing coaching and training to assist them in professional development. I plan to relocate back to the Memphis area and would welcome the opportunity to join your team. I am confident that I possess the necessary technical knowledge and skills to add value to your company. May we meet to discuss your needs further?

Sincerely,

Steve Sanders

This paragraph-style letter communicates important information in every paragraph. Note the objective—clearly spelled out in the opening paragraph—and the rationale for making a move, detailed in the closing sentences.

# 83

*Writer: Bill Kinser, MRW, CPRW, JCTC, CEIP, CCM; Fairfax, VA*

WILLIAM WASHINGTON

1941 Bluebird Lane, Reston, VA 20194
571.815.0906 ❑ wwashington@email.com

May 9, 2010

Mr. Edward Kennedy
Vice President of Human Resources
Evolution Communications
7101 Innovation Boulevard
Dulles, VA 20101

**SUBJECT: Senior Software Engineer Position**

Dear Mr. Kennedy:

Adaptability, determination, and innovative thinking are the key attributes that have contributed to my success during my last 12 years in increasingly responsible information technology (IT) positions. Through a balanced combination of technical "know-how," interpersonal skills, and leadership initiative, I offer Evolution Communications a demonstrated ability to exceed customers' expectations with products and services that will make their jobs easier, save time, and increase revenue. Because my skills and experience closely complement your requirements for the senior software engineer position, my résumé is enclosed for your review and consideration.

In my current position with Global Telecom, I have played a primary role in improving a number of critical applications. An example of my success in this regard was achieved when I became the key production support person for one of our largest billing applications. I took over this role one week before the monthly production cycle of 20,000 invoices was to be completed. While performing the "pre-run" test, a number of variables changed, including customers and pricing. As we completed the preliminary and actual runs, I kept track of areas for improvement and within two weeks had automated six manual systems.

Recognizing that being an effective IT professional involves more than working with machines, my efforts are focused on making things less burdensome for users and strengthening my team's relationship with our customers. When it comes to problem solving, I am quick to adopt the users' perspective in order to define the human side of the IT equation. In summary, my work is rewarded when my customers are happy because I've made their work easier and less time intensive by meeting their needs through improved technology.

In exploring new professional opportunities, I am eager to repeat and surpass my past achievements in a new environment. Naturally, the possibility of joining Evolution Communications is an exciting prospect. As such, I would appreciate the opportunity to meet with you to discuss your needs and to demonstrate how I can add to your bottom line through innovative IT solutions. Thank you. I hope to hear from you soon.

Sincerely yours,

William Washington

Enclosure

An eye-catching graphic helps this letter stand out, and important skills and traits are clearly communicated in each paragraph. Note the subject line, which calls immediate attention to the reason for writing.

# 84

*Writer: Helen Oliff, CPRW, CFRWCC, CEC; Reston, VA*


## Eugene R. Accent

81 Ferry Street
Minneapolis, MN 55304
etraccent@hotmail.com
Phone: (763) 123-4455
Fax: (763) 123-4456


May 12, 2010

Mr. Terry Ransom
Chief Executive Officer
Global CIO Solutions
1832 East 38th Street
Minneapolis, MN 55407

Dear Mr. Ransom:

***Information technology is a large investment for your company today. Estimates are that companies typically spend an average of 3.94% of their budgets on IT. Are you sure you're getting the best financial and performance return from your company's investment in IT? I can help you optimize your returns.***

I am seeking new career challenges and opportunities with a company where I can get away from the nomadic lifestyle of consulting. Currently, I am a strategic partner with a leading provider of management and technology services to diverse companies worldwide. I consult with clients on strategic IT investments, cost reduction, and effectiveness. Under my leadership, Fortune clients have gained significant improvements in IT speed-to-value and performance, such as

- Approving $300M investments in critical new core systems over 2 years
- Reducing low-value IT projects and enhancements by 15% to 25%
- Increasing utilization of internal IT resources from 50% to 60%
- Reducing IT project schedule overruns by 15% to 20%

Throughout my career, I have held various positions in IT—including sales, management, consulting, and strategy—and have worked with businesses in the financial services, manufacturing, and high-tech industries. I have helped companies improve their business and IT performance and profitability by selling, planning, and implementing new IT processes and systems. Additionally, I have helped IT organizations globalize and shift from traditional to business-oriented service models. Repeated successes demonstrate my ability to communicate, motivate, build, and lead organizations that want to make the changes required to improve their IT value and performance.

I would welcome an opportunity to deliver similar results for your organization. May we talk at your earliest convenience?

Sincerely,

Eugene R. Accent

Enclosure: Resume

Designed to set the stage for a follow-up phone call, this letter starts off with highlighted information that is sure to catch a senior executive's attention in today's cost-conscious environment.

*Writer: Teena Rose, CPRW, CEIP; Springfield, OH*

# 85

## Dorothy M. Rose

5522 Robert Pike, Bedford, PA 15522
Home: (814) 622-1821 ▪ Cell: (814) 622-9191
E-mail: drose@jitaweb.com

March 23, 2010

David T. Ross, CFO
Allegheny Manufacturing
252 Mt. Washington Avenue
Pittsburgh, PA 15235

*"Project Leader with 10+ years of IT Experience, Accentuated with PC, Networking, Programming, Telecommunications, Systems Development, and Data Communications Support."*

**Re: IT Director Position**

Dear Mr. Ross:

For this position, you're seeking a qualified professional with 3 or 4 key ingredients: management, networking, programming, and systems development experience. Am I right? I'll outline how my background "hits the bullseye," so that you can easily see I'm the perfect candidate for this job.

First, I possess in-depth experience as a manager and supervisor. In my current position, serving as team leader, I supervise more than two dozen installation technicians. I guide and assist each tech through all aspects of the installation process, ensuring each customer receives top-quality service and is given the support needed—whether it applies to PC support, networking, programming, telecommunications, or data communications. My management experience stems from the late 1990s and progresses throughout my career—up to current positions with HT Technical Resources and $S^3$ Business Techs.

Second, you're seeking a candidate with intricate knowledge of technical operations. As mentioned above, I serve as team leader for HT Technical Resources along with supervising the teams for HT Technical Programs. Whether managing the team or handling internal administrative processes, I possess extensive knowledge and I've done a great job overseeing a technical operation.

Matching every facet of your job description, I'm a perfect match for this position.

To discuss my qualifications further, or to answer questions, call me at (814) 622-1821 or (814) 622-9191. I look forward to meeting with you. Thanks for giving my request your consideration.

Sincerely,

Dorothy M. Rose

Attachment

The boxed quote—taken directly from the company's want ad—makes the purpose of this letter crystal clear. Throughout, the focus is on showing how closely the candidate matches the company's specifically stated needs.

# 86

*Writer: Jennifer Nell Ayres*

VIVIENNE R. TABERT
*ViviTabert@yahoo.com*

1240 Primrose Court ▪ Clarkston, MI 48347
248.969.9933 Residence

**INFORMATION TECHNOLOGY EXECUTIVE**

April 29, 2010

Charles T. Stanstead
CEO
Midwest Financial Advisors, Inc.
2525 Michigan Avenue, Suite 7-B
Chicago, IL 60601

Dear Mr. Stanstead:

Are you interested in meeting an IT professional dedicated to achieving the goals of your organization, with the ability to adapt quickly to shifting market conditions in an expedited, yet cost effective manner? As these points are critical for organizations to remain competitive and profitable, my successful history at the executive level, managing and delivering high-quality systems, makes me uniquely suited for today's economic environment. I am confident that my leadership and passion to build and direct complementary teams of bright, knowledgeable professionals can benefit your organization.

An overall achievement summary of my career includes the following:

- Established an international software development center in Brussels, Belgium, for the global leading financial firm Merrill Lynch that saved $5.3 million annually.
- Developed a mutual fund advisor system at Bear Stearns, enabling the firm to manage more than $1.7 billion in customized asset portfolios.
- Developed a certificate registration system that enabled Chase Manhattan to save $4 million annually.
- Created a P&L reconciliation system, which saved Merrill Lynch $750K annually.
- Created the first data warehouse at Chase Manhattan containing a complete 15-year history of all financial transactions, including but not limited to trades, commissions, and journal entries.

I am a hands-on manager who enjoys and is experienced in motivating people to excel. I am driven, lead by example, and demonstrate professional integrity in my work and with customers. My talents include a profitable combination of strong leadership skills, technical savvy, and instinctive business insight firmly rooted in client-centered focus and interpersonal dynamics.

Although I understand that a resume cannot fully detail my background, it's a great starting place. Enclosed is a concise synopsis of my career path to date. If you are interested in exploring mutual interests, I am open for discussion.

Regards,

Vivienne R. Tabert

Enclosure

The bullet format is used effectively to highlight impressive achievements with well-known companies in the same industry as the company to which this person is applying. These are sure to catch the reader's eye!

# 87

*Writer: Jean Cummings, M.A.T., CPRW, CPBS, CEIP; Concord, MA*

**Robert P. Barnes, CBCP**
***Certified Business Continuity Professional***

RobertPBarnes@earthlink.net

1434 Madison Boulevard
Orlando, FL 38917

Residence: 954-555-1212
Mobile: 954-555-1212

April 8, 2010

Samuel Ryan, CIO
Global Financial Services, Inc.
495 Central Avenue
Orlando, FL 38917

Dear Mr. Ryan:

Development of a comprehensive, state-of-the-industry business-continuity program is critical to a company's ability to achieve its core mission. Employee safety, shareholder value, corporate reputation, revenues and profits, data integrity, and IT systems—these are some of the corporate interests that an effective business-continuity program is designed to protect. My expertise is the ability to deliver, within a complex multinational organization, innovative business-continuity plans that are integrated with overall corporate strategy and aligned with corporate goals.

In my work as Business Recovery Manager at Morgan Summers Financial Services, I established just such a program. My groundbreaking thinking and writing promotes business-continuity planning as a strategic, business-driven process in which IT plays a supporting role. My contributions helped ensure that the company would mitigate risk, survive potential disruptions, and recover in a timely manner. Achievements included the following:

— Developed and executed business-continuity plans for an organization with $176 billion in assets under management, 40 business units, 800 employees, and 19 different IT systems running 200 applications.

— Promoted my visionary concept of the role of business-continuity planning throughout the organization and achieved buy-in for plan initiatives from 40 business units (including six IT business units) and two disaster-recovery vendors.

— Implemented a multifaceted employee-awareness program to help ensure that employees knew how to implement plans in the event of a business disruption.

I came up through the ranks as an IT professional and earned both my M.B.A. degree and my bachelor's degree in Business Computer Information Systems. As an experienced BCP manager who is a Certified Business Continuity Professional, I am well credentialed for assuming a leadership position in business-continuity planning.

Please contact me if you are interested in my demonstrated ability to help a company mitigate risk and protect critical assets. I look forward to an opportunity to speak with you in person about your business requirements. Thank you.

Sincerely,

Robert P. Barnes

Enclosure

The need to safeguard data and quickly resume operations in the event of a business interruption is on the "hot list" of many companies. This candidate emphasizes his strong background in the emerging field of business continuity.

# 88

*Writer: Deborah S. James, CCMC, CPRW; Rossford, OH*

## WENDELL L. JAMES

1010 Schreier Road
Rossford, OH 43460

wjames@mac.com

O: 419-666-4518
C: 419-345-0000

August 28, 2010

Glenn P. Rossmeyer
Executive Search of Northwest Ohio
894 Vann Avenue
Toledo, OH 43605

Dear Mr. Rossmeyer:

Over the past two years, the telecom industry has gone through turbulent times. The demands to determine the right strategic approach and execute on the chosen strategy have never been higher. If you have a client who is looking for a proven leader to develop a real-world integrated business strategy with a focused view on implementing the necessary steps to achieve the stated goals, I would like to be considered for the opportunity.

My credentials clearly demonstrate my role as a creative problem solver with a focus on real-world business problems. I bring a results-driven leadership style to an organization and a unique ability to blend a market view into a technically focused company. My background includes extensive experience in developing positive working relationships with major suppliers, customers, and partners. Because of my strong industry contacts, I have been able to achieve surprising results with minimal resources.

Briefly, some of my accomplishments include the following:

- **Packaged and sold a midstage telecom company for $257M.**
- **Extensive international experience:**
  - Created and managed a start-up's international operations and sales force in Latin America.
  - Directed a midstage company's international product management, vendor relations, customer education, and type acceptance in Germany.
  - Assisted a Fortune 500 regional telco in its international market entry and operations throughout Europe.
- **Personally handled angel and mezzanine fund-raising for a telecom start-up.**
- **Invented, developed, and rolled out nationwide telemetry data network.**
- **Inventor of 11 U.S. and multiple international patents.**

I am currently seeking a leadership position as the CEO or Corporate Development Director with a growth company. Due to my results-oriented focus, I will favorably consider a position with significant equity ownership or an upside bonus potential. My enclosed résumé outlines my credentials and accomplishments in more detail.

My experience is diverse and my ambition for steering growth and continuous improvement is high. Please call me to schedule a convenient time to discuss client opportunities in more detail. For the record, I am willing to relocate. Thank you for your time and consideration.

Best regards,

Wendell L. James

*Enclosure*

This letter was written to a recruiter. It combines informative paragraphs with hard-hitting bullet points that enable a quick skim of highly relevant information.

**89**

*Writer: Deborah Wile Dib, CPBS, CCM, NCRW, CPRW, CEIP, JCTC, CCMC; metro NY*

# GAYLE M. PATRICK

**INFORMATION TECHNOLOGY SENIOR EXECUTIVE**

September 17, 2010

Jessminda Kumar
Chief Executive Officer
Platinum Technologies
100 Technology Drive North
Woodbury, NY 11797

Dear Ms. Kumar:

Building corporate value through intrapreneurial information technology management is my expertise. Using the IT function to increase revenues, improve earnings, reduce operating costs, and deliver more competitive and sustainable market advantage is what I've done best for more than 15 years while working with global leaders including CSFB (where I am CIO of the retail banking group) and KPMG Consulting.

If this record of accomplishment is what Platinum Technologies values in a leader, I would like to explore the possibility of a senior management role within your information technology group or your core executive team.

My passion for transforming an entrepreneur's drive into effective corporate technology initiatives has generated millions of dollars in cost reductions and efficiency enhancements. I routinely manage staffs in the hundreds and direct multimillion-dollar projects and budgets. I am consistently the number-one selection for high-value projects requiring disciplined management. Prime initiatives include

- Revitalizing a "backwater" server farm organization into a "world class" eBusiness data center.
- Assisting in transforming CSFB into the nation's number-two online banking firm.
- Generating nearly $10 million in productivity enhancements and operational savings.
- Shaping a splintered group of unhappy employees into a cohesive team of top performers.
- Delivering numerous application, network, and system management projects for major clients.

Each of these milestones was achieved using mission-critical leadership abilities that include seeing, understanding, and strategizing the "big picture"… communicating and translating technical jargon and business needs into terms understandable by both business and tech groups… building great teams by respecting and acknowledging individual contributions while motivating the whole… and maintaining a calm and effective management style, even in the face of critical situations or restructurings.

Ms. Kumar, you will find me to be an excellent investment. I offer a breadth and depth of leadership and management abilities that blend corporate goals, customer focus, and team-building skills into win-win results. If you believe, as I do, that a brief fact-finding meeting to determine a mutual interest might be appropriate, let's get together. I will call you next week to set up a time that works with your schedule.

With best regards,

Gayle M. Patrick

Enclosure

**192-23 35th Avenue, Flushing, NY 11358 • Home: 718-111-1111 • Work: 212-555-5555**
**Cell: 212-111-1111 • Fax: 718-555-5555 • E-mail: gayle.patrick@optonline.net**

Note how the bullet points—each only one line, yet containing a wealth of impressive information—break up the paragraphs and immediately pull in the reader.

# 90

Writer: *Debbie Ellis, MRW, CPRW*

## Gary W. McBride

**4114 Burberry Mews**
**New York, New York 10010**
**Mobile (212) 555-5555 • Residence (212) 555-1212**
**gmcbride@syscom.net**

### SENIOR INFORMATION TECHNOLOGY & SYSTEMS EXECUTIVE

**Architectures / Platforms / Software / Networks / Databases / Voice & Data Communications**
**Internet & Intranet Technologies / E-Commerce Technologies / Conversion & Migration**

John Johnson
Management Recruiters International
295 Madison Avenue
New York, New York 10017

**IN RE: SENIOR INFORMATION TECHNOLOGY / SYSTEMS EXECUTIVE OPPORTUNITIES**

Dear Mr. Johnson:

I am a well-qualified **Information Technology and Systems Design Executive,** successful in identifying organizational needs and leading the development / implementation of emerging technologies. With extensive experience in both private and government sectors, I have been highly successful in the conceptualization of effective system design, as well as improving productivity, quality, and operating performance. Presently, I am focused on providing support for a 300,000-seat, multibillion-dollar IT infrastructure management project in conjunction with the U.S. Department of the Navy.

The scope of my responsibility transcends the entire project management lifecycle, from initial needs assessment and technology evaluations through vendor selection, internal systems development, pilot testing, technical and user documentation, and full-scale implementation. Most notable are my strengths in facilitating cooperation among cross-functional project teams to ensure that all projects are delivered on time, within budget, and as per specifications. Highlights of my professional career include the following:

- Led the development of a streamlined eCommerce solution for the Navy/Marine Corps Intranet's (NMCI) Asset Management Process valued in excess of $6 billion.
- Responsible for data modeling, application development, and project management representing $82 million in new revenue.
- Received the *Hammer Award* for "Reinventing Government" and the USAG Surgeon General's *Coin of Excellence* for my work developing full-lifecycle software products.
- Earned the *Commander's Plaque* for setting up the Combat Ammunition System-Base Level (CAS-B) at Holloman AFB while serving in the United States Air Force as a commissioned officer.

Secure in my current position, I am confidentially exploring challenging new opportunities and am therefore enclosing my résumé for your review. My goal is a CTO, CIO, or CKO position where I can affect positive results for start-up, turnaround, or high-growth operations. My current compensation package exceeds $200K, and I am available for travel and / or domestic relocation.

If one or more of your clients is looking for a dynamic, aggressive leader, we should talk. I would welcome the opportunity to speak with you regarding your clients' needs, and appreciate both your time and consideration of my qualifications.

Sincerely,

Gary W. McBride

The heading on this letter—mirroring the resume—is a powerful statement of the executive's expertise and capability. The second-to-last paragraph includes personal and compensation information appropriate to its recruiter audience.

A Magic Example

91

*Writer: Susan Britton Whitcomb, PCC, CCMC, MRW, NCRW; Fresno, CA*

**JOSÉ ROMERO**

555 Skyline Drive
Mountain View, CA 95555

E-résumé: www.joseromero.com

Cell: (555) 555-5555
jromero@aol.com

December 30, 2010

Mr. Victor Petrocelli
Procurement Manager
MajorTech Company
555 Granite Bay Road
Granite Bay, CA 95555

Re: Software VAR Procurement Specialist

Dear Mr. Petrocelli:

Gene Mortillano spoke to me recently about your need for a Software VAR Procurement Specialist at the Granite Bay site. Although I am not actively pursuing a career change, I am very interested in the position for a number of reasons. First, MajorTech's name is synonymous with "best-of-breed" product engineering and technology solutions. Further, the company's reputation for attracting and retaining quality individuals isn't happenstance. In part, it is attributable to MT's commitment to diversity, employee development, mentoring, and performance-based advancement opportunities.

What would I bring to the table? A record that represents a good mix of creativity, drive, intellect, and leadership, along with solid knowledge of OS and Web applications. Highlights of my recent contributions for ABC Services (a software subscription/upgrade outsource company) are these:

- ✓ Supported a 23% increase in revenue and a 32% increase in profit (recent quarter), primarily through development and management of VAR channel programs for software companies and partnership support to UNIX install base.
- ✓ Doubled company's sales with launch of new Web products division as a result of relationship selling and a partnering commitment with industry leaders such as 3Com and Intel.
- ✓ Earned Netscape's Preferred Reseller award, reserved for top-performing groups among 400 reseller partners.

Given my technical knowledge, management skills, and partnership-management strengths, I believe I have much to offer MajorTech as it approaches an exciting turning point. I will be in touch and look forward to learning more about your needs for this position.

Sincerely,

José Romero

The candidate mentions up front that he was referred for the position. Then he follows with specific reasons the reader should be interested in his background and capabilities.

# Chapter 13

# Winning Cover Letters for Career Changers

## Top 5 Cover Letter Writing Tips for Career Changers

1. Let your current career objective "drive" your entire resume writing, formatting, and design process. Focus on what you want to do now and not necessarily on what you've done in the past.
2. Be sure to include keywords that are specific to the profession or industry in which you are pursuing employment. By using keywords that reflect your current career goals, you make yourself an immediate "insider."
3. Place a heavy focus on your transferable skills, experiences, knowledge, and qualifications. Sometimes this requires disentangling those skills from the position in which you acquired them, to clearly demonstrate their transferability to your new career objective.
4. Highlight "alternative" experiences that might be more appropriate to your current career objectives than your past employment experience. Those experiences might include volunteer activities, involvement in community or professional associations, board affiliations, or a host of other activities.
5. Do not feel as though you must include all of your past work experience. Use only what's relevant or that demonstrates skills transferability.

# 92

*Writer: Annemarie Cross, CEIP, CPRW, CARW, CCM, CECC, CERW, CWPP; Hallam, Victoria, Australia*

## PAUL SIMMONS

879 West Lane • Atlanta, GA 30374 • psimmons@hotmail.com • (770) 485-7857 (A/H)

April 24, 2010

Mr. Bob Smith
Chief Firefighter
Metropolitan Fire Brigade
P.O. Box 10268
Atlanta, GA 30374-0268

**RE: FIREFIGHTER POSITION**

Dear Mr. Smith:

Achieving results and proficiently performing the duties of a professional firefighter requires exceptional concentration, team collaboration, and understanding of the complex nature of the job, while explicitly listening and responding appropriately to instructions—our lives and those within the community we serve demand it. I believe my skills, experience, personal aptitude, overall dedication, and passion to serve the community while upholding the professional values of the MFB would certainly be transferable to this role.

My enclosed resume highlights my professionalism, commitment, and proven competencies to which I add the following achievements:

- Served as an active CFA team member for five years in a voluntary capacity, undergoing training and responding and assisting at residential property fires and road accidents.
- Participated at CFA training/information at Statesville, experiencing first hand firefighting techniques such as ladder and hose skills and other complex exercises.
- Commitment to further firefighting professional development with current studies involving Certificate IV in Fire Technology.
- Proactive agent for health & safety compliance with current First Aid Workplace Level 2 Certificate; received numerous "no lost time" records due to zero workplace accidents.

In addition, I add my ability to

- Utilize sound written and mathematical competencies with the successful completion of a Numeracy and Literacy course.
- Administer strong communication, interpersonal, and presentation skills with certification in Public Speaking, and with the proven ability to communicate with people from a diverse range of backgrounds.

I thank you for your consideration and would welcome the opportunity to discuss the needs of your organization and further demonstrate my enthusiasm and commitment towards this role.

Sincerely,

Paul Simmons

Enclosure

Seeking his dream job—as a firefighter—following a career in logistics, this candidate highlighted his relevant volunteer experience and recent training along with highly transferable skills.

**93**

*Writer: Kristin Coleman; Poughkeepsie, NY*

**Alexandra Tamburro**

856 Hillcrest Drive ❧ Poughkeepsie, NY 12603 ❧ (845) 485-1234 ❧ alextam@hotmail.com

June 12, 2010

Ms. Taylor Raine, Superintendent
Arlington Central School District
123 Mandalay Drive
Poughkeepsie, NY 12603

Dear Ms. Raine:

Please accept this letter of introduction and enclosed résumé for consideration of a teaching position within your district. Specifically, I am seeking a secondary position working with students with special needs.

After several years of being an "at-home" mom, I made a decision to complete my education and become a teacher. Making the transition into education was a natural progression for me. While mothering gave me knowledge of child development across school-age years, I have always, separately, had a desire to be a classroom educator. Throughout the years, I have devoted a significant amount of time to the development of young people and have always been actively involved with my own children's school community. Now that I have earned my degree and fulfilled the NYS teaching requirements, I am ready to pursue this new avenue of service to children.

Having a child in the special education program, I am especially drawn to this discipline. I believe that I have a unique perspective from which to draw, and I am sympathetic to children with learning difficulties. As a student teacher, I demonstrated a strong level of commitment to appropriate teaching practices and excelled at providing individualized instruction. I was also successful in finding ways to integrate technology into lessons, keeping students interested and focused, and minimizing disruptions.

By far, my strongest asset is my positive language. Whatever the subject area or approach, I seize any opportunity to encourage children's relationships with one another and always find ways to foster self-esteem and boost confidence levels. Although I am a new teacher, I have years behind me and the maturity that comes with that. My training is current, and I have up-to-date knowledge of the most recent research-endorsed classroom practices.

Thank you for your consideration. I look forward to hearing from you soon.

Sincerely,

Alexandra Tamburro

Enclosure

This candidate makes a very strong case for moving from mom to teacher. Her personal experiences with her own child are included because they are 100 percent relevant to her goal.

# 94

*Writer: Carolyn Braden, CPRW*

**SELENA GAIL COOPER**

2131 Aaronwood Drive – Gallatin, Tennessee 37066

Home (615) 206-4413 – sgcooper@comcast.net

November 1, 2010

Ronald B. Siegel, Esquire
Law Offices of Grosso, Greene & Siegel
135 East Main Street, Suite 210
Gallatin, Tennessee 37066

Re: Paralegal Position

Dear Mr. Siegel:

Today's successful law firm desires to provide clients with maximum value and welcomes the growing involvement of paralegals. In a recent survey of attorneys conducted by a leading legal-staffing service, 61% of respondents said that the increased use of paralegals has reduced costs and 96% praised this practice for its positive impact on client service. As a graduate of the Paralegal Program at Nashville Career Center, I am eager to apply the skills and training I have acquired to a paralegal position with your firm. The attached résumé briefly summarizes my background.

My diverse work history has allowed me to develop many of the skills needed to be a successful paralegal. The nature of my demanding work as a Store Manager with McDonald's taught me the same communication skills, organizational abilities, leadership qualities, and tenacity needed to be a good paralegal. In addition, I offer energy, enthusiasm, solid research skills, and strong writing abilities. You will find that I am well prepared to play a critical role in handling many of the details necessary for litigation support and other projects.

I am confident that my education, skills, and professionalism will be a welcome addition to your legal team, and I believe I will be equally rewarded by the experience I will gain in your law office. Thank you for your time and consideration, and I look forward to a favorable response from you in the very near future.

Sincerely,

Selena Gail Cooper

Enclosure

After completing an 18-month paralegal-training program, this candidate was looking for her first job in this field. She references her prior experience (in fast-food management and operations) to give herself a competitive edge.

Writer: *Peter Hill, CPRW; Honolulu, HI/Shanghai, China*

# 95

**EDWARD KUMAMOTO**
kumamotoed@islandnet.com

P.O. Box 775
Mililani, Hawaii 96789

Home: 808-555-4563
Cellular: 808-555-5457

May 1, 2010

Ms. Janice Glassman
Director of Human Resources
ABC Pharmaceuticals, Inc.
789 Lancing Avenue
San Diego, California 92109

**Re: Pharmaceutical Sales Representative—Zone 12, Hawaii**

Dear Ms. Glassman:

ABC Pharmaceuticals is *Making the World a Healthier Place.* I can help you do exactly that.

Recently I "rode" with a pharmaceutical sales representative here in Honolulu and quickly understood that, in addition to excellent product knowledge, building and maintaining relationships with physicians is key. I offer you the skills and background to handle this job.

My résumé details a proven record of utilizing **communication and presentation skills** in various capacities in both the airline industry and as a member of the media. My **bachelor's degree** is in Journalism and I enthusiastically believe that this complements my communication and presentation skills perfectly.

Your advertisement states that the ideal candidate will have outside sales experience. Although I have not held an outside sales position, I have sold duty-free products on international flights while employed as a flight attendant. Volume averaged between $1,200 and $1,500 per flight, generating revenue in the millions of dollars for the company.

There is one very important piece of information my résumé does not tell you. I was **born and raised in Hawaii.** I took it upon myself to leave the islands, living and traveling extensively throughout the mainland United States and around the world. Through these experiences I acquired the ability to relate to all types of people. Hawaii is a melting pot of inhabitants native to our islands, like myself, and of folks from all over the world. I offer ABC Pharmaceuticals the ability to relate to, and to build relationships with, your physician customers here in our unique island communities.

I look forward to speaking with you soon and will gladly make myself available for a telephone or teleconference interview.

Sincerely,

Edward Kumamoto

Enclosure

Pharmaceutical sales is a very competitive field. This letter makes a strong case for a job seeker who has no formal sales experience.

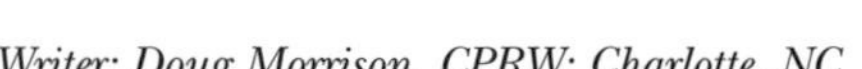

# 96

*Writer: Doug Morrison, CPRW; Charlotte, NC*

**DAVID LIVINGSTON**

3530 Brighton Place
Charlotte, NC 28215

Home (704) 442-3650
dlivingston@aol.com

April 1, 2010

Mr. Charley Cassavetes
Senior Vice President & General Manager, Football Operations
Houston Tuxedos
711 Oil Boulevard, 17th Floor
Houston, TX 77002

Dear Mr. Cassavetes:

At the start of any football season, you'll see a back on one of the teams, a runt of a fellow (compared to the bellicose behemoths surrounding him), keep breaking through the line for long gains. Fans and commentators alike praise him for his deft footwork—giving him *all* the credit for the yards gained.

But under closer scrutiny, you'll notice that this little fellow had very little to do with evading tacklers. His teammates opened the holes for him, and all he had to do was grab the ball and run.

Practicing good teamwork is as essential to business operations—and to the game of life—as it is to on-field play. I believe in the power of teamwork. When an organization pulls together, much more is accomplished.

For this and other reasons, I would like the opportunity to try out for another position—as a coach or a public/community relations liaison with the Houston Tuxedos organization.

As an NFL wide receiver for 12 years (Jets, Packers, and Patriots), and currently a free agent, I am interested in exploring other options. Off-field experience includes substantial volunteer work with numerous community organizations (e.g., Adopt-a-Family, Blue Cross Caring Team, the Children's Hospital, D.A.R.E., M.A.D.D., the Salvation Army, and Special Olympics). In addition, I interned with the F.B.I. for eight years.

I'd like to earn the privilege of playing on your team and would appreciate the opportunity for a personal interview. Together, I believe we could both gain more ground! May I have a tryout?

Sincerely,

David Livingston

What do professional athletes do when they retire? This individual wanted to work for a pro football team in player development, coaching, or community relations. He pulls his diverse experiences together to support his case.

# 97

*Writer: Debra O'Reilly, CPRW, IJCTC, CEIP; Brandon, FL*

**Janet M. Wills**
17 Terryville Avenue
Bristol, CT 06010
**860-555-5555**
janmw@ct.com

June 17, 2010

Mr. Robert Pinewood
Pinewood Lumber & More, Inc.
2003 Century Avenue
Uniontown, CT 06000

RE: Clerical Position in Fast-Paced Dispatch/Operations Office

Dear Mr. Pinewood:

High-quality work, customer satisfaction, and company loyalty have been a strong focus for me throughout my career. Recently, after 28 years with Modern Insurance, I accepted early retirement. A funny thing happened on the way to my retirement party, though: I found that I miss my daily contact with people, the challenge of fast-paced problem-solving, and a sense of service to the local community.

Your job posting on CareerBuilder.com convinced me that such opportunities still exist. The functions I have mastered provide the skills you are seeking:

- ***Clerical and administrative:*** At Modern, I performed clerical functions in several settings, as data entry operator, tape librarian, customer service worker in Data Communications, and, more generally, as Access Control Administrator.
- ***Computer:*** I have utilized MS Office (Word and Excel), PeopleSoft, Oracle, and a variety of company-specific systems and applications to manage, edit, and update data; track workflow; and enhance security.
- ***Quality:*** My work ethic has steadily earned high marks, demonstrated by the regularity of performance evaluations stating, "Exceeded goals."
- ***Dedication to tasks:*** Whenever there was a tough assignment, I was the one called in to "get the job done."
- ***Customer service:*** I served for five years with Modern's Customer Service Focus Group, helping to increase satisfaction levels with both internal and external corporate customers.

In the office, I was known as "the answer person." Whatever the challenge, people came to me for research and solutions, and I never let them down. At home, I have renovated two houses, gaining valuable knowledge of construction, building materials, and tools. (And as a community-theater stage manager, my set building is unparalleled!)

I look forward to discussing your needs and my possible contributions. I'm ready, willing, and able to fit in wherever I am needed, to uphold your tradition of **"Quality & Customer Service, Always."** Thank you for considering both my qualifications and my potential contributions to your company and its legacy.

Sincerely,

Janet M. Wills

This broadcast letter (sent without a resume) describes a multifaceted professional with a lengthy, strong interest in the insurance industry. She is seeking a less-strenuous but still-challenging position after retirement.

# 98

*Writer: Jennifer Rushton, CERW, CARW, CEIC, CWPP; Sydney, New South Wales, Australia*

## SUSAN R. ROACH

98 Ben Franklin Drive
Cherry Hill, NJ 07896

srroach@aol.com

Home: (609) 666-1111
Home Fax: (609) 666-7777

October 4, 2010

Sally J. Thomason
President
Athena Packaging, Inc.
234 Sampras Parkway
Cherry Hill, NJ 07895

Dear Ms. Thomason:

It is with great interest that I am forwarding my résumé for consideration as Creative Manager within your organization. Throughout my career, I have focused on empowering my students to succeed by encouraging them to develop their strengths and grow both academically and personally. With a background in education and learning, combined with outstanding interpersonal and communication skills, I am confident that my qualifications and experience will be of great benefit to your organization.

I am known as a detail-oriented individual determined to excel, with proven organizational, communication, and leadership skills that are necessary to transform concepts into operating realities. With a keen eye for detail and strong time-management abilities, I offer project-administration and communication skills that would transfer to many other environments.

From my résumé you will gather the facts about my success as an educator, but what may not be obvious is the fact that I possess a strong interest in creative design. The qualities that have made me effective as a teacher will, I am confident, help me become successful in a new field: my persuasive style of communication, ability to put others at ease, and persistent dedication to quality results.

Although I have thoroughly enjoyed the challenge of educating young minds and stimulating young children to excel academically, I have reached a juncture in my career where it is time to examine new professional opportunities. I thrive in challenging environments, and it is these qualities that attract me to a highly competitive and exciting career in creative design. My promise is that a meeting will not be a waste of time, yours or mine.

I would welcome the opportunity to discuss how my credentials and expertise can benefit your organization, and I will therefore contact your office next week to arrange a mutually convenient time for us to meet. In the interim, I thank you for reviewing this letter and the accompanying material.

Sincerely,

Susan R. Roach

Enclosure

Teachers seeking to transition to another field face a difficult hurdle. This individual used her teaching experiences as a "plus" for the creative design position she was targeting.

# 99

*Writer: Janice Shepherd, CPRW, JCTC, CEIP; Bellingham, WA*

## Anthony J. Winters

777 East Mountain Way
Wellington, WA 98888
(777) 333-3377
tony@att.com

September 21, 2010

General Manager
Maris Gardens at Cordelia
5511 Columbine Drive
Wellington, WA 98888

RE: Community Relations Director

I enclose my résumé in response to your September 18, 2010, ad in *The Wellington Gazette* for a Community Relations Director. It seems a surprisingly good match for my background, and I would welcome an opportunity to discuss it with you personally.

My considerable experience as a highly successful, respected, and beloved pastor / counselor / teacher, briefly summarized on the enclosed résumé, testifies to my relationship-building expertise—I am confident in my ability to represent Maris Gardens to prospective residents and their families. My work with diverse populations has honed my innate ability to recognize needs and present workable solutions—I can easily relate to your customers. Of course, successful networking with civic and religious leaders in local and state communities, office personnel, administrators, executives, children, and adults is one of my fortes.

With my experience in volunteer recruitment, public speaking, presentations, and training, I have well-developed powers of persuasion—easily translated to sales and marketing skills—and certainly ministry and teaching can be considered long-term-care industries.

I hope you can see the potential here for my making a significant contribution to your business. I will give you a call next week to determine a mutually convenient time to discuss the position further. Thank you for your consideration.

Sincerely,

Anthony J. Winters

enc: résumé

Clergy, too, sometimes seek to transition to another field. This letter clearly conveys how the professional skills this candidate used as a pastor will translate to a role in community relations.

# 100

*Writer: Igor Shpudejko, CPRW, JCTC, MBA; Mahwah, NJ*

**RICHARD KIMBLE**

rkimble@aol.com

12 Norwood Avenue
Oakland, NJ 07420

(201) 739-1458 (H)
(201) 983-4598 (W)

---

February 18, 2010

Tamara Danson
Corporate Recruiter
National Financial Advisors, Inc.
7525 Madison Avenue, Suite 25
New York, NY 10025

Dear Ms. Danson:

After 20 years as a successful small-business owner, I'm changing career directions to follow my longtime desire to be a financial planner. To that end, I am currently enrolled in a CFP program.

Although I have no professional experience as a financial planner, I have frequently advised others on investment strategies. In my own case, I developed an investment strategy for my portfolio that yielded an annual return of 10.5% for a 10-year period ending 12/31/09. I also managed the disbursement of assets for two estates.

I can be characterized as an entrepreneur with sound business judgement, maturity, good sales skills, and high integrity. I enjoy challenges that require learning new skills and interacting with the public. I am steady and patient, having built my own business from the ground up to more than $500,000 in annual revenues.

My goal is an exciting and rewarding position with a company facing new prospects. I am eager to participate in any training process that will build on my skills and provide the knowledge I need to be successful.

I prefer to stay in the metropolitan New York City area but will consider attractive opportunities in the tri-state region.

Sincerely,

Richard Kimble

Enclosure

This letter was written for a professional photographer seeking to become a financial planner. It emphasizes business experience, transferable skills, maturity, and sound business judgment.

**101**

*Writer: Jacqui Barrett-Poindexter, MRW, CPRW, CEIP; Kansas City, MO*

# DOUGLAS PELKEY

**8091 N. 85th Place West**
**Tulsa, OK 74133**

**918-254-1234**
**dougpelkey@hotmail.com**

April 3, 2010

Ms. Jane Mathiesen
Senior Vice President
Marriott International
Marriott NCED Conference Center
2801 East Highway 9
Norman, OK 73160

Dear Ms. Mathiesen:

If you are seeking a forward-thinking, performance-driven, and quality-focused Group Sales Manager who consistently delivers solid results, you will be interested in the experience and accomplishments highlighted in the enclosed resume.

Tenacious in my efforts to transition into the hotel and lodging industry, I am presently networking with key industry leaders to focus my efforts. Additionally, I have enrolled in the Hotel and Lodging Association's Education Institute in pursuit of credentialing to fortify my efforts. Furthermore, my career history demonstrates a determination to exceed quality and customer service expectations, attributes that are key in the hotel and lodging industry.

During my 12-year sales and marketing career, I have made significant contributions to the development and implementation of marketing and sales programs to boost bottom-line performance. Additionally, I am exceptionally people focused and continually "wow" my customers into ongoing relationships. As such, my record of performance includes the following:

- Spearheading premium marketing programs to thwart the competition and expand market share.
- Penetrating difficult-to-access "hierarchical" professionals via my out-of-the-box sales and marketing strategies.
- Delivering triple-digit percentage sales increases year over year.
- Continually analyzing problems, offering solutions, and maintaining a healthy and growing bottom line.

My success in the past and my future successes stem from my strong commitment, work ethic, and desire to become an extremely valuable employee. It is my goal to transfer these attributes to your organization.

I look forward to speaking with you personally so that we may discuss the specific needs of your company and how I can fulfill them. Feel free to contact me at 918-254-1234.

Sincerely,

Douglas Pelkey

Enclosure

This letter was instrumental in the successful career transition of a medical-equipment sales manager into the hospitality industry.

# 102

*Writer: Donna Farrise, JCTC; Hauppauge, NY*

**KIMBERLY BLAKELY**
22 Romeo Drive
Commack, NY 11725
(631) 462-6917
kblakely@optonline.net

---

Dear Sir or Madam:

Reflecting on my professional experience within the insurance industry, it is at this point in my career that I am seeking to pursue my long-term personal and professional goal of a challenging career within **Human Resources.** Let me briefly highlight the skills, values and contributions I will bring to your organization:

- Dedicated commitment to a long and successful career within **Human Resources.**
- Excellent customer service/relations, time-management, troubleshooting, and communications skills, developed through many years in the insurance industry as a **Claims Specialist.**
- Ability to perform independently or as part of a team, building cooperative working relationships among management and support staff in order to meet goals and achieve successful results.
- An energetic, enthusiastic approach with proven success in prioritizing time and resources to attain goals and meet project deadlines.

My personal and professional education, work experiences, interests, and strengths have all contributed to outstanding business achievements. I am accountable for diverse responsibilities, including servicing clients and the general public. My acquired knowledge and experience as a contributing individual in the business world will prove to be a quality that will enhance the goals and standards of any Human Resources department.

Please take the time to review the aforementioned credentials. I firmly believe you will find them to meet the needs of your company, and I am confident my contributions to your organization will prove to be lasting, if given the opportunity. Thank you for your time and consideration.

Very truly yours,

KIMBERLY BLAKELY

Enclosure

This letter very clearly spells out what the candidate is seeking (a career in human resources) and why she should be considered—she shows she knows what's important in an HR role.

# 103

*Writer: Marcy Johnson, CPRW, CEIP, NCRW, CPBS; Story City, IA*

## Rees D. Tyler, Sr.

reesdtyler@aol.com

555 Little Wall Lake Road • Green Rock, IL 61241
Home: (217) 222-2222 • Cell: (217) 778-8778
Office: (217) 266-6622

January 14, 2010

Mitchell O'Rourke, Senior Vice President
Sales, Service & Marketing
Indian Motorcycle Corporation
200 East Fourth Street
Houston, TX 77025

Dear Mr. O'Rourke:

The opportunity to unite common interests and provide organizational structure to a group impassioned by its proud past and bright future is an opportunity that might come along once in a lifetime. With excitement and enthusiasm, I am submitting my resume for your review. A 30-year infatuation with motorcycles, a strong leadership background, and a career as an attorney seem like the perfect fit for your needs to direct and grow the Indian Riders Group.

Twenty years of my career have involved managing day-to-day, strategic, and financial administration of a successful law practice, managing a multimillion-dollar budget for a county attorney's office, and managing a real estate firm. As a member of the local executive steering committee of Boy Scouts of America, I was instrumental in raising more than $400,000 for various organizational activities. But the common thread tying my career together is a fascination with motorcycles. My wife and I both own bikes and ride up to 8,000 miles each year. We have attended the Sturgis Rally, participated in Daytona Bike Week, and ridden to both coasts from our home in the Heartland. We enjoy travel, embrace relocation, and look forward to participating in group rides.

With only 6.8% of 51,000 vintage and new-era Indian bike owners currently participating in the Indian Riders Group, the sky is the limit for building the organization. I want to help lead and unite this diverse group of people and promote the wealth of benefits, including travel discounts, roadside assistance, and new incentives listed on your Web site. Colleagues compliment my "gift of persuasion," and frankly, I have been extremely successful in defending clients as a defense attorney in a large metropolitan area in Illinois. Another accomplishment is prosecuting the first Class A felony in Woodbury County—and winning.

There is a reason some associations are more successful than others. If you are looking for a progressive, efficient Executive Director who can meet your needs, exceed your expectations, and continue the dynamic growth toward your goal of "providing a safe riding environment celebrating the friendship of motorcycling and freedom of the road," please consider my qualifications. Spending the second half of my career building the Indian Riders Group is a calling that I anticipate fulfilling with enthusiasm. Thank you for your consideration.

Sincerely,

Rees D. Tyler, Sr.

Resume enclosed

A high-powered attorney wanted to follow his love of motorcycles into an association-management position in the motorcycle industry. He did his homework and, in his letter, connected his experience and skills to the organization's needs.

*A Magic Example*

# 104

*Writer: Susan Britton Whitcomb, PCC, CCMC, MRW, NCRW; Fresno, CA*

## RHONDA HALLIER

555 Loveland Street ~ Sudbury, MA 01776 ~ 978.495.5355 ~ Mobile: 978.500.5556 ~ rh@email.com

August 20, 2010

Gerald Genner
Zena's Island Day Spa
555 Simpson Lane
Sudbury, MA 55555

Dear Mr. Genner:

What do you look for in an aesthetician? From a customer's perspective, I know what brought me back again and again…

- **Relationship:** An aesthetician who connects with her clients…one with a consultative style who asks questions to uncover needs, avoids offering cookie-cutter skincare solutions, and promotes daily use of products that will keep me looking like I just stepped out of a salon.
- **Holistic Resources:** An aesthetician committed to continuing education and professional development…one who is seen as a go-to person for information on new trends, products, online resources, and more.
- **Results:** An aesthetician who can improve the health and radiance of my skin and, in turn, enhance my overall sense of well-being.

As you might guess, I value these qualities and practice them myself as an aesthetician. In addition, I bring a profit perspective to the picture.

Unlike most aestheticians, I have a strong background in business, previously working for more than a decade as a senior banking executive (in several instances, I was recruited to turn around underperforming regions and led them to become the #1 ranked in the region). This past year, I made the decision to pursue a career transition that would combine my long-time interest in health, provide greater contact with people, and allow me to do what I do best…consultative sales.

Unfortunately, I have visited several salons where my aesthetician missed the opportunity to ask questions and suggest products that would solve my personal needs. With my experience developing national sales strategies and training top sales performers for the financial sector, I'm confident I could not only service your clientele but also boost your numbers for product sales. In addition, my banking background has given me extensive contacts and relationships with high-net-worth individuals in the area—all potential customers for your salon.

I'd appreciate the opportunity to visit with you about potential opportunities and will give you a call in a few days to see how I might bring value to your salon.

Best regards,

Rhonda Hallier

Enclosure

This letter makes a strong and convincing case for a career transition from banker to aesthetician. It focuses not only on fundamental skills, but also on the added value this individual offers.

# The Total Job Search: Thank-You Letters, Recruiters, and Resumes

# Chapter 14

# Winning Thank-You Letters

Ask yourself this question: "When should you send a thank-you letter after an interview?"

If you answered "always," you're right! Regardless of the circumstance, the position, or your level of interest in the opportunity, you should *always* send a thank-you letter. It's proper job search etiquette, and it can give you an advantage in an intensely competitive job search market.

Remember back when you were a child, when your mother forced you to sit down and write thank-you notes after each holiday season? You thought it was a laborious task, and you simply didn't understand why you couldn't just go play with your new toys. Well, believe it or not, and whether your mother knew it or not, she was teaching you an extremely valuable business skill.

> *Tip* Simply put, sending a thank-you letter after an interview is good manners!

People remember other people who go the "extra mile" and put forth the extra effort. When you send a thank-you note after an interview, you are communicating the following:

- I appreciate your time and consideration in interviewing me.
- I am interested in the opportunity. (Even if you're not, you certainly do not want to "burn any bridges." In fact, you want to leave every door open for future opportunities.)

- I am well versed in business etiquette and protocol.
- I know how to deal with people and win their trust.
- I am a good communicator with excellent interpersonal skills.
- I follow through on tasks I have initiated.
- I will put forth extra effort for you and for the company.
- I am determined to get what I want.

Remember the discussion from the Introduction about the history of cover letters and how they have transitioned from transmittal letters to cover letters to marketing communications over the past several decades? Well, the same can be said about thank-you letters. Fifteen years ago, you sent a thank-you letter that communicated two key concepts:

1. Thank you for your time.
2. I'm quite interested in the position.

Here's an example:

Dear Mr. Marsh:

Thank you for taking the time to meet with me last Thursday. I enjoyed learning about Triple X and meeting the other members of the Engineering department. As I mentioned, I am quite interested in your position for an Engineering Manager and look forward to returning for a second round of interviews. I'll wait to hear from Sally about scheduling.

That's it. The letter was brief and to the point. It was simply a formality.

Today, thank-you letters have evolved into what we refer to as "second-tier" marketing communications—letters that highlight your qualifications and "sell" you for a specific position. Consider that your resume and cover letter were your "first-tier" marketing tools. They got you in the door for the interview and, thus, served their purpose. Now, you're ready to go on the attack again, marketing your skills and qualifications, communicating your expertise, and demonstrating your value to that specific organization with your "second-tier" tool—your thank-you letter.

## How Thank-You Letters Can Help You Land a Job

Well-written thank-you letters can be powerful marketing communications that can advance your candidacy in a number of important ways.

### Reinforce Points from the Interview

Thank-you letters give you the opportunity to reiterate the skills, qualifications, and experiences you bring to the company that are directly related to its current and long-range needs.

Your interviewer cannot possibly remember every detail that was discussed during your interview. It is your responsibility to highlight the information about yourself and your career that is most relevant to the position and to the company. Don't ever leave your interviewer wondering whether you can or cannot do something. Spell it out so that your qualifications are clear and readily identifiable.

Here's an example. With the following two sentences, not only did we highlight years of experience and success, we focused on the individual's technical expertise as it relates directly to that company's current needs.

> As you will recall, I bring to your company six years of progressively responsible experience in insurance claims processing, along with award-winning performance in customer service/customer satisfaction. In addition, I spearheaded the implementation of new client/server technology to support our growing infrastructure, much like the project that you are currently undertaking.

### Communicate New Information

Thank-you letters enable you to share new information that was not addressed during the interview. Although you go into each interview with your own agenda of information that you want to share, in some instances you might not have been able to communicate everything you had intended. It might be that the allotted interview time was too brief or the interviewer's agenda did not lend itself to a discussion of a particular topic. Or it might be that you simply forgot to mention something that, in hindsight, you consider essential to communicate. Use your thank-you letter to share that information and bring it to your interviewer's attention. Here's an example:

> One key facet of my career that we did not discuss on Friday is my experience in vendor sourcing. With Chevron, I am responsible for researching and identifying new vendors worldwide to supply both our administrative and field operations. To date, I have contracted with more than 200 vendors for more than $100 million in annual purchases. In addition, I am currently in the final stages of implementing a vendor quality program that is projected to cut 8 percent from our costs.

This paragraph highlights what the candidate forgot to mention during the interview, using concrete numbers to demonstrate the scope of his responsibility. He then follows up with an achievement that communicates two critical concepts: performance improvement (vendor quality) and cost savings.

## Respond to Objections from the Interview

Thank-you letters give you the opportunity to respond to any objections that were discussed, or inferred, during the interview.

Often during an interview, your interviewer will identify one or two concerns she has about your qualifications, experience, skills, and candidacy for the position. This is where your thank-you letter can have a tremendous impact. It provides you with a vehicle to respond to those objections and, hopefully, overcome them.

Suppose you were applying for a position in real estate in a city in which you had never worked. To really excel in that position, you must have local contacts that you can leverage to your advantage. This is what the hiring company is most concerned about in relation to your ability to handle the job. Here's an example of how to deal with that in your thank-you letter:

> You're right. I have never worked in the San Diego market. However, I have worked in other new markets nationwide where I have quickly integrated myself into the local business community and driven significant revenue growth. Furthermore, I have extensive business contacts in San Diego who are more than willing to open new doors and introduce me to the people in town who I need to know.

In this paragraph, the candidate communicated the fact that he has successfully met the challenge of building new markets in his earlier positions. All of a sudden, he's not an outsider; already he has contacts in San Diego.

## Share Relevant Personal Information

Thank-you letters are an excellent vehicle for sharing personal information when, and only when, you believe it to be relevant to the position, the company, or the people you will be working with.

Although job seekers are generally told to refrain from sharing personal information, there are situations in which this type of information can be valuable in facilitating a positive hiring situation. Consider the following example:

> In reference to our discussions regarding relocation, let me share with you that my wife is a Nursing Administrator; therefore, it should be relatively easy for her to find a position in Detroit. If you have any specific contacts or recommendations, I'd appreciate it. In addition, during our interview I noticed several photographs of you on the golf course. I am also an avid golfer and would like to know where the best course in town is. Maybe, on my next trip, we can fit in nine holes.

What has this paragraph communicated? Simply put, it says that the candidate and his wife are quite interested in the position, are willing to relocate, and can quickly assimilate into the community. What's more, the candidate and the interviewer share a common interest. This type of information is obviously most appropriate for more senior-level candidates for whom relocation and spousal employment are primary considerations.

## Keep Your Qualifications on the Manager's Mind

Thank-you letters keep you and your qualifications in the forefront and on the mind of the hiring manager.

Consider this. You're applying for a pharmaceutical sales position and you know that the competition is stiff. There might be perhaps 200 or more candidates for one opening. The interviewer has reviewed all of the resumes and talked with more than 50 people. At that point, everyone blurs together and the interviewer really can't remember who's who.

Just then, your thank-you letter appears on her desk. All of a sudden, not only does she remember who you are, she also remembers your past track record of sales performance, your outgoing personality, and your knowledge of pharmaceutical products. You've just positioned yourself in the forefront of her mind! When you call the next day to follow up, she knows who you are and immediately invites you back for a second round of interviews.

## Distinguish Yourself from Other Candidates

Thank-you letters competitively distinguish you from other candidates, particularly those who do not put forth the extra effort to send a thank-you letter.

We'll use the same scenario as in the preceding section. By sending a thank-you letter, you have not only put yourself in the forefront of the hiring manager's mind, but you've also put yourself ahead of the other candidates for the position. Those who have not gone to the effort of sending a thank-you letter are simply lost in the shuffle and will most likely never hear back from her.

### Build a Relationship

Thank-you letters help you build a relationship with influential hiring authorities.

A typical job search involves many interviews. Obviously, not all of these will result in a job offer. But it is always in your best interest to create a positive image of yourself and your professional capabilities. Who knows where this might lead! It's not inconceivable that you could build a referral network with people who interview you but don't select you for a specific position. Your thank-you letters help you build a relationship and convey a consistently positive and professional impression.

> *Tip* Thank-you letters really do make a difference. Our professional colleagues who are recruiters or hiring managers tell us that they're "astounded" at how few candidates take the time to send a thank-you letter. There are no negatives to sending a thank-you letter—provided that it is well written and relevant to your interview situation. Send your thank-you letters today and give yourself a competitive edge!

## Frequently Asked Questions About Thank-You Letters

Here are some of the most common questions that people ask about writing and sending thank-you letters:

- **How many pages should my thank-you letter be?** Again, as with most other activities in your job search campaign, there are no definite answers and no specific rules. Generally speaking, we recommend that thank-you letters be one to two pages long, depending entirely on the amount of information you want and need to communicate to your interviewer.

- **Should my thank-you notes be handwritten or word-processed?** We recommend that thank-you letters be typed for a professional appearance. Use the same paper, typestyle, and format that you used for your cover letter. Handwriting is difficult to read and does not convey a businesslike image. Although a brief, handwritten note can be a charming and personal touch, do not attempt to convey more than a few sentences by hand.
- **Should I send more than one thank-you note to a company?** When you've interviewed with more than one person, either individually or in a group, take the time to write a separate thank-you letter to each person. And be sure that the content of each letter is unique, because there's a good chance your letters will be shared or added to your interview file. Focus on an area of rapport you developed with each interviewer, and try to connect your letter to what you feel are each person's strongest interests and concerns.
- **How soon should I send my thank-you note?** Send your letter as soon as possible, within a day of your interview. It will arrive while you as an individual are still somewhat fresh in an interviewer's mind and before a final hiring decision has been made. Plus, it's good etiquette.
- **Should I send my thank-you letters by postal mail or by e-mail?** As we've mentioned earlier, e-mail is fully accepted for most business correspondence today. As such, it is perfectly fine to send your thank-you letters by e-mail. In fact, an e-mail letter is easier to circulate than a hard-copy letter, so your thank-you letter might be viewed by more people at the hiring company. And it will arrive at its destination almost immediately. On the other hand, a letter printed on high-quality paper and mailed the "old-fashioned" way has a lot of appeal. For one thing, it's different, and that alone will help it stand out. For another, it presents a more formal appearance and elevates the entire job search process and correspondence from casual to a bit more stately and significant. The bottom line is that you can use either method to send your thank-you letters—just be sure you send them!

## Thank-You Letter Checklist

After you've written a thank-you letter, take a quick moment to review this list. Does your thank-you letter communicate the following?

- Performance
- Success
- Energy
- Enthusiasm
- Personality
- Commitment
- Results
- Interest in the position
- Interest in the company
- Your value to the company
- Your potential contributions to the company

If your letter communicates most of this, great. Proofread it one more time and get it out ASAP. If it doesn't, you might want to go back and rewrite or edit it. Remember that you are writing a marketing letter, so be sure to *sell yourself!*

> *Tip* No two thank-you letters you write will be the same, because no two situations are ever the same. To have impact, thank-you letters must be individually written to highlight what is most significant to that person and that company.

## One Final Recommendation

When you are sitting in an interview and you think of something that would be important to include in your thank-you letter, jot down a quick note—a word or two—to remind yourself. It communicates a positive message if your interviewer sees that you're so interested in the position that you have to take notes! If the situation does not lend itself to note-taking, the moment you leave the interview, find a quiet place and write a few notes to yourself about the company's core issues, needs, and challenges. You'll then know what to focus on when writing your thank-you letter that same day or the next.

## Sample Thank-You Letters

Following are four thank-you letters. Each is quite different from the others in style, tone, format, and message. Each was written for a particular person in a particular situation. Some are traditional; some are more creative. Some are short and to the point; others are much more detailed. These samples give you an idea of what thank-you letters are all about.

*Writer: Carole S. Barns*

**CALISTA MARIE KINGSTON**

12 North Terrace View Drive ◆ Fresno, CA 93714 ◆ (559) 325-3232
lakeview@seanet.com

February 16, 2010

Ms. Wilhelmina Jackson
Director of Training
SunSystem.com
123 Highline Circle
San Jose, CA 95150

Dear Ms. Jackson:

Gracias! Merci! Danke schoen! Thank you!

In any language, my appreciation is genuine for the time you, Linda, and Darrell gave me Tuesday. It's such a joy when a job interview is not only informative, but also filled with interesting conversation. I was particularly impressed with the depth of your commitment to quality training. Obviously you "walk the talk" that knowledgeable employees are critical to an organization's success *and* necessary to continue SunSystem.com's phenomenal growth. I left your offices totally psyched—energized, enthusiastic, and eager to put into play for SunSystem.com a variety of personnel-training and staff-development projects as a member of your team.

Based on my broad credentials in training, coaching, project management, vision-based strategic planning—as well as knowledge of UNIX, Web-based design systems, and HTML—I am uniquely qualified to fill the role of Learning Content Manager. We discussed in detail most of my qualifications on Tuesday. Let me itemize some additional reasons to hire me:

- ***Responsibility for anticipating, designing, and implementing changing training needs.*** In both current and former positions, I created programs to meet changes in procedures, cultures, and economic situations that provided each individual with strong support and overall direction in keeping with company core values, mission, and key deliverables.
- ***Management of personnel.*** Not only do I have experience and skill in managing people of diverse responsibilities, levels, ages, and cultures, I am aware of the special considerations that are needed to guide co-workers in a matrix/project management setting with other managers.
- ***Development and administration of budgets.*** Key to the success of my Education for Success clients has been the attention I've given to developing strong business plans, short- and long-term budgets, and solid P&L statements.

My vision for the Learning Centers is to work with you to develop a team of individuals who are customer-focused, have performance standards aimed at meeting the needs of their constituency, and possess the tools to support that direction and the company's mission and goals. Throughout my career I have been characterized as a decisive business leader who is able to envision and deliver results and who has earned the respect of all personnel in each organization, from those in entry-level positions to members of the senior executive team. It is this strength in leadership and dedication that I bring to SunSystem.com.

Thank you, again, for such an interesting and informative meeting. I look forward to moving to the next step in the selection process.

Sincerely,

Calista Marie Kingston

This letter recaps key qualifications and closes by sharing the candidate's "vision." It is detailed, yet entirely relevant.

*Writer: Mark Berkowitz, MS, NCC, NCCC, CPRW, IJCTC, CEIP*

# *Graham T. Johnson*

*235 Shady Hill Lane*
*Thornwood, NY 10504*
*(914) 747-5555*
graham@aol.com

---

November 2, 2010

Rev. Monsignor Trent P. James, Pastor
St. Bernadette Roman Catholic Church
1127 Main Street
Danbury, CT 06810

Dear Pastor James:

It was a pleasure meeting you and the Director-of-Music Search Committee on Sunday, October 29th. I wanted to take the opportunity to thank you and the committee for taking the time to both interview and audition me.

I found St. Bernadette Church to be an exciting and liturgically rich and active parish and am totally confident that my qualifications are head-on with your position requirements. I am certain that with my education and experience, I would quickly become a valuable asset to the life and ministry of St. Bernadette.

In conversations with committee members, I learned that they believe my expertise would be a welcome addition to the music ministry and staff of St. Bernadette, as they were impressed with the following:

- My knowledge of Catholic liturgy/ritual
- Proficiency in organ
- Proven ability to recruit and direct youth/children, contemporary and adult choirs/cantors

I look forward to meeting with you again so that we may take matters to the next level, as I am convinced that my background and expertise make an excellent match for the needs of your parish. In the interim, thank you for your consideration, attention, and time.

Sincerely,

Graham T. Johnson

The position the candidate interviewed for is with a church. The thank-you letter connects with the unique culture of this employer by evoking more empathy and feeling than might be appropriate for a corporate position.

*Writers: Wendy S. Enelow and Louise M. Kursmark*

**MASON BROWN**
**1024 Miller Park Avenue**
**Baltimore, Maryland 22110**
**Home (410) 757-7981 Email mason.brown@mac.com**

---

March 15, 2010

Fortunat F. Mueller-Maerki
Egon Zehnder International
55 East 59th Street
New York, NY 10022

Dear Mr. Mueller-Maerki:

Thank you for your time on Friday and for sharing such helpful information about the opportunity with Abrams Corporation. In anticipation of our second meeting next week, I have given considerable thought to the position, the expectations of the European parent company, and the challenges inherent in the assignment. To that end, I would like to bring several key points to the forefront:

- I am accustomed to change and growth, a critical factor for this position as outlined in the job description. Most recently, during my tenure as General Manager of Advantage Corporation, I led the organization through tremendous transition with annual growth of more than 24%.
- My expertise in sales, marketing, new business development, and key account management has been a critical foundation for the profitable growth of both Advantage and General Corp. For each, I spearheaded the design and delivery of new product initiatives that consistently accelerated growth and improved financial performance.
- With 11 years of experience in the consumer goods industry, I know the market, the players, and the competition. This will provide Abrams with a tremendous competitive advantage throughout the Americas market.

On a more personal note, I am excited about returning to my hometown of Chicago. I look forward to meeting with you on the 23rd and would be delighted to provide any additional information that will help you establish my fit for the Abrams opportunity. Thank you.

Sincerely,

Mason Brown

Specific success stories, industry expertise, and personal considerations are all used to reinforce this executive's fit for the position. Note that a letter does not have to be very long to be effective.

*Writer: Elizabeth Axnix, CPRW, JCTC, CEIP; Riverside, IA*

# HEATHER CARTER

103 South Burlington, #1 | 641.472.7360 | Fairfield, IA 52556
h.carter@aol.com

March 22, 2010

Mr. Richard Torres
General Manager
Royal Flush Corporation
555 Golden Street
Deadwood, SD 55555

Dear Mr. Torres:

Thank you for your time and hospitality in meeting with me this past weekend. I appreciated very much the opportunity to interview for the general manager position and learn more about your company. Enclosed is a list of my professional references.

The astute business manager bases decisions on in-depth research, empirical evidence, and documented numbers. When I'm faced with making a critical business decision, I certainly use all three tools. However, in making personal decisions, I add one more criteria—intuition. My business sense indicates that my management skills and knowledge of the hospitality industry would easily transition to a general management role with your company, while my sense of intuition tells me that I would be very happy making my home in the Deadwood area.

My decision to relocate to the Deadwood area is equally divided between business and personal. The term "culture shock" was mentioned frequently in the interview. I currently live in a town of 350 people in one of our nation's most rural states, Iowa. My husband and I have researched the suitability of the Deadwood area very carefully through frequent and lengthy visits and, frankly, it is the isolation that attracts us primarily. The economic opportunities are also attractive. The growth in the area's gaming industry has spurred corresponding growth in the hospitality sector, and that's where my expertise lies.

Although my gaming experience is very limited, I have successfully addressed a number of situations from which parallels could be drawn. I've had guests expire in the parking lot, I've assisted law enforcement authorities in apprehending armed drug smugglers (in front of a full lobby, of course!), and I've dealt with hundreds of rabid, unruly, and inebriated sports fans. To my way of thinking, guests intent on playing games of chance do not compare with athletes suffering from high levels of testosterone and steroids! In any event, I am a very quick learner and am eager to expand my knowledge of the hospitality industry.

I fully understand the economic, cultural, and demographic realities of Deadwood. I've experienced its hospitality, and I have calculated the risks and rewards of relocating to the area. You will not make a poor business decision if you hire me, because my business sense tells me that I can strengthen guest and employee loyalty, control variable expenses, and deliver consistent, profitable results for Royal Flush Corporation.

Sincerely,

Heather Carter

Enclosure

P.S.: Doesn't your gut feeling have you wanting me to work for you rather than your competitor?

This letter makes a persuasive case for relocation, attempting to overcome a potential obstacle that was uncovered during the interview. The P.S. is a perfect, attention-getting finish to the letter.

Chapter 15

# Cover Letter Tips and Techniques from Recruiters

At this point, you've probably devoted several hours, if not more, to writing your cover letter. You've read this book, flipped back and forth between sections, written, edited, rewritten, and proofread. Now, you've finally got a letter ready to go. Great! You've got the right marketing materials (your resume and cover letter) and are ready to move your job search full steam ahead.

However, have you considered the changes you might make to your letter if you are sending it to a recruiter and not to a company directly? This is an important consideration because recruiters are often interested in information that might be a bit different from what you would normally submit to a human resources manager at a company.

## Advice from the Recruiters

To be sure that you include the "right" information in your recruiter cover letters, we interviewed several respected recruiters across the country and asked them each to address the following questions:

- What type of information should job seekers include in their cover letters?
- What type of information catches your attention and encourages you to contact a job seeker?
- What type of information immediately disqualifies a job seeker, in your opinion?

- Is it essential that job seekers include salary requirements in their cover letters?
- Are there any other insights you can offer to job seekers to help them write better cover letters?

Following are the responses to these questions. Pay close attention to each recruiter's opinions so that you can translate that information into great copy for your next cover letter.

## Randy Block: Retained Recruiter Information Technology, High-Tech

Randy Block, JCTC, CCMC, and Staffing Consultant
Block & Associates, Larkspur, CA
www.randyblock.com
randy@randyblock.com
(415) 383-6471

Cover letters are a "weird bird" in the recruiting industry. Many, many recruiters simply skip reading the cover letter and go right to the resume. As such, to increase the chance that your cover letter will be read, *keep it short.* It should be no more than three paragraphs and should fit comfortably on one page.

There are basically two types of cover letters that you should send to recruiters. In fact, these letters are often easier to write than cover letters you'll be sending directly to companies. Pay close attention to the "formulas" for each type of letter.

### Position-Specific Letters

*(Use this formula when you're submitting your resume and cover letter for a specific position that the recruiter is trying to fill.)*

1. At the beginning of the first paragraph, mention any third-party referral (for example, "Joe Johnson suggested I contact you…").
2. In the first paragraph, mention which position you are applying for.
3. In the second paragraph, highlight your strengths, skills, experience, and accomplishments as they best fit the position.
4. In the third paragraph, let the recruiter know exactly how you can be reached 24/7.

### General-Contact Letters

*(Use this formula when you're submitting your resume and cover letter for any current or future openings that might be appropriate for an individual with your qualifications.)*

1. At the beginning of the first paragraph, mention any third-party referral (for example, "Joe Johnson suggested I contact you…").
2. In the first paragraph, state the kind of position or positions you desire and that best complement your strengths and skills.
3. In the second paragraph, use bullets to highlight your strengths, skills, and accomplishments.
4. In the third paragraph, let the recruiter know exactly how you can be reached 24/7.

### Online Cover Letters

The emergence of e-mail as a primary job search vehicle has also changed the structure and content requirements of cover letters. Consider these important tips when preparing your electronic cover letter (e-letter):

1. The subject line should reflect the specific opening that the recruiter is trying to fill and/or the name of the third party referring you to the recruiter.
2. If you are sending a general-contact letter for any current or future openings, indicate your title or function in your subject line.

*Note* Leaving the subject line blank or saying "resume attached" will almost always result in an immediate delete.

### Position-Specific E-letters

1. The body of the text should be short so that the recruiter doesn't have to scroll to read it all.
2. At the beginning of the letter, include the name of the third party who referred you (if applicable).
3. Specify the position for which you are applying.
4. Briefly highlight your top three or four applicable qualifications.
5. Ask the recruiter for a reply to your e-mail.

### General-Contact E-letters

1. The body of the text should be short so that the recruiter doesn't have to scroll to read it all.
2. At the beginning of the letter, include the name of the third party who referred you (if applicable).
3. Specify the types of positions for which are you most qualified.
4. Briefly highlight your top three or four applicable qualifications.
5. Close with a confident statement (for example, "I will add value to your clients' bottom line.").

### Immediate Turnoffs

And, finally, when I'm reviewing cover letters, there are several things that immediately turn me off:

1. Letters that are longer than one page.
2. Letters that are jam-packed with words and have little white space.
3. Letters that look and read just like every other cover letter I receive (for example, taken from a template and not personalized).
4. Letters that don't have a resume. I typically "can" these immediately. I know that it's not that the candidate forgot to send a resume, but rather they sent the cover letter as a "teaser" ("news at 11" approach), saying, "I'll send you my resume after you read my cover letter."
5. Letters that are cute or humorous. Comedy is very hard to do in movies, plays, and so on. Don't try it with your cover letter!

## Shelly Goldman: Retained and Contingency Recruiter
## Health Care, Finance, Accounting, and Technology Industries

Shelly Goldman, CPCC, CEIP
The Goldman Group Advantage, Reston, VA
www.TheGoldmanGroupAdvantage.com
shelly@thegoldmangroupadvantage.com
(888) 858-8518

A succinct, well-written, and vibrant cover letter really gets my attention. A well-thought-out cover letter lets me know the author can communicate the winning messages he or she is trying to project to the audience.

I enjoy reviewing cover letters that are not too long (one page is great!). Information should be relevant and not added just to fill up space. All information should be in support of creating a positive impression. Candidates should address why they have decided to send a resume and cover letter and what professional attributes, characteristics, and skills they possess that demonstrate the reasons they should be considered. A comfortable, professional, and relaxed style of writing can really help set them apart from the crowd.

I like to feel that the cover letter is customized for me (even if it's not) and that each job seeker has taken the time to highlight the key facts that might be of interest to me specifically. The candidate should emphasize noteworthy and appropriate accomplishments and the attributes that contributed to his or her record of success. Addressing the cover letter to a specific person is essential.

If the candidate is writing in response to a specific position, it's important to see that he or she has taken the time to directly address what in his or her background relates to the current position. Effectively responding to and addressing key points definitely grabs my attention. Any additional value-added skills the candidate might bring to a potential employer, whether required for the position or not, would also be of interest.

Candidates who send a cover letter and resume for nonspecific career opportunities should immediately identify their career objectives in the beginning paragraph of their cover letters. Candidates should also include key accomplishments from their backgrounds and should be able to draw positive attention to what makes them unique, innovative, and interesting candidates who will stand out from the crowd.

Whether the cover letter is sent for a specific or nonspecific position, it's always a good idea to thank the reader for his or her time and consideration. Asking for a follow-up response is also important. Acknowledging that the candidate would enjoy and appreciate an opportunity to discuss his or her qualifications in more detail is encouraged. A candidate might also choose to close the cover letter by letting me know he or she will follow up with a direct phone call on a specific day and at a specific time. Either way, it's important to close with a next-step plan. This creates an impression that the job seeker possesses self-assurance and pride.

Compensation information is not vital to include in the cover letter because that information can be discussed at a later date if I am interested in a candidate. Also, if the candidate is open to relocation, that fact is appropriate to include in the cover letter.

On a final note, I will generally immediately disqualify candidates who use cover letters as a vehicle for "bashing" past or current employers, or candidates who seem deceptive in their approach. Another real killer in the search process is bad grammar, bad spelling, a poorly constructed cover letter, or numerous typographical errors. If a job seeker is going to take the time to prepare a resume and cover letter, he or she must be positive that the document is 100 percent error free.

## Darrell Gurney: Retained and Contingency Recruiter

Darrell Gurney, CPC, JCTC, CCMC, RSCP
A Permanent Success National Career Coaching & Search Partners, Los Angeles, CA
www.HeadhuntersRevealed.com
CareerMeister@CareerSecrets.com
(310) 842-8864

In discussing cover letters, we must first have a brief conversation about how recruiters work. From my experience, and that of many others I've interfaced with in the recruiting world, the first and foremost item we look at is a candidate's *resume.* From the resume alone, a recruiter can tell whether the individual fits into the specialty niche of positions the recruiter fills, whether the candidate is marketable (in other words, no bouncing around, stable and steady path of progressive growth within a niche, and so on), and whether the candidate is superior (for example, shows results, accomplishments, rankings, and so on). A recruiter looks for these factors sequentially, not moving on to explore the next until the prior requirement is satisfied. For example, if a recruiter sees in three seconds that the candidate doesn't fit his niche, he doesn't even delve more deeply into the candidate's marketability. If, and only if, these requirements are satisfied by the recruiter's examination of *the resume only,* then he or she will look at the cover letter.

Regarding the cover letter itself, recruiters aren't interested in candidates' self-analytical exposes of themselves but, rather, just some basic facts: positions/industries of interest, salary history and desires, and location preferences. The reason a recruiter doesn't need the candidate to elaborate is because the recruiter already *knows* what he or she can sell about this person from the resume. He or she can see from the resume whether the person is an XYZ person to fill an XYZ job. Therefore, anything pertinent to the candidate's fulfilling the recruiter's three requirements needs to be on the resume itself, with the cover letter giving only some basic, secondary information.

The basics of a good cover letter include the following:*

- **All contact information.** It's not enough to include that information only on your resume; it must also be included on your cover letter in case the two get separated.
- **Reasons for leaving.** Describe briefly why you're in the market and, in a short sentence for each position, why you've moved in the past. This is especially important for a resume that smells of "rubber" (lots of bouncing around). To possibly attract a recruiter, you'd better strike preemptively with a good reason for moving before you strike out. But *keep it short!*
- **Positions and industries of interest.** Include position titles and industries for which you would like to be considered. The more specific you are, the better.
- **Salary history and expectations.** It doesn't matter that you are "flexible" or "open to compensation commensurate with duties and responsibilities." You do have a bottom line, although recruiters won't focus on *your* bottom line, but rather on theirs. Remember, the more you make, the more most recruiters (contingent) will make. Regardless of how much you don't want your last salary to impact your next, 99 percent of the time it will, so deal with it! Employers generally offer at least some increase over your last salary, and a recruiter can negotiate for as much as possible, but the company isn't going to give you a 60 or 80 percent raise! Simply spell out what you've earned in each of your positions so that the recruiter can see

*Excerpted from *Headhunters Revealed! Career Secrets for Choosing and Using Professional Recruiters*, Hunter Arts Publishing, © 2000. All Rights Reserved.

your progression. Then, be sure to state the salary range you're willing to consider.

- **Locations of interest.** State either that you want to stay within a certain locale (city or state) or spell out exactly which cities, states, or regions of the country or world you would consider. This information can be extremely valuable in a database search, especially for recruiters who work on a nationwide or worldwide basis.

One other important consideration when writing your cover letter is the keyword-searchable database that virtually all recruiters now use. Note that cover letters are often scanned into these databases, along with resumes. Therefore, it is essential to include relevant keywords in your letters that might or might not be included in your resume.

Consider a case where someone wants to move into a field in which he doesn't have prior experience. It's rare that an individual without experience in a particular position or industry could be placed into that field by a recruiter, but I can't say it hasn't happened. For example, a young salesperson recently sent me his information. His resume spoke of his top-ranked experience in copier sales, but his cover letter mentioned that he wanted to move into pharmaceutical or medical sales. In *some* instances, those types of moves are possible. Pharmaceutical companies are often looking for people with great sales backgrounds regardless of industry experience, so this is an instance in which it might help to have a cover letter databased in addition to the resume. When I did a keyword search using the word "pharmaceutical," this young man's cover letter and resume popped up. If he had submitted a resume alone or not mentioned pharmaceutical sales (his industry target) in his cover letter, he would simply have been passed over.

## Mitch Halaby: Executive Recruiter—Accounting and Finance

Mitch Halaby
Rockville, MD
mitch.halaby@ajilonfinance.com
(301) 545-6151

### What to Include in Your Letter

As a senior executive recruiter, when I think about the type of information you should include in a cover letter, the first thing that comes to mind is, "the less information, the better." Recruiters don't read every cover letter they receive. If you want recruiters to read your cover letter, make it easy for them. If your cover letter is three to five paragraphs and each paragraph has six to twelve lines, most recruiters won't read it.

The type of information you include in your cover letter should be very specific to the position you're applying for and should not repeat information that is already on your resume. A good recruiter knows that when you do this, it's only to fill space in your cover letter.

Recently I received a resume with an e-mail text message—no formal cover letter—and was particularly intrigued. This is how the text message looked and what it said:

> Very smart, high energy, outgoing controller. Helped take a company public. Go-to person always driving for change and efficiency. Very operationally oriented. Large public experience. CPA, University of Illinois—top 1%.

When I read the text message, the first thought that came to my mind was that this person must have been referred to me by one of my fellow recruiters from my Chicago office. The reason I felt that way was that the format (incomplete sentences) and the limited information is how recruiters communicate with each other. I responded to the e-mail to determine whether the sender was a candidate or indeed a recruiter from my office in Chicago. I was amazed when I discovered that it was a candidate who sent the message.

There are two points to consider in reference to the preceding example. First, if the candidate had tried to communicate in a three-to-four-paragraph formal cover letter what he communicated in three-and-a-half sentences, I probably would not have read it. Second, he spoke my language—to the point and brief. By the way, this candidate is scheduled for a final interview with my client.

As a recruiter, I seldom look at cover letters for staff or mid-management positions. However, when it comes to senior management/C-level positions, it's a different story. Let me tell you what I mean. For senior-level positions, I tell the potential candidate the specific experiences (implementing a software package, taking a company public, or building a department) my client is looking for. I then ask the candidate to describe to me in detail, in a cover letter, similar events in his or her past that most closely relate to what my client is looking for. If the candidate doesn't follow those simple instructions, it's over! My responsibility as a recruiter is to provide my client with the best talent. At least 75 percent of that effort involves screening people out.

### The Salary Question

When I was a student at the University of Massachusetts, I had an economics professor who would answer all difficult and complex questions from students with "It all depends." I think what he was trying to teach us was that not everything is black and white. The same is true when we are discussing whether to include salary history or salary requirements in a cover letter. Here are my recommendations:

1. If salary requirements are not requested, do not make any reference to salary in your letter.
2. If a potential employer or recruiter states in the job description that you should include salary requirements in your cover letter, you had better do so. Nothing disqualifies a candidate quicker than not being able to follow simple instructions.

The question then becomes, how do you communicate your salary requirements? The first step is to know the salary range you require. I can't tell you the number of times I have pre-closed candidates on their salary requirements 5% to 12% below what they first indicated. In other words, within just a few minutes they have agreed to accept a lower salary than their "required range" in order to be considered for a position. Clearly, their "required range" was a wish rather than a requirement. They should have done more research and presented a range closer to reality, or a broader range.

When you know your real salary range, you are ready for step two. What is your potential employer's salary range? Think about this. If a company is trying to determine your salary expectations before you have even met them, they are usually trying to screen you out based on your salary requirements. That's fair. However, what's good for the goose is good for the gander. You can employ the same strategy: "Does the company meet my salary requirements?"

The job description might or might not mention the salary range. If it doesn't, you have to research and discover what it is. Call anonymously to the human resources department and ask. Do research on the company size, geographic location, and industry; then go to the Internet and come up with a salary range.

Now that you have determined what the company's range is, one of three scenarios will play out: Your salary range is either below, within, or above theirs. All things being equal:

1. If your range is below the company's, pick a range that begins with your maximum and ends with their minimum.
2. If your salary range is within theirs, pick the midpoint of their range as the minimum you are willing to consider and their maximum as the top end.
3. If your salary requirements are above theirs, you need to determine why. Did your work experience begin when the employment market was paying a premium for recent college graduates? Does the differential in salary have to do with demographics or where the company is located? Does the company historically pay less than what the market will bear for the type of position they are trying to fill? Once you determine the reason why, *and this is key,* if you still want to pursue the opportunity, pick the top end of their salary range and add 5 to 7 percent.

An important question to ask yourself is who is looking at your cover letter. Is it an administrative assistant, who is looking for candidates who do not answer the question about salary in the cover letter so that she can throw out their cover letters and resumes? Or is it the CFO, who is willing to stretch on salary if the candidate has the exact experience he's looking for?

In my opinion, as an experienced recruiter, the single most critical piece of advice I can offer to job seekers is to follow instructions! I am willing to give candidates the benefit of the doubt if they don't know how to construct a strong resume. I am less forgiving if they choose not to follow simple instructions (such as including a salary history or salary requirements).

## Rolande LaPointe: Contingency Recruiter—Generalist

Rolande LaPointe, CPC, CIPC, CPRW, IJCTC, CCM, CSS, CRW
RO-LAN Associates, Inc., Lewiston, ME
rlapointe@aol.com
(207) 784-1010

As a recruiter, it is important that I have as much information about a candidate as possible. This includes personal data as well as professional information. In order for me to best introduce an individual, I need to know the following:

- Complete contact information (address, phone, fax, cell, e-mail)
- Types of positions the candidate seeks
- Industries in which the candidate is interested in working or in which he or she has experience
- Summary of qualifications and skills (not relying solely on the resume for this information)
- Geographic preference(s), if any
- Salary requirements
- Benefit expectations
- Special family needs (for example, health care, education)
- Availability for interviews
- Starting date to begin a new position

If this takes two pages to accomplish, I do not mind. My goal is to know my candidate well enough to be able to effectively introduce him or her to my client companies.

What catches my attention is a well-prepared letter that introduces the candidate as a person. The personal and professional information should be presented in a way in which the candidate's personality comes through in the letter.

The cover letter also gives the candidate an opportunity to demonstrate his or her communication style. In reading the cover letter, I instinctively assess communication skills and search for any typos or grammatical errors.

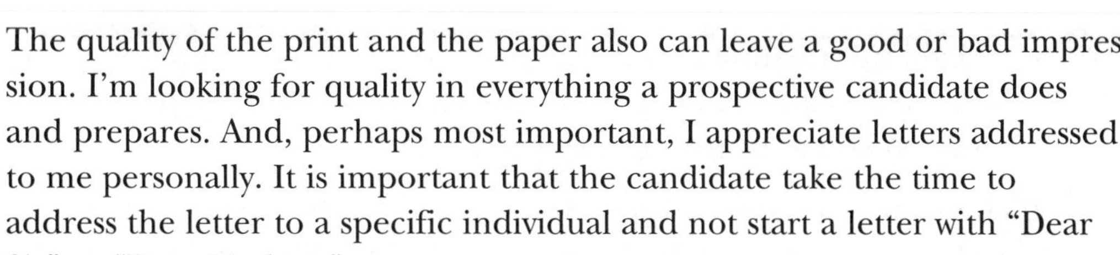

The quality of the print and the paper also can leave a good or bad impression. I'm looking for quality in everything a prospective candidate does and prepares. And, perhaps most important, I appreciate letters addressed to me personally. It is important that the candidate take the time to address the letter to a specific individual and not start a letter with "Dear Sir" or "Dear Madam."

It is also important that the candidate be absolutely up front with the recruiter concerning any possible issues regarding past work history or any other possible "negative" employment-related situations that might need further explanation. Of course, none of the specifics should be introduced in the cover letter; these should be discussed with the recruiter during the first interview. In many cases, the recruiter can help defuse a potential problem.

I'm sure I operate much like many other recruiters: I consider it essential for a job seeker to include compensation requirements when contacting me—even if it is only a salary range or a salary history. Along with this information, it is also helpful for me to know whether the person is willing to negotiate salary and benefits.

Conversely, the type of information that immediately is a turn-off for me in a cover letter is a mention that the candidate already has contacted several other recruiters, having posted his or her resume on various sites online, and basically giving the impression of coming to me as an afterthought. This sort of information is better brought up at the initial interview with a recruiter and *not* in the cover letter.

## Key Points to Remember

In reading through all of the recruiter recommendations, several key points become immediately obvious:

- Cover letters to recruiters must be brief. Although there are situations in which letters might extend onto a second page, most recruiters prefer letters that are short and to the point.
- Include specific information about your job targets. The more specific you are in terms of the type of position(s) you are seeking and your industry preference(s), the more valuable a recruiter will be as part of your job search team.

- Highlight information that depicts your greatest career achievements, most notable skills, and experience as they relate to the type of position(s) you are currently exploring.
- Include salary history and requirements so that the recruiter immediately knows *where* you fit in. Even if all you do is "define the ballpark," be sure to at least give recruiters some idea of your past compensation and current expectations.
- Pay special attention to the particulars of writing e-letters (electronic cover letters). These letters are different in style and content from traditional printed cover letters. They are more brief and should include important position information in the subject line.

Follow all of these "rules" for writing cover letters targeted to recruiters, and you'll instantly improve the number of recruiter responses you receive. Remember, the recruiter playbook is different from the company playbook. Be sure you're playing the right game!

Chapter 16

# Next-Generation Job Search Letters

Up until now, this book has focused entirely on writing powerful cover letters and thank-you letters, both of which are essential to every job seeker's successful campaign. In this chapter, we're going to introduce you to what we refer to as *next-generation letters*—the newest strategies and techniques for writing letters that will further accelerate your search and help you land that great new job.

In this chapter we will discuss four different types of next-generation letters:

- High-impact networking letters
- Personal branding letters
- Reconnecting letters
- Career-update letters

Each of these letters has a specific purpose and a specific goal, which we'll explore in greater detail as we work our way through this chapter. After each section, you'll find two examples of the type of letter discussed. You can use these as the foundation for writing your own letters.

*Tip* Adding these special letters to your job search toolkit can give you a strong and competitive advantage over other candidates.

People remember other people who distinguish themselves from the crowd, and these letters can accomplish just that. When well written, they instantly communicate a strong and sustainable message that will prompt action and results—the only *true* purpose of a letter.

- High-impact networking letters prompt your network contacts to take action by offering you job leads, search recommendations, and other contacts to expand your network.
- Personal branding letters prompt prospective employers and recruiters to offer you an interview as a result of your brand (your unique value proposition).
- Reconnecting letters remind individuals and companies that you're in the market for a great new opportunity.
- Career-update letters notify recruiters and companies that you've accepted a new position, while reminding them that you *may* be available for future opportunities.

Throughout this book, we've communicated the importance of individuality—of writing letters that represent the very best *you* have to offer. This next generation of job search letters does just that by allowing you to communicate, in a fresh and upscale style, *who* you are, *what* you have to offer, and the *value* of that offer.

> *Tip* Although the letters in this chapter are shown in print format, you can send your next-generation job search letters by e-mail if you prefer. In fact, e-mail works especially well given the informal tone that characterizes letters to people you know.

## High-Impact Networking Letters

Networking letters are written specifically to build your own network of contacts, expand your network, and generate job leads, but you probably already know that. You might then be asking yourself, "What is the difference between traditional networking letters and high-impact networking letters?" The answer is simple—high-impact networking letters are characterized by a dual emphasis on both the personal connection and your professional information.

When writing a high-impact networking letter, you want to accomplish three distinct objectives:

- Leverage your personal relationships with business colleagues, mentors, managers, peers, and professional contacts.
- *Quietly* market the strength of your experience, qualifications, and achievements.
- Encourage your contacts to take action by contacting you, sharing information about potential leads and opportunities, and referring you to others in their network to further expand your own network.

When writing your networking letters, you want to ask your contacts for their help and *never* ask them for a job. Most likely, your contacts will be happy to help and support you in your search; few, however, will have specific job openings. By asking for their assistance, you're allowing them to help you as they are able and deem most appropriate. When you ask for a job, it can be an immediate turn-off, and because they usually cannot offer you a job, you generally will not hear back from them. That, in and of itself, defeats the entire purpose of networking; namely, to capture new leads and contacts and expand your network. To get the most out of your networking efforts, be sure to approach each of your contacts with the *right* message!

There are two distinct schools of thought about how to write networking letters. We'll start with the more traditional networking letter that, to some degree, is much like the traditional cover letter in that it showcases certain highlights of your career and entices the reader to take action. Two samples of this type of networking letter follow. The first (Drew Michaelson) uses a bulleted format to pinpoint his most notable achievements. This makes it easy for networking contacts to quickly review the information and determine where they can refer him. The second (Louise Fulton-Greene) is written in a paragraph format and "tells the story" of what's happened in her career since the time that she and her contact worked together in years past. Note that each letter begins with an immediate personal connection, the most important characteristic of every networking letter.

**DREW R. MICHAELSON**

drewrm@verizon.net

1221 Ross Road
New Orleans, LA 77873

Phone: (508) 555-9362
Fax: (508) 555-9255

May 23, 2010

Arnold Tilley
Executive Vice President
Triangle Product Associates
3899 River Boulevard
Austin, TX 79083

Dear Arnie:

Arnie, I'm looking for a really unique professional opportunity and I need your help. Specifically, I'm interested in senior-level consulting and interim executive assignments, Board of Director appointments, and, perhaps, another full-time President/CEO position. Most important, I am NOT looking for the "typical" job. What I want is a new challenge, a new project, a new venture, a turnaround, or any one of a number of other opportunities where the focus is on building something new or reenergizing what already exists.

To refresh your memory just a bit, I've included a copy of my resume, which highlights the strength of my experience in the manufacturing, distribution, and aftermarket products industries. Let me also highlight a few key points of particular interest:

- As the President/CEO of Rohell, I built a start-up venture from concept into a $120 million company with 4 locations, 50 employees, and annual profit margins averaging 28%.
- Established a global distribution network with 150 domestic and 100 international partners. Total combined revenues from both distribution channels exceeded $48 million annually.
- Created a multi-site offshore manufacturing operation that reduced cost of goods by as much as 50% annually. In addition, led project team in developing and bringing to market 10 new product lines (more than $200 million in combined revenues over 10 years).
- Substantial leadership responsibilities for all core management disciplines (e.g., strategic planning, finance, sales, marketing, technology, human resources, administration).

Now, after two years of golf, my handicap is the best it's ever been and I'm delighted! Unfortunately, I'm bored and miss the challenges I was so accustomed to in the past. The break has been revitalizing, but I'm now ready to move forward.

If you are aware of a company or consulting group that could benefit from my experience, I would welcome the contact information and your referral. I'll follow up with you in a week or so to see if you have any recommendations. Thanks so much for your assistance, and I'm happy to return the favor whenever you need it.

Sincerely,

Drew Michaelson

**LOUISE FULTON-GREENE**
22 Walker Road
Selma, New Jersey 08579
908-555-3829 / lfg@aol.com

August 12, 2010

Susan Shadon
Chief Executive Officer
Citibank Investment Holdings
900 Citibank Boulevard
Chicago, IL 60937

Dear Susan:

When I reflect back on my career at J&J, it's hard to believe that I left more than five years ago. Seems like only yesterday! Despite all the transition, what a great company it was and what a tremendous learning ground for so many of us.

As you're aware, I resigned my position with J&J to assume a VP of Finance position with a high-growth communications company. Our growth was phenomenal, building J&J from $18 million in annual revenues to more than $120 million with 28 distinct operating companies/divisions. In fact, after just three years, I was promoted to the #1 finance position in the company's largest and most profitable operating division.

Then, in 2007, I was enticed to join an early-stage merchant banking group in need of strong financial and operating leadership. I thought this would be a tremendous opportunity and, in many ways, it has been. Over the past two years, I orchestrated a major acquisition and its complete reorganization and have recently launched the start-up of a new high-tech venture. Our long-term goal is an IPO; however, there have been so many changes within the investor group that I have begun to question their long-term commitment.

Thus, I'm contacting a select group of my colleagues to inquire whether you are aware of any executive opportunities for a candidate with my qualifications. I'm interested in a position that will combine my financial and operating expertise; I would consider a start-up venture, a rapid turnaround situation, or a high-growth company.

I would appreciate any ideas, recommendations, or referrals that you could offer and will, in the future, be delighted to do the same for you if the situation ever arises.

I've enclosed my resume and will follow up with you shortly to get your feedback. Thanks so much.

Sincerely,

Louise Fulton-Greene

Enclosure

The second and entirely different networking approach comes to us from Kathy Condon of KC Solutions in Vancouver, Washington. Kathy is a well-known and well-respected networking expert who firmly believes that *no* mention should be made of work or wanting a job when first making a networking contact. Furthermore, Kathy is a firm believer that networking notes should be handwritten for that all-important personal touch and recommends including a business/contact card so your information is readily available. She reminds us that networking notes are about building relationships, not getting jobs. Here are two great examples from Kathy:

Ralph, I appreciated your taking the time to talk with me at the Chamber event last Thursday. It was good to share your excitement about your forthcoming vacation in the Caribbean. Do call if you have any other questions before you leave. Otherwise, I will plan to call you after the 17th so we can have a cup of coffee.

Mary Hellmich

Linda, I enjoyed talking with you at the Habitat for Humanity dinner last night. Congratulations, again, on your promotion. Your enthusiasm for the new challenges was most apparent. I will give you a call next week and let's see if we can get our calendars to match so we can have that cup of coffee.

Harry James

## Personal Branding Letters

Branding letters are written specifically to communicate your own personal brand and the value your brand brings to an organization. In many respects, these letters are an extension of more traditional cover letters that you would send in response to advertisements or to companies and recruiters directly. The one distinguishing characteristic that sets these letters apart from other letters is their focus on communicating your brand and demonstrating the success of that brand.

To develop your own branding letters, you must first be able to clearly communicate what your brand is. Begin by asking yourself these all-important questions:

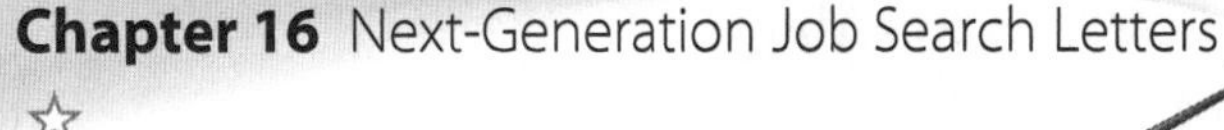



1. What is unique about me and my career?
2. What are my strongest skills and qualifications?
3. What are my most notable achievements and contributions?
4. What have I done—in my current and past positions—that distinguishes me from my peers?
5. What gives me a competitive advantage in the employment market?
6. What is the most important message that I want to communicate to a prospective employer or recruiter?

Take time to carefully think about your answers to the preceding questions. Then, use that specific information to develop your own branding statement—a statement that communicates your unique value and the value that a company will enjoy if they make you an offer.

In selecting the branding letters to showcase in this book, we contacted one of our colleagues, Deborah Wile Dib of ExecutivePowerBrand.com. Deb is well-known and well-respected throughout the professional resume-writing community for her expertise in developing branded documents (e.g., resumes, letters, executive profiles). We decided that if we were going to feature two branding letters, we should give you the very best.

In Deb's first example, Carmen Santiago's brand is clearly communicated with distinct components of her cover letter. First, you'll notice the headline under her name:

**Global Business Development & Technology Executive:**
**Special Expertise in Emerging Markets & Creative Capitalism**

With one quick glance at the letter, you immediately know *who* Carmen Santiago is. Her brand is then further substantiated with the branding statement that opens her letter:

Building stronger pathways to profit (even within tangled markets) is at the core of everything I do.

This is a powerful statement that gives her a strong and distinct market position—precisely what a branding letter is intended to do. Note, also, that her contact information includes her LinkedIn profile, her Web portfolio, and her blog—named, appropriately, Creative Capitalism. All of these additional information sources support her brand image and establish Carmen as a thought leader and innovator.

Deb's second example (Jonathan Heidrick) appears at first glance to be a traditional cover letter, like many you'll read in this book. And it's an excellent letter—sharply focused, a quick read, with short paragraphs and concise bullet points. Jonathan's brand is conveyed in two key parts of this letter. First, read the first sentence of the second paragraph. Jonathan discusses what he does—and then tells *how* he does it, clearly conveying his unique value:

> I drive exceptional revenue and margin growth with little or no cost of sales—by leveraging emerging trends, creating ethical best practices, and developing loyal teams of customer evangelists.

Finally, the footnote of Jonathan's letter is in itself a powerful branding statement:

> Visit www.JHeidrick.com to see how linking trends, people, and innovation creates aggressive growth and revenue.

Not only has Jonathan enticed readers to visit his Web site, he's used precise, on-brand language that communicates who he is, what he does, how he does it, and the value he delivers—and all in one sentence!

**Carmen Santiago**

US Mobile: +1 (555) 555-5555
Email: Carmen@CarmenSantiago.com
LinkedIn: www.linkedin.com/in/CarmenSantiago
Portfolio & Blog: www.CarmenSantiago.com
2125 Mirror Lake Road, Seattle, WA 98136 USA

**Global Business Development & Technology Executive**
**Special Expertise in Emerging Markets & Creative Capitalism**

March 15, 2010

James Franklin, CEO
Global Products, Inc.
2909 Pacific Highway, Suite F290
Renton, WA 98058

Dear Mr. Franklin:

Building stronger pathways to profit (even within tangled markets) is at the core of everything I do. In 10+ years at Trio Technologies, I extended the company's leadership into numerous emerging markets and delivered turnarounds and growth in its existing channels:

**Corporate strategy:** Conceived and drove Trio Technology's renowned "Global Reach" program, a $1B initiative launched in multiple countries to revitalize thought leadership in emerging markets and create new avenues for profit.

**Global team leadership:** Delivered $80M in new revenue and improved brand perception by doubling Trio's share to 60% in the Internet café market, one of China's largest PC markets.

**Passionate visionary with bold, achievable goals**: Pioneered a new P&L business group in China, growing operations in six countries with $75+M revenue in the first year and delivering groundbreaking, industry-stimulating products.

**Big ideas, big revenue impact, when it counts:** Created and executed an expansion of Trio's channel business into emerging markets, bringing in new revenue when business languished after the dot-com technology recession of 2000 to 2003.

**Extensive international management expertise:** Worked on the ground in 43 emerging and mature countries and 100+ cities, meeting all levels of stakeholders and leading highly diverse international teams of 100+ people.

If creating new markets and channels or revving up stagnant regions or product lines is a strategic imperative—while leading the pack in profitable, yet socially responsible development—let's schedule a conversation. I'll touch base with you early next week.

Sincerely,

Carmen Santiago

P.S. To view my resume, online portfolio, and Creative Capitalism blog, visit www.CarmenSantiago.com.

**Growth • Turnarounds • Emerging Markets • Strategy • General Management • Marketing • Channels • Sales**

**JONATHAN HEIDRICK**
128 Tan Ling Road, #02-09, Singapore 088271
Jon@JHeidrick.com
+65 55555555

March 15, 2010

Vivienne Rowan, President
Worldwide Logistics, Inc.
890 Golden Gate Boulevard
San Francisco, CA 94513

Dear Ms. Rowan:

Are aggressive growth, significantly increased revenue, and reduced expenses your strategic imperatives in today's volatile market?

As Managing Director of the Singapore office for global logistics company Regent Ltd, I drive exceptional revenue and margin growth with little or no cost of sales—by leveraging emerging trends, creating ethical best practices, and developing loyal teams of customer evangelists. Using these techniques I...

- Transformed the Singapore office to become the firm's #2 revenue producer, moving it from 8th of 9 global offices in just 3 years.
- Increased the office's gross profitability up to 600%, with Q3 figures already doubling the previous year's historic gains.
- Won a mission-critical $10M, 5-year contract with Viro Petroleum; reduced staff turnover by 50% in 2 years; expanded China / Japan markets; and opened an Australian office to tap the region's energy market.

With the goal of permanent relocation to San Francisco, I would like to speak with you to discuss possibilities for senior-level employment within Worldwide Logistics. I will be in San Francisco in April, meeting with key companies from the 15th through the 22nd. Have you availability?

Sincerely,

Jonathan Heidrick

Visit www.JHeidrick.com to see how linking trends, people, and innovation creates aggressive growth and revenue.

## Reconnecting Letters

The sole purpose of a reconnecting letter is to contact prospective employers, network contacts, recruiters, sponsors, and others in your job search community who you've been out of touch with for six or more months. You can often leverage these contacts to uncover new career opportunities that you would most likely not have been aware of unless you'd reconnected with these individuals, no matter the length of time that has passed.

Reconnecting letters are really an extension of networking letters. You will use the same successful networking principles discussed previously in this book, simply expanding those concepts and actions to include individuals with whom you have not been in touch for quite a while.

As with the other next-generation letters that we're showcasing in this chapter, reconnecting letters generally have two distinct objectives:

- Communicating with individuals with whom you've not been in contact for an extended period of time.
- Alerting individuals to your current *employment* situation and either asking for information about prospective opportunities or letting them know about opportunities you may be offering.

Look carefully at the two sample reconnecting letters that follow to understand how to best use these letters to your advantage. You can see how powerful these letters can be in rekindling past collegial relationships, opening new doors, and uncovering new opportunities.

In the first example, Jacqueline Grove talks about the excitement of retirement, yet also communicates what she is missing from the "corporate" world. She then offers her financial expertise—at no charge—as a way of getting herself in front of her contact and other potential employers who would be interested in a candidate looking for only part-time or project work.

Compare that letter with the second letter (Michael Spinelli), in which he is contacting one of his most valuable mentors to inquire about new opportunities where he could again work under this individual's leadership. Note that this job seeker is currently employed and simply reconnecting with professionals from years past to help him secure a new executive position.

**JACQUELINE D. GROVE**
**grovejackied@aol.com**

**11 Juniper Street**
**Charleston, SC 22909**
**302-999-3827**

August 27, 2010

Lisa R. Newton
Chairman of the Board
Dryman Industries
9000 Dryman Boulevard
Ames, IA 59883

Dear Lisa:

Life is great! Since taking advantage of an early retirement opportunity from Belmont Financial Industries, I've had time to spend with family and friends, thoroughly enjoyed my eldest daughter's wedding, and have actually been able to have a full conversation with my husband. I don't think that had happened since somewhere in the mid-1990s!

After years and years of an intense work schedule, unending deadlines, and complex financial and organizational transactions, I can now breathe again! I've also had the opportunity to reflect a bit on my career and those who contributed so significantly to my personal and professional success. Undoubtedly, you are one of those who, through your efforts, spurred my achievement and strengthened my performance.

Retirement is an "odd bird." Although I am enjoying myself, I miss the business relationships, interactions, and intellectual challenges associated with ESOPs, privatizations, and other sophisticated financial transactions. I also miss having the opportunity to mentor and develop other top-notch finance professionals, sharing my strategic and management expertise to complement their "technical" qualifications.

To meet that need and give back to those who have so freely given to me, I am now offering my services on a "project" or "consulting" basis to a select group of individuals and organizations. And the best part is that I do not expect any compensation, other than associated travel costs as applicable. I'm pleased to have the opportunity to contribute and am delighted to find myself in the most unique position of being able to do so.

I'll follow up with you in a week or two and hope you realize that this offer comes from my heart and not my pocket! You know me, and you know that I operate at the highest level of professional and ethical standards.

The best to you and yours. We'll talk soon.

Very truly yours,

Jackie Grove

**MICHAEL D. SPINELLI**

12 Woolridge Drive
Pierson, FL 33890
mdsp@bellsouth.net

Phone: 907-555-3827
Cell: 249-909-3827
Fax: 907-555-0087

August 15, 2010

Dr. Max Myerson
Director
The AMGETTE Corporation
22 Grove Street
Cincinnati, OH 45202

Dear Max:

One of my most triumphant "corporate" moments was a day shortly after you and Bob had acquired Delta Labs. The three of us, along with Henry, Celia, and Ralph, sat in the board room strategizing our next actions to recover market share. It was then that I recommended our first-ever value branding and pre-pricing programs. I can vividly remember everyone's reaction, summarized as "it will never work." But you, and you alone, trusted my instincts and gave me the go-ahead. It was a monumental day for me and the day that you can be credited with a dramatic turnaround. In fact, if you recall, we were able to recapture 12 share points within just three weeks!

Since that day, more than five years ago, I've continued to forge innovative marketing and business development programs that have consistently generated strong revenues, double-digit profits, and industry-leading market share ratings.

- One company grew by more than 50% in revenues in two years and yielded 41% gross margins as a result of a 100%+ price increase in value-added products.
- Another company grew from $3.5 million to $15 million in just 16 months through my innovations in branding and product positioning.
- A third firm delivered total profit growth of 100% adjusted EBIT under my leadership.

These achievements are indicative of the quality and caliber of my entire career. Relying on my innate marketing intuition, I identify opportunities, build markets, and generate dramatic revenue and profit gains. Whether spearheading an emerging venture, high-growth company, or turnaround, I have excelled.

Now, at this juncture in my career, I am interested in affiliating with a company that rewards innovation, risk, and success. Thinking back on all the people I know, the projects I've directed, the companies I've been associated with, and more, I kept thinking about you and the tremendous opportunities you afforded to me. As such, I'd be delighted to meet with you, catch up, and hear about your latest "corporate adventures."

I'll phone next week to discuss your availability and schedule a meeting at your convenience.

Sincerely,

Mike Spinelli

## Career-Update Letters

Career-update letters have two distinct purposes. First, they are used to notify personal and professional contacts, recruiters, and companies that you've accepted a new position and to provide them with any new contact information. Second, and perhaps more importantly, these letters can be used to position yourself for new opportunities by

- Encouraging them to do business with you at your new company.
- Reminding them that you are available for future opportunities that might include permanent positions, consulting engagements, or special project assignments.

Look carefully at the two sample career-update letters that follow to understand how to best use these letters to your advantage. They're an excellent way to stay in touch and continue to build your network of contacts even when you're currently employed.

In the first example, George Abramson used his letter to alert his colleague that he's accepted a new position and encourages the recipient to consider doing business with him at his new company. In the second letter, Marilyn Secrist also notifies the recruiter that she's accepted a new position, but at the end of her letter she clearly communicates that she would like to be considered for any new opportunities that might arise for a candidate with her qualifications.

**GEORGE G. ABRAMSON**

22 Elm Boulevard
Waco, TX 77372

(925) 555-5555
gabramson@msn.com

November 23, 2010

Edward Morgenstern
President
Woodworth Manufacturing Group
4344 Lewis Valley Road
Lehigh, PA 19903

Dear Ed:

It's been some time since we've spoken, and I hope you do not think it too presumptuous, but I wanted to update you on the latest opportunity my career has presented to me.

Most of my friends and colleagues know me as "George, the HR Guy." And, indeed, that is who I was for years and years. It was a tremendously rewarding career path that I look back on with pride and self-satisfaction. But, at this point in my life, I was ready for new challenges and new opportunities. However, I still wanted to keep my hands in the "HR pot." It's what I do best.

Then, the perfect opportunity presented itself—a position allowing me to leverage my past HR experience in a new direction—executive recruitment. So now I'm "George, the Executive Recruiter," specializing in the recruitment, selection, and placement of senior-level executives for emerging technology companies.

Having made this transition only within the past few weeks, I am just beginning to launch my recruiting efforts and am really excited about the potential. From my experience working closely with recruiters throughout my career (from the HR side of the table), I completely understand the dynamics of this unique relationship. What's more, I know and appreciate the needs and expectations of my client companies.

If, in the future, you have any executive staffing requirements, I hope that you will consider contacting me and letting me work with you to find the perfect candidate.

Thanks for your attention and your support throughout my search campaign. Let's stay in touch, and be sure to tell Beth that Lisa sends her best wishes. Please note my new contact information above.

Your colleague,

George Abramson

**MARILYN SECRIST**

890 Coleman Road
Granite, CA 90988

(707) 555-3927
msec@adelphia.net

September 17, 2010

Larry Holbrook
Managing Partner
Management Recruiters of CA
PO Box 909
San Diego, CA 99902

Dear Larry:

I wanted to drop you a quick note to let you know that I've accepted a new opportunity and to thank you for the assistance and support you've offered throughout my career.

In August, I joined Michelin Tire as their new Sales Performance Vice President. This is a new direction for me and I'm really excited about the potential. Plus, with more than 15 years' senior-level sales and marketing experience, I have a unique perspective of the needs and expectations of my clients.

Most important, I want to let you know that if you are ever engaged in a search for a senior-level corporate sales executive, I would still welcome your consideration. I have accepted the position with Michelin to broaden my product and market knowledge and, in turn, position myself for even greater opportunities over the coming years.

I've enclosed a copy of my resume just to be sure you have an updated version.

Again, thank you for everything. I hope to hear from you when just the "perfect" opportunity comes across your desk, whether it be a full-time permanent position, a consulting engagement, or a special project assignment.

Sincerely,

Marilyn Secrist

Enclosure

By adding these next-generation letters to your job search portfolio, you will better equip yourself to compete in today's job search market. What's more, you'll have a broader array of job search tools that you can use to help position yourself for new career and better career opportunities.

Keep in mind, your aim in your job search is to make yourself memorable to as many people as possible—potential employers, direct network contacts, and referrals. You never know when an opportunity that's perfect for you will arise, and you want to be on the "radar screen" so that when it does arise, your name and your qualifications will immediately come to mind. Because they are somewhat out of the ordinary, next-generation job search letters will help you stand out from the crowd. They can add a powerful edge to your job search and lifelong career management.

# Chapter 17

# Winning Resume Strategies

This chapter was the greatest challenge of all for us. How could we write just one chapter on resumes when, between the two of us, we've written more than a dozen whole books? Yet we felt that it was important to include some basic information on resume strategy, development, writing, and presentation. After all, we assume the reason that you're reading this book is because you

- Are just starting or are in the midst of a job search.
- Have either a completed resume or one under development.
- Need to know how to write powerful cover letters to accompany that resume.
- Frankly, we can't think of any other reason why you'd be reading this book!

First, we address three critical components of resume preparation: strategy, writing, and presentation. Then, to illustrate these concepts, we've included a detailed section with recommended resume formats and samples. Each of these formats has been designed for specific job search situations and types of job seekers. Wouldn't it be great if you could select one of these samples and just plug in your career information? Ten minutes and you'd be done! However, the chances of that happening are quite slim. Each job seeker has different skills, qualifications, and experiences, and each resume must be custom-designed. No two situations are ever exactly the same. These samples are offered simply to give you ideas for content, format, presentation, and impact. Use them wisely and to your advantage.

The final section in this chapter, "Magical Tips on Resume Writing," contains ideas, techniques, and insights that we have learned through our 25+ years in resume writing and career marketing. If you're interested in a more comprehensive discussion of resume writing, we refer you to this book's companion, *Résumé Magic,* by Susan Britton Whitcomb.

## Resume Strategy

We've spent a great deal of time in this book discussing the fact that cover letters and thank-you letters are really marketing communications. They should be designed to "sell" your qualifications and position you for a new career opportunity. This concept is even more critical when you're writing your resume! Consider your resume your own personal advertisement that highlights the features, benefits, and value of the product you are selling—*you!*

You will want to address several vital strategic issues before you write one word of your resume because they will provide the foundation for virtually everything you include in your resume *and* everything you omit.

### Focus and Perception: Who You Are

Who are you, and how do you want people to perceive you? A resume does not work if your reader cannot immediately understand who you are, your primary skill sets, and the value you bring to the organization.

*How do you accomplish that in your resume?* To quickly give a snapshot overview of who you are, use either of these two strategies to begin your resume:

- **Strategy 1:** Write a clear and well-defined Objective that states the type of position you are most interested in. For example:

  *Example*

  Seeking a challenging management position leading customer service operations for a high-growth consumer products company.

- **Strategy 2:** Omit an Objective and start your resume with a Summary or Career Profile that succinctly describes who you are and quickly grabs your reader's attention. For example:

*Example*

**SENIOR SALES & MARKETING EXECUTIVE**

**Building Revenues and Market Share Throughout National Markets**

Dynamic 15-year career leading sales, marketing, and service organizations. Delivered strong and sustainable revenue gains in both emerging and mature business markets. Excellent sales training and team leadership skills. Wharton MBA.

Whether you decide to use an Objective or a Summary, your reader will be able to quickly and accurately define who you are and where you fit into the organization.

> *Tip* Without a doubt, current resume styles favor the use of the Summary or Profile rather than an Objective. From a marketing standpoint, it's more beneficial to use a Summary, which tells the reader, "Here's what I have to offer," than an Objective, which states, "Here's what I want." If you do use an Objective, try to include language that implies benefit to the organization and not just what is important to you.

For guidance on writing Objectives and Career Summaries, refer to pages 337–339 of this chapter.

## Career Goals and Objectives: Who You Want to Be

Always remember the following: *Your resume needs to focus on the type of position you are currently seeking, which might or might not be in line with what you have done in the past.* Your current objectives will determine what information you include in your resume and how you present it. Your challenge is to write a document that positions you for the type of job you are currently seeking, not a document that simply reiterates what you have done in the past.

In theory, you want to take everything you have ever done in your career and lay it out on a table. Then choose those items that are most closely related to where you are currently headed in your career. Those are the items you will want to highlight in your resume. Does this strategy sound familiar? It should! It's precisely the same approach we recommended for preparing your cover letters. Bring to the forefront the items you want someone to "see" about you and your career.

> *Tip* Just as with cover letters, your resume should include only relevant information. It is not a "biography" and does not have to include everything you've ever done. Always keep your career goals in mind when choosing information to include on your resume.

*How do you define how you want to be perceived in a resume?* Consider this example. For the past 12 years, you've worked as a Laboratory Specialist for the American Red Cross. If you were interested in remaining in this line of work, your Summary might read something like this:

> Twelve years of progressively responsible experience in high-volume blood-bank operations for the American Red Cross. Excellent technical, scientific, and laboratory-management skills. Extensive experience in the use of sophisticated laboratory equipment and instrumentation.

Now suppose that you're ready to shift your career focus to a position in Healthcare Administration that has nothing to do with laboratory operations. Your Summary might read something like this:

> Twelve years of progressively responsible experience with a major healthcare organization. Excellent qualifications in project planning and management, budgeting, materials acquisition, technology procurement, and team building/leadership. Introduced processes that increased productivity, improved quality of operations, and contributed to double-digit cost savings.

These two summaries sound like they're about two different people. Yet you were 100 percent honest and accurate, simply shifting your focus from one set of skills to another to support your current objective. In the resume trade, this is referred to as "painting the picture you want someone to see while remaining in the realm of reality."

### Sales and Merchandising: What You Have Accomplished

Your resume should be more than a list of past jobs. It is the first opportunity you have to distinguish yourself from the competitive crowd of other candidates, and it should be written as a personal sales and marketing tool that attracts and impresses employers. Your qualifications, words, format, and presentation must all be favorably presented to attract your reader's interest. Take credit for your experience and accomplishments, know what makes you marketable, and sell it!

*How do you accomplish this in a resume?* You can most positively position your qualifications by defining the scope of your responsibilities and then highlighting your achievements and successes. That means not just saying what you did, but also how well you did it.

**Poor Example:**

- Managed accounting and finance operations for a $22 million company.

**Good Example:**

- Independently planned and directed a team of 27, responsible for accounting and financial affairs for a $22 million NASDAQ company with three operating locations and 500 employees.

**Poor Example:**

- Supervised IT operations in Dow Chemical's headquarters facility.

**Good Example:**

- Chief Information Officer with full responsibility for the strategic planning, development, and leadership of the entire information technology organization for Dow Chemical's $800 million headquarters facility. Introduced PC-based client/server architecture, SAP and SPC technologies, and an internal software-development team to optimize performance and productivity.

**Poor Example:**

- Coordinated office affairs for the President and Executive Committee.

**Good Example:**

- Independently and sensitively managed all administrative affairs on behalf of the President and Executive Committee of a $42 million industrial manufacturing company.

To create a hard-hitting resume, ask yourself what you have accomplished in your career, what quantifiable achievements you have delivered, what special projects you have managed, what honors and awards you have won, what unique skills and qualifications you have developed, and what distinguishes you from other candidates applying for the same position. Then use that information as the ammunition for your resume. This will enable you to write a document that is powerful, positive, and competitive.

For more information on writing job descriptions, refer to pages 340–342 of this chapter.

## Resume Writing

Now that you've given some thought to the strategy behind your resume, let's look at how to compose each of the distinct sections that make up most resumes. We'll address both content—what to include—and writing—how to communicate this information for maximum impact.

The most difficult part of resume writing is getting started. Where do you begin? You've got lots of information, but you aren't sure what to do with it all. Here's a step-by-step action plan that will make the process easier and faster. Follow it closely, and you will see that it is not nearly as difficult a task as you imagined.

### Content

Begin by compiling the raw information about yourself and your career, some of which will be included in your final resume, and some of which will not. Then, proceed through the following steps:

1. Type your name, address, home phone number, and e-mail address. Include your work phone, cell phone, fax, and pager numbers if appropriate.
2. Write your objective(s) and a list of *all* the skills you possess that support that objective.
3. List your job titles, employers, locations, and dates for each position you've held, along with basic information about that job, your responsibilities, the company, and your achievements. Jot down this information in note form, and don't waste time on specific wording and sentence structure. We'll worry about that later.
4. Type a list of all your academic experience: college degrees, college attendance, professional certificates and licenses, and continuing education.

5. List any of the following information that is applicable to you and your career:

   Professional memberships

   Civic memberships

   Computer and technology skills

   Honors and awards

   Volunteer experience

   Publications

   Public-speaking experience

   Media recognition

   Foreign-language skills

   International experience

## Objectives and Career Summaries

Now that you have compiled the raw data for your resume, it's time to begin actually writing the text. The most important thing to consider in this process is what your current career objectives are. This will dictate what information you include, where you include it, and how you include it. Remember, you're "painting a picture."

### Objectives

Begin by deciding whether you want to include an Objective on your resume. Including an Objective is optional and depends entirely on you and your goals. If you know that you are looking for a position as a Field Service Dispatcher and nothing else, you might want to include an Objective. However, if you're looking at several different opportunities, we recommend that you leave off the Objective. In this situation, your Objective would be either limiting or so broad that it said nothing.

Here's an example of a well-written Objective:

> Seeking a Customer Service Management position in the Telecommunications industry.

Why is this Objective so good? Because it clearly states what type of position this individual is seeking and in what industry. There are no unanswered questions about what this person wants to do. If she had wanted to take it a step further, she could have written this:

Seeking a Customer Service Management position where I can apply my six years of experience in the Telecommunications industry.

This Objective is even better, because not only does it communicate the type of position and industry in which the candidate is interested, it also communicates that she has experience that is directly relevant.

### Career Summaries

If you do not use an Objective, consider using a Career Summary, Professional Profile, or Qualifications Statement at the beginning of your resume. When you write an Objective, you are telling your reader what you want from them. When you write a Summary, you are communicating what you have to offer—your value. It is a much more powerful introduction that immediately entices someone to read on. Consider these examples:

**SENIOR FINANCE EXECUTIVE**

Corporate Finance Executive with 18 years of experience leading the financial-management functions of a multinational corporation. Combine strong analytical skills and creative thinking with outstanding financial and investment expertise. Delivered consistent gains in revenues and profitability while reducing annual operating costs and optimizing organizational productivity. MBA in Finance.

- Strategic Business & Financial Planning
- Acquisitions / Joint Ventures / LBOs
- Treasury, Banking & Cash Management
- Equity & Debt Financing
- U.S. & Foreign Tax Regulations
- ESOP & 401K Plans
- International Trade Finance & Credit
- Information Systems & Technologies

OR

**QUALIFICATIONS PROFILE:**

Special Events – Meeting & Conference Planning – Trade Shows – Fund-raising

Creative professional successful in planning, coordinating, and managing programs and special events for up to 5,000 guests. Sourced vendors, negotiated contracts, managed budgets, coordinated schedules, recruited volunteers, and facilitated press coverage. Outstanding organizational, communication, decision-making, problem-solving, and project-management skills. Enthusiastic and energetic.

Now, wouldn't you agree that these sample Summaries are dramatically more powerful than a traditional Objective? We certainly believe so. Each individual's career goals are clearly communicated, not with a passive Objective statement, but with a powerful presentation of their skills and qualifications.

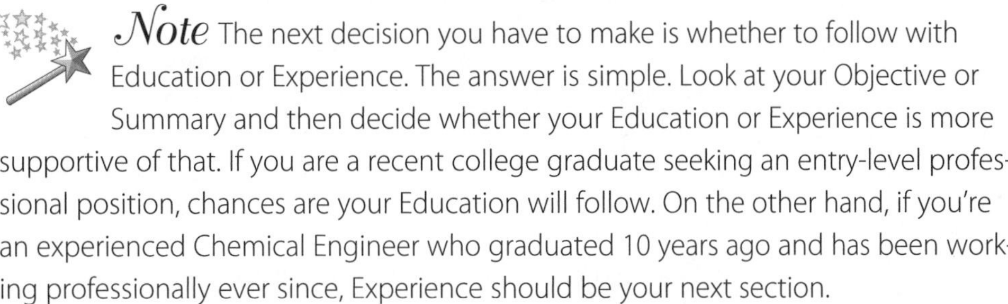

*Note* The next decision you have to make is whether to follow with Education or Experience. The answer is simple. Look at your Objective or Summary and then decide whether your Education or Experience is more supportive of that. If you are a recent college graduate seeking an entry-level professional position, chances are your Education will follow. On the other hand, if you're an experienced Chemical Engineer who graduated 10 years ago and has been working professionally ever since, Experience should be your next section.

## Education

The Education section of your resume should include college degrees (or the name of the college you attended if you do not have a degree), certificates, licenses, seminars, workshops, and other continuing education. Be sure to include all relevant information (for example, major courses of study, names of colleges and universities, academic honors, and demonstration of leadership capabilities). If your education ended with high school, list the name of the school, its location, and your graduation date. If you are a college graduate, there is no need to include high school unless you graduated from a prestigious private institution.

Here are a few examples to get you started:

**EDUCATION:**

M.B.A.—Harvard University—2000

B.A.—Management & Economics—Princeton University—1998

**Graduate,** 200+ hours of continuing professional education

OR

**EDUCATION & PROFESSIONAL CERTIFICATIONS:**

CENTRAL MICHIGAN UNIVERSITY
Grand Rapids, Michigan

Bachelor of Arts—1995
**Business Administration**
Internship: Langley & Stewart Investors, London, England, 1994
Foreign Exchange: Paris, France, Summer 1993

NASD Registered Investment Representative, 2002

Certified Insurance Counselor (CIC), 2000

Life & Health Insurance License, 2000

Real Estate Sales License, 1997

OR

CENTRAL VIRGINIA COMMUNITY COLLEGE, Lynchburg, Virginia

Currently pursuing **A.A. Degree in General Studies** (to be conferred in June 2010)

**High School Graduate,** Virginia Episcopal School, Lynchburg, Virginia, 2007

## Employment Experience

The Experience section of your resume will most likely be the longest and the most detailed. It will also take you the longest to write. In this section you want to highlight, as briefly as possible, the key responsibilities and accomplishments of each of your positions using powerful words to create an effective presentation.

By now you should realize that resumes are not job descriptions. They might certainly include some information that is in your job description, but a resume is a sales document, not just a listing of duties and responsibilities. It must be well worded and carefully merchandised to capture your reader's attention. You must include precise information about your job functions and achievements, not just generalized statements of overall responsibilities. Include specific figures, percentages, and results when describing your accomplishments to clearly communicate your skills and expertise.

Here's an excellent example of a high-impact experience description. It effectively communicates overall scope of responsibility in the first paragraph and then presents measurable accomplishments in an easy-to-skim bullet format.

Directed the planning, staffing, budgeting, and operations of a six-site logistics operation for $800 million plastics distributor. Scope of responsibility was diverse and included purchasing, vendor management, materials handling, inventory control, distribution planning, and field delivery operations. Managed a staff of 55 through six supervisors. Controlled a $45 million annual operating budget.

- Introduced continuous improvement and quality-management programs throughout the logistics organization. Results included a 25% increase in productivity and a 64% increase in customer satisfaction.

- Spearheaded cost-reduction initiatives that reduced labor costs by 18%, overtime by 34%, and material waste by 42%.

- Renegotiated key vendor contracts for a 28% reduction over previous year's costs.

- Facilitated the integration of logistics and supply-chain management operations following the $2.8 million acquisition of Ellerson Plastics Components.

Prospective employers who read this description can quickly sense the scope of this candidate's responsibilities (size of company, number of people, budgets) and clearly identify his achievements (cost savings, productivity improvements, waste reductions, acquisition integration, customer satisfaction). Remember, recruiters and employers won't read between the lines for relevant information. You must spell it out.

As you're writing your job descriptions, remember that they should generally get shorter as you go back further in time. Obviously, you are not going to include as much information about a job from 10 years ago as you are about your current position. Use your previous positions to highlight notable achievements, major responsibilities, special projects, and performance improvements.

## "Older" Experience

If you've been working for 15, 20, or more years, you will have to decide how much of your older experience you want to include. This will depend entirely on how relevant that information is to your current career objectives. If you can optimize that experience and demonstrate value, include it, but be brief and leave off the dates (particularly if they're prior to 1980) if you're concerned that they might immediately exclude you from consideration. Here's an excellent example:

> Previous professional experience includes several responsible operations-management positions with Ryder Dedicated Logistics, FedEx, and DHL.

Note that the value you get from this sentence is the impressive name recognition of your past employers.

OR

> Promoted rapidly throughout early career in sales and customer service. Personally negotiated and closed a $17 million sale to Chrysler, the largest sale in the history of IBM.

Here the value is the financial result you delivered.

## Spelling, Punctuation, Grammar, and Syntax

Your resume must be perfect, with absolutely no errors. A typographical error, poor word choice, inconsistency in syntax, or incorrect punctuation can be the kiss of death. Ask yourself whether you'd hire someone who sent a resume that was filled with errors. Your answer is most likely no. So why would anyone else? Remember, your resume demonstrates the quality of work you will produce on that company's behalf. If it's not perfect, it's not acceptable.

Proofread your resume not just once or twice, but repeatedly to identify and correct any typographical or wording errors. Then ask three to five of your friends or colleagues to review it as well, just to double-check that you have not missed anything.

Also, be sure to choose language that is appropriate to the position you are seeking. If you're an entry-level professional, don't use "Ph.D." language. On the other end of the spectrum, if you're in line for a CEO slot, use appropriate management and leadership terminology to create a resume that has the right tone and impact for a candidate at that level.

## Writing in the First Person and in the Correct Tense

Write your document in the active first-person voice, never the third-person. There are no exceptions to this rule.

One quirk in resume writing that sometimes causes confusion about which voice is being used is the fact that, almost invariably, pronouns are omitted. For instance, you would not say "I direct a six-person sales administration team that supports all 47 of our field sales engineers." Instead, you would word this statement in the following idiosyncratic "resume language": first person, pronouns omitted.

> Direct six-person sales administration team that supports all 47 of the company's field sales engineers.

Another question that frequently arises is whether to write in the present or past tense. As a rule, you should write the activities and responsibilities of your current position in the present tense, and all past positions and all completed accomplishments in the past tense.

## Length

The same one-page versus two-page dilemma that we explored with cover letters is also a major point of discussion in relation to resume writing. Twenty years ago, it was standard practice to have a one-page resume. Today, the rules have changed, the market has changed, and the competition has increased phenomenally. Most individuals would now agree that a resume does not necessarily have to be just one page. Unlike cover letters, which overwhelmingly remain one page, resumes are frequently two or even three pages in length. If you have more than 10 or 15 years of relevant experience, you would probably shortchange yourself if you rigidly followed the so-called "one-page resume rule."

What your resume does have to be is a document that sells you. We recommend that you begin by writing the text and then determining whether it will fit most comfortably on one page or two. However, if you're going to use a second page, be sure that you do indeed need it. If you have only two or three lines on the second page, go back and edit your text, delete a line here and there, and get your resume onto one page.

*Tip* You will find that the response to your resume will be directly proportional to how well you've marketed your qualifications and achievements, not the number of pages in your resume.

## Resume Presentation

There are countless ways to arrange the contents of your resume, and dozens of different fonts and formatting styles you can choose. The underlying foundation for all of your design decisions should be to communicate the most important information about your qualifications quickly, easily, and logically. Your resume should be inviting and easy to read, yet provide enough detail to convey the depth of your experience. The reader should be able to grasp the key points in a 10-second skim-through. All formatting enhancements (such as headers, bold type, bullet points, underlining, and so forth) should help readers notice and remember your strongest "selling points."

### Format

Format should *not* be your primary consideration when writing your resume. Often job seekers will see a format they like and then try to make their information fit into it. It simply doesn't work! You can review other resumes for ideas, but you must craft your document to sell only you.

A much better strategy is to decide on a resume format after you have written the text and seen what information you have to work with. At this point, the most effective format should easily present itself just from the type of information you have written. Then all you'll need to do is

- Set your headings and margins.
- Adjust spacing for readability and impact.
- Insert horizontal rules or other graphic elements to improve appearance and organization.
- Select which type enhancements (**bold,** *italics,* or underlining) you want to use and where.
- Edit the text to comfortably fit on each page.

We strongly recommend that you adhere to these formatting guidelines:

- Don't expect readers to struggle through paragraphs that are 10 to 15 lines long. Substitute two or three shorter paragraphs or use bullets to set off new sentences and sections.
- Don't overdo your use of bold, italics, or underlining. Excessive use defeats the purpose of these enhancements. If half of the type on the page is bold, nothing will stand out.
- Use a readable font size. This is a subjective assessment and will vary from about 9 points to 12 points depending on the specific font you choose. If you want employers to review your resume, make sure they don't need a magnifying glass!
- Don't clutter your resume. Everything you've heard about "white space" is true. Let your document "breathe" so that readers don't have to struggle through it. Ease of readability is a key factor in the effectiveness of your resume.
- Use an excellent printer. Smudged, faint, heavy, or otherwise poor-quality print will discourage red-eyed readers.

### Visual Presentation

Because your resume is actually a marketing document, its appearance is critical. To survive in the job search market and outperform other well-qualified candidates, your resume must be sharp and powerful in its presentation. Keep in mind that even if you submit your resume electronically to a resume database, at some point it will be viewed by humans. So you must design it to appeal to human eyes as well as to keyword-selecting software.

We recommend that you create a look that is "conservatively distinctive." Use a commonly accepted typeface such as Times New Roman, Arial, Bookman, Verdana, Tahoma, or Georgia. Unless you're seeking a position in graphic arts or some other creative career track, don't put logos or artwork on your resume.

Your choice of paper color is entirely based on your personal preference, although we do recommend something conservative—such as white, ivory, or light gray—because you never know who might be looking at your resume, and you can't go wrong with these selections. However, a bit of creativity can give you a real boost and help your resume stand out from the crowd. Review the discussion on cover letter paper in chapter 5, and choose matching or complementary paper for all of your job search materials.

## Recommended Resume Formats

Following are nine resume formats (with full sample resumes) that were designed with specific types of job seekers in mind.

## Blue-Collar Job Seeker

# Peter Swann

(203) 555-7854 75 Beech Street, North Branford, CT 06471 peterswann@aol.com

**VACUUM FURNACE OPERATOR**

Recognized for quality, productivity, and work ethic. In every position, contributed to improved operations and positive results through dedication, leadership, and effective problem-solving.

**EMPLOYMENT**

**Vacuum Furnace Operator—ACME MACHINE COMPANY, BRANFORD, CT** **2004–Present**

Perform extremely close-tolerance metal fabrication work for the aerospace industry as an outsourced service provider to customers including Pratt & Whitney, Boeing, General Motors, the U.S. Navy, and the Department of Defense. As sole Vacuum Furnace Operator on shift, operate three furnaces simultaneously to keep fabricators supplied and maintain productivity in cell-based, ISO 9000 manufacturing environment.

Troubleshoot furnace problems to sustain high quality within the vacuum environment. Maintain outstanding quality record, consistently complying with stringent close-tolerance standards.

- Successfully completed training in ***Basic Vacuum Practices*** (Varian, Chicago, Illinois) and ***Vacuum Furnace Operation*** (Vacuum Furnace Systems, Pittsburgh, Pennsylvania).
- Increased productivity of the vacuum furnace operation by eliminating redundant paperwork and shortening several required forms.
- Took initiative to plan and orchestrate furnace move during recent plant consolidation. Successfully completed move with no unscheduled downtime.

**Building Manager—EAST END APARTMENTS, NEW HAVEN, CT** **2001–2004**

Served as on-site manager for 14-unit apartment building. Scheduled all repair and remodeling work.

- Raised occupancy from 30% to 100%.
- Organized and led neighborhood pride events that were featured on local TV (WNHT-TV).

**Corporal—UNITED STATES MARINE CORPS, SAN DIEGO, CA** **1997–2001**

As Equipment NCO, responsible for approximately $350,000 of equipment.

- Recognized for exemplary performance and outstanding dedication by Commanding Officer.

**Commercial Painter—ELM CITY PAINTING, NEW HAVEN, CT** **1996–1997**

**EDUCATION**

**Southern Connecticut Technical College** **2004–Present**
**Major: MECHANICAL ENGINEERING TECHNOLOGY (DESIGN) PROGRAM**

**INTERESTS**

Church choir, golf, biking, and reading.

This format is recommended because it highlights skills, training, and experience, and the job seeker's profession is clearly evident.

## Graduating Student with Minimal Work Experience

**LAURA S. LEWIS**
4998 Irene Avenue, Apt. #202
Baltimore, MD 21211
(555) 783-2372 / lslewis@aol.com

**CAREER OBJECTIVE: Entry-Level Professional Position in Corporate Law & Litigation**

**QUALIFICATIONS PROFILE:**

- Legal Research & Writing
- Case Strategy & Management
- Client Negotiations
- Legal Briefs & Memoranda
- Pleadings & Motions
- Depositions & Interrogatories

PC proficient. Strong organizational and project management skills. Analytical and decisive.

**EDUCATION:**

**UNIVERSITY OF MARYLAND SCHOOL OF LAW,** Baltimore, Maryland
**J.D. Degree,** December 2008
Honors & Activities: Top 35% of Class; Member, Moot Court Board

**UNIVERSITY OF SAN DIEGO,** San Diego, California
**B.A. Degree in History; Minor in English; Cum Laude,** May 2005
Honors & Activities: Top 10% of Class; Dean's List; Golden Key National Honor Society
Phi Alpha Theta (National History Honor Society)
Sigma Kappa Sorority (Scholarship Chair)

**EMPLOYMENT EXPERIENCE:**

**Server / Customer Service Associate** — 2007 to Present
KIVA GRILL, Baltimore, Maryland
CRATER'S, Baltimore, Maryland
Fast-paced customer service positions with two upscale restaurants. Emphasis on quality service, up-selling, cross-selling, public relations, and customer loyalty/retention.

**Law Clerk** — Summer 2007
OFFICE OF ATTORNEY GENERAL, Baltimore, Maryland
Selected from a competitive group of more than 50 candidates for a 4-month intensive clerkship. Assisted staff attorneys with client interviews and investigations. Researched and wrote memoranda, documented findings, and prepared legal materials for courtroom litigation.

**Law Clerk** — Summer 2006
LAW OFFICE OF JACK GREENE, ESQ., Baltimore, Maryland
Three-month clerkship with private law firm specializing in contracts, torts, and real estate transactions.

**Server** — 2004 to 2006
PUSSER'S, San Diego, California
GREEN STREET INN, San Diego, California
HYATT REGENCY, San Diego, California
Worked in several exclusive privately owned and hotel restaurants. Recognized for outstanding customer service and selected to train newly hired wait staff.

This format is effective because it brings the job seeker's relevant skills to the forefront (based on her objective) and highlights her strong academic career.

## Young Professional Uncertain About Career Objectives

# Kelly Townsend

kellytown@yahoo.com

27-A High Street
Danbury, CT 06811
203.555.8910

## Summary of Qualifications

- **Exceptional customer service skills... strong written and oral communications abilities...** creation of customer-response scripts adopted company-wide.
- **Team leadership and staff management abilities...** talent for building and leading high-performing, goal-focused teams.
- **Operations management experience...** development of procedures, benchmarks, training manuals, and training procedures.
- **Proven problem-solving and analytical skills...** well organized, with excellent planning and follow-through.
- **Record of rapid advancement** based on demonstrated competence and leadership abilities.

## Professional Experience

**THE STORE,** Danbury, CT 2003–Present

*Advanced through progressively challenging customer communications/management positions during rapid growth of The Store's online business from 30 to 700 employees.*

**Team Leader: Online Customer Communications,** 2005–Present

Lead and direct three-member team that responds to and resolves customer issues and complaints related to online orders. Also supervise corporate sales team that manages the selection and fulfillment of special and bulk orders; oversee mailroom; perform daily audit/balancing of gift certificate, check, and credit voucher accounts.

**HIGHLIGHTS: Human Resources**

- Effectively manage diverse employees, adapting management and communication style for best results with each individual.
- Successfully resolved staff problems, including negative attitude, lackluster performance, and poor attendance; built a productive team that delivers exemplary customer service.
- Initiated daily team meetings to promote communication and consistency.
- Wrote training manuals for department operations and all specific position functions.
- Trained all team members on new electronic communications system.

**HIGHLIGHTS: Operations Management**

- Recommended organizational restructuring that resulted in creation of two specialized communications teams, enabling rapid response and high levels of expertise on specific issues.
- Created performance benchmarks for communications team, establishing goals for speed, accuracy, and rapid resolution. Personally perform at *twice* the pace of rest of unit (averaging 23 responses per hour); team consistently performs 2%–4% above goals.
- Authored 29 customer-response templates that have been adopted for use in all domestic and international electronic and verbal customer messages.
- Developed key-word sorting methodology that allows automatic routing of e-mail messages to correct department for rapid and efficient response.
- Twice recognized for excellence in customer relations problem-solving; one of only four employees earning these awards among 65 in the department; only employee honored twice.

We endorse this format because it highlights a cross-section of skills and qualifications that are relevant to a number of different types of positions, companies, and industries. This format is

*(continued)*

*(continued)*

**Kelly Townsend**
**Page 2**

kellytown@yahoo.com
203.555.8910

**THE STORE** continued

**E-mail Specialist: Exceptions and Customer Research,** 2004–2005

Oversaw responses to customer electronic communication routed to Customer Research and Exceptions queues. Reviewed customer claims and verified credit-card information.

- Provided exceptional customer service that directly contributed to reduced merchandise loss and increased profits for all brands.

**Customer Service Representative: Exceptions and Customer Research,** Feb–Oct 2004

Investigated and evaluated customer claims received by phone, mail, and e-mail related to missing items and packages.

- Initiated the separation of the electronic communication representatives to a separate team by documenting need over several months and recommending organizational restructuring solution.

**Customer Service Representative,** 2003–2004

Answered customer calls, processed orders, resolved problems, and provided assistance/service to nationwide customer base.

- Achieved record daily sales results.
- Recognized for excellence in customer satisfaction and problem-solving.

## Education

**BACHELOR OF ARTS IN COMMUNICATION,** 2003 University of Connecticut, Storrs, CT

- **Public Relations Internship** with UConn Marketing Department, Spring 2003
- **Public Relations Award for Excellence:** Case Study/Program Planning, Winter 2000
- **Teaching Assistant:** Careers in Communication, Professor John Rodriguez
  One of a handful of undergraduate students at UConn selected as Teaching Assistants.

## Additional Information

- Computer skills include comprehensive knowledge of Microsoft applications... working knowledge of Lotus Notes... expert ability in Kana e-mail system (departmental trainer for this application).
- Available for relocation.
- References gladly provided on request.

flexible and appropriate in countless different situations—it allows the job seeker to explore a variety of career opportunities while still giving readers a sense of her skills and strengths.

## Career Changer

**JOHN T. STANDISH**
789 Craigmont Avenue
Duluth, Minnesota 33383
555-333-3726 / stand@earthlink.net

---

**SENIOR EXECUTIVE PROFILE**
**Strategic Human Resources Leadership / Organizational Development / Change Management**
**Performance Optimization / Leadership Training & Development / P&L Management**
**Harvard MBA Degree**

Dynamic management career leading organizations through start-up, change, revitalization, turnaround, and accelerated growth. Cross-functional expertise with proven success in optimizing organizational growth, productivity, and efficiency. HR Generalist experienced in benefits, compensation, recruitment, training, and HRIS technology. Expert team-building, team leadership, communication, and interpersonal relations skills. Strategic and analytical with outstanding problem-solving and negotiating skills.

---

**PROFESSIONAL EXPERIENCE**

**Chief Executive Officer** 2005 to Present
MED HEALTH SOLUTIONS, Duluth, Minnesota

***CHALLENGE:*** *Lead the organization through a comprehensive organizational development and change-management program to support growth, diversification, and expansion.*

Senior executive recruited to plan and orchestrate a complete redesign of strategic planning, HR/OD, administrative, information technology, marketing, and operating functions to increase revenues and bottom-line profitability. Manage within a tightly regulated and competitive industry.

- One of two senior executives credited with transitioning Med Health Solutions from 2008 revenues of $7,000 per month to current revenues of $1.5 million per month (57% increase within two years). Drove profit growth by better than 45%.
- Architected and implemented an aggressive internal change initiative. Partnered core operations to support organizational redesign and performance reengineering initiatives.
- Built a best-in-class HR organization, implemented advanced HRIS technology, designed benefit and compensation programs, established a formal salary structure, and introduced employee training, counseling, and coaching programs.
- Revitalized all core financial functions, implemented client/server architecture to optimize technology performance, and created a team-based/customer-based corporate culture.
- Negotiated $2.8 million acquisition of competitive company and facilitated seamless integration of personnel, technology, and product lines.

**President / General Manager** 1998 to 2005
DYNAMIC SOLUTIONS, INC., Tampa, Florida

***CHALLENGE:*** *Launch and build an entrepreneurial venture within an intensely competitive consumer market and create a strong organizational infrastructure to support continued growth and market penetration.*

Senior executive with full responsibility for strategic planning, business development, staffing, HR administration, operations, marketing, and P&L performance of an independent venture. Built the entire organizational infrastructure, created accounting and financial reporting processes, and implemented computer technology to support operations.

This format is recommended because it transitions every position to focus on the candidate's new HR career path and not on what he has really devoted the vast majority of his time to (CEO responsibilities). By using this strategy, we can change how someone perceives this individual. He is no longer

*(continued)*

*(continued)*

**JOHN T. STANDISH** / Page Two 555-333-3726 / stand@earthlink.net

- Built new venture from concept to over $1 million in annual sales with a 23% profit margin.
- Created performance-based training programs for all hourly and management personnel.
- Achieved and maintained a stable workforce with less than 5% turnover in an industry with average turnaround of better than 20%.
- Launched a series of innovative community outreach programs as part of the corporation's strategic marketing and business development efforts.

**Chief Executive Officer** 1991 to 1998
LSI SOCIEDAD, S.A., Santo Domingo, Dominican Republic

***CHALLENGE:*** *Orchestrate the growth of a new international venture within the financial services industry, and transition through organizational change and market repositioning.*

Senior management executive, senior sales manager, and HR director with full P&L responsibility for building new professional services organization. Created organizational infrastructure, recruited/trained personnel, designed marketing and business development programs, and created all administrative and internal reporting systems.

- Built new company from concept into a $12 million annual revenue producer with EBTA of $1 million annually. Achieved/surpassed all corporate revenue and profit objectives.
- Led the organization through a successful internal transition and recreated core business processes to support massive change and recreate corporate image.
- Recruited and trained a team of more than 60. Introduced incentives linked to performance and focused on customer development, retention, and growth.
- Negotiated health and insurance benefit contracts for the corporation. Designed salary structures, incentive programs and executive compensation plans.

**Personal Assistant to CEO** 1989 to 1991
BANCO DEL COMBRERO, Santo Domingo, Dominican Republic

***CHALLENGE:*** *Facilitate market and revenue growth for a specialty import/export company.*

Recruited by CEO to assist with building a profitable international business venture. Scope of responsibility spanned all core executive functions with particular emphasis on organizational design, policy/procedure development, recruitment and training, sales, and marketing.

- Instrumental in driving growth from $2.5 million to $5.5 million in annual revenues.
- Recruited former Procter & Gamble executive to the organization to provide critical industry and market leadership. Recruited sales producers from leading Latin American companies.
- Created organizational infrastructure and HR support to facilitate diversification and expansion into both emerging and established consumer markets.
- Designed HR policies, compensation plans, performance review schedules, and a series of employee training and development programs.

**EDUCATION**

Executive MBA—Harvard University—1997 (Distinguished Alumnus Award)
BS Business Administration—Lillymount University—1989

**PROFESSIONAL AFFILIATIONS**

Society for Human Resource Management (SHRM)
American Society for Training & Development (ASTD)

"John the CEO," but rather "John the HR executive." In addition, note that his Summary highlights skills and qualifications directly related to his current objectives and not his past experience, immediately "painting a picture" of an accomplished HR executive.

## Industry Changer

**EDWARD EDGERLY**
**edgerly@inmind.com**

1 Mission Circle
Miami, Florida 33389

Phone: 555.315.3334
Fax: 555.315.3332

**SENIOR MANUFACTURING INDUSTRY EXECUTIVE**
**President / Vice President / Chief Operating Officer / General Manager**
**Incorporating Advanced Information & Manufacturing Technologies to Optimize Productivity**

- Multi-Site Operations Management
- Global Sales & Marketing Leadership
- Key Account Relationship Management
- Process Redesign & Performance Optimization
- Opportunity Development & Profitability
- Multi-Site P&L Management
- Budgeting, Finance & Cost Reduction
- Joint Ventures & Acquisitions
- Product R&D & Commercialization
- Robotics & Automated Processes

Entrepreneurial spirit and drive with outstanding strategic-planning, problem-solving, decision-making, and negotiating skills. Creative with strong communication, team-building, leadership, and interpersonal skills. Bottom-line driven.

**PROFESSIONAL EXPERIENCE**

**Vice President & General Manager** 2008 to Present
**PREMIER PLASTICS CORPORATION,** Reading, PA
*($40 million manufacturer with state-of-the-art technology center)*

Recruited as #2 executive in a small, growth-driven, global manufacturer. Given full responsibility for recreating the business infrastructure, redesigning domestic and international sales and market-development programs, realigning engineering and manufacturing operations, eliminating excessive costs, and introducing advanced information and manufacturing technologies. Joint P&L responsibility with company president.

- **Revenue & Profit Growth.** Reduced breakeven by $1.5 million within first nine months. Currently projecting 30% revenue growth and 400% income growth in 2010.
- **E-Commerce.** Established the corporation's first website to launch massive e-commerce initiative currently on track to generate $2.5 million in first-year sales.
- **Technology Advances.** Directed technology team responsible for software development, customization, and implementation of advanced EDI system. Spearheaded acquisition of $200,000 in automated manufacturing technologies, systems, and processes.
- **Sales & Marketing Leadership.** Created a best-in-class global sales organization that captured three multimillion-dollar exclusive customer accounts with Flint Ink, PPG Industries, and Sherwin Williams. Currently negotiating final agreement with DuPont. Total value of $5–10 million in revenue.
- **International Business Development.** Built and led a completely new European sales organization projected to deliver $8 million in sales in 2010 and $15 million in 2011.
- **Product Engineering & Development.** Revitalized engineering, introduced automated productivity-improvement tools, implemented accurate tracking and reporting systems, and launched major initiative to develop and market new products. Currently completing applications for four new product patents.
- **Manufacturing Operations.** Spearheaded cost-reduction, quality-improvement, and productivity-improvement programs projected to reduce annual expenses by 12% while enhancing product quality and customer satisfaction/retention. Currently finalizing ISO 9001 for certification.

For a candidate seeking to transition his skills from one industry to another, this format is ideal. The presentation focuses on the candidate's transferable qualifications with virtually no mention of his

*(continued)*

*(continued)*

**EDWARD EDGERLY** – Page Two

**Vice President & Chief Operating Officer** 2006 to 2008
**NEUMANN, INC.,** Gladstone, PA
*($20 million U.S. division of $300 million world-class manufacturer)*

Recruited to U.S. division of German-based manufacturer supplying major corporations worldwide (e.g., BASF, DuPont, Hershey, Sun Chemical) to revitalize lackluster operations and reposition for long-term growth and profitability. Full operating, engineering, manufacturing, R&D, sales, marketing, HR, and P&L responsibility for U.S. operations supplying customers throughout North America.

- **Revenue & Profit Growth.** Delivered first-year revenue growth of 50.3% and profit growth of 544.6%, achieving 10% EBIT in a traditionally low-margin market. Sustained performance results through year two and positioned for continued accelerated growth.
- **Information Technology.** Led transition from UNIX-based to PC-based technology infrastructure.
- **Sales & Marketing Leadership.** Transitioned sales into a value-added partner to the manufacturing organization. Recruited direct sales force, introduced incentive program, developed website and product catalog, expanded product line offerings, and created a targeted sales/market penetration program.

**General Manager & Chief Operating Officer** 1999 to 2006
**TECHFORM CORPORATION,** Valley Forge, NJ
*($35 million international division of $350 million manufacturer)*

Recruited to plan and orchestrate an aggressive reengineering and turnaround of this specialty manufacturer faced with tremendous competition, cost overruns, poor market penetration, and faltering sales performance. Held full planning, operating, marketing, HR, technology, and P&L responsibility for the entire international division, including 14 manufacturing locations, 2 company presidents, and a 200-person staff. Challenged to drive earnings growth and ROA while repositioning and stabilizing the organization.

- **Revenue & Profit Growth.** Drove revenues from $18 million to $35 million over seven years with a better than 18% increase in bottom-line profitability. Credited with creating the business and marketing plans that successfully revitalized and repositioned the organization.
- **Technology Development.** Led project team in the design, development, prototyping, and full-scale manufacturing of several new product technologies to advance market positioning.
- **Cost Reduction & Performance Improvement.** Launched a massive cost-reduction initiative, introduced automated production techniques, lowered headcount, and reduced production costs by 30–70% over two years. Added $500,000+ to profits.
- **Operating Turnaround.** Reversed $250,000/month negative cash flow in Latin American division and restored to positive cash position.
- **High-Growth Performance.** Increased revenues and net income year-over-year in Mexico and Brazil during periods of hyperinflation (2000%) resulting from economic and political turmoil.

**Previous Professional Experience** with Automatic Lighting Company ($250 million industrial manufacturer) in Griswold, NJ. Promoted from Sales Engineer to Engineering Manager to Manager of International Operations with full operating responsibility for $30 million international division.

- **International Business Development.** Five-year senior management career developing international distribution channels throughout Europe, South Africa, Latin America, Canada, and Australia. Led buyout of Japanese joint venture. Heavy focus on international technology transfers.
- **Product R&D.** Five-year management career in product R&D included one patent, three major new product lines, and numerous line extensions to meet expanding customer demand. Led 30-person team.

**EDUCATION** **BS, Industrial Engineering**—Newark College of Engineering—Newark, NJ

previous and long-time experience in the plastics industry. His technology experience is brought to the forefront in each of his positions.

## Mid-Level Management Candidate

# Susan C. Boone

2525 Dogwood Trail
Raleigh, NC 27612

sueboone@earthlink.net

Home: 919-555-2929
Mobile: 919-200-3030

## Marketing & Sales Management Professional

**Clearly articulating value proposition and developing strategic, consultative, business-building solutions for client companies in diverse industries.**

Repeatedly successful in capturing new business and establishing relationships with decision makers at Fortune 500 firms. Expert in developing consultative business partnerships—assessing needs, learning marketing objectives, and devising creative strategies that deliver desired benefits. Demonstrated ability to introduce new concepts and nontraditional services at the highest corporate level. Background in management consulting/organizational performance; MBA.

- Strategic Marketing Planning
- Campaign Strategy & Execution
- Marketing Staff & Department Leadership
- Marketing Collateral / Corporate Identity
- Consultative Needs Assessment
- Executive-Level Presentations & Sales
- National Account Management & Retention
- Trade-Show Marketing & Lead Conversion

## Experience and Achievements

UNMIXED MESSAGES, Raleigh, NC 2006–Present

Advertising and information service company specializing in radio broadcast information.

### National Director of Marketing

**Developed millions of dollars of new business with high-profile national accounts (Coca-Cola, Frito-Lay, Home Depot, Johns Hopkins Medical Center); overcame longstanding objections by developing executive-level relationships and creating marketing programs aligned with brand image and business objectives.**

Develop strategic marketing plans for national accounts, successfully promoting a nontraditional marketing vehicle (radio program sponsorship) through needs-based analysis and custom proposal development. Combine heavy new business development with ongoing management and growth of key accounts. Develop marketing plans and proposals; negotiate contracts; implement programs; follow through with a strong emphasis on service and development of client relationships.

**Marketing, Sales & New Business Development:**

- Achieved 100% or more of sales objectives every year—in 2009, performed at 130% of goal.
- Over 90% of sales represent new business.

**Representative Accounts:**

- Captured the firm's first contract with Coca-Cola—a strategic target for 20 years. Built relationships with top decision makers and developed creative/consultative proposals that tied programs to specific brands. Grew the account from $13K first contract to more than $1M annually.
- Created innovative sponsorship program for Home Depot, a national account with a limited local-marketing budget. Aggressively promoted program tie-ins and carefully tracked results. Grew annual business from $500K to projected $1.5M by year-end 2010.
- Capitalized on program format (live reading of sponsorship announcements) to gain new business with Johns Hopkins—sold account based on proposal to customize the marketing message daily.
- Leveraged relationships and results with Frito-Lay to capture additional business with multiple brands within the company.

This suggested format clearly presents both broad management skills and strong, quantifiable accomplishments.

*(continued)*

*(continued)*

**Susan C. Boone** Home: 919-555-2929 ▪ Mobile: 919-200-3030 ▪ sueboone@earthlink.net

TRIANGLE CONSULTING, Durham, NC 2001–2006

Boutique management-consulting firm whose clients included Bayer, Oriel Therapeutics, Cronos Integrated Systems, AT&T, and Lucent.

### Management Consultant

**Developed performance-improvement strategies for diverse businesses,** participating in all phases of consulting projects from presentation and sale through assessment, analysis, recommendation and report development, and delivery of findings to executive management at client companies nationwide.

- Efficiently managed multiple consulting engagements and ongoing account relationships.
- Delivered client training programs to build business skills and enable achievement of identified goals.
- Co-created a computer program that analyzed organizational climate by relating employee emotions with work attitudes.

CHEM PRODUCTS INTERNATIONAL, Raleigh, NC 1998–2001

Chemical manufacturer and distributor.

### Product Manager, 1999–2001 ▪ Bulk Sales Specialist, 1998–1999

**Brought on board to drive sales growth of bulk-chemicals business.** Developed comprehensive marketing strategy and aggressively pursued new business while actively managing existing accounts. Developed proposals and negotiated sales.

- Increased sales 55% in less than 3 years.
- Introduced first catalog for bulk sales—researched, designed, and launched.

TEACHING AND TRAINING EXPERIENCE

- **Contract Communications Facilitator,** Communispond, Raleigh, NC, 2002–2004: Presented “Effective Business Communications” seminars to employees of major corporate clients, including Bayer and Oriel.
- **Adjunct Management Instructor,** North Carolina State University, Raleigh, NC, 2000–2002: Taught Organizational Behavior, Leadership Skills, and Team Building to undergraduate business students.

## Education

**MBA** in Marketing, 2000 ▪ **BSBA** in Marketing, 1997 North Carolina State University, Raleigh, NC

## Technologist or Scientist

# ROSE ANNE LARKIN

75 Broad Street, Melrose, MA 02176 ▪ 781-594-2345 ▪ roseanne@boston.rr.com

**Developing clean, elegant, highly functional code... creating attractive and functional user interfaces... providing advanced technology solutions that boost productivity and efficiency across the organization.**

**TECHNICAL PROFILE**

**Certification:** Sun Certified Java 6 Programmer

**Programming Languages:** Java, J5EE, Java Servlet, JSP, JDBC, JINI, JavaSpaces, JavaScript, XML, XSLT, CSS, DHTML, SQL, Oracle PL/SQL

**Development Tools:** IDEA, Ant, CVS, JMeter, JUnit, Big Brother, Oracle9i, Oracle JDeveloper

**Web Application Servers:** Apache, Tomcat

**Operating Systems & DBM Systems:** UNIX, Windows 2007, Windows XP, Oracle

**EDUCATION**

**MS Computer Science,** summa cum laude, Boston University, 2006

**BS Electrical Engineering,** summa cum laude, Tufts University, 2002

**JAVA DEVELOPER**

**Experienced application developer/Sun certified Java 6 programmer** recognized for initiative, problem-solving skills, and creativity in both programming and web design. Master's degree in computer science. Strong project planning and project-management skills. Meticulous attention to testing and documentation. Fast and reliable; quick learner; team player.

**EXPERIENCE**

**Web Developer:** Mediquick Systems, Cambridge, MA 2006–2010

In fast-paced team environment, devised technical solutions to support smooth and productive operations at the company's call center and 27 outpatient surgery centers nationwide. Developed and introduced new web applications; troubleshot and improved existing technology; readily took on new projects and gained reputation for devising clean, fast, elegant solutions to diverse technical challenges that often required on-the-job learning.

- **Appointment book application:** Created new application 10x faster than existing, using dynamic HTML to create user-friendly interface with advanced functionality—the company's first-time use for several functions. (HTML and JavaScript on the client side; Java Servlets, JDBC, XML, XSLT, CSS, JINI, and JavaSpaces on the application side; Oracle SQL and PL/SQL on the database side.)
- **Web interface for new services package:** Developed one of the main interfaces in the intranet site, providing dynamic and customized content for all components of service packages at individual centers.
- **Report administration:**
  — Accounting and financial reports: Developed multi-level administration tool with easy customization at the department level. Created login screen for desktop access to customized reports based on user group.
  — Exam-book reports: Designed and developed dynamic exam book, giving users statistical information that enables comparisons and projections.
- **JavaSpaces e-mail follow-up:** Set up JavaSpaces service, and then wrote remote objects to JavaSpaces to allow sending of e-mail to clients using JavaMail—adding functionality and speed without taxing server capacity.
- **Web application enhancement and troubleshooting:** Repeatedly fixed bugs and found faster, more efficient solutions.
- **Set up web development environment and services:**
  — Installed and configured Apache, Tomcat.
  — Set up Big Brother system that monitors our main websites and immediately sends notification when problems are detected.
  — In UNIX environment, set up Ant as Java-based build tool; CVS as version control system; JUnit as unit testing system.
  — Set up Apache JMeter to load-test the web application performance.

**Web Projects:** Freelance programming 2002–2006

This format is effective because it highlights specific technical qualifications (languages, operating systems, and applications) while also detailing the specific business benefits that have resulted from this candidate's technology projects.

## Candidate Leaving the Military or Government for a Corporate Position

**CHRISTOPHER CRAIG**
432 Colonel Marshall Way
Lovingston AFB, Colorado 38837

Phone: (555) 352-4726
Fax: (555) 354-3827

Voice Mail: (555) 352-3827
E-mail: commander@aol.com

---

**CAREER PROFILE:**

High-caliber Management Executive with more than 15 years of experience building and leading top-performing, efficient, and cost-effective operations for a global organization. Strong general management qualifications in strategic planning, reengineering, process redesign, quality, and productivity improvement. Excellent experience in personnel training, development, and leadership. Skilled public speaker and executive liaison.

**PROFESSIONAL EXPERIENCE:**

**MANAGEMENT EXECUTIVE** 1984 to Present
UNITED STATES NAVY—U.S. & WORLDWIDE ASSIGNMENTS

*Fast-track promotion through a series of increasingly responsible management positions directing large-scale operating, resource management, finance, and human resource organizations. Acted in the capacity of* ***Chief Operating Officer, General Manager,*** *and* ***Management Executive,*** *developing and leading high-profile business units supporting global operations. Expertise includes the following:*

**General Management / Operations Management**

- Planned, staffed and directed business affairs for organizations with up to 4,200 personnel assigned to more than 15 different sites worldwide. Held full decision-making responsibility for developing annual business plans and long-range strategic plans, evaluating human resource and training requirements, and implementing advanced information technologies.
- Consulted with senior executive management team to evaluate long-term organizational goals and design supporting business and financial systems to control operations.
- Managed more than $300 million in annual budget funds allocated for operations, research and development, and general expenses. Slashed 22% from the budget through reallocation of resources, personnel, and technologies.
- Conducted ongoing analyses to evaluate the efficiency, quality, and productivity of diverse operations (e.g., administrative, equipment, maintenance, transportation, human resources, inventory control). Streamlined operations and reduced staffing requirements by 18%.
- Negotiated and administered multimillion-dollar vendor contracts supporting more than $80 million in field construction and renovation projects. Delivered all projects on time and within budget.
- Appointed to several headquarters committees working to professionalize the U.S. Navy, introduce proven business management strategies, and enhance internal accountabilities.

We recommend this style because it uses a format that highlights the candidate's general business skills and qualifications. By using "corporate" language, not military or government lingo, it appears as though the candidate already belongs in "corporate America."

**CHRISTOPHER CRAIG** – *Page Two*

**Human Resource Leadership**

- Directed staffs of up to 100+ technical, professional, and support personnel. Fully accountable for personnel scheduling, job assignments, performance reviews, merit promotions, and daily supervision. Coordinated manpower planning to meet operational requirements and realigned workflow to optimize productivity.
- Designed and led hundreds of personnel training and professional skills development programs throughout career. Topics included budgeting/finance, leadership, team building, information technology, communications, reporting, and diversity.
- Introduced innovative training technologies (e.g., remote, video, telecommunications).

**Information & Telecommunications Technology**

- Spearheaded the selection, acquisition, and implementation of more than $45 million in technologies over the past 10 years (e.g., Internet and intranet, data mining, data warehousing, CAD/CAM, Microsoft Office, GIS).

**Asset Management**

- Controlled more than $175 million in capital equipment, materials, and supplies. Redesigned logistics support programs and reduced inventory costs by $3 million annually.

**Career Path**

**Commanding Officer** (2004 to Present)
**Resource Management Director** (2000 to 2004)
**Executive Officer** (1996 to 2000)
**Business/Finance Manager** (1994 to 1996)
**Operations Officer** (1988 to 1994)
**Administrator / Program Coordinator / Educational Officer** (1984 to 1988)

*Received several distinguished awards and commendations for outstanding leadership qualifications, management expertise, quality/productivity improvements, and cost reductions.*

**EDUCATION:**
**MS—Executive Management**—Naval Postgraduate School—1992
**BS—Management**—U.S. Naval Academy—1984
**Graduate**—500+ hours of leadership and executive management training

**AFFILIATIONS:**
Who's Who Worldwide (2005)
Sydney Roads Total Quality Management Council
American Society of Military Leaders
American Management Association

## Senior Manager or Executive

# ROBERT SANTIAGO

312-700-0101 | 2775 Hyde Park Place, Chicago, IL 60616 | santiago@att.net

---

## COO / CFO / GROUP CONTROLLER / VP FINANCE

**Industrial & Consumer Products Manufacturing**
**U.S. Steel—Aramark—Tech-Soft—Turnaround & High-Growth Ventures**

Strategic and hands-on executive, an accomplished change agent with a 20-year track record of revitalizing, restructuring, accelerating growth, and maximizing ROI for manufacturing operations in intensely competitive international markets. Repeatedly delivered rapid and sustainable performance improvements in turnaround and rescue assignments: restored profitability, transformed operational systems, spurred revenue growth, improved morale, and positioned businesses for growth and sale.

Recognized for ability to distill complex issues to fundamentals, create blueprints for growth, and implement systems to guarantee profitability and sustainable competitive advantage.

- Strategic Planning & Tactical Execution
- Financial & Operations Analysis
- Leading-Edge Technologies & Methodologies
- Revenue & Profit Growth
- M&A Due Diligence
- Contract Negotiations

---

## EXPERIENCE AND ACHIEVEMENTS

GREAT LAKES INDUSTRIES, Palatine, IL (chemicals manufacturer and distributor) 2005–2010

**Chief Operating Officer**

**Recruited by owner/CEO to take plateaued company to the next level. Transformed antiquated processes, met strict cost-reduction milestones, grew revenues 50% in 18 months, and structured the organization for profitable sale.** With full accountability for all functional areas of the company, installed vital internal controls, budget compliance, strategic planning, and employee training; instilled customer focus and addressed performance improvement at every level of the organization.

- Introduced 21st-century technology and methodologies, purchasing essential capital equipment and implementing Lean Manufacturing, Six Sigma, ISO 9002, performance benchmarking, and OSHA/Hazmat training (and successfully averting threatened EPA and OSHA actions).
- Grew revenues from $12M to $18M, primarily as a result of increased manufacturing capacity due to dramatic productivity gains—e.g., cut production time for one product by 80%.
- Slashed inventory, modernized warehouse, and cut labor costs.
- Secured federal and state grants, tax cuts, and empowerment-zone concessions to fund capital improvements and technology investments.
- Created a culture of employee "ownership" and pride in work well done.

KRAKOW ASSOCIATES, Chicago, IL ($70M commodities brokerage firm) 2001–2005

**CFO / COO**

**Reversed alarming trend of spiraling costs and declining profitability;** implemented cost controls and fiscal accountability that supported profitable growth from $12M to $70M in four years. Oversaw P&L and all financial, IS, and business operations.

- Captured immediate $250K profit contribution and 28% reduction in operating costs by reviewing and renegotiating numerous supply and service contracts and establishing disciplines for day-to-day business practices.
- Implemented tight financial controls. Within 15 months, brought all accounts into compliance, improved cash flow, eased bank tensions, and saved $80K in interest payments.
- Structured sale of company assets for profitable payout to owners.

This resume is distinguished by its executive-level language, tone, style, and impact. All of these combine to create a powerful, upscale, and executive presentation.

312-700-0101 **Robert Santiago** santiago@att.net

TECH-SOFT, INC., Naperville, IL ($650M manufacturer of hand-held computers and software) 1999–2001

**Senior Director, Financial Planning & Analysis**

**Through top-down business analysis, set the stage for transformational product shift that boosted profit margins 45% and positioned company for dramatic growth.** Participated in executive decision-making that steered business toward profit opportunities. Set financial controls and formalized planning processes.

- Orchestrated reduction in product offerings from 500 to 16, enabling 30% reduction in plant operating costs and profit growth from $8M to $26M within one year.
- Introduced performance benchmarking and pushed accountability to the lowest levels, leading to headcount reductions, commission-structure adjustments, and elimination of inefficient practices.
- Championed adoption of Oracle-based ERP system to streamline, standardize, and improve the efficiency of company operations in 65 countries worldwide.

CHEMICAL SPECIALTIES, INC., Gary, IN (manufacturer of chemical specialty products) 1993–1999

**CFO / VP Finance**

**Rescued business on the brink of bankruptcy, achieving profitability, explosive revenue growth, dramatic productivity gains, and recognition as a "Top 100 Fastest-Growing Company" in Indiana.** Began by negotiating with creditors, resolving existing bank-covenant violations, and securing new capital for automation and equipment. Continued to deliver financial, operational, and product improvements that drove sales from $17M to $45+M in a six-year period.

- Reversed $290K loss to $1M profit within seven months.
- Improved manufacturing productivity 25%.
- Drove automation initiatives, including smooth implementation of CAELUS-based ERP system.
- Revitalized product development; remarketed existing products; realigned sales territories.
- Introduced contract manufacturing to utilize excess capacity. Established lucrative contracts with major manufacturers. Identified and negotiated acquisition of manufacturing plant with complementary products that further spurred contract manufacturing revenues.

KRAFT FOODS, Iowa City, Iowa ($25B food products manufacturer and distributor) 1987–1993

**Plant Controller,** 1990–1993

**Selected for a "fix now or close" turnaround assignment with one of Kraft's largest manufacturing facilities.** Led team that assessed operations, identified immediate and ongoing cost reductions, established operational controls, and laid the foundation for 12 years of profitable operation.

- Identified $600K in first-year cost reductions and year-over-year savings in the millions of dollars. Improved efficiency, introduced manufacturing line changes, and reduced headcount.
- Empowered employees and opened lines of communication with union officials to instill ownership.

**Manufacturing Cost Manager (Group Controller),** 1989–1990

**Identified cost savings and operational improvements** as roving analyst for six Kraft plants.

EARLY CAREER (progressive accounting positions with U.S. Steel and Aramark) 1982–1987

## Professional Profile

EDUCATION
Villanova University, Villanova, PA
**MBA, Quantitative Analysis,** 1987; **BS, Accounting,** 1982

CERTIFICATION
**Certified Management Accountant,** ICMA, 1998

AFFILIATIONS
Association for Financial Professionals
American Association of Accountants
Institute of Management Accountants

## Consultant

**RAYMOND R. PALANSKI**
82 Grisham Road
Seafert, DE 19898
Phone: 555-839-2876 E-mail: rrpalanski@aol.com Fax: 555-839-9643

---

**EXECUTIVE PROFILE**

**Corporate Development Executive / Business Development Strategist** with 15+ years across broad industries, products, services, and technologies in U.S. and foreign markets. Intuitive, insightful, creative, and intelligent. Confidential advisor to CEOs, CFOs, chairmen, and other senior executives. Impeccable ethics and integrity. MBA Degree. CPA.

- Growth & Development Strategy, Value Analysis, Vision & Leadership
- Mergers, Acquisitions, Joint Ventures, Strategic Alliances & Partnerships
- Capital Formation, Investment Banking & Venture Capital Funding
- Complex Financial Analysis, Modeling & Transactions Structuring
- Executive Mediation, Negotiation, Facilitation & Partner/Liaison Affairs
- Acquisition Integration & Post-Integration Leadership

---

**CAREER PROFILE**

**CORPORATE DEVELOPMENT CONSULTANT** 2000 to Present
**THE PALANSKI COMPANY,** Dover, DE

**Strategic & Financial Advisor / Investment Banker** to U.S. and foreign corporations committed to acquisition-focused growth strategies. Provide turnkey leadership for major acquisition, strategic alliance, joint venture, and refinancing programs, from initial business planning, candidate/partner selection, due diligence, deal structuring, and negotiations through final execution. Project highlights include

- **Forum International**—Developed and executed strategy to employ high market capitalization of U.K. medtech company for U.S. expansion. Delivered strategy that achieved profit targets to counter R&D costs; product/service outsourcing; and roll-up consolidation. Point person for two acquisitions, driving client revenues from $2 million to $30+ million. Listed company on the London Stock Exchange.
- **Leverson Global**—Authored business plan for strategic alliance to establish a U.S. consulting firm joint venture for $2 billion Dutch corporate division. Executive committee voted full funding for $750,000.
- **Bross & Company**—Architected competitive strategy for Fortune 1000 Bross client to increase market share and profitability within the changing healthcare reimbursement market.
- **Biotech Partners**—Currently leading effort to acquire larger, publicly held competitor to build critical mass, expand product line, and achieve public listing with less-costly and more-creative "back door" strategy.

**VENTURE PROJECTS DIRECTOR** 1994 to 2000
**LOUISIANA GENERAL HOSPITAL (LGH),** Baton Rouge, Louisiana

Recruited by Chairman of the Board as **Venture Projects Director** to orchestrate an aggressive expansion throughout highly competitive healthcare industries, technologies, and services. Conceived, developed, and led successful corporate development projects (strategic alliances, joint ventures, start-up ventures). Served as **CFO, Treasurer, or Director of Finance** for new projects. Member—Corporate Strategies Committee. **Board Member**—MGH portfolio companies.

- **CRESSTAR, Inc.**—CFO tasked to either restore this medical imaging technology transfer venture to profitability or close. Sought funding to energize company, expand operations, and strengthen financial performance. Achieved all financial objectives.
  - — Negotiated $2 million strategic alliance with 3M and $5 million contract with Procter & Gamble.
  - — Developed capital strategy and business plan leading to acquisition by French merchant bankers.
- **Fox Runn Partnership**—Partnered with two for-profit companies to develop a $100 million retirement community. Negotiated complex $75 million construction loan and subsequent permanent mortgage financing package. Restructured loan status when FDIC took over bank. Structured and negotiated successful buyout of corporate partner facing bankruptcy to eliminate partnership liability.
  - — Returned $7+ million profit on $2.3 million investment (despite poor regional real estate market).

This format is recommended because it places the emphasis on depth and scope of consulting projects, notable results and achievements, and reputation and diversity of clients.

**RAYMOND R. PALANSKI**—*Page Two* Phone: 555-839-2876 E-mail: rrpalanski@aol.com Fax: 555-839-9643

**VENTURE PROJECTS DIRECTOR** *(Continued):*

- **Louisiana Biomedical Research Corporation**—Single-handedly structured a complex financial model for $125 million bond financing for development of 650,000 sq. ft. of biomedical research labs. Met debt covenants, grant restrictions, market lease rates, FASB 13, and debt burden limits.
  - Created financial plan in place for six years. Co-led company's $30 million operations during tenure.
- **Acute Disease Care Center**—Authored strategic, financial, and business plans approved for $22 million in new venture funding by the Board of Trustees.
- Conceived, developed, and/or launched several other successful new ventures/portfolio companies:
  - **XRT**—Partnered with Paris-based VC firm to develop international telemedicine partnership.
  - **LGHIC**—Launched diagnostic imaging venture. Increased reimbursement by $5 million.
  - **American Express**—Partnered hospital with American Express to establish profitable in-house travel agency.

**VENTURE PROJECTS CONSULTANT / INTERIM CFO** 1991 to 1994

- **LGH**—Developed and implemented strategic business plan to establish innovative marketing initiative. Subsequently recruited as Venture Projects Director with this $1+ billion corporation.
- **Crescent Ventures**—Developed and automated accounting and financial management systems for seven partnerships of this $160 million new venture firm (*now one of the world's largest VC firms*). Directed investor relations with corporations and pension funds. Managed $40 million cash fund.
- **Paris Stores, Inc.**—Created and implemented financial and administrative infrastructure to lead Canadian-based retail chain into U.S. market (18 stores in Eastern and Midwestern regions).
- **Seventh Avenue Deli**—Developed strategic business plan for retail food company that attracted majority ownership investment offer from Beatrice Foods.

**CHIEF FINANCIAL OFFICER / SENIOR VICE PRESIDENT** 1989 to 1991
**BUCKMAN & LEWISTON,** Boston, Massachusetts (*22-office regional investment brokerage*)

Promoted from Vice President of Finance to CFO with full leadership responsibility for the firm's finance, investment, credit, accounting, MIS, and human resource operations. Teamed with Chairman and CEO in negotiating the profitable sale of the firm in 1991 (*declined offer to remain with new corporation*).

**MANAGER—INVESTOR RELATIONS** 1986 to 1989
**DRG CORPORATION,** Westborough, Massachusetts

Communicated financial results and strategic direction to Wall Street, strengthening DRG's market credibility (*despite negative industry press*). Authored corporate press releases and speeches.

**ASSISTANT TO THE PRESIDENT** 1984 to 1986
**MID-EAST ROYALTIES,** Chattanooga, Tennessee

Managed SEC affairs through two security offerings for $100 million oil and gas company.

**EDUCATION**

**MBA—Finance** EMORY UNIVERSITY—1991
**BA—Economics** UNIVERSITY OF TENNESSEE—1983
**CPA** STATE OF LOUISIANA—1983

**HUMANITARIAN EFFORTS**

Conceived, planned, solicited, and integrated corporate partners, and spearheaded Bosnian famine relief effort in 2007. Led project in cooperation with local network television affiliate to create local fund-raising and corporate giving campaigns. Raised $600,000+ in donations and relief supplies.

# Magical Tips on Resume Writing

With more than 25 years of resume-writing experience between the two of us, we've come to know certain things that will help you create resumes that get noticed. Follow these magical tips to ensure that your resume is appropriate, on target, and a powerful sales document.

## No Rules—Just Write

If anyone ever tells you that there are "rules" to resume writing, walk away. The fact that there are no rules is what makes the resume-writing process so challenging. What works for one individual does not work for another. Each document must be custom-designed to that individual's specific experiences, qualifications, credentials, and track record of performance.

## Sell It to Me; Don't Tell It to Me

The "sell it to me; don't tell it to me" strategy is one of the most effective in resume writing. Read the following sentence carefully:

> Responsible for recruitment, training, benefits, compensation, and employee relations.

That sentence very succinctly "tells" the reader what you did.

A much better strategy is to "sell" your accomplishments by using a sentence such as this:

> Directed recruitment, training, benefits compensation, and employee relations for a 400-employee corporation with 25% annual growth and worldwide market presence.

Can you see the difference? The first is passive; it simply states overall responsibilities. The second is assertive; not only does it highlight responsibilities, but it clearly communicates the large and dynamic environment in which the job seeker worked. Sell your success. No one else will!

## Be Honest, but Not Modest

If you are ever going to "toot your own horn," now is the time, and the vehicle is your resume. You *never* want to lie or misrepresent yourself. However, you do want to sell what you have accomplished and capture your reader's interest. It is time to remember all the great things you've done throughout your career and let the world know about them.

## The Essentials: Employment and Education

Your resume must include your employment history and academic credentials. Although we have said that there are no rules for resume writing, it is expected that you will include your employment history and education qualifications. A prospective employer or recruiter must be able to quickly review your employment (companies and positions) and your academic credentials (college degrees, certificates, and continuing education). If you do not include this information, you leave the reader with virtually nothing to evaluate your skills, competencies, and potential value to that company.

## It's OK to Leave Out Some Things

Your resume *does not* have to include each and every position you've ever held. Understand that we are not recommending that you misrepresent anything about yourself or your career. However, at some point in time, your older work experience becomes less important to your current career objectives, particularly if you've been working for 20 or more years.

If this is your situation, you might elect not to include your earlier experience, or you might summarize it if it is relevant to your current goals or offers you some competitive distinction from other candidates. This might include names of prominent companies you worked for, prominent client accounts you managed, significant and quantifiable achievements, or interesting and unusual experiences.

The other situation in which you might not include each and every position you've ever held is when you had a job that was particularly short in tenure. Suppose you worked in real estate sales for six months in 2004 between your two industrial sales management positions. Unless that experience is directly related to the type of position for which you are currently applying, you might elect to delete it from your resume. It was short in duration, it was six years ago, and it is unrelated to your professional career. It was simply a "filler."

Be advised that we recommend that at the time of an interview you share any information you left out of your resume. You don't want to create a veil of misconception. When you're face to face in an interview, tell the interviewer about those other positions so that you are disclosing all information. Just explain that the experience was irrelevant to your current career goals and, therefore, not worth including on your resume. You never want the interviewer to have any question as to your personal integrity, ethics, and values.

### Never Include Salary Information on Your Resume

If a prospective employer or recruiter has asked for that information and you choose to comply, include it in your cover letter. That is the appropriate place, not your resume. See chapters 1, 3, 6, and 15 for more on this subject.

### Wording to Avoid

Do not start job descriptions with the words "Responsible for" or "Duties included." These phrases are dated and make for boring resume reading. You will significantly improve the tone and impact of your resume if you write using action verbs such as *managed, directed, trained, supervised, designed, developed, improved, increased, saved, reduced, facilitated, spearheaded…* the list goes on and on. For a comprehensive list of action verbs, refer to appendix B.

Compare these two sample resume sentences to see the difference that action verbs can make:

> Responsible for planning and managing new product introductions.

> Spearheaded the introduction of six new products that generated more than $2 million in first-year revenues.

See the difference in impact and tone? The first is passive. The second is energizing and immediately communicates success and achievement.

### Presentation Counts

Your resume's visual presentation must be powerful, attractive, and easy to read. When your resume first passes in front of someone, you have only a few seconds to catch his or her attention. You can best accomplish this by preparing a document that is visually pleasing, has lots of white space, and can be quickly perused. If you don't catch the reader's attention visually, he or she might never read your resume, and you might never have the opportunity for an interview.

## Include Your E-mail Address

Be sure to include your e-mail address it on your resume (and in your cover letter). Virtually the entire business world now communicates via e-mail. Let people know that you're "in the loop" by providing your e-mail contact information. Not only does this demonstrate that you're keeping up with the times, it also provides a prospective employer or recruiter an easy and fast channel to communicate with you.

Don't use your current employer's e-mail address on your resume! Not only is this "bad form," implying that you use business tools for personal use, but there is the very real chance that you could jeopardize your current position if someone at your company intercepts or sees your job search–related e-mail messages. With numerous sources of free e-mail access widely available, it's a simple task to sign up for a personal e-mail address when you start your job search.

## Take Everyone's Advice with a Grain of Salt

No matter who you speak with or who reviews your resume, you will get different opinions. Remember, that's part of what makes the entire job search process such a challenge. It is not an exact science, but rather is open to extensive personal interpretation. Listen carefully to what everyone says to you about your resume, and then integrate only the information you believe is appropriate to your career, your current objectives, and your personal situation.

## Is Your Resume Working for You?

Take this short quiz. If you can't check off every box, go back and work on your resume some more.

- ☐ Are you proud when you look at your resume?
- ☐ Does your resume leave a memorable visual impression?
- ☐ Is your resume easy to peruse and easy to read?
- ☐ Have you left adequate white space?
- ☐ Are your career objectives and strongest qualifications crystal-clear upon quickly scanning the resume?
- ☐ Have you included all relevant work experience?

- ☐ Have you included relevant degrees, training, and educational credentials?
- ☐ Does your resume highlight your most significant career accomplishments?
- ☐ Have you included measurable results that demonstrate your contributions?
- ☐ Does your resume include your e-mail address?
- ☐ Have you triple-checked for grammar, punctuation, and spelling errors?
- ☐ Does your resume highlight your technical qualifications (if appropriate)?
- ☐ Does your resume clearly communicate your value to a prospective employer?
- ☐ Does your resume *sell* you?

# Chapter 18

# Strategies, Tips, and Techniques to Recession-Proof Your Career

Now that you've worked your way through the earlier chapters of this book, you should have created an outstanding portfolio of cover letters and thank-you letters and written a best-in-class resume. If you're an active job seeker, you can use these letters, along with your resume, to apply for new positions and move your job search forward. If you're a passive job seeker, you'll watch the employment market carefully and then use your letters when that great opportunity crosses your path. Either way, you're all set to go. Now comes the hard work: the actual job search!

In decades past, job search was a relatively straightforward process. If you wanted to work for a company, you applied to the company, interviewed with a hiring manager or human resources specialist, and, hopefully, got the job offer. It *was* a remarkably clean, efficient, and easy-to-manage process for almost all job seekers.

Not today! In the past few years there have been remarkable changes in job search and career management—specifically where the jobs are, how we look for those jobs, the obstacles we have to overcome and the pitfalls we have to avoid to get to those jobs, and the volume of competition that we have to "beat" in order to get the job offer. Today's job search can be tough, intense, time-consuming, expensive, and remarkably frustrating. However, once you land that great new opportunity and are happily and profitably employed, it will all have been worth it.

To help you with that process, this chapter outlines the knowledge, information, tools, and insights you need to plan and manage a successful job search campaign and create a proactive, lifelong career-management plan.

*Tip* Recession-proof your career by taking control and proactively managing your career. Look beyond "getting a job" and think, plan, and act to achieve your goals today, tomorrow, and into the future. You will feel more in control and will make smarter choices about the opportunities that come your way. Start today!

## Job Search in a Challenging Economic Environment

In decades past, managing your job search and your career were so much easier than today. You graduated from high school or college, accepted a position with a reputable company, and often worked for that same company until you retired. Maybe you switched companies once or twice, but that was usually it. Companies offered their employees a stable working environment, great benefits, a retirement package, and much more.

Now, everything is different. Job change is today's status quo, and you should expect to change jobs or employers at least seven or eight times during your career, if not more. So much for stability! Much of the reason for this massive change in the job market is a direct result of

- Economic globalization
- Industry collapse
- Global recession
- Increased workforce competition
- Increased global competition
- Offshoring of major manufacturers and suppliers
- And countless other factors

However, we're not going to focus on why finding a job is more competitive than in years past. Rather, we're going to tell you how to win at job searching: how to get noticed, get interviewed, get offers, and get hired.

## The Eight Most Important Elements of Job Search Success

To plan and manage a successful job search campaign, there are eight critical things you must know:

1. **Job search is sales—pure and simple.** You have a product to sell: yourself. As such, your challenge is to advertise, market, merchandise, and position that product for sale in today's competitive employment market. Most significantly, how can you distinguish that product from all of the other products? What makes you special, different, more qualified, and a better hire? A lot of that is what should be the foundation for your resume and cover letters because they're your best marketing and merchandising tools—the things that will entice someone to "pick up" the merchandise and invite you in for an interview. Once you're interviewing, you need to negotiate the sale of the product by clearly communicating its features and benefits—your qualifications, experience, achievements, project highlights, financial contributions, and more—to close the deal and get the job offer.
2. **You must have a great 30-second introduction.** Knowing who you are and the value you bring to a company is critical to your job search success. When someone asks you what you do for a living, you must have a powerful yet brief summary that you can flawlessly communicate to them. Here's a great example:

   *I'm a sales professional who has delivered double-digit revenue increases in product sales for more than 10 consecutive years. Most notably, I've excelled in launching new products in both U.S. and Latin American markets, doubling and tripling the volume of sales with existing customers and capturing new key accounts across a broad range of new industrial markets. In fact, based on my successes last year, I was honored as the #1 sales associate in ABC Company's 400-person global sales organization. It was really quite an honor.*

3. **Don't worry about what you can't control.** There are scores of things you cannot control in your job search. You cannot control the downfall of an industry and the subsequent evaporation of those positions. You cannot control a company's loss of a major contract and the associated jobs. You cannot control an economic recession and the resulting massive layoffs. You cannot control the fact that you are not free to relocate because of your child's special healthcare needs. And, most importantly, you can't control someone else's agenda for who they need to hire, when, and for how much. Instead of worrying about what you cannot control, focus your energies on the things that you can control: namely, how you plan and manage your job search campaign.
4. **It's all about who you know—or who you can get to know.** Whether or not you like it, successful job search has a lot to do with who you know and who they know. If a colleague, friend, relative, acquaintance, or anyone else can help you get an interview, you're one step closer to a job. In the next section, "The Bicycle Model of Job Search," we discuss how to best plan, manage, and optimize your networking efforts. For now, just know that you'll want to work hard to positively leverage your relationships to help land a new position.
5. **Think in bullet points.** When you're networking with a colleague, interviewing for a job, or telling someone about your career, think in bullet points. Sometimes it's easy to get lost in your own answer when responding to an interview question or an inquiry about what you do for a living. To prevent that from happening, think about your answers as though they were bullet points, highlighting your most notable two to three accomplishments, projects, activities, or responsibilities as they relate to the specific question. Start with a quick introduction; for example:

   *Yes, I've led the development and rollout of staff-training programs throughout my career with AT&T. Most notably, I…*

   Then, highlight your bullet points—your achievements. Not only does this format help you stay organized, it makes it easier for your interviewer or network contact to understand who you are and take special note of your career successes.

6. **Listen, and listen hard.** When you're in an interview, it can be very difficult to listen intently because your mind is racing to come up with your next answer. However, you must listen, and listen hard. Any experienced interviewer can tell when someone is listening intently, and it communicates that you're sincerely interested in the position, the company, the person you're speaking with, and more. Plus, you'll learn what's most important about the position and can use that detailed information in your thank-you letter.
7. **Ask for the job.** When you're actively interviewing, always remember the following. As your interview is coming to a close, be certain that you boldly, yet appropriately, communicate that you want the job. Don't simply shake hands, say thanks, and leave. Rather, shake hands and tell your interviewer that you're really interested in the position, believe that you have just the right combination of skills and qualifications they require, and would love to accept the opportunity. Then ask what you can do to make that happen. Most likely you won't get an immediate offer because that's not the way of the world anymore, but you will have differentiated yourself from everyone else who just walked out the door and didn't ask for the job. And isn't that why you're there in the first place?
8. **Wait your turn.** We hear it all the time: "I was perfect for that job, but someone else got the offer." Well, that person was probably in the job market longer than you, had been passed over a number of times for positions that he or she believed were a perfect fit, and had echoed those exact sentiments time and time again. Instead of allowing the situation to frustrate you, cross that opportunity off your list and you'll see that you're one step closer to your turn for an offer!

## The Bicycle Model of Job Search

Today's job search is a complex process that involves a diversity of channels to effectively market yourself and your resume. You can no longer simply rely on newspaper advertisements, online job postings, or any other single activity to find your next opportunity. Rather, you must build an integrated job search program that mixes together a combination of the following activities:

- Ad responses and online job postings
- Online resume postings
- Traditional networking
- Web 2.0 networking
- Recruiter contacts
- Company contacts
- Venture-capital contacts
- Job fairs

The easiest way to look at this integrated job search strategy concept is to think of it as a bicycle wheel with you at the very center and each of the spokes representing one specific job search channel (see figure 18.1).

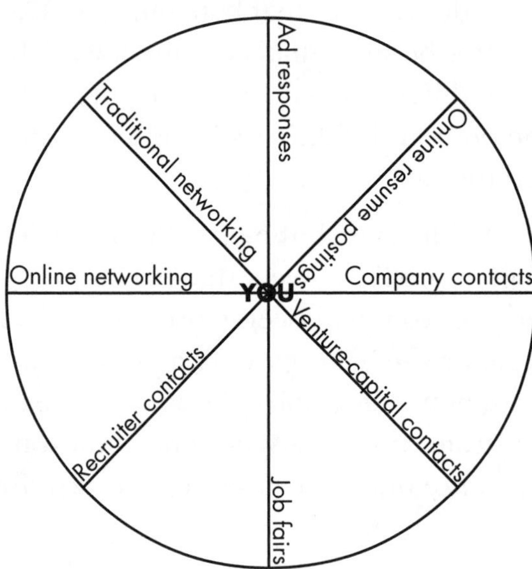


*Figure 18.1: The Bicycle Model.*

Now, think about the bicycle in action and you'll see that the spoke is in motion. The same is true about every person's job search. Nothing is stagnant; there is constant movement, change, and progression as you work your way through your search, using all available (and appropriate) job search channels.

Before we discuss these job search channels in more detail, it is important to note that not all channels will be right for you. Certain channels are better for people in certain industries or professions or at certain levels or in different geographies. For example, the senior executive's search campaign will be different than that of the graduating student; the marketing manager's campaign will differ from the scientist's campaign; the person who's willing to relocate will have a different campaign than the person who cannot relocate; and so forth. Do not think that you have to use every one of these job search channels. Rather, use only the channels that are right for you.

*Tip* Each person's job search strategy and action will be different. The specific job search activities you engage in depend entirely on you, your experience, and your career objectives. No two job search campaigns look the same!

## Ad Responses and Online Job Postings

It's obvious that one of the easiest and perhaps best ways to search for a new position is to find companies that are looking to hire. This job search channel is really a no-brainer. Of course, you're going to look for advertisements in your local newspaper, in professional journals, in business publications, and at online job posting sites for positions that are appropriate for a candidate with your qualifications. If you meet most (not necessarily all) of the qualifications, submit your resume and cover letter. With ads and job postings, it's always a numbers game. The more jobs you apply for, the better your odds of getting a response and an interview. And that's what this process is all about.

It's also important to recognize that you will probably never get a reply to many of your applications. In many cases, you won't be able to follow up because the ad will be "blind," not revealing the company name or any contact information. Even when applying to a respected, well-known company, you might find that you are totally ignored unless you are called for an interview. Don't obsess over it; concentrate on other strategies and move on.

Be certain that you have a quick and easy process for applying to posted jobs. Don't spend hours tweaking and perfecting your resume to make yourself a perfect match—this is not the best use of your valuable time. Do, of course, customize your cover letter as much as possible in a reasonable time frame. Then send in your application and devote your time and energy to other, more worthwhile pursuits.

Although we'd like to assure you that 100 percent of the job postings you'll see are for legitimate opportunities, unfortunately, they're not; but you probably already know that. Our philosophy is that if it seems like a good fit, apply. The worst-case scenario is that you get a phone call, an e-mail, or an invitation to interview for a position that you don't want. In that case, of course, you can respectfully decline the offer to interview. However, you never know what one interview might lead to or what other jobs might present themselves. As such, we recommend you rarely, if ever, turn down an interview offer. Take a chance and go ahead with the interview; you never know where it might lead.

*Tip* Job search is all about building relationships with lots and lots of different people. Never turn down the opportunity to interview, even if you don't think you want the position. You don't know who you might meet or what other opportunities you might uncover.

## Online Resume Postings

One of the greatest things about the Internet is that it gives you the ability to quickly and easily post your resume on various Web sites. By doing so, you're making your resume available for review by human resource professionals, hiring managers, recruiters, and others who are looking for a candidate with your experience and qualifications. Because posting your resume is relatively easy and usually free, you can quickly post it on scores of Web sites, from the large general sites such as CareerBuilder.com and Monster.com to the profession-specific Web sites such as SalesJobs.com and MechanicalEngineeringCareer.com.

*Tip* Posting your resume wildly all over the Internet is *not* a proactive job search strategy; rather, it's largely a waste of your time and incorrectly creates the illusion of being productive. Post your resume only on select sites that are likely to be looking for candidates with your specific experience and qualifications. Otherwise, you're just spinning your wheels.

## Traditional Networking

The single most effective job search strategy and action is networking with people you know and people *they* know. Think about networking in terms of levels. Your level-1 networking contacts are the people you actually know. This group will include past and current coworkers, past and current managers, relatives, friends, neighbors, and community contacts. If you speak to these people in person or on the phone, be certain to follow up with them via e-mail so that you can send them a resume. Even if you know these people very well, they probably do not know all of the specific details of your career. Don't be shy; send each of them a copy of your resume so that they can learn more about your career and make the appropriate referrals.

When you reach out to these people, use a friendly and no-pressure approach. Never ask them for a job. If they have a job to offer, they'll let you know about it. What you really want from them are three to five names of other people they know that you can contact about your job search. Those new names, e-mail addresses, and phone numbers become your level-2 networking contacts. New contacts from them become level 3, and so the process goes. With each new level, you'll uncover new opportunities, get more interviews, and move closer to the ultimate job offer.

*Tip* When networking, never ask for a job. Rather, ask people for their help. Most will want to help, but few will have a job in their back pocket!

## Web 2.0 Networking

The Internet has revolutionized how we network. It has created entirely new networking channels for all of us. No longer do we have to rely on our Rolodex for contacts. Now, we can reach out to our contacts on a much larger scale through a variety on Web 2.0 offerings. We both consider

LinkedIn to be at the top of the list of online networking venues, because we experience it on a daily basis. And, in fact, just like traditional networking, LinkedIn networking relies on the same system of levels of contacts. You can reach out to one of your level-1 contacts and ask for an introduction to a level-2 contact. We've seen how miraculously it can work in connecting the right people with the *other* right people who have the right job.

Other Web 2.0 sites, best known as social networking sites, are increasing in their acceptance as professional networking venues. These include Facebook, MySpace, and Twitter. Even YouTube, when used in an appropriate business manner, can be a remarkably effective networking tool that you can use to showcase your skills, qualifications, and expertise.

*Tip* Be careful what you post on these social networking sites. If it's not something you'd want your next employer to see or hear, don't post it. The frat party pictures are *not* your best selling tool for an interview at Verizon Wireless!

## Recruiter Contacts

There are thousands and thousands of third-party recruiting companies in the U.S. whose only job is to fill job postings for companies. For example, Dow Chemical may be looking for a new Packaging Director. Instead of running an advertisement or posting a job on its Web site, Dow can hire a recruiter to do all of the legwork for it. That way, the company is not overwhelmed with hundreds, if not thousands, of applicants. Instead, the recruiter will find several candidates that meet the company's specifications to a tee and then present those select candidates to the company.

The landscape of the recruiting industry has changed significantly over the past decade as a result of both the Internet and economic recession. As you know, the Internet has created entirely new channels for job searching, and as a result some companies have been able to minimize or eliminate their need for third-party recruiters and the huge expense involved. The economic recession has also taken its casualties in the recruiting industry just as in so many other industries. However, recruiting still thrives and many companies rely exclusively on it for most of their hiring.

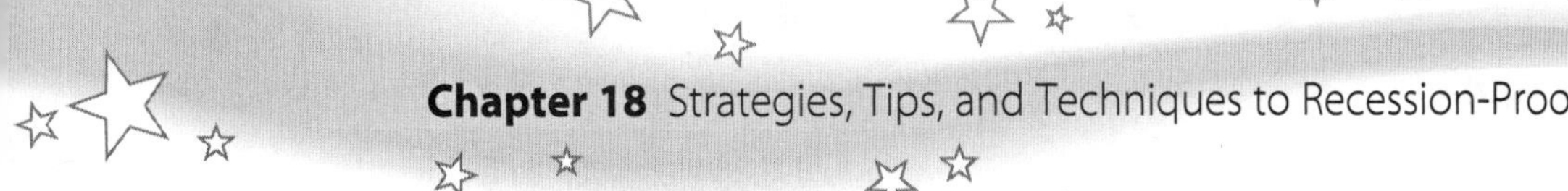


If you're considering contacting recruiters for help with your job search, contact only recruiters who specialize in your profession and your industry. If you're a sales professional in the pharmaceutical industry, reach out to recruiters who specialize in sales positions within that industry. If you're an accountant who's worked in several different industries, contact recruiters who specialize in accounting positions and leave the industry wide open. Put yourself where you belong when working with recruiters and you'll be a much more marketable commodity for them.

A common misconception is that a recruiter will work with you to find you a job. Nothing could be further from the truth! Recruiters work for the companies that pay them—the hiring companies. True, they are in the business of filling openings, and they want *someone* to be chosen, but that someone could be you or any other person. Recruiters are not invested in your career, so don't pin your hopes on their efforts. Use them as just one channel for marketing yourself to potential employers.

Of special note when contacting recruiters is the amount of information you'll share with them. This will include your compensation and benefit expectations, geographic preferences, and any other special requirements you might have (such as access to educational facilities or healthcare services). Recruiters work to make the perfect match between job seeker and company, so you need to be honest and upfront about your needs and objectives.

And, finally, two other very important considerations when contacting recruiters: First, work with as many recruiters as possible so that you'll have a strong job search team. There is no advantage to working with just one or two recruiters, unless you know them well. Second, send your resume via e-mail. All recruiters now scan resumes into their resume databases so that they can search them as they get orders for new positions. If you mail a resume, it will most likely not be scanned into their system and you'll have lost out on future opportunities.

### Company Contacts

Reaching out to companies that you're interested in working for can be a great strategy. It's an even better strategy if you happen to know someone at the company (a network contact) who can help you get in the door for an interview. However, if you don't know anyone or can't make a connection to someone through your network, you can cold-call the company with a cover letter and resume that you'll send via e-mail. You'll select these companies based on your industry and geographic preferences.

Write a letter that focuses on the company and its issues, why you want to work for them, and why they'll be interested in you. Send your correspondence to either the senior hiring manager in the department/division/organization you want to work in; or, if you can't identify that person, send your material to the human resources manager. It's always best to go directly to the hiring manager whenever you can because they are most likely to be the ultimate hiring decision maker.

Spend some time researching the company before you contact them, not only to get the correct contact names, but also to learn as much about the company as you can. Then, if you're fortunate enough to have the opportunity to interview, you'll be well informed about the company and its products and services, mission statement, expansion plans, competition, key markets, critical initiatives, and whatever other information you've been able to uncover. A smart job seeker = a new hire!

### Venture Capital Contacts

Venture capital and private equity firms can be a very fruitful job search channel for individuals with the appropriate skill sets. Consider this: If you contact a venture capital firm that specializes in the hospitality industry, you're positioning yourself for two different types of opportunities. First, the venture capital firm might be looking to bring someone on board who can help them identify and select potential acquisition candidates and then help integrate them into the venture capital firm's portfolio of companies. Second, they might be looking to hire someone to work in one of the companies that they own. As such, when you reach out to venture capital and private equity firms, you're double-hitting for career opportunities.

Just as you do for other companies, you'll select these firms based on their industry specialization. However, we do not recommend that you limit your search geographically. Although a venture capital firm itself might be headquartered in San Jose, California, that does not mean its companies are in that same location. To the contrary, its companies will probably be scattered throughout various locations statewide, nationwide, or worldwide.

Be advised that we do not recommend this job search channel to all job seekers. Generally, this channel is best for managers and executives who would work within the firm's companies, or for individuals with a wealth of experience in mergers and acquisitions, corporate and investment finance, contracts, and related functions who would work directly for the venture capital or private equity firm itself.

> *Tip* When preparing a targeted e-mail campaign to recruiters, companies, or venture capital firms, select your targets carefully and put yourself and your resume in front of people who would be specifically interested in a candidate with your qualifications. Don't waste your time or money reaching out to organizations that don't hire individuals with your specific skills or experience.

## Job Fairs

When you attend job fairs, you should have only one goal in mind—and it's not to get a job. Getting a job at a job fair is a one-in-a-million shot. Rather, know that the reason to attend these events is to meet people and get their business cards so that you can follow up with them *after* the event. Most job fairs get phenomenal attendance these days, and it's difficult to have more than a minute or so to speak with someone. As such, your 30-second introduction (see item #2 in the previous section, "The Eight Most Important Elements of Job Search Success") must be well worded, well rehearsed, and ready at a moment's notice when someone says to you, "Tell me about yourself."

## Choose Your Strategy

One final, yet very important concept about the integrated model of job search: The reason this model works so well is because of the diversity of the activities, contacts, and outreach that is involved. Don't fool yourself into thinking that you can do just one thing and get the same results. That simply won't happen. Occasionally, a job seeker is lucky and a great new opportunity falls into his or her lap, but that's the exception in today's marketplace.

> *Tip* No one job search channel is better than another. It's the cumulative impact of them all that will lead you to your career success.

Now that you've taken the time to review all of the information on job search, your challenge is to select the job search channels that will work best for you based specifically on your experience, profession, qualifications, career achievements, and more. Just remember, diversification in job search strategy is key. The more channels that you use, the more opportunities will come your way, and the faster you'll find your next great career opportunity.

### Lifetime Career Management

In generations past, individuals looked to companies to manage their careers. If you worked for Hilton and worked hard, did a great job, and met or exceeded all of your performance requirements, you felt secure in the fact that the company would take care of you. Well, no more. Now it's your responsibility to proactively manage your career, from the day you start working to the day you stop, and every day in between. If you don't manage it, no one else will, because no one else cares. That may be brutal, but it's the reality of today's employment market. You must take the reins of control over your career, know where you want to go, figure out how you're going to get there, and then make it happen. It's that simple, yet that complex.

Today's savvy professional knows that managing his or her career is a lifelong responsibility. Whether you're a young college graduate just launching your career, an experienced senior executive, or anyone in between, you must realize that managing your career is up to you.

## The Top Eight Lifelong Career-Management Strategies for Success

Here are the top eight critical strategies and actions that you must employ to successfully manage your career—today, tomorrow, and over the many years to come.

1. **Follow your occupational instinct.** As authors, both of us are hard-wired to be writers. Have you discovered what you're hard-wired to do? What excites you? What invigorates you? Ultimately, you'll find joy in your work and your career if you follow your occupational instinct and do what you love. Unfortunately, all too many people don't figure this out until they're well into their careers, when it becomes more difficult—yet not impossible—to make a change.

   If you're still young and just beginning your lifelong career, be certain that you're following your occupational instinct and you will find career fulfillment. If you're already well into your career and not fulfilled, consider making a change if you have the resources to sustain yourself and your family through a career transition. Begin by hiring a career coach or career counselor and completing some career assessment and exploration activities that should help you uncover your occupational instinct. Then, if you have the guts that it takes to make a big career change, go for it. We've worked with thousands of job seekers and can guarantee that lifelong career fulfillment is possible for just about everyone. All you have to do is determine what you're supposed to be doing and where you're supposed to be, and then figure out a plan to get there. And remember to enjoy the journey and not just the destination!

2. **Keep an ongoing record of your career achievements, successes, project highlights, honors and awards, and other notable activities.** Although you might think you'll remember it all when it's time to update your resume, you won't. And because you never know which of those achievements or projects might be relevant to a future career opportunity, it's important to document it all. Create a Career Success Journal, a Project Highlights Journal, or a Career Successes file folder and keep a running list of everything that you do, achieve, and contribute. Then, when it's time to update your resume, interview for a new position, network with a new contact, or perform any one of a number of other job search activities, you'll have everything you need at your immediate disposal.

   Remember that the quality of your resume can only be as good as the information that you remember to include. The most powerful resumes are always those for the job seeker who has maintained an ongoing record of his or her career so that all the facts and figures are available.

3. **Update your resume every six months—at a minimum.** You never know when someone might ask you for a resume for a unique opportunity, when the job of your dreams will be posted on the Internet, or when a new opening will become available within your company and you will have only have 24 hours to respond. When a great opportunity presents itself or you're working within a tight deadline, the very last thing you want to have to do is scramble to get your resume updated. Mark it on your calendar, do it every six months, and you'll find you're well prepared for any opportunity at a moment's notice.

   If you have strong writing skills, you should easily be able to maintain and update your resume on a regular basis. However, if writing is not your strongest talent, consider working with a professional resume writer who can better sell, market, and merchandise you and your achievements. A minor investment in a talented resume writer can translate into thousands and thousands of dollars in your pocket when you land a great new opportunity.

4. **Work your network before you need your network.** Have you ever been contacted by a past colleague who you haven't spoken to or heard from in years? Now, all of a sudden, they need your help to introduce them to one of your associates. It might have been nice to have heard from them at some point prior to when they needed you to do something for them.

   Staying in touch with your network contacts is a great idea and can go a long way in maintaining and strengthening your professional relationships. Don't misunderstand; we're not recommending that you call your contacts every month, or even every quarter. However, you could send a holiday card once a year, or perhaps a holiday card in December and a short e-mail in July to touch base, send good wishes, and tell them you're available to offer any help they may need in moving their career forward. Remember, networking is a two-way street. You do for them and they do for you.

5. **Know your market.** One of the most critical keys to long-term successful career management is market intelligence. Specifically, this refers to intelligence about geographic markets, industry markets, product markets, competitive markets, economic markets, and more. The more intelligence you have, the more knowledgeable you are and, therefore, the more control you will have over your career.

Intelligence is power, and to succeed in anything—including your career—you need power.

Collecting intelligence is, generally, relatively easy and rarely involves more than simply reading. Here's a great example. Suppose you're a manufacturing plant manager living in Baltimore, Maryland, and employed with the same company for 10 years. Although you feel as secure as one can in these times, you do consider yourself a passive job seeker and are always on the lookout for new and better opportunities. One of the things that you do every week is read the *Baltimore Business Journal*, from which you capture all kinds of market intelligence about new corporate formations, new construction contracts, new corporate real-estate signings, competitive contract awards, company bankruptcies, and lots of other very valuable information. By keeping abreast of all of this information, you'll be one of the first to know if a company signs a contract to build a new manufacturing facility or if a company wins a large manufacturing contract and will need to hire and expand to meet the deadlines.

6. **Go where the action is.** Industries fluctuate as the world changes. The automotive manufacturing industry is a great example of an industry that used to lead our nation and is now teetering on the brink of financial disaster. As such, people employed in automotive manufacturing have had to retool their skills and qualifications to transition into different industries. If these individuals were savvy, they would have transitioned into what are termed growth industries—industries that are projected to increase in demand over the years to come.

   According to the U.S. Bureau of Labor Statistics (www.bls.gov), some of the fastest-growing industries in the U.S. include Technology, Energy, Environmental Services, Healthcare, Professional Services, and Personal Services. As such, as you take control of your career, build your skills, talents, and competencies to favorably position yourself within the growth industries that are leading the U.S. and the world.

7. **Realize that your goals will change and that your career choices and decisions will also change as you move through the career pathways of your life.** For most people in their 20s and 30s, it's all about getting ahead in their careers, moving up the ladder, and finding new

opportunities. Most people in their 40s are concerned about solidifying their professional positions and continuing to move up into even higher and more responsible positions. Then, in your 50s and 60s, things might start to change. Of course your career is still important, but your personal life tends to become increasingly important as you begin to reprioritize. It's that whole work/life balance concept that so many of us struggle with.

Speaking of work/life balance, is it balance or blend that you strive for? Let's clearly distinguish between the two:

- **Work/life balance** is finding the perfect balance between how much time you devote to work and how much time you devote to your personal life. When you're trying to achieve this, it's a constant balancing act to find just the right balance and then retain it. Realizing that life is much more complicated—both personally and professionally—than it was when the work/life balance phrase was first coined decades ago, all too many people are fighting to find their right balance and all too many are feeling as though they've failed. As such, many of us have decided to focus on blend instead of balance.

- **Work/life blend** is when you're able to blend the two things together in such a way that it works for you. Both of us are entrepreneurs and, therefore, we tend to work much more than the average 40-hour work week. In fact, sometimes we'll work twice that amount of time in a week. But that's okay, because that's our choice! It's the blend of the two that works best for us. On the other hand, your blend might look totally different. Perhaps your work/life blend is 30 hours of work a week and absolutely no more. Well, if that's what works for you, perfect. Ask yourself what your perfect blend would be and then strive to achieve that goal.

8. **Today's status quo in the employment market is distinguished by three characteristics: change, movement, and transition.** The employment market will never be as stable as it was in the past. Rather, today's market is fluid, dynamic, and constantly changing. For some job seekers, that change and flexibility can be remarkably energizing and fulfilling. For others, however, it can be difficult to navigate, particularly for people who like everything to stay the same.

No matter which category you fall into, you must learn to go with the flow because the current of our global employment market will continue to change and reinvent itself over and over throughout your working life. We encourage you to embrace that change and realize the tremendous opportunities that it can hold for you.

## Moving Forward

After reading this chapter, you should be prepared to

- Plan and execute a winning job search campaign that will land you a great new opportunity.
- Develop a lifelong career-management plan that will lead you through a fulfilling and prosperous career pathway.

If nothing else, we hope that you feel more in control of your career destiny.

Today's employment market can be a frightening place. Everything is changing, and companies that have been around for decades are disappearing every day. Instead of focusing on the negative, however, look to the positive. As one business closes, another business opens. As some industries falter, other industries—particularly in healthcare, energy, and technology—are soaring. Become an agile and intelligent job seeker, proactively manage your career, and you will come out on top!

# Appendixes

Appendix

A

# Using Keywords to Win in Your Job Search

Ten years ago no one had ever heard of *keywords*. Today, they are everywhere!

- You talk to a resume writer, recruiter, career counselor, corporate human resources professional, or career coach, and each of them mentions the importance of keywords.
- You read about the Internet and online job search, and the emphasis is on keywords and keyword scanning.
- You listen to a CNN news brief about the latest employment trends, and the reporter highlights the importance of keywords in today's competitive job market.
- You attend a job search training and networking seminar, and the focus is on keywords.
- You purchase a book on resume writing and job search, and the emphasis is on keywords and their importance in the development of resumes, cover letters, broadcast letters, and other job search marketing communications.

Then, you ask yourself:

- What are keywords, and where did they come from?
- What is all this talk about keywords and scanning?
- How do I use keywords in my cover letters?
- Which keywords are right for me, my profession, and my industry?

The following sections answer all of your keyword questions.

## What Are Keywords, and Where Did They Come From?

Keywords are nothing new. They are buzzwords—the "hot" words associated with a specific industry, profession, or job function—that clearly and succinctly communicate a specific message about a job function, qualification, accomplishment, or responsibility. Keywords are usually nouns or groups of nouns—words such as *benefits plan design* (for human resources), *market share ratings* (for marketing and sales), *logistics management* (for transportation), and *platform architecture* (for information technology).

Trends today, greatly influenced by the tremendous competition in the job market, require that resumes, cover letters, and other job search communications clearly present your skills and qualifications in an action-driven style. Your challenge when preparing these documents is to demonstrate that you can deliver strong performance results. And there is no better manner in which to accomplish this than with the use of powerful keywords and phrases that demonstrate your qualifications, capabilities, skills, and value to a hiring organization. Keywords get you noticed rather than passed over.

Here are some "general management" and "professional" keywords for use in your resume and cover letter. Use these keywords to supplement the keywords for your designated profession or industry (we give some examples of these later in this chapter).

- Strategic planning
- Performance and productivity improvement
- P&L responsibility
- Continuous process improvement
- Organizational design

- Business process design and reengineering
- Infrastructure development
- Business process optimization
- Team-building and leadership
- Business turnaround and revitalization
- Change management
- Start-up ventures and new enterprises
- Information technology
- New media, Internet, and e-commerce
- Consensus-building
- Executive presentations and negotiations
- Project design and management
- Competitive market and product positioning
- Investor and board relations
- New-product and new-service introductions
- Oral and written communications
- Problem-solving and decision-making

The list could go on and on. You can probably think of many more to integrate into your job search materials.

## What Is All This Talk About Keywords and Scanning?

Keywords are the standard by which thousands of companies and recruiters screen applicants' resumes to identify core qualifications and skills.

Upon arriving at a company that uses scanning technology, all resumes, and sometimes their accompanying cover letters, are scanned into the company's database. This process makes all the words in the resume accessible via a computerized search. What criteria are used for the search? Quite simply, they are the keywords that match the specific hiring criteria. As you can imagine, these keywords are vastly different from position to position even within a company, and perhaps for similar positions with different companies. The companies themselves select the keywords they will use for the search. Therefore, it is critical that you include an appropriate assortment of keywords in your resume, cover letter, and all other job search communications so that your documents will be "found" by the scanning technology used at your target company.

Whether or not this strategy and mechanism for evaluating a candidate's qualifications is appropriate, the fact remains that keyword scanning has become an increasingly dominant tool in today's hiring market. Make certain you give yourself every chance for consideration. Do not allow yourself to be passed over because you do not have the right words in your resume and cover letter. Integrate the keywords in this chapter into your resume as they accurately reflect your experience. Not only will you meet the technological requirements for keyword scanning; you will also create powerful career marketing tools. And, we all know that the winners in job search are those who can "sell" their qualifications, highlight their achievements, and distinguish themselves from the competition.

## How Do I Use Keywords in My Cover Letters?

Keywords are remarkably effective tools to use in developing your cover letters, broadcast letters, thank-you letters, and other job search correspondence. They strengthen the presentation of your skills, qualifications, and experience, as well as demonstrate your competencies, achievements, and successes. Use keywords to highlight information as it directly relates to the position for which you are applying.

As on your resume, you can use keywords in various cover letter sections, styles, and formats. The following brief cover letter excerpts demonstrate how best to integrate keywords into your letters.

### Integrating Keywords into the Text

> My career is best summarized as follows: Years of senior management experience with two global corporations—Excelsior Bank and Voice of America—and now my current position as President/CEO of a start-up technology venture. The breadth of my experience is remarkably broad, from managing VOA's entire Latin American operation to the more finite functions of building an operating architecture and business infrastructure for a new and highly specialized enterprise.

## Using Keywords in a Separate Skills Section

Highlights of my professional skills that might be of particular interest to you include the following:

- Strategic sales and market planning
- New-product introduction
- Competitive sales negotiations
- Sales team training and leadership
- Account development and management
- Client retention and loyalty
- New-product design and development
- U.S. and international sales management

## Using Keywords in a Career Highlights Paragraph

Highlights of my career that might be of particular interest to you include the following:

- Ten years of experience as Managing Director, Senior VP, Executive VP, COO, and now President/CEO.
- Success in start-ups, acquisitions, turnarounds, high-growth companies, and multinational organizations.
- Innovative performance in business development through internal growth, mergers, acquisitions, joint ventures, and strategic alliances.
- Outstanding P&L performance measured via revenue and profit growth, cost reduction, market penetration, and other key indices.
- Expertise in sales, marketing, and the entire customer development/management/retention process.
- Strong information technology expertise.

*Example*

## Using Keywords in a Comparison-List Format

| Your Qualifications | My Experience |
|---|---|
| M.B.A. degree | M.B.A. degree from Harvard Business School |
| Human Resource Management | 10 years of experience in HRM and OD |
| HRIS technology | Implementation of $2.8 million HRIS technology system |
| Benefits and compensation | Design of IBM's benefits and compensation systems |
| Management recruitment | Recruitment and development of IBM's newest executive team |

> *Tip* Keywords are also powerful tools to incorporate into your other job search materials (such as resumes, leadership profiles, career biographies, Internet postings, and networking letters). In fact, you can also use them in general business correspondence, proposals, reports, capital financing requests, venture capital and Wall Street solicitations, advertisements, marketing communications, publicity, publications, and public-speaking presentations. Their usefulness in professional documents is unlimited! Retain your keyword list for use in future writing and documentation.

## Which Keywords Are Right for Me, My Profession, and My Industry?

The easiest way to find the right keywords for you is to peruse newspaper advertisements and online job postings for positions that are a great fit. These descriptions are chock-full of keyword qualifications, and you should use them appropriately in your cover letter and resume.

Where else can you find appropriate keywords? We've made it easy for you! The following is a comprehensive list of keywords for your use as a tool and resource. Review each keyword and ask yourself whether it represents one of your important qualifications or job functions. Then make certain that you include the most relevant of these keywords in your resume and cover letters.

Not only will you be delighted with the impact of your new job search communications, you can rest assured that your documents will be located by the scanning software whenever a company is searching to fill a position that matches your skills.

### Administration

Administration
Administrative infrastructure
Administrative processes
Administrative support
Back-office operations
Budget administration
Client communications
Confidential correspondence
Contract administration
Corporate recordkeeping
Corporate secretary
Customer liaison
Document management
Efficiency improvement
Executive liaison affairs
Executive officer support
Facilities management
Front-office operations
Government affairs
Liaison affairs

Mail and messenger services
Meeting planning
Office management
Office services
Policy and procedure
Product support
Productivity improvement
Project management
Records management
Regulatory reporting
Resource management
Technical support
Time management
Workflow planning/prioritization

## Association and Not-for-Profit Management

Advocacy
Affiliate members
Board relations
Budget allocation
Budget oversight
Chapter
Community outreach
Corporate development
Corporate giving
Corporate sponsorship
Education foundation
Educational programming
Endowment funds
Foundation management
Fund-raising
Grass-roots campaign
Industry association
Industry relations
Leadership training
Marketing communications
Media relations
Member communications
Member development
Member-driven organization
Member retention
Member services
Mission planning
Not-for-profit
Organization(al) leadership
Organization(al) mission
Organization(al) vision
Policy development
Political affairs (political action committee–PAC)
Press relations
Public policy development
Public/private partnerships
Public relations
Regulatory affairs
Research foundation
Speakers bureau
Special-events management
Volunteer recruitment
Volunteer training

## Banking

Asset-based lending
Asset management
Audit examination
Branch operations
Cash management
Commercial banking
Commercial credit
Consumer banking
Consumer credit
Correspondent banking
Credit administration
Credit analysis
*de novo* banking
Debt financing
Deposit base
Depository services
Equity financing
Fee income
Foreign exchange (FX)
Global banking

Investment management
Investor relations
Lease administration
Letters of credit
Liability exposure
Loan administration
Loan processing
Loan quality
Loan recovery
Loan underwriting
Lockbox processing
Merchant banking
Non-performing assets
Portfolio management
Receivership
Regulatory affairs
Relationship management
Retail banking
Retail lending
Return on assets (ROA)
Return on equity (ROE)
Return on investment (ROI)
Risk management
Secondary markets
Secured lending
Securities management
Transaction banking
Trust services
Unsecured lending
Wholesale banking
Workout

## Customer Service

Account relationship management
Customer communications
Customer development
Customer focus groups
Customer loyalty
Customer management
Customer needs assessment
Customer retention
Customer satisfaction
Customer service
Customer surveys
Field service operations
Inbound service operations
Key account management
Order fulfillment
Order processing
Outbound service operations
Process simplification
Records management
Relationship management
Sales administration
Service benchmarks
Service delivery
Service measures
Service quality
Telemarketing operations
Telesales operations

## Engineering

Benchmark
Capital project
Chemical engineering
Commissioning
Computer-aided design (CAD)
Computer-aided engineering (CAE)
Computer-aided manufacturing (CAM)
Cross-functional team
Customer management
Development engineering
Efficiency
Electrical engineering
Electronics engineering
Engineering change order (ECO)
Engineering documentation
Environmental engineering
Ergonomic techniques
Experimental design

Experimental methods
Facilities engineering
Fault analysis
Field performance
Final customer acceptance
Hardware engineering
Industrial engineering
Industrial hygiene
Maintenance engineering
Manufacturing engineering
Manufacturing integration
Mechanical engineering
Methods design
Nuclear engineering
Occupational Safety and Health Administration (OSHA)
Operating and maintenance (O&M)
Optics engineering
Plant engineering
Process development
Process engineering
Process standardization
Product design
Product development cycle
Product functionality
Product innovation
Product lifecycle management
Product manufacturability
Product reliability
Productivity improvement
Project costing
Project management
Project planning
Prototype
Quality assurance
Quality engineering
Regulatory compliance
Research and development (R&D)
Resource management
Root cause
Scale-up
Software engineering
Specifications
Statistical analysis
Systems engineering
Systems integration
Technical briefings
Technical liaison affairs
Technology development
Test engineering
Turnkey
Work methods analysis

## Finance, Accounting, and Auditing

Accounts payable
Accounts receivable
Asset disposition
Asset management
Asset purchase
Audit controls
Audit management
Capital budgets
Cash management
Commercial paper
Corporate development
Corporate tax
Cost accounting
Cost avoidance
Cost/benefit analysis
Cost reduction
Credit and collections
Debt financing
Divestiture
Due diligence
Employee stock ownership plan (ESOP)
Equity financing
Feasibility analysis
Financial analysis
Financial audits
Financial controls
Financial models
Financial planning
Financial reporting

Foreign exchange (FX)
Initial public offering (IPO)
Internal controls
International finance
Investment management
Investor accounting
Investor relations
Job costing
Letters of credit
Leveraged buyout (LBO)
Liability management
Make/buy analysis
Margin improvement
Merger
Operating budgets
Operational audits
Partnership accounting
Profit gains
Profit/loss (P&L) analysis
Project accounting
Project financing
Regulatory compliance auditing
Return on assets (ROA)
Return on equity (ROE)
Return on investment (ROI)
Revenue gain
Risk management
Shareholder relations
Stock purchase
Strategic planning
Treasury
Trust accounting
Workpapers

## General Management, Senior Management, and Consulting

Accelerated growth
Acting executive
Advanced technology
Benchmarking
Business development
Business reengineering
Capital projects
Competitive market position
Consensus building
Continuous process improvement
Corporate administration
Corporate communications
Corporate culture change
Corporate development
Corporate image
Corporate legal affairs
Corporate mission
Corporate vision
Cost avoidance
Cost reduction
Crisis communications
Cross-cultural communications
Cross-functional team leadership
Customer-driven management
Customer loyalty
Customer retention
Decision-making authority
Efficiency improvement
Emerging business venture
Entrepreneurial leadership
European Economic Community (EEC)
Executive management
Executive presentations
Financial management
Financial restructuring
Global market expansion
High-growth organization
Infrastructure
Interim executive
Leadership development
Long-range planning
Management development
Margin improvement
Market development
Market-driven management
Marketing management
Matrix management

Multifunction experience
Multi-industry experience
Multisite operations management
New business development
Operating infrastructure
Operating leadership
Organization(al) culture
Organization(al) development
Participative management
Performance improvement
Policy development
Proactive leadership
Process ownership
Process reengineering
Productivity improvement
Profit and loss (P&L) management
Profit growth
Project management
Quality improvement
Reengineering
Relationship management
Reorganization
Return on assets (ROA)
Return on equity (ROE)
Return on investment (ROI)
Revenue growth
Sales management
Service design/delivery
Signatory authority
Start-up venture
Strategic development
Strategic partnership
Tactical planning/leadership
Team-building
Team leadership
Total quality management (TQM)
Transition management
Turnaround management
World-class organization

## Health Care

Acute care facility
Ambulatory care
Assisted living
Capital giving campaign
Case management
Certificate of need (CON)
Chronic care facility
Clinical services
Community hospital
Community outreach
Continuity of care
Cost center
Electronic claims processing
Emergency medical systems (EMS)
Employee assistance program (EAP)
Fee billing
Full-time equivalent (FTE)
Grant administration
Health-care administrator
Health-care delivery systems
Health maintenance organization (HMO)
Home health care
Hospital foundation
Industrial medicine
Inpatient care
Long-term care
Managed care
Management service organization (MSO)
Multihospital network
Occupational health
Outpatient care
Patient accounting
Patient relations
Peer review
Physician credentialing
Physician relations
Practice management
Preferred provider organization (PPO)
Preventive medicine
Primary care
Provider relations
Public health administration

Quality of care
Regulatory standards (JCAHO)
Rehabilitation services
Reimbursement program
Risk management
Service delivery
Skilled nursing facility
Third-party administrator
Utilization review
Wellness programs

## Hospitality

Amenities
Back-of-the-house operations
Banquet operations
Budget administration
Catering operations
Club management
Conference management
Contract F&B operations
Corporate dining room
Customer retention
Customer service
Food and beverage operations (F&B)
Food cost controls
Front-of-the-house operations
Guest retention
Guest satisfaction
Hospitality management
Inventory planning/control
Labor cost controls
Meeting planning
Member development/retention
Menu planning
Menu pricing
Multi-unit operations
Occupancy
Portion control
Property development
Purchasing
Resort management
Service management
Signature property
Vendor sourcing
VIP relations

## Human Resources

Americans with Disabilities Act (ADA)
Benefits administration
Career pathing
Change management
Claims administration
College recruitment
Compensation
Competency-based performance
Corporate culture change
Cross-cultural communications
Diversity management
Employee communications
Employee empowerment
Employee involvement teams
Employee relations
Employee retention
Employee surveys
Equal Employment Opportunity (EEO)
Expatriate employment
Grievance proceedings
Human resources (HR)
Human resources generalist affairs
Human resources partnerships
Incentive planning
International employment
Job task analysis
Labor arbitration
Labor contract negotiations
Labor relations
Leadership assessment
Leadership development
Management training and development

Manpower planning
Merit promotion
Multimedia training
Multinational workforce
Organization(al) design
Organization(al) development (OD)
Organization(al) needs assessment
Participative management
Performance appraisal
Performance incentives
Performance reengineering
Position classification
Professional recruitment
Regulatory affairs
Retention
Safety training
Self-directed work teams
Staffing
Succession planning
Train-the-trainer
Training and development
Union negotiations
Union relations
Wage and salary administration
Workforce reengineering

## Human Services

Adult services
Advocacy
Behavior management
Behavior modification
Casework
Client advocacy
Client placement
Community-based intervention
Community outreach
Counseling
Crisis intervention
Diagnostic evaluation
Discharge planning
Dually diagnosed
Group counseling
Human services
Independent life skills training
Inpatient
Integrated service delivery
Mainstreaming
Outpatient
Program development
Protective services
Psychoanalysis
Psychological counseling
Psychotropic medication
School counseling
Social services
Social welfare
Substance abuse
Testing
Treatment planning
Vocational placement
Vocational rehabilitation
Vocational testing
Youth training program

## Information Systems and Telecommunications Technology

Advanced technology
Applications development
Architecture
Artificial intelligence (AI)
Automated voice response (AVR)
Backbone
Benchmarking
Capacity planning
CASE tools
CD-ROM technology
Cellular communications
Client/server architecture
Computer science
Cross-functional technology team

Data center operations
Data communications
Data dictionary
Data recovery
Database administration
Database design
Database server
Desktop technology
Disaster recovery
Document imaging
E-commerce
E-learning
Electronic data interchange (EDI)
Electronic mail (e-mail)
Emerging technologies
End-user support
Enterprise systems
Ethernet
Expert systems
Fault analysis
Fiber optics
Field support
Firewall
Fourth-generation language (4GL)
Frame Relay
Geographic information system (GIS)
Global systems support
Graphical user interface (GUI)
Hardware configuration
Hardware development/engineering
Help desk
Host-based system
Imaging technology
Information technology (IT)
Internet
Joint application development (JAD)
Local area network (LAN)
Mainframe
Management information systems (MIS)
Multimedia technology
Multiuser interface
Multivendor systems integration
Network administration
Object-Oriented Programming (OOP)
Office automation (OA)
Online
Operating system
Parallel systems operations
PC technology
Pilot implementation
Process modeling
Project life cycle
Project management methodology
Rapid application development (RAD)
Real-time data
Relational database
Remote systems access
Research and development (R&D)
Resource management
Satellite communications
Software configuration
Software development/engineering
Systems acquisition
Systems configuration
Systems development methodology
Systems documentation
Systems engineering
Systems functionality
Systems implementation
Systems integration
Systems security
Technical documentation
Technical training
Technology commercialization
Technology integration
Technology licensing
Technology needs assessment
Technology rightsizing
Technology solutions
Technology transfer
Telecommunications technology
Teleconferencing technology
User training and support

Vendor partnerships
Voice communications
Web hosting
Webcasting
Webinar
Wide area network (WAN)

## Law and Corporate Legal Affairs

Acquisition
Adjudication
Administrative law
Antitrust
Briefs
Case law
Client management
Competitive intelligence
Contracts law
Copyright law
Corporate bylaws
Corporate law
Corporate recordkeeping
Criminal law
Cross-border transactions
Depositions
Discovery
Due diligence
Employment law
Environmental law
Ethics
Family law
Fraud
General partnership
Intellectual property
Interrogatory
Joint venture
Judicial affairs
*Juris Doctor* (JD)
Labor law
Landmark decision
Legal advocacy
Legal research
Legislative review/analysis
Licensing
Limited liability company (LLC)
Limited partnership
Litigation
Mediation
Memoranda
Mergers
Motions
Negotiations
Patent law
Personal injury
Probate law
Real estate law
Risk management
SEC affairs
Settlement negotiations
Shareholder relations
Signatory authority
Strategic alliance
Tax law
Technology transfer
Trade secrets
Trademark
Transactions law
Trial law
Unfair competition
Workers' compensation litigation

## Manufacturing and Production

Asset management
Automated manufacturing
Best-in-class
Capacity planning
Capital budget
Capital project

Cell manufacturing
Computer integrated manufacturing (CIM)
Concurrent engineering
Continuous improvement
Cost avoidance
Cost reductions
Cross-functional teams
Cycle time reduction
Distribution management
Efficiency improvement
Environmental health and safety (EHS)
Equipment management
Ergonomically efficient
Facilities consolidation
Inventory control
Inventory planning
Just-in-time (JIT)
Labor efficiency
Labor relations
Logistics management
Manufacturing engineering
Manufacturing integration
Manufacturing technology
Master schedule
Materials planning
Materials replenishment system (MRP)
Multisite operations
Occupational Safety and Health Administration (OSHA)
On-time delivery
Operating budget
Operations management
Operations reengineering
Operations start-up
Optimization
Order fulfillment
Order processing
Outsourcing
Participative management
Performance improvement
Physical inventory
Pilot manufacturing
Plant operations
Process automation
Process redesign/reengineering
Procurement
Product development and engineering
Product rationalization
Production forecasting
Production lead time
Production management
Production output
Production plans/schedules
Productivity improvement
Profit and loss (P&L) management
Project budget
Purchasing management
Quality assurance/quality control
Quality circles
Regulatory compliance
Safety management
Safety training
Shipping and receiving operations
Spares and repairs management
Statistical process control (SPC)
Technology integration
Time and motion studies
Total quality management (TQM)
Traffic management
Turnaround management
Union negotiations
Value-added processes
Vendor management
Warehousing operations
Work in progress (WIP)
Workflow optimization
Workforce management
World-class manufacturing (WCM)
Yield improvement

## Public Relations and Corporate Communications

Advertising communications
Agency relations
Brand management
Brand strategy
Broadcast media
Campaign management
Community affairs
Community outreach
Competitive market lead
Conference planning
Cooperative advertising
Corporate communications
Corporate identity
Corporate sponsorship
Corporate vision
Creative services
Crisis communications
Customer communications
Direct-mail campaign
Electronic advertising
Electronic media
Employee communications
Event management
Fund-raising
Government relations
Grass-roots campaign
Investor communications
Issues management
Legislative affairs
Logistics
Management communications
Market research
Marketing communications
Media buys
Media placement
Media relations
Media scheduling
Meeting planning
Merchandising
Multimedia advertising
Political action committee (PAC)
Premiums
Press releases
Print media
Promotions
Public affairs
Public relations
Public speaking
Publications
Publicity
Sales incentives
Shareholder communications
Special events
Strategic communications plan
Strategic planning
Strategic positioning
Tactical campaign
Trade shows
VIP relations

## Real Estate, Construction, and Property Management

Acquisition
Americans with Disabilities Act (ADA)
Asset management
Asset valuation
Asset workout/recovery
Building code compliance
Building trades
Capital improvement
Claims administration
Commercial development
Community development
Competitive bidding
Construction management
Construction trades
Contract administration
Contract award

Critical path method (CPM) scheduling
Design and engineering
Divestiture
Engineering change orders (ECOs)
Environmental compliance
Estimating
Facilities management
Fair market value pricing
Field construction management
Grounds maintenance
Historic property renovation
Industrial development
Infrastructure development
Leasing management
Master community association
Master scheduling
Mixed-use property
Occupancy
Planned-use development (PUD)
Portfolio
Preventive maintenance
Project development
Project management
Project scheduling
Property management
Property valuation
Real estate appraisal
Real estate brokerage
Real estate development
Real estate investment trust (REIT)
Real estate law
Real estate partnership
Regulatory compliance
Renovation
Return on assets (ROA)
Return on equity (ROE)
Return on investment (ROI)
Site development
Site remediation
Specifications
Syndications
Tenant relations
Tenant retention
Turnkey construction

## Retail

Buyer awareness
Credit operations
Customer loyalty
Customer service
Distribution management
District sales
Hardgoods
In-store promotions
Inventory control
Inventory shrinkage
Loss prevention
Mass merchants
Merchandising
Multisite operations
POS promotions
Preferred customer management
Pricing
Product management
Retail sales
Security operations
Softgoods
Specialty retailer
Stock management
Warehousing operations

## Sales and Marketing

Account development
Account management
Account retention
Brand management
Business development
Campaign management
Competitive analysis
Competitive contract award
Competitive market intelligence
Competitive product positioning
Consultative sales
Customer loyalty
Customer needs assessment
Customer retention
Customer satisfaction
Customer service
Direct-mail marketing
Direct-response marketing
Direct sales
Distributor management
E-business
E-commerce
Emerging markets
Field sales management
Fulfillment
Global markets
Global sales
Headquarters account management
High-impact presentations
Incentive planning
Indirect sales
International sales
International trade
Key account management
Line extension
Margin improvement
Market launch
Market positioning
Market research
Market-share ratings
Market surveys
Marketing strategy
Mass merchants
Multichannel distribution
Multichannel sales
Multimedia advertising
Multimedia marketing communications
National account management
Negotiations
New market development
New product introduction
Product development
Product launch
Product life cycle management
Product line rationalization
Product positioning
Profit and loss (P&L) management
Profit growth
Promotions
Public relations
Public speaking
Revenue growth
Revenue stream
Sales closing
Sales cycle management
Sales forecasting
Sales presentations
Sales training
Solutions selling
Strategic market planning
Tactical market plans
Team building/leadership
Trend analysis

## Security and Law Enforcement

Asset protection
Community outreach
Corporate fraud
Corporate security
Crisis communications
Crisis response
Electronic surveillance
Emergency planning and response
Emergency preparedness
Industrial espionage
Industrial security
Interrogation
Investigations management
Law enforcement
Media relations
Personal protection
Public relations
Safety training
Security operations
Surveillance
Tactical field operations
VIP protection
White-collar crime

## Teaching and Education Administration

Academic advisement
Accreditation
Admissions management
Alumni relations
Campus life
Capital giving campaign
Career counseling
Career development
Classroom management
Conference management
Course design
Curriculum development
Education administration
Enrollment
Extension program
Field instruction
Grant administration
Higher education
Holistic learning
Instructional media
Instructional programming
Intercollegiate athletics
Leadership training
Lifelong learning
Management development
Peer counseling
Program development
Public/private partnerships
Public speaking
Recruitment
Residential life
Scholastic standards
Seminar management
Student-faculty relations
Student retention
Student services
Tenure
Textbook review
Training and development

# Appendix B

# Action Verbs for Cover Letters

When it comes to writing your cover letters, resumes, thank-you letters, and other job search communications, you have two choices:

1. You can write passively, using phrases such as "I was responsible for" and "My duties included."

OR

2. You can write assertively and professionally, using action verbs to communicate what you have done and what you have accomplished.

To help you with this task, we've assembled a list of 250 action verbs. Use the words in this list to transform passive sentences into powerful achievements.

*Note* The verbs here are given in the present tense, which you would use for writing descriptions of your current job and activities. For past accomplishments, you would translate these verbs to the past tense.

Accelerate
Accomplish
Achieve
Acquire
Adapt
Address
Advance
Advise
Advocate
Analyze
Apply
Appoint
Arbitrate
Architect
Ascertain
Assemble
Assess
Author
Authorize
Brief
Budget
Build
Calculate
Capture
Catalog
Champion
Clarify
Classify
Close
Coach

Collect
Command
Communicate
Compare
Compel
Compile
Complete
Compute
Conclude
Conduct
Conserve
Consolidate
Construct
Contract
Coordinate
Counsel
Counteract
Craft
Create
Decrease
Delegate
Deliver
Demonstrate
Deploy
Design
Detect
Determine
Develop
Devise
Direct
Discover
Dispense
Display
Distribute
Diversify
Divert
Drive
Earn
Edit
Educate
Effect
Elect
Eliminate
Emphasize
Encourage
Energize
Enforce
Enhance
Enlist
Ensure
Establish
Estimate
Evaluate
Examine
Exceed
Execute
Exhibit
Expand
Expedite
Experiment
Export
Facilitate
Finalize
Finance
Forge
Formalize
Formulate
Generate
Govern
Graduate
Guide
Hasten
Hire
Hypothesize
Identify
Illustrate
Imagine
Implement
Import
Improve
Improvise
Increase
Influence
Inform
Initiate
Innovate
Inspire
Install
Institute
Instruct
Integrate
Intensify
Interpret
Interview
Introduce
Invent
Investigate
Judge
Justify
Launch
Lead
Lecture
License
Maintain
Manage
Manipulate
Manufacture
Map
Market
Mastermind
Measure
Mediate
Mentor
Model
Modify
Monitor
Motivate
Navigate
Negotiate
Nominate
Observe
Offer
Officiate
Operate
Orchestrate
Organize
Orient
Originate
Outsource
Oversee
Participate
Perceive
Perform
Persuade
Pilot
Pinpoint
Pioneer
Plan
Position
Predict
Prepare
Prescribe
Present
Preside
Process
Procure
Promote
Propose
Publicize
Purchase
Qualify
Rate
Realign
Rebuild
Recapture
Receive
Recognize
Recommend
Reconcile
Record
Redesign
Reduce
Reengineer
Rejuvenate
Reorganize
Reposition
Represent
Research
Resolve
Respond
Restore
Restructure
Retrieve
Revamp
Review
Revise
Revitalize
Satisfy
Schedule
Select
Sell
Simplify
Solidify
Solve
Spearhead
Specify
Standardize
Stimulate
Streamline
Structure
Succeed
Suggest
Summarize
Supervise
Supply
Support
Surpass
Synthesize
Systematize
Tabulate
Target
Teach
Terminate
Test
Train
Transcribe
Transfer
Transform
Transition
Translate
Troubleshoot
Unite
Update
Upgrade
Use
Utilize
Verbalize
Verify
Win
Write

Appendix

C

# Recommended Job Search and Career Web Sites

The Internet has changed job search forever. Information that used to take days or even weeks to find can now be accessed in just minutes. It truly is a revolution.

However, the pace of development and the number of new Internet sites that emerge every day make it impossible to provide a comprehensive list of *all* Web sites related to employment, careers, and job search. The following list includes some of our favorite sites, some of the largest sites, and some of the best sites.

This list is by no means comprehensive. We strongly suggest that you devote the time necessary to conduct your own independent Web-based research as applicable to your specific job search campaign and career path.

Enjoy the surf!

## Dictionaries and Glossaries

Outstanding information on keywords and acronyms.

| | |
|---|---|
| Acronym Finder | www.acronymfinder.com |
| Babelfish Foreign-Language Translator | http://babelfish.yahoo.com |
| ComputerUser | www.computeruser.com/resources/dictionary/noframesindex.html |
| Dave's Truly Canadian Dictionary of Canadian Spelling | www.luther.ca/~dave7cnv/cdnspelling/cdnspelling.html |
| Duhaime's Legal Dictionary | www.duhaime.org |
| InvestorWords.com | www.investorwords.com |
| Law.com Legal Industry Glossary | www.law.com |
| Merriam-Webster Collegiate Dictionary & Thesaurus | www.m-w.com/home.htm |
| National Restaurant Association Restaurant Industry Glossary | www.nraef.org/pdf_files/IndustryAcronymsDefinitions-edited-2-23.pdf |
| Nolo's Legal Glossary | www.nolo.com/lawcenter/dictionary/wordindex.cfm |
| TechWeb TechEncyclopedia | www.techweb.com/encyclopedia/ |
| Verizon Glossary of Telecom Terms | www22.verizon.com/wholesale/glossary/0,2624,P_Q,00.html |
| Washington Post Business Glossary | www.washingtonpost.com/wp-srv/business/longterm/glossary/index.htm |
| Webopedia: Online Dictionary for Computer and Internet Terms | www.webopedia.com |

| | |
|---|---|
| Whatis?com Technology Terms | http://whatis.techtarget.com |
| Wordsmyth: The Educational Dictionary/Thesaurus | www.wordsmyth.net |

## Job Search Sites

You'll find thousands and thousands of current professional employment opportunities on these sites.

### General Sites

| | |
|---|---|
| 6FigureJobs | www.6figurejobs.com |
| AllStar Jobs | www.allstarjobs.com |
| BlackWorld Careers | www.blackworld.com/careers.htm |
| BlueCollar.com (Australia) | www.bluecollar.com.au |
| Canada WorkinfoNET | http://mb.workinfonet.ca/en/other-workinfonets/index.php |
| CareerBuilder | www.careerbuilder.com |
| Career Exposure | www.careerexposure.com |
| CareerJournal | www.careerjournal.com |
| Careermag.com | www.careermag.com |
| Career OneStop | www.jobbankinfo.org/ |
| Contract Employment Weekly | www.ceweekly.com |
| EmploymentGuide.com | www.employmentguide.com |
| Excite | http://careers.excite.com |
| Futurestep | www.futurestep.com |
| GETAJOB! | www.getajob.com |

| | |
|---|---|
| Help Wanted | www.helpwanted.com |
| JobBankUSA | www.jobbankusa.com |
| Job Circle | www.jobcircle.com |
| Job.com | www.job.com |
| Job-Hunt.org | www.job-hunt.org |
| JobHuntersBible.com | www.jobhuntersbible.com |
| Career Services (New Zealand) | www.careers.govt.nz/ |
| Monster.com | www.monster.com |
| NationJob Network | www.nationjob.com |
| Net Temps | www.net-temps.com |
| NowHiring.com | www.nowhiring.com |
| Online-Jobs.Com | www.online-jobs.com |
| The Riley Guide | www.rileyguide.com |
| Saludos Hispanos | www.saludos.com |
| Spherion | www.spherion.com |
| The Ladders | www.theladders.com |
| TrueCareers | www.truecareers.com |
| Vault | www.vault.com |
| Yahoo! HotJobs.com | http://hotjobs.yahoo.com |
| WorkTree | www.worktree.com |

## Career-Specific Sites

### Accounting Careers

| | |
|---|---|
| American Association of Finance and Accounting | www.aafa.com |
| Career Bank | www.careerbank.com |
| CFO.com | www.cfo.com |
| CPAnet | www.CPAnet.com |
| SmartPros Accounting | www.accountingnet.com |

### Arts and Media Careers

| | |
|---|---|
| Auditions.com | www.auditions.com |
| Fashion Career Center | www.fashioncareercenter.com |
| Playbill (Theatre Jobs) | www.playbill.com/jobs/find/ |
| TVJobs.com | www.tvjobs.com |

### Education Careers

| | |
|---|---|
| Chronicle of Higher Education Career Network | www.chronicle.com/jobs |
| Council for Advancement and Support of Education | www.case.org |
| Education Jobs.com | www.educationjobs.com |
| Teachers-Teachers.com | www.teachers-teachers.com |
| Teaching Jobs | www.teaching-jobs.org |
| TopSchoolJobs.org | www.topschooljobs.org |
| University Job Bank | www.ujobbank.com |

### Food Service Careers

| | |
|---|---|
| Escoffier On Line | http://escoffier.com/phpnuke/html/index.php |
| Foodservice.com | www.foodservice.com |

### Government Careers

| | |
|---|---|
| Federal Jobs Net | www.federaljobs.net |
| FRS Federal Jobs Central | www.fedjobs.com |
| GetaGovJob.com | www.getagovjob.com |
| GovExec.com | www.govexec.com |
| USAJOBS | www.usajobs.opm.gov |

### Health Care/Medical/Pharmaceutical Careers

| | |
|---|---|
| Great Valley Publishing | www.gvpub.com |
| HealthJobSite.com | www.healthjobsite.com |
| J. Allen & Associates (physician jobs) | www.NHRphysician.com |
| MedHunters.com | www.medhunters.com |
| Medzilla | www.medzilla.com |
| Monster Healthcare | http://healthcare.monster.com |
| Nursing Spectrum | www.nursingspectrum.com |
| Pharmaceutical Company Database | www.coreynahman.com/pharmaceutical_company_database.html |
| Physicians Employment | www.physemp.com |
| RehabJobsOnline | www.rehabjobs.com |
| Rx Career Center | www.rxcareercenter.com |

### Human Resources Careers

| | |
|---|---|
| HR Connections | www.hrjobs.com |
| HR Hub | www.hrhub.com |
| Human Resources and Skills Development Canada | www.hrsdc.gc.ca/en/home.shtml |
| Jobs4HR | www.jobs4hr.com |
| Society for Human Resource Management | www.shrm.org/jobs |

### International Careers

| | |
|---|---|
| EscapeArtist.com | www.escapeartist.com |
| International Career Employment Center | www.internationaljobs.org |
| LatPro | www.latpro.com |
| OverseasJobs.com | www.overseasjobs.com |

### Legal Careers

| | |
|---|---|
| Greedy Associates | www.greedyassociates.com |
| Legal Career Center | www.attorneyjobs.com |

### Sales and Marketing Careers

| | |
|---|---|
| American Marketing Association | www.marketingpower.com |
| MarketingJobs.com | www.marketingjobs.com |
| NationJob | www.nationjob.com/marketing |
| SalesJobs.com | www.salesjobs.com |
| Sales Ladder | http://sales.theladders.com |

## Technology/Engineering Careers

| | |
|---|---|
| American Institute of Architects | www.aia.org |
| American Society for Quality | www.asq.org |
| Chancellor & Chancellor Resources for Careers | www.chancellor.com/fr_careers.html |
| ComputerWork.com | www.computerwork.com |
| Computerworld Careers Knowledge Center | www.computerworld.com/careertopics/careers?from=left |
| Dice | www.dice.com |
| IEEE-USA Job Service | www.ieeeusa.org |
| Jobserve | www.jobserve.com |
| National Society of Professional Engineers | www.nspe.org |
| National Technical Employment Services | www.ntes.com |

## Sites for Miscellaneous Specific Fields

| | |
|---|---|
| AG Careers/Farms.com | www.agcareers.com |
| American Public Works Association | www.apwa.net |
| AutoCareers.com | www.autocareers.com |
| CEOExpress | www.ceoexpress.com |
| Environmentalcareer.com | www.environmental-jobs.com |
| Environmental Career Opportunities | www.ecojobs.com |
| Pilot Jobs | www.findapilot.com |
| Hire Vets First | www.hirevetsfirst.gov |

| | |
|---|---|
| Logistics Jobs | www.jobsinlogistics.com |
| MBACareers.com | www.mbacareers.com |
| Social Work Jobs | www.socialservice.com |

## Company Information

Outstanding resources for researching specific companies.

| | |
|---|---|
| 555-1212.com | www.555-1212.com |
| Brint.com | www.brint.com |
| EDGAR Online | www.edgar-online.com |
| Fortune Magazine | http://money.cnn.com/magazines/fortune/ |
| Hoover's Business Profiles | www.hoovers.com |
| infoUSA (small business information) | www.infousa.com |
| OneSource CorpTech | www.corptech.com |
| SuperPages.com | www.bigbook.com |
| U.S. Chamber of Commerce | www.uschamber.com |
| Vault | www.vault.com |

## Interviewing Company Research Tips and Techniques

Expert guidance to sharpen and strengthen your interviewing skills.

| | |
|---|---|
| About.com Interviewing | http://jobsearch.about.com/od/interviewsnetworking/ |
| Bradley CVs Introduction to Job Interviews | www.bradleycvs.demon.co.uk/interview/index.htm |
| Dress for Success | www.dressforsuccess.org |
| Job-Interview.net | www.job-interview.net |

| | |
|---|---|
| Northeastern University Career Services | http://careerservices.neu.edu/job_search/interviewing.php |
| Wendy Enelow | www.wendyenelow.com/articles/?page_id=11 |

## Salary and Compensation Information

Learn from the experts to strengthen your negotiating skills and increase your salary.

| | |
|---|---|
| Abbott, Langer & Associates | www.abbott-langer.com |
| America's Career InfoNet | www.acinet.org/acinet/select_occupation.asp?stfips=&next=occ_rep |
| Bureau of Labor Statistics | www.bls.gov/bls/wages.htm |
| Clayton Wallis Co. | www.claytonwallis.com |
| Economic Research Institute | www.erieri.com |
| Janco Associates MIS Salary Survey | www.psrinc.com/salary.htm |
| JobStar | www.jobstar.org/tools/salary/index.htm |
| Monster.com Salary Info | salary.monster.com/ |
| Salary.com | www.salary.com |
| Salary Expert | www.salaryexpert.com |
| WorldatWork: The Total Rewards Association | www.worldatwork.org |

## Top 10 Career Blogs

Online weblogs, or blogs, can provide a wealth of career advice and assistance in real time. Here are 10 of the best that we recommend you read regularly:

1. **Alison Doyle:** http://alisondoyle.typepad.com/
2. **CareerSolvers** (Barbara Safani): www.careersolvers.com/blog/
3. **Best Job Interview Strategies Blog:** www.best-interview-strategies.com/job-interviews-blog.html
4. **Business Exchange Executive Job Search Blog:** www.bx.Businessweek.com/Executive-Job-Search/Blogs/
5. **Career Hub:** www.CareerHubBlog.com
6. **Career Management Alliance:** www.careermanagementalliance.com/blog
7. **JibberJobber** (Jason Alba): www.jibberjobber.com/blog/
8. **Monster Blog:** www.Monster.Typepad.com/MonsterBlog
9. **Quintessential Careers:** www.QuintCareers.com/Career_Blog
10. **RiseSmart Outplacement Blog:** www.risesmart.com/risesmart/blog/

Appendix D

# Index of Contributors

The sample cover letters, resumes, and thank-you notes in this book were written by professional resume and cover letter writers. If you need help with your job search correspondence, you can use the following list to locate the career professionals whose samples you admire.

*A note about credentials:* Nearly all of the contributing writers have earned one or more professional credentials. These credentials are highly regarded in the careers and employment industry and are indicative of the writer's expertise and commitment to professional development.

**Georgia Adamson, MRW, ACRW, CCM, CEIP, CPRW, JCTC, CCMC**
A Successful Career
180-A W. Rincon Ave.
Campbell, CA
Phone: (408) 866-6859
Fax: (408) 866-8915
E-mail:
success@ablueribbonresume.com
www.AblueRibbonResume.com;
www.asuccessfulcareer.com

**Elizabeth Axnix, CPRW, JCTC, CEIP**
The Axnix Advantage
110 N. Knisel St.
Riverside, IA
Toll-free: (800) 359-7822
Fax: (319) 648-4819
E-mail: axnix@earthlink.net

**Jacqui Barrett-Poindexter, MRW, CPRW, CEIP**
President, Career Trend
Kansas City, MO
Phone: (816) 584-1639
Fax: (801) 382-5842
E-mail: jacqui@careertrend.net
www.careertrend.net

**Janet Beckstrom, CPRW, ACRW**
Owner, Word Crafter
1717 Montclair Ave.
Flint, MI
Toll-free: (800) 351-9818
Fax: (810) 232-9257
E-mail: janet@wordcrafter.com
www.wordcrafter.com

**Martin Buckland, CPRW, CJST, CEIP, JCTC, CPEC**
Elite Resumes
200 Winston Park Dr., Suite 100
Oakville, Ontario, Canada
Phone: (905) 825-0490
Toll-free: (866) 773-7863
Fax: (705) 835-0952
E-mail: martin@aneliteresume.com
www.AnEliteResume.com

**Diane Burns, CCMC, CPRW, CCM, IJCTC, CLTMC, CPCC, FJSTC, CEIP**
Career Marketing Techniques
3079 N. Columbine Ave.
Boise, ID
Phone: (208) 323-9636
E-mail: diane@polishedresumes.com
www.polishedresumes.com

**Kristin M. Coleman**
Coleman Career Services
Poughkeepsie, NY
Phone: (845) 452-8274
E-mail:
kristin@colemancareerservices.com

**Annemarie Cross, CEIP, CPRW, CARW, CCM, CECC, CERW, CWPP, Reach Certified Personal Branding Strategist, Reach Certified Online Identity Strategist**
Advanced Employment Concepts
Hallam, Victoria, Australia
Phone: +613 9708 6930
Fax: +613 9796 4479
E-mail: success@aresumewriter.net
www.aresumewriter.net/

**Jean Cummings, M.A.T., CPRW, CPBS, CEIP**
President, A Resume For Today
Concord, MA
Phone: (978) 254-5492
Toll-free: (800) 324-1699
E-mail: jc@aresumefortoday.com
www.AResumeForToday.com

**Laura DeCarlo, MCD, CCM, CERW, JCTC, CECC, CCMC, CEIC**
President, A Competitive Edge Career Service, LLC
Melbourne, FL
Toll-free: (800) 715-3442
Fax: (801) 752-7517
E-mail:
success@acompetitiveedge.com
www.acompetitiveedge.com

**Deborah Wile Dib, CPBS, CCM, NCRW, CPRW, CEIP, JCTC, CCMC**
Executive Power Brand
Metro NY
Phone: (631) 475-8513
Fax: (501) 421-7790
E-mail:
debdib@executivepowerbrand.com
www.executivepowerbrand.com

**Kirsten Dixson, CPBS, JCTC**
Exeter, NH
Phone: (603) 580-2208
E-mail: kirsten@kirstendixson.com
www.kirstendixson.com

**Nina Ebert, CPRW/CC**
A Word's Worth Résumé and Writing Service
Central NJ
Phone: (609) 758-7799
Toll-free: (866) 400-7799
Fax: (609) 758-7799
E-mail:
nina@keytosuccessresumes.com
www.keytosuccessresumes.com

**Debbie Ellis, MRW, CPRW**
President, Phoenix Career Group
Toll-free: (800) 876-5506 (U.S. and Canada)
International: (281) 458-5040
E-mail:
debbie@phoenixcareergroup.com
www.PhoenixCareerGroup.com

**Donna Farrise, JCTC**
President, Dynamic Resumes of Long Island, Inc.
Hauppauge, NY
Toll-free: (800) 528-6796
Fax: (631) 952-1817
E-mail: donna@dynamicresumes.com
www.dynamicresumes.com

**Arthur I. Frank, MBA**
President, Resumes "R" Us
Flatrock, NC
Phone: (828) 696-2975
Toll-free: (866) 600-4300
Fax: (828) 696-2974
E-mail: af97710@bellsouth.net
www.powerresumesandcoaching.com

**Louise Garver, MA, CPRW, CEIP, JCTC, CMP, MCDP, CLBF, CPBS, CCMC, CJSS, COIS**
President, Career Directions, LLC
Broad Brook, CT
Phone: (860) 623-9476
Fax: (860) 623-9473
E-mail:
Louise@careerdirectionsllc.com
www.CareerDirectionsLLC.com

**Susan Guarneri, MS, NCC, NCCC, LPC, CPRW, CEIP, IJCTC, MCC, CERW, CPBS, DCC, CCMC, COIMS, CMBS**
President, Guarneri Associates/ Resume-Magic
6670 Crystal Lake Rd.
Three Lakes, WI
Toll-free: (866) 881-4055
E-mail: Susan@Resume-Magic.com
www.resume-magic.com

**Michele Haffner, CCMC, CPRW, JCTC**
Advanced Resume Services
1314 W. Paradise Ct.
Glendale, WI
Phone: (414) 247-1677
Fax: (414) 434-1913
E-mail:
michele@resumeservices.com
www.resumeservices.com

**Cheryl Ann Harland, CPRW, JCTC**
Resumes by Design
25227 Grogan's Mill, Ste. 125
The Woodlands, TX
Phone: (281) 296-1659
Toll-free: (888) 213-1650
E-mail: cah@resumesbydesign.com
www.resumesbydesign.com

**Beverly Harvey, CPRW, JCTC, CCM, CCMC, CPBS, CJSS**
Beverly Harvey Resume and Career Services
Pierson, FL
Phone: (386) 749-3111
Toll-free: (888) 775-0916
Fax: (386) 749-4881
E-mail: beverly@harveycareers.com
www.harveycareers.com

**Maria Hebda, CPRW, CCMC**
Career Solutions, LLC
Trenton, MI
Phone: (734) 676-9170
Fax: (734) 676-9487
E-mail: maria@writingresumes.com
www.writingresumes.com

**Loretta Heck**
President, All Word Services
Prospect Heights, IL
Phone: (847) 215-7517
Fax: (847) 215-7520
E-mail: siegfried@ameritech.net

**Peter Hill, CPRW**
Principal Consultant, PHI Consulting
Honolulu, HI/Shanghai, China
U.S. Phone: (808) 384-9461
Shanghai Phone: +86 137-7448-0436
E-mail: pjhill@phi-yourcareer.com
www.phi-yourcareer.com

**Deborah James, CCMC, CPRW**
President, Leading Edge Resume & Career Services
Rossford, OH
Phone: (419) 666-4518
Toll-free: (800) 815-8780
Fax: (419) 791-3567
E-mail:
djames@leadingedgeresumes.com
www.leadingedgeresumes.com

**Marcy Johnson, CPRW, CEIP, NCRW, CPBS**
President, Executive Career Move/ First Impression Resume & Job Readiness
Story City, IA
Phone: (515) 733-4998
Fax: (515) 733-9296
E-mail:
marcy@executivecareermove.com
www.resume-job-readiness.com;
www.executivecareermove.com

**Bill Kinser, MRW, CPRW, JCTC, CEIP, CCM**
President, To The Point Resumes
Fairfax, VA
Phone: (571) 276-8342
E-mail:
info@tothepointresumes.com
www.tothepointresumes.com

**Myriam-Rose Kohn, CPRW, IJCTC, CCM, CEIP, CCMC, CPBS, CJSS**
President, JEDA Enterprises
Valencia, CA
Phone: (661) 253-0801
Fax: (661) 253-0744
E-mail:
myriam-rose@jedaenterprises.com
www.jedaenterprises.com

**Cindy Kraft, CPBS, CCMC, CCM, CPRW, JCTC**
President, Executive Essentials
Valrico, FL
Phone: (813) 655-0658
Fax: (813) 354-3483
E-mail: cindy@cfo-coach.com
www.cfo-coach.com

**Lorie Lebert, CPRW, IJCTC, CCMC**
President, The Loriel Group—
Coaching ROI/Resume ROI
Phone: (662) 287-0777
Toll-free: (800) 870-9059
Fax: (810) 222-0101
E-mail: Lorie@DoMyResume.com
www.DoMyResume.com;
www.CoachingROI.com

**Linsey Levine, MS, MCDP, LMHC**
CareerCounsel
Ossining, NY
Home Office Phone: (914) 923-9233
White Plains Office Phone:
(914) 948-9286
E-mail: linsey@linseylevine.com
www.linseylevine.com

**Ross Macpherson, MA, CPRW, CJST, CEIP**
Career Quest
Whitby, Ontario, Canada
Phone: (905) 438-8545
Fax: (905) 438-4096
E-mail: ross@yourcareerquest.com
www.yourcareerquest.com

**Meg Montford, MCCC, CMF**
Abilities Enhanced
Kansas City, MO
Phone: (816) 767-1196
E-mail: Meg@abilitiesenhanced.com
www.abilitiesenhanced.com

**Doug Morrison, CPRW**
Career Power
Charlotte, NC
Phone: (704) 365-0773;
(704) 527-5556
E-mail: dmpwresume@aol.com
www.careerpowerresume.com

**JoAnn Nix, CPRW**
A Great Resume Service, Inc.
Van Buren, AR
Phone: (479) 410-3101
Toll-free: (800) 265-6901
Fax: (479) 474-4013
E-mail: info@agreatresume.com
www.agreatresume.com

**John O'Connor, MFA, CRW, CPRW, CCM, CECC, CFRW**
Career Pro, Inc.
Raleigh, NC
Phone: (919) 787-2400
Toll-free fax: (866) 447-9599
E-mail: john@careerproinc.com
www.careerproinc.com

**Helen Oliff, CPRW, CFRWCC, Certified Executive Coach**
Turning Point
Reston, VA/Phoenix, AZ
Phone: (703) 346-8888
Fax: (801) 601-0077
E-mail: helen@helenoliff.com
www.helenoliff.com

**Debra O'Reilly, CPRW, IJCTC, CEIP**
A First Impression Resume Service/ ResumeWriter.com
Brandon, FL
Toll-free: (800) 340-5570
Fax: (813) 315-6634
E-mail: debra@resumewriter.com
www.resumewriter.com

**Don Orlando, MBA, CPRW, JCTC, CCM, CCMC, CJSS**
Executive Master Team—Career Management Alliance
President, The McLean Group
Montgomery, AL
Phone: (334) 264-2020
Fax: (334) 264-9227
E-mail:
yourcareercoach@charterinternet.com

**Jane Roqueplot, CPBA, CWDP, CECC**
JaneCo's Sensible Solutions
Sharon, PA
Phone: (724) 342-0100
Toll-free: (888) 526-3267
Fax: (724) 346-5263
E-mail: info@janecos.com
www.janecos.com

**Teena Rose, CPRW, CEIP**
Resume to Referral
Springfield, OH
Phone: (937) 325-2149
E-mail:
admin@resumetoreferral.com
www.resumebycprw.com

**Jennifer Rushton, CERW, CARW, CEIC, CWPP**
Keraijen—Certified Resume Writer
Sydney, NSW Australia
Phone: +612 9994 8050
Fax: +612 9994 8008
E-mail: info@keraijen.com.au
www.keraijen.com.au

**Janice Shepherd, CPRW, JCTC, CEIP**
Write On Career Keys
Bellingham, WA
Phone: (360) 738-7958
Fax: (360) 306-8225
E-mail:
janice@writeoncareerkeys.com
www.writeoncareerkeys.com

**Igor Shpudejko, CPRW, JCTC, MBA**
President, Career Focus
Mahwah, NJ
Phone: (201) 825-2865
Fax: (201) 825-7711
E-mail: ishpudejko@aol.com
www.CareerInFocus.com

**Laurie Smith, CPRW, JCTC**
Creative Keystrokes Executive Resume Service
Charlotte area, NC
Toll-free: (800) 817-2779
E-mail:
ljsmith@creativekeystrokes.com
www.creativekeystrokes.com;
www.executive-resumes.com

**Lisa LeVerrier Stein, CPRW, CEIP, JCTC**
Deerfield Beach, FL

**Vivian VanLier, CPRW, JCTC, CEIP, CCMC, CPRC**
President, Advantage Resume & Career Services
Los Angeles (Valley Glen), CA
Phone: (818) 994-6655
Fax: (818) 994-6620

E-mail:
vivian@cuttingedgeresumes.com
www.CuttingEdgeResumes.com

**Susan Britton Whitcomb, PCC, CCMC, MRW, NCRW**
Job Search Academy/Career Coach Academy
Fresno, CA
Phone: (559) 222-7474
Toll-free fax: (888) 795-2725
E-mail:
susan@jobsearchacademy.com
www.jobsearchacademy.com;
www.careercoachacademy.com

**Karen Wrigley, CPRW, JCTC**
AMW Resume Service
Austin, TX
Phone: (512) 337-7343
Fax: (512) 672-6226
E-mail:
karen.wrigley@amwresumes.com
www.amwresumes.com

## Location Unknown

**G. William Amme, JCTC**
A CareerPro Inc.

**Lynn Andenoro, CPRW**
My Career Resource

**Jennifer Nell Ayres**
Nell Personal Advancement Resources

**Carole S. Barns**
A Great Career, Inc.

**Mark Berkowitz, MS, NCC, NCCC, CPRW, IJCTC, CEIP**
President, Career Development Resources

**Kathryn Bourne, CPRW, JCTC**

**Carolyn Braden, CPRW**

**Kristie Cook, CPRW, JCTC**
Absolutely Write

**Salome A. Farraro, CPRW**

**Christine Ferguson, CPRW**

**Nancy Karvonen, CPRW, JCTC, CCM, CEIP, CJST**

**Shanna Kemp, M.Ed., JCTC**
Kemp Career Services

**Rhoda Kopy, BS, CPRW, JCTC, CEIP**

**Jean West, CPRW, JCTC**

# Index

## D



## E



## F

## G



## H



## I



## J

## Q–R

## S

## U



## V



## W



## X–Z

# Notes

# Notes

# Notes